J.L. GRANATSTEIN

The Ottawa Men: The Civil Service Mandarins, 1935–1957

With a New Introduction

UNIVERSITY OF TORONTO PRESS
Toronto Buffalo London

© University of Toronto Press Incorporated 1998
Toronto Buffalo London

First published by Oxford University Press © 1982

Printed in Canada

ISBN 0-8020-8181-9 (paper)

Printed on acid-free paper

Canadian Cataloguing in Publication Data

Granatstein, J. L., 1939–
The Ottawa men: the civil service mandarins, 1935–1957

Includes bibliographical references and index.
ISBN 0-8020-8181-9

1. Government executives – Canada.   2. Civil service – Canada.
3. Canada – Officials: employees.   4. Canada – Politics and government –
1935–1957.   I. Title.

FC610.G73 1998   352.3′092′271   C97-932508-0
FC1034.G73 1998

University of Toronto Press acknowledges the financial assistance
to its publishing program of the Canada Council for the Arts and the
Ontario Arts Council.

This book was originally published with the help of a grant from the
Social Science Federation of Canada, using funds provided by
the Social Sciences and Humanities Research Council of Canada

FOR MY FATHER

CONTENTS

LIST OF ILLUSTRATIONS

INTRODUCTION TO THE 1998 EDITION

Robert Bryce, the last of the Ottawa Men in this book and perhaps the last in actual fact, had a very frugal streak. The university
economist A.W. Currie worked briefly in Ottawa during the war
and after, and he remembered lunching with Bryce and other
mandarins in the Chateau Laurier cafeteria during the 1950s.
'Once I remarked to Bryce that he invariably had tea rather than
coffee. "Yes," he said, "each cup costs ten cents but with coffee
you get only a single cup. With tea you get an empty cup, a tea
bag, and a pot that holds two cups of hot water for two cups
of tea."' At the time, Currie added, Bryce was the highest-paid
public servant.[1]

As a senior official of the Department of Finance and the Treasury Board, Clerk of the Privy Council, and then Deputy Minister
of Finance, Bryce had a major role in shaping Canada's fiscal and
social welfare policies, and his attitude to public moneys was not all
that different than to his own. When he died, in July 1997, *Maclean's*
gave him a handsome, laudatory obituary. One reader was not
amused, however. Bryce's forty years of influence on government
policy, he wrote, 'left us with an employment insurance system that
encourages people not to work, an unaffordable medicare system,
old age pensions we cannot afford and a horrendous national debt.
... Some nation builder.' Another *Maclean's* reader read the obituary
differently. 'It indicates the lack of men of that calibre in Canada
today.'[2] Much water has flowed under the national bridge since *The
Ottawa Men* was published in 1982, but I still side with those who
see Bryce's influence as positive, remarkable, and the very antithesis
of the spendthrift approach suggested by the letter-writing critic.
The same holds for those other mandarins I chronicled.

Why do I say this? Historians are supposed to be sensitive in
their work to the spirit of the era in which the men and women

they write about lived. The irate *Maclean's* letter-writer, on the other hand, is applying his take on current problems to events that spanned the years from the 1930s to the 1970s, an ahistorical approach to say the least. Those decades were shaped by the Great Depression, the Second World War, the postwar boom, and the Cold War, and the spirit of the age was very different from that of our mean-spirited 1990s.

In 1944 and 1945, when the postwar Reconstruction policies were crafted, no one wanted to see the return of economic depression, for one thing. Everyone recognized the necessity not to repeat the mistakes of the post–Great War years, when returned men were treated badly, and this obliged the government to develop programs to compensate and reward male and female veterans, a challenge that was met in a generous, magnificent way.[3] And once the war was all but won, the government's planners recognized the need to prepare for Reconstruction carefully and, to them, that meant putting purchasing power in the hands of Canadians to avoid the economy's faltering. This led to unemployment insurance, family allowances, and a wide variety of government programs that pumped money into the reconversion of industry from war to peace, the building of homes, and the expansion of Canadian trade.

Later, because the economy showed extraordinary resilience and the annual budgets tended to be in surplus, the federal government expanded the social safety net to include more generous old age pensions, the Canada Pension Plan, and hospital insurance and Medicare. Certainly the Canadian people welcomed these measures—the Liberals who put them into place held power from 1935 to 1957 without interruption, and after John Diefenbaker's stint from 1957 to 1963 they remained in office for another twenty-one years, again without interruption except for the blink of the Joe Clark government.

Today, however, with a huge national debt and with services from all levels of government drying up, the world is a very different place, and nowhere more so than in the Canadian public service. In Bryce's time, in the era of the mandarins, the public service was an exciting place. Salaries were good in relative terms, there was room for men with ideas, and the excitement of building a nation out of a geographically and racially divided Dominion was palpable. Not so today. The federal government of the 1990s is scrambling to dispense with or disperse its powers, the provinces—not least an *indépendentiste*-minded Quebec—are setting the agenda, and the bean-counters rule. The Canadian public service has been dramatically downsized, by 20 per cent, in the 1990s, and whole departments have been all but eliminated. Recruiting has dried up, and the senior cadre is overwhelmingly white, male, and aging in a country that is now multicultural and where women expect and are entitled to good jobs.

Worse yet, the surviving public servants face public scorn. Civil servants are pronounced lazy and expendable and are told that they can't manage their way out of a paper bag; proponents of the right-wing ethos that holds sway in business declare proudly that the best government is no government at all.[4] There are few if any proud mandarins any more.

The Ottawa Men, therefore, tells the story of a very different time than today's. It was a period of growth and optimism, a time of expanding horizons and near-religious fervour to improve the lot of ordinary Canadians and establish Canada's place in the world. It was a period when a small country could be dramatically changed by the efforts of a few public servants working hand in hand with their political masters. It was a better time.

When reviewers examined *The Ottawa Men*, one point that many did not fail to note was the arbitrary nature of my definition of just who qualified as a mandarin. I had selected the key figures in what I took to be the power departments and agencies of the period—Finance, External Affairs, the Bank of Canada, the Privy Council Office, and the Prime Minister's Office. The group of officials from those departments was all male, white, anglophone, well-educated, and overwhelmingly from central Canada. With some of my selections no one could disagree. With the demographic traits that characterized them, there could be little argument, for the civil service of the era *was* white, male, and English-speaking. The mandarins, in a very real sense, were the vanguard of the new middle class, and they were armed by the end of the 1930s with the powerful new tool of Keynesian economics. With the War Measures Act smoothing out the bumps that might be thrown up by Opposition politicians, the media, and special interest groups, the Second World War gave them virtually free rein to act in their conception of the national good.

But where in *The Ottawa Men* were officials such as Arthur Mac-Namara, a key shaper of Ottawa's manpower and labour policies? Or James Coyne, one of the brightest men in the Bank of Canada? Or Hugh Keenleyside of External Affairs, an organized man in a department best known for its administrative chaos? Where was David Sim, a major player in the Customs and Excise department and in the area of trade? Or Hector McKinnon, another trade expert? And what of Walter Turnbull, Mackenzie King's Principal Secretary, R.A. MacKay, an academic who served on the Rowell-Sirois Royal Commission and joined External Affairs during the war, to remain there into the 1960s, or Maurice Pope, who served as military adviser to the Prime Minister and in External Affairs? Where was C.J. Mackenzie, the engineering dean who took over the National Research Council and became the key figure in scientific affairs in Ottawa? His predecessor at the NRC, General Andrew G.L. McNaughton, might also have been included, for his postwar role in diplomacy and Canada–United States relations was significant indeed. So too might Walter Woods, the key figure in designing the Veterans Charter that made Canada's treatment of its veterans a model for the world.

Any of these men might have been included—in a different book. They were good managers, as capable and dedicated to the public weal as Skelton, Clark, and Towers and their colleagues. The indisputable keys to inclusion in the mandarinate, in my view, were influence and power. The men I selected for study had both; in my view, those omitted did not have such an impact, or at least not in critical areas.

This is a biased view, of course. For the period to 1957, the key areas of government, to my mind, were foreign policy, finance, social welfare, and the organization of government. A bureaucrat in the Geological Survey might have played—and probably did play—a critical role in mapping the nation and locating its mineral resources, but this was not power and influence in the areas under study. A mercurial figure such as Hugh Keenleyside might have done excellent work in various positions. For a variety of reasons, however, he was never selected to fill the key posts. The same might be said of Pope and MacKay or even of Coyne, arguably the most intelligent of them all. Even Woods, a major player in a critical area that touched on all postwar questions, was not quite at the centre. Others might reach different conclusions and, as I said in my original preface, they might well be right, but I would disagree with them today just as I did in 1982.

Another criticism levelled at this book was that the relationship between the public servants and the politicians was not explored sufficiently. It was the task of the bureaucrats to advise on policy and even to originate it, but their actions were always subject to the approval of their political masters. Their role was not a public one; it could not, in their view, withstand the light of publicity. This was not because what they did and said was shameful; far from it. But the proper functioning of the public service required a confidential relationship between minister and adviser, with everyone understanding, *pace* R. MacGregor Dawson, that the minister was ultimately responsible for the policies that came forth.

Even so, there is some justice in the criticism that the nature of the relationship might have been given closer scrutiny in *The Ottawa Men*. Certainly Mackenzie King, Canada's most unloved but highest-ranked Prime Minister,[5] played a critical role in determining who joined the public service at the highest ranks and who rose and fell. King's selection of O.D. Skelton in the mid-1920s was an absolutely critical determinant of the future of the Canadian public service, the *fons et origo* of it all. King's choice of Norman Robertson as Skelton's successor in 1941 similarly plucked a man from relative obscurity and put him into a genuinely crucial wartime role in which he performed brilliantly. King's favourites included Lester Pearson and Clifford Clark, superb choices in anyone's eyes, but his harsh gaze undoubtedly constrained the career of the troublesome but brilliant Hume Wrong, an External Affairs officer who, notwithstanding King's disfavour, was able to rise on sheer ability.

For all his astuteness and skill in selecting the men who would serve his purposes well, King was a disorganized man. The business of his office and his Cabinet was a shambles until Arnold Heeney and J.W. Pickersgill came on the scene at the end of the 1930s. These two (with Skelton and Robertson) worked directly with the Prime Minister. There seems to have been little admiration for the leader, almost no sense that he was a great man. His personal traits were so disconcerting, his abuse of his staff so consistent, his dilatoriness (interrupted by terrific bursts of work and concentration) so pervasive that none who worked with him could admire King. And yet, ... his caution, his political nose, his sure grasp of public opinion, his ever-present concern with preventing the worst from happening proved astonishingly effective. Under King, the Liberal Party became the master pattern for a Canadian political party, and if he was assisted in this achievement by his key public servants, so be it. King chose them and assigned them their tasks, after all.

At the same time, the public service remade Canada into a modern state. The reforms that Sir Robert Borden's government had put into place at the end of the Great War in the search for efficiency had further bureaucratized an already cumbersome bureaucracy. Thanks to King's and Skelton's wisdom, however, there was still room for the talented generalist. Men like Pearson and Robertson, Bryce and Wilgress could tackle almost any job, draw on the experts as needed, and deal with their own and foreign bureaucracies skilfully. Other nations were undergoing similar transformations at the same time, to be sure; the New Deal, for example, transformed the American bureaucracy, and administrative reform pushed the governments of Britain and France towards similar efficiency. What is significant, however, is that Canada's transformation took us into the war and into the peace with a public service that was recognized by everyone—except, perhaps, Canadians—as one of the very best anywhere. King and Skelton built better than they knew.

Almost invariably, King tried to respect the line that divided the public welfare and the party's good, because he understood instinctively that what was good for Canadians was good for the Grits and for his leadership. Arnold Heeney, on the other hand, always agonized over the division between politics and government, and Pickersgill almost certainly crossed the line: before the end of the period covered here, he was a minister in St Laurent's government. Pearson also made the transition from the public service to partisan politics in 1948, and when he formed a government in 1963, he put Mitchell Sharp and Bud Drury, former public servants, into his Cabinet.

The Conservatives, condemned to Opposition by what they saw as the unholy marriage between the bureaucrats and the politicians, naturally fumed and fulminated. They may have been right to do so, but they were wrong to come into office in 1957 fearful that the civil servants would try to sink them. Mackenzie King had always understood that public servants were there to help the government in power, and he had no qualms about turning to Clifford Clark, R.B. Bennett's choice for Deputy Minister of Finance, when he returned to office in 1935. To his credit, Bennett had quickly come to recognize O.D. Skelton's great worth when he took power in 1930, even though Skelton had been a partisan Liberal before he joined the public service and had played a quasi-partisan role, for example, during the 1926 constitutional crisis in the advice he offered King.[6]

Mackenzie King was not the only political player, however, though his power was unquestioned. What is certain is that the power and influence of the mandarins depended to a substantial extent on the intelligence of their respective ministers and on the power they wielded. If the minister was a power in Cabinet, his senior officials had power, too. Whatever his portfolio, when C.D. Howe directed his officials to act, they were listened to, and no one doubted that they spoke for their master. When Pearson acted as Under-Secretary of State for External Affairs in 1946 and 1947, everyone recognized that he had the support of his minister, Louis St Laurent, and few doubted that the Quebec lawyer was the likely successor to Mackenzie King. On the other hand, Ian Mackenzie, first the Minister of National Defence, then Minister of Pensions and National Health, and finally the first Minister of Veterans Affairs, had some influence with Mackenzie King because the Prime Minister liked him. His portfolios were important, but Mackenzie allowed Defence contracting to slip out of control in the late 1930s, and that fatally weakened his position in Ottawa. Even though his portfolios were critical in designing the social welfare and veterans' policies that were so important for postwar Canada, Mackenzie's reputation as a bibulous bon vivant and womanizer did him little good. This, as much as anything else, explains why Mackenzie's Deputy Minister, Walter Woods, able as he was, important as his role unquestionably was, could never quite make it into the first rank of the Ottawa Men. Power and influence were for ministers and bureaucrats the keys to success in the era of the mandarins.

Was this the golden age of public administration in Canada? Surely not, if representativeness is a test, as it might be in today's excruciating atmosphere of political correctness. But if the efficacy of policy is the only test, as it should be, then the answer has to be yes. It was not that the problems Canada faced were minor— depression, war and Cold War, reconversion, and the implementation of the social welfare state were major crises by any standard.

What made the age golden was political stability, the arrival in Ottawa of a cadre of able policy thinkers and skilful administrators, and the circumstances that let them feel free to act without the dead hand of budgetary pressure weighing heavily upon them. Indeed, as much as anything else, the key to the golden age was probably the blank cheque that the federal government seemed to have at its disposal from the war through to 1957. There was relatively little that the government wanted to do that could not be undertaken because of fiscal constraints. Canada could fight a war *and* re-arm for a Cold War *and* implement social welfare. In this respect, the era was unique.

It was also unique in that the war had altered the balance of global power. The old, important players were either removed from the scene by defeat, like Germany and Japan, or substantially weakened by the effort to achieve victory, like Britain, France, and the Netherlands, creating an opportunity for a brash, upstart nation to make its mark. Canada seized that opportunity. The hesitant Dominion became the confident middle power, a nation that had few qualms about stepping into the most difficult arenas and a sufficient sense of itself to take on confidently the British or the Americans on matters of great import. The window of opportunity soon closed, however; it took no more than a half-generation before most of the old balance of power was restored, albeit under the shadow cast by the conflict between two superpowers.

Above all, however, what made the golden age was the quality of the Canadian players, both political and bureaucratic. The King and St Laurent governments had powerful, determined ministers who wanted to move and shape the nation. In this they were assisted, sometimes pushed, by their officials. Intelligent, shrewd, political in the best sense (in that they knew the limits of the art of the possible), the mandarins played a critical role in turning Canada from a marginal colony with few rich and many poor into a confident nation with the highest standard of living in the world. This was a miracle of the first order, and only those among us who delight in focusing on the warts can fail to recognize this. The mandarins did not achieve all this on their own, of course. Canada's transformation was brought about by the labour and sweat of countless ordinary men and women. But leadership was necessary, and it was at hand. Canadians should be so fortunate today.

NOTES

1. Letter to author, 31 August 1982.

2. 'The Mail,' *Maclean's*, 25 August 1997, pp. 4–5.

3. See Peter Neary and J.L. Granatstein, eds., *The Veterans Charter and Post–World War II Canada* (Montreal and Kingston, 1998).

4. Carol Goar, 'Beleaguered Civil Service Sets Sights on Recovery,' *Toronto Star*, 23 August 1997.

5. See Norman Hillmer and J.L. Granatstein, 'Historians Rank the Best and Worst Canadian Prime Ministers,' *Maclean's* (21 April 1997), 34ff.; Val Ross, 'Restoration of a Tarnished King,' *Globe and Mail*, 31 May 1997.

6. I have benefited here from reading the draft chapters of Norman Hillmer's biography of Skelton.

PREFACE

The Ottawa Men were an extraordinary group of civil servants who collectively had great influence and power in Ottawa from the Depression through to the late 1950s. Some called them civil servants or mandarins—often with a sneer, attributing to them the worst characteristics of pettifogging bureaucrats, or of an élitist and separate caste out of touch with the reality of Canada. Others saw them as public servants in the best sense of that term, men who changed the way government operated and whose overall influence and impact were positive in the extreme. This account, generally speaking, undoubtedly leans towards the latter view.

The mandarins of this period were a remarkable group, a collection of friends and colleagues who looked, sounded, and spoke alike; lived close together; and, to a surprising extent, socialized with each other during the work week and on vacations. Their backgrounds were more disparate than many believe, though their education and training were notably similar. They were all generalists recruited into the public service because of their brains and their non-specialized approach, rather than for their skills in particular disciplines. Their openness to ideas set them apart from the rest of the bureaucracy and determined their reaction to the country's problems, which were major ones. In a momentous twenty-year period that encompassed the Depression, the Second World War, and the Cold War, the Ottawa Men had to face the challenge of creating a governmental structure, a foreign policy, and an international monetary policy for a country that had never had them. There were also the difficulties of working within what amounted to a one-party system, for the Liberals were in power from 1935 to 1957.

This book studies the Ottawa Men by combining a biographical approach and a policy-oriented one. I have attempted to look at the most important mandarins both collectively and individually, and to trace the establishment of the key departments, agencies, and offices in which they served. The Department of External Affairs, the Department of Finance, the Bank of Canada, and the Privy Council Office/Prime Minister's Office were the institutional focuses for the mandarins studied here. From those bases they set out to remodel the nation, and they did. They created a sophisticated economic policy for Canada that recognized that this nation had to trade to survive, that made use of all the political muscle Canada could muster during and after the war, and that worked to improve the lot of the Canadian people through planned and co-ordinated government activities and social-welfare programs. They also created a foreign policy for Canada that was at once nationalist and internationalist, aggressive and responsible, practical and idealistic. In the East Block itself, the mandarins created the mechanisms—notably in the Privy Council Office and Prime Minister's Office—through which the Prime Minister and Cabinet could shape, direct, and control the course of events in Canada to the extent they chose or were able. In the process they also created a central government structure and system in which great power and influence flowed to them as well—a necessary, and probably not entirely unwelcome or unplanned, concomitant.

In my view the most important mandarins were those who served in departments and agencies at the centre of the Ottawa nexus from 1935 to 1957, and these are the Ottawa Men of this book. I realize other historians could make a different selection, of both important mandarins and key departments, and they might be correct. My choice, however, has also been influenced by two other factors: the availability of research material that would make detailed treatment possible; and my desire to fit the mandarins' careers together so as to allow me to trace the evolution of a bureaucracy, the way it made policy, the relationships between the policy-makers, and their dealings with the politicians whom the electoral process had placed atop the nation's government structure.

ACKNOWLEDGEMENTS

This book, like most, could not have been written without the assistance of a great many people. The Hon. J.W. Pickersgill, R.B. Bryce, Escott Reid, Louis Rasminsky and the Hon. Mitchell Sharp all submitted to my prying with good grace and patience. Mrs A.D.P. Heeney, Professor Brian Heeney, Mrs N.A. Robertson, Kenneth Clark and Margaret Clark Johnston, Mrs John Deutsch, and Mrs W.A. Mackintosh all proffered invaluable help. No author could have asked for better co-operation.

Messrs. Pickersgill, Bryce, Reid, Rasminsky, Heeney, and Mrs Robertson all read sections of the work and offered voluminous (and sometimes very critical) comments. So too did Mrs C.H.A. Armstrong, Professor Douglas Owram, Professor John English, Professor Robert Bothwell, and Dr Norman Hillmer. This assistance has greatly enhanced the finished product, although I absolve all of them from any blame for its shortcomings. Also deserving of my thanks are William Toye of the Oxford University Press—an editor in the grand manner and one to whom this book and its author owe much—and Patricia Sillers for her helpful attention to typescript and proofs.

I must also thank the Bank of Canada archives, the Queen's University archives, and the Public Archives of Canada for splendid co-operation. I have occasionally felt obliged to criticize the PAC's policies and practices, but I am happy to acknowledge that it continues to be the pre-eminent national archives in the North Atlantic area. Long may it remain so. Several friends shared their archival research with me, and I am much obliged to Robert Cuff, Norman Hillmer, Robert Bothwell, and John English for this generosity. Photographic research was done on short notice by Bill Young. Others who helped were Ms Jane Witty of the Bank of Canada Archives, Mrs P. Christie, Alexandra Skelton, and the Hon. J.W. Pickersgill.

Sections of this book have been delivered as papers and/or published elsewhere in slightly different forms. I am grateful to the *Journal of Canadian Studies, Policy Options*, the Royal Military College of Canada, and the history departments of the University of Western Ontario (particularly Peter Neary and Jack Hyatt) and the University of New Brunswick (T.W. Acheson especially) for their kindness.

Finally much of the research for this book was undertaken while I was simultaneously working on a study of Norman Robertson, one of the leading men of influence in Ottawa. I must again express my gratitude to the Department of External Affairs for its great assistance and to the Social Science and Humanities Research Council of Canada for its support.

JLG

THE OTTAWA MEN
The Civil Service Mandarins, 1935-1957

1

THE MANDARINS

'The Civil Service', one official of the Treasury in London told a scholar in the early seventies, 'is run by a small group of people who grew up together.'[1] As a simplification of Whitehall and the mandarins who control it through a network of school, family, class, and intellectual ties, this is true enough. In England there is a mystique about the public service. It has a romantic aura composed of power, associations with Empire, and first-class intellects singularly devoted to the service of Britain's permanent national interests, whatever they might be. Politicians come and go, the occupants of 10 Downing Street change their party labels, but the national interest endures. And the mandarins are its keepers.

Though Whitehall's power has gone now, and the British national interest is no longer as clear as it once was, the austere and noble image of Whitehall's élite remains. Britain's Permanent Undersecretaries carry weak briefs these days, but who can doubt that their traditions comfort them on cold, damp nights?

Canada, of course, is different. Here there is no such thing as a public service dominated by class, family, and tradition. The men in charge who carry their briefcases, flow-charts, and print-outs across the land, wrestling uncertainly with the intractable problems of a half-continent and a divided population, come from a wide range of social and educational backgrounds. Recent events have revealed that they, along with the politicians they serve— men and women worn down by the weight of their tasks—seem incapable of affecting national problems.

But it was not always so in Ottawa. Once there was a civil service in the Whitehall tradition that was dominated by a small group of men of undisputed ability and great power. The problems they faced, though no less awesome than those of today, appeared soluble, and their confidence in dealing with them was enormous.

From the 1930s to the 1950s Canada's civil-service mandarins—like those of Whitehall—had many things in common. They were a coherent group, united not only by their work but by their friendships and those of their wives and children. They operated almost anonymously within a tight and private little world—offices moments away from each other, homes nearby, clubs close at hand. Yet this mandarinate was not a closed circle. It was remarkably open to new men throughout most of its ascendancy; its members were constantly on the alert for able recruits who would fit in. O.D. Skelton, who founded the mandarinate after his appointment as Under-Secretary of State for External Affairs in 1925, saw potential in Clifford Clark, one of his former students at Queen's University, whom he had hired as a colleague in the Department of Political Science and Economics. After two years of persuasion, Skelton convinced Prime Minister R.B. Bennett to bring Clark to Ottawa as Deputy Minister of Finance in 1932. Skelton and Clark together selected Graham Towers as the man to be Governor of the Bank of Canada. These three, with the assistance of W.A. Mackintosh, another student and colleague at Queen's, later enticed to Ottawa the best of the bright young men they could locate in universities across the country. Skelton, Clark, and Towers trained, polished, and force-fed these recruits on the proud ethos, which they themselves honoured and practised, of public service as a duty and a privilege.

There can be no doubt that in the process they created an élite. But it was a meritocratic élite. If a dirt-poor boy from a Saskatchewan farm or a Winnipeg tenement could make it to university and do well, he was entitled to—and received—the same consideration for admittance to the civil service as the son of a professor or a mining-company president. Ability was the key; capability a necessity. Influential friends could be important but were by no means essential.

Any listing of the mandarins of 1935 to 1957 has to be arbitrary to some degree; but for this study the mandarinate consisted of the following men, all of whom greatly influenced government policy.

DEPARTMENT OF EXTERNAL AFFAIRS
O.D. Skelton, Loring Christie, Hume Wrong,
Lester Pearson, Norman Robertson, Escott Reid

DEPARTMENT OF FINANCE

W. Clifford Clark, R.B. Bryce, W.A. Mackintosh,
Mitchell Sharp, A.F.W. Plumptre

BANK OF CANADA

Graham Towers, Donald Gordon, Alex Skelton,
John Deutsch, Louis Rasminsky

PRIVY COUNCIL OFFICE/PRIME MINISTER'S OFFICE

Arnold Heeney, J.W. Pickersgill

DEPARTMENT OF TRADE AND COMMERCE

Dana Wilgress

Finance, External Affairs, Trade and Commerce, the Bank of
Canada, the Privy Council Office, and the Prime Minister's Office
were the key departments and organizations because the times
made them so. In the late 1920s External Affairs acquired prestige
mainly because it was headed by Skelton, the closest adviser to
Prime Minister Mackenzie King. But with the international
storm-warnings of the 1930s, the intensification of Canada's
struggle for status and responsibility during the war, and the Cold
War that began with Igor Gouzenko's disclosure of the U.S.S.R.
embassy's espionage documents in September 1945, External Affairs was brought, and remained, to the fore, even though it was
not ordinarily involved in day-to-day domestic policy-making.
Arnold Heeney, who had left the Privy Council Office for External Affairs in 1949, referred to his departmental colleagues only
half-jokingly as ' "the boys" on the Olympian team.'[2]

Finance and the Bank of Canada secured their importance in the
latter years of the Depression when government, for the first time,
began to cast aside its dedication to *laissez-faire* and intervene with
increasing effectiveness in all the affairs of the nation. Both maintained their importance because of the war's extraordinary fiscal
demands, and because the Canadian government's wholesale
adoption, during and after the war, of social-welfare economics
guaranteed their pre-eminence in peacetime.

The Privy Council Office and the Prime Minister's Office
(PCO and PMO) gained influence from the increased power that
the workings of the new interventionist state and the war thrust
on the Prime Minister and the Cabinet. As the government assumed greater responsibilities, it became essential to provide

much more organization for the Ministers of the Crown. As this was accomplished, the Clerk of the Privy Council and the Prime Minister's secretary almost automatically became powerful officials, privy to all bureaucratic and political secrets. These offices also acquired importance because King and St Laurent trusted the men in charge of them implicitly—for both their competence and devotion and because the two Prime Ministers believed, correctly, that on the most significant issues these officials shared their views.

Although its weight in Cabinet and in bureaucrats' committees was negligible in the 1930s, Trade and Commerce is included in the list because its deputy minister from 1940 to 1943, Dana Wilgress, commanded a high personal reputation—but he was esteemed despite his department of origin, not because of it. Not until January 1948, when C.D. Howe was made minister, did Trade and Commerce become powerful, a state of affairs that was confirmed when Mitchell Sharp and Alex Skelton, two of the younger mandarins, signed on. Some departments were strong because of their function; Trade and Commerce became powerful because of its minister.

What of the mandarins themselves? Their common gender must be noted. At the beginning of the period covered by this book, for example, women could not serve as officers in the Department of External Affairs; not until the war were some women brought in as temporary appointments. The first genuine appointment of a woman to an important post, that of Agnes McCloskey as Consul in New York City in 1943, resulted more from a decision to rid External Affairs of this unpopular and tyrannical accountant who had arrogated to herself total control of the department's administration than from a recognition of her ability. There were virtually no women filling 'officer'-level positions elsewhere in key departments and offices before the war; indeed, during the war the only senior post held by a woman in Ottawa was Chief of the Oil and Fats Administration in the Wartime Prices and Trade Board, a position filled by Mrs Phyllis Turner.[3] The mandarin world was exclusively male.

Nor was there a single French-Canadian member of the mandarin group. In some ways that fact is more striking—and more shameful. Women at least suffered similar discrimination elsewhere in the world. But for one of the charter groups in a nation to be completely unrepresented at the top level of the bureaucracy was a true reflection of the concentration of power in Canada: only English Canadians had it. Not only were Québécois not represented at the very top, but they were also denied a share of power at lower levels. For example, a report on employees in Finance noted on January 8, 1940 that there were no French Canadians in the Deputy Minister's office, only 17 (out of 147) in the Administration Branch, and 6 (out of 65) in the Accounts Branch.[4] More than a dozen years later, in 1953, John Porter's study of the bureaucratic élite noted that French Canadians held only 13.4 per cent of the top posts in the public service (his sample being 202, or ten times the number used here)—and a French Canadian had been Prime Minister for five years.[5]

Why? The most likely reason is that Clark, Skelton, and Towers knew few French Canadians personally and had few contacts in francophone Quebec. Canada was 'two solitudes' then far more so than now, and while these men were not anti-Quebec or opposed to bringing French Canadians into government, they were under little serious pressure to do so. Whenever pressure was applied, as it was at various times on External Affairs, the recruits, with few exceptions, proved to be less than able. Experience seemed to suggest that those French Canadians with political muscle behind them were not first-rate; that those who came without it suffered by association with those who did have patrons and had failed to gain entry to the officer ranks, let alone to the select company of the mandarinate; and presumably that many first-rate French Canadians did not choose to work in 'English' Ottawa.*

Thus government business in Ottawa was conducted in one language only. (Only one or two of the mandarins—Pickersgill and Heeney were the exceptions—had any fluency in French.) Clerks and typists might have spoken French among themselves, but no matter how much they fumed, the work they prepared was solely in English; a researcher has to hunt extensively in the files of the key departments (or any of the others) to find a paper, memo, or

---

* Another reason may have been the examination system itself. Although applicants could, of course, write in French, the examinations 'even when translated into French, reflected the patterns of thought and cultural style of English-speaking Canada'. (*Report of the Royal Commission on Bilingualism and Biculturalism*, vol. IIIa, (Ottawa, 1969), 101. See also J.E. Hodgetts *et al.*, *The Biography of an Institution*, (Montreal, 1972), 474ff. Copies of 1930s External Affairs examinations, for example, are readily available in PAC, External Affairs Records and PAC, Laurent Beaudry Papers.)

report in French. If a French-speaking officer tried to speak French at work, or to function in his native tongue, he could quite literally have been considered unstable. Certainly that was how Mackenzie King viewed the actions of Laurent Beaudry when, as Acting Under-Secretary of State for External Affairs in 1937, he tried to run his department's business in the other language of Canada.[6] It was an unhappy and unhealthy situation, one that more than justified Pauline Vanier's recollection that the few of her compatriots who were willing to work in an anglophone environment were treated 'like natives' in Ottawa.[7] The nation would pay dearly for these sins of omission and commission by its leaders.

On the other hand, it must be said, there were relatively few economists being produced in Quebec at the time when most of the mandarins joined the civil service. But even if that lack might have closed off Finance and the Bank to French Canadians, the alleged bias in favour of intelligent generalists that was the rule in External Affairs and in Heeney's Privy Council Office should at least have encompassed the lawyers, classicists, and others that the Quebec educational system did produce. Some able men *were* recruited just before or during the war—Jules Léger, Jean Chapdelaine, and Marcel Cadieux in External Affairs, to cite only three—but their numbers were small, and these three mandarins-in-training did not reach the heights until much later. This cultural blindness in Ottawa has to be seen as an unconscious expression of the English-Canadian view of Quebec as a land of happy (if slightly disloyal) peasants, notaries, and priests.

The absence of French Canadians in the top ranks effectively meant that Roman Catholics were under-represented as well. Only one member of the mandarin class, John Deutsch, was a Catholic, and there was only one Jew, Louis Rasminsky of the Bank of Canada. Deutsch and Rasminsky were the only two in the group who did not have a British heritage—all the rest were WASPs. Most of the mandarins attended church infrequently, if at all. Rasminsky and Deutsch were faithful adherents, but among the Protestants only Arnold Heeney was notably religious (surprising when it is considered that the fathers of Reid, Pearson, and Wrong, as well as Heeney, were all clergymen), and Skelton and Robertson were firmly agnostic.

Who were these mandarins and where did they come from? Heeney, Reid, Pearson, and Wrong, as clergymen's sons, were *de facto* members of the middle class (the dominant trait of the mandarins). Clark, Deutsch, and Pickersgill were from poor rural backgrounds; Sharp rose from poverty in Winnipeg; Gordon from a desperate family situation in Toronto; and Rasminsky came from a lower-middle-class ghetto of Toronto. Graham Towers, on the other hand, was a descendant of one of the founders of the Bank of Montreal; Bryce's father owned mining companies, the family's fortune rising and falling with the market and the business cycle; Robertson's father was a classics professor at the University of British Columbia, and Wrong's, though nominally a clergyman, was head of the history department at the University of Toronto. None of the parents were prominent politically, although Robertson's father was well known as a Liberal in Vancouver and Plumptre's mother was involved in Toronto politics.

All the mandarins except Donald Gordon were born in Canada and all were remarkably young. In 1939 Pearson was 43, Wrong 45, Gordon 38, Pickersgill 34, Rasminsky 31, Robertson 35; among the most senior, Clark was 50, Wilgress 47, Towers 42, and Skelton, the dean of the mandarinate, 61. Most of them had come of age in the 1920s and early 1930s to finish their education and set about their careers. All were bright and well educated. Of the group all had at least one university degree, except for Donald Gordon. He had gone to work for the Bank of Nova Scotia as a teenager, but had taken a Canadian Bankers' Association course by correspondence at Queen's and had done well enough to be spotted as a comer by Mackintosh and steered to the Bank of Canada when it was established in 1935.[8] Four of the group were Rhodes Scholars—Robertson, Reid, Heeney, and Alex Skelton—and Pearson, Wrong, Plumptre, Rasminsky, and Pickersgill had attended Oxford, Cambridge, or the London School of Economics. Curiously, some of the brightest stars in the group failed to get a 'first'. Taking seconds were Pearson in modern history, Robertson in modern greats, and Heeney in history. Wrong graduated with 'distinction' in the shortened post-war course in history, the equivalent of a first-class degree, and Escott Reid won a first in philosophy, politics and economics.[9] Six attended graduate school in the United States—Skelton, Clark, Mackintosh, Robertson, Bryce, and Christie—but a surprising number of the mandarins did not complete their doctoral dissertations: Clark, Robertson, Bryce, Reid, and Rasminsky all turned away before their theses were written. A large number—Skelton *père et fils*, Clark, Robertson, Wrong, Pearson, Reid, Deutsch, Plumptre,

Mackintosh, and Pickersgill—taught in universities before joining the public service.

Among Canadian universities attended by the group, Queen's and Toronto stood out. Skelton taught both Clark and Mackintosh at Queen's and brought them into his department as colleagues. Deutsch and Alex Skelton were students there. Towers and Wilgress had both attended McGill and studied under Stephen Leacock. Reid, Plumptre, Bryce, Pearson, Wrong, and Rasminsky were Toronto graduates; Sharp, Heeney, and Pickersgill had gone to Manitoba, Christie to Acadia, and Robertson to UBC. The level of education was impressive, and the mandarins had been selected to some extent because of their advanced training. When O. D. Skelton was beginning to recruit a staff for External Affairs in 1927, he told his academic correspondents that his standards were about the same as those required for an assistant or associate professor;[10] roughly similar standards prevailed with Clark and Towers. A good education was the prerequisite for joining the élite. (Donald Gordon was the exception that proved the rule.)

But if the quality of one's education could help in getting a job in Ottawa, it did not help very much in determining who made it into the élite group. That seems to have depended on talent alone. Norman Robertson, for example, had been a Rhodes Scholar, a doctoral candidate at the Brookings Graduate School, and an instructor at Harvard. But these accomplishments guaranteed him nothing at all with Skelton. Over his first half-dozen years in Ottawa, Robertson had to earn his way into the inner circle by hard, slogging work at a vast array of subjects, and particularly by making himself into an expert on trade policy at a time, in the 1930s, when such expertise was of great importance. It was Robertson who handled the trade negotiations with Britain and the United States that produced a succession of treaties in 1935, 1936, 1937, and 1938. His success drew him favourably and forcibly to the attention of Mackenzie King. When Skelton died in 1941, Robertson seemed his logical successor as head of External Affairs, even though he was only 36. Similarly, when Robert Bryce joined Finance in 1938, he came with good recommendations and with a reputation as a Keynesian. That may have impressed Clark, but what must have sold him on his new recruit was Bryce's remarkable ability to produce long, polished memoranda with amazing speed. Similarly, when Arnold Heeney joined the Prime Minister's Office in 1938, he could have been quickly broken—like previous functionaries—by Mackenzie King's ill-treatment, imperious demands, and insistence on worrying those around him to distraction with his finicky sensibility. But Heeney had the right stuff, the talent to impose organization and system on a Prime Minister (and a Cabinet) desperately in need of them, along with the nerve to withstand King's demands when they clashed with his conscience. Ability mattered most, and the mandarins earned their way to the top.

This was about all they earned, for their salaries were low when compared to those received by men with similar responsibilities in business (although quite good in comparison, say, to university salaries). When Clark started as Deputy Minister of Finance in 1932, his annual salary was $12,000—less ten per cent, a deduction suffered by all civil servants as an economy measure. That was a high salary by comparison with the average wage and his Queen's University pay, but even in the Depression years it was not close to the salaries of businessmen who ran, not the financial affairs of the nation, but corporations. Presidents of the chartered banks earned four or five times the salary of Clark; presidents of railways received even larger sums; and many corporations paid figures that were at least comparable. Who could deny that Clifford Clark's responsibilities were at least as great as those of the president of the Bank of Montreal? Clark was at the top end of the civil-service-officer pay-scale; Norman Robertson, however, began at the bottom, receiving $2,520 when he joined External Affairs in 1929. It was ten years before he received $4,580, and that was only because his promotion had been accelerated.[11] Throughout this period, Robertson was negotiating trade agreements affecting millions of dollars in exports and imports—and wearing suits that were shiny with use. When he became Under-Secretary in 1941, his salary jumped to $10,000—a very good wage for 1941; but considering the responsibility, the work-load, and the strain, no one could seriously have suggested that he was overpaid. Nor would anyone have argued that Dana Wilgress or Bryce received too much in January 1940 when their salaries reached $7,800 and $4,020 respectively.[12] The only mandarin whose salary was out of line was Graham Towers. His salary in 1940 was $30,000, but he had been hired at this figure in 1934.[13] Towers, however, was not strictly a civil servant. As Governor of the Bank of Canada he was *sui generis*, and his salary had been deliberately set to equal the annual income he would have received if he had stayed with his previous employer, the Royal Bank.

The relatively low salaries did not make it easy to hold good people in Ottawa. The situation was particularly acute at the end of the war, when the patriotic impulse that had kept men and women working in Ottawa under terrific pressure disappeared or diminished. How could the problem be overcome? the mandarins wondered.[14] The solution proposed by Arnold Heeney at the end of 1945, clearly after widespread canvassing of opinion, was a Royal Commission on the civil service; this commended itself to the Prime Minister and led in the next year to the creation of the Royal Commission on Administrative Classification in the Public Service. Walter Gordon, a friend of most of the mandarins, a Liberal in good standing, and a wartime recruit to the Finance Department, was appointed Commissioner. He cheerfully admitted in his memoirs that Clifford Clark had selected him because he was 'a friendly ex-member of his department' able to 'set salaries, [Clark's] own included. . . .'[15]

Gordon did what he had been appointed to do.[16] His Royal Commission recommended a higher salary scale for the top positions in the civil service, and particularly those in External Affairs, Finance, and the PCO. The recommendations, soon accepted by the government, were just and necessary, and Arnold Heeney wrote to his wife, before the public announcement, that 'There's a good prospect of our raise coming through . . . and it may even be $15,000 which we could certainly use. Mike [Pearson] is to go to External Affairs & at the new salary so that should help to push the rest of us along . . .'[17] It did, although there was not one who could not have made more money in the private sector. The mandarins did not stay in Ottawa because of the pay.

They remained because they liked their work and because they believed that what they were doing was the most important job in the country, but primarily because they shared a belief that public service was a civic virtue: they felt a duty to serve their country and its people. If that sounds trite and pious today, it is only because our age is more cynical. Those mandarins were sincere in their belief and lived it. Of course they wanted a comfortable salary, but almost all would have remained at their posts without it. The ethos that governed them was probably attributable in part to the Oxford background of so many of them—Balliol and St John's had for generations been the training-ground for Whitehall's mandarins. Robertson may have reinforced his Oxford training at Brookings, an institution that deliberately prepared men and women for the American public service. But wherever their devotion came from, all shared it.

The mandarins also shared a common lifestyle. Those who had been in Ottawa in the 1930s, with their salaries of $3,000 or $4,000 on which they raised young families, did not live extravagantly. Nevertheless, almost all were able to employ a full-time maid, and possibly a nanny or mother's helper to assist with the children. That sounds very odd today, but it was not unusual in Depression-era Ottawa, when domestic service was one of the few respectable jobs open to working-class women, and where almost every member of the middle class had a maid—at $15 or $25 a month plus room and board.

Most of the mandarins lived initially in the New Edinburgh district of Ottawa, although some quickly found their way into the more exclusive Rockcliffe Village, where house prices ranged in 1937 from $10,000 to $20,000 and ten years later from $20,000 to $36,000.[18] A few lived in the Glebe. But Ottawa was very small—the population was 127,000 in 1931 and 155,000 in 1941—and if one had a car (several did not, and Robertson never learned to drive), no spot in town was more than ten or fifteen minutes away. Most of the mandarins walked to work each day, or rode the streetcar, talking shop as they travelled. Arnold Heeney, Jack Pickersgill, Louis Rasminsky, and often Lewis Clark, the Chargé d'Affaires at the American Embassy from 1943, regularly hiked into town each day from Rockcliffe during the war, eventually securing a pass from the Governor General, the Earl of Athlone, that allowed them to cut through the grounds of Government House. Heeney and Rasminsky continued this daily walk for years. After it became too much for the ailing Heeney, Rasminsky arranged to have his Bank of Canada car pick up the two of them near the Prime Minister's residence on Sussex Drive.[19]

Through the Second World War and well beyond, most of the key officials had offices in the East Block. Indeed, it is now difficult to believe that in this building so much political and bureaucratic power was concentrated. The Prime Minister, the Clerk of the Privy Council, and the Under-Secretary of State for External Affairs all had their offices there, and the Cabinet met there. The officers of the Department of External Affairs, the staffs of the Prime Minister's Office and the Privy Council Office, were also located there. Finance was close by, the Bank of Canada was across Wellington Street, the Library of Parliament was at hand, and scarcely any of the mandarins was more than a two- or three-minute walk from all the rest. It was a close-knit government.

The mandarins met regularly for lunch. During the Depression and war years, the favoured meeting-place was the Château Laurier cafeteria, which had large tables where friends could get together over inexpensive but good food. Later, as the mandarins grew older and became more senior, the Rideau Club replaced the Château. Although there were some common tables there where anyone could sit, there was far less informality, and the food, though more expensive, wasn't as good.

Nor was it enough that the officials spent all their working days together. The social life of Ottawa proper held few attractions for most of the bureaucrats, and indeed it was a bleak and somewhat rough town. Unaccountably, however, most of the mandarins loved it, and the nearby Gatineau. James Eayrs has referred to the 'trials of trying to eke out a civilized existence in that "sub-Arctic town transformed by a stroke of Victoria's pen into the cockpit of malodorous politics" ' in attempting to explain why the 'senior members of its bureaucracy huddle so exclusively together in their private retreats . . . keeping their own company and secrets . . .'*[20] And Kildare Dobbs has observed that 'The constant intimacy of their social life fosters an official unanimity unmatched in other English-speaking capitals.'[21]

The wives also tended to group together, doing volunteer work, sharing Gatineau cottages in the summer, shopping together—although there were tensions at various points, as when a husband's career did not seem to be advancing, or when one mandarin's good fortune caused minor jealousies or spitefulness. As for the mandarins, they considered themselves the best company in town, and most of their socializing, at least in the 1930s and 1940s, was with each other. As late as the 1960s one young academic attending a conference at Mount Gabriel, Quebec, noted that Rasminsky, Plumptre, and other bureaucrats clumped to-

* That intimacy left many retired Deputy Ministers in a sad state. Walter Woods, a Deputy in Veterans' Affairs, wrote in his memoirs that 'we had decided to leave Ottawa when I left the service [in 1950]. I had seen too many former Deputy Ministers haunting the streets of Ottawa looking like lonesome ghosts in the years following their retirement.' Walters Woods, *The Men Who Came Back* (Toronto, 1956), 167.

gether, ignoring the other conferees, while the American delegates circulated.[22]

Because they shared a sense of nationalism, most of the Ottawa men had joined the clubs and associations that were forming in those years and that appealed to well-educated young men of talent: the Canadian Club, the Canadian League, the Canadian Institute of International Affairs, the League of Nations Society. Heeney and Robertson, for example, were members of the Canadian League in the 1920s; virtually all in the group belonged to the CIIA; and most, if not all, were in the conference circuit that Edgar Tarr of Winnipeg, the CIIA's heart and soul, kept alive. These connections brought them together with men who chose different routes to power and success. For example, Brooke Claxton, an able Montreal lawyer and later Minister of Health and Welfare and National Defence who was much involved in the CIIA, the Canadian League, and the Canadian Broadcasting League, became a friend of Heeney, Pickersgill, Robertson, and Graham Spry, that lobbyist *extraordinaire*, who was also a good friend of Heeney and Robertson, with whom Spry had been at Oxford. The web of interconnections was intense, embracing family, class, school, associations, and work.[23]

There were further connections. Hume Wrong's father had been a divinity-school classmate of the father of Dean Acheson, later American Secretary of State and before that an American mandarin. The sons were close friends and allies in Washington from 1927 to 1953; their friendship was much to Canada's advantage and helped to determine Wrong's career in the Department of External Affairs. The fathers of both Robertson and Heeney had been classmates at McGill, and their sons met when both won Rhodes scholarships in 1923. Heeney grew up in Winnipeg with Maryon Moody, the future wife of Lester Pearson. Rasminsky and Plumptre were classmates and friendly rivals in the Department of Political Economy at the University of Toronto, and Bryce, although a few years younger than Plumptre, moved in the same circles at the University. Pickersgill and Alex Skelton were at Oxford at the same time, while Pearson and Wrong were both members of the history department at the University of Toronto in the mid-1920s. Skelton, Clark, and Towers all served together on the executive of the Canadian Political Science Association at the beginning of the 1930s (Norman Robertson was secretary when Skelton was president) and worked together to establish the

Canadian Journal of Economics and Political Science. Finally, Hume Wrong and Loring Christie were related by marriage.

All these connections suggest that the educated middle class in Canada in the first thirty years of this century was incredibly small; that those among the two or three per cent of school leavers who went on to university tended to meet others of similar good fortune; and that bright people, not surprisingly, gravitated toward other bright people.

There were other links in Ottawa in those days before television. During the war the Shakespeare Club met to read plays, and this brought the John Deutsches together with the ablest members of the Ottawa Press Gallery, notably Grant Dexter, Bruce Hutchison, and Max Freedman.[24] Deutsch's brief departure from the civil service at the end of the war to join the *Winnipeg Free Press* as an editorial writer was certainly attributable to those contacts, and to his long and confidential relationship with Dexter and Hutchison. There was the Dance Club, apparently originated by Maryon Pearson and much frequented by the Heeneys and the Blair Frasers.[25] And there was The Dining Club, which had come into existence some time after the Great War and brought together a variety of compatible men, all of whom enjoyed talk and gossip. The leading figures in the beginning, and for the next twenty years and more, were representative of old Ottawa: Sir Lyman Duff, Chief Justice of Canada; Col. O.M. Biggar, a lawyer and the Chief Electoral Officer after the Great War; and John Stevenson, the Canadian correspondent for the *Times*, the *Round Table*, and other British journals. Mandarin members of The Dining Club at various times included Loring Christie, Norman Robertson, R.B. Bryce, Arnold Heeney, Louis Rasminsky, and others. Even politicians belonged—men such as Norman Lambert, the Liberals' key organizer from the 1930s through the war, M.J. Coldwell of the CCF, and others.[26]

The mandarin club, however, was the Five Lakes Fishing Club. Located in the Gatineau thirty-one miles from the city, it brought the friendly bureaucrats face to face with the myth of the wilderness. The Club was rustic, a large cottage with rough sleeping accommodations for eighteen to twenty, no electricity, a communal kitchen where each fended for himself (although washing-up was provided by the resident caretaker and his wife), and for many years outdoor plumbing of the most primitive type. There were five lakes with sometimes good angling, a collection of rowboats and canoes (no powerboats were permitted), and some splendid treed country for walking. The Club was a safety valve, a refuge. And always the talk was of policy.

As there has been some misinformation published on the Five Lakes Fishing Club, there may be merit in setting the story of its creation straight. Clifford Clark was its founder, much as he had largely shaped the mandarinate. A keen fisherman, he enjoyed and needed the relief that could be gained by a few days away from Ottawa. As early as 1935 he had begun looking for suitable properties that might be made into a fishing club,[27] but the best spots seemed either too expensive or too far from Ottawa. In 1937 he began to search in earnest, writing to Onesime Gagnon, the Minister of Mines, Game and Fisheries in Quebec City, about the possibility of leasing lakes in the Gatineau.[28] But not until May 1939 did Clark finally find the ideal site: the John Gilmour estate in Wakefield Township. This property included four lakes wholly within its bounds—Trout, Long, Dunning's, and Round; a corner of Forked Lake, on the Gilmour property, made a fifth lake to fish in. That May, Clark and some of his friends had fished in Trout Lake, 'and while the day selected was too early in the season, we had excellent results—14 red trout running up to 2½ lbs.'[29]

Long negotiations followed before Clark could swing the deal. In August Clark and three friends, including Donald Gordon of the Bank of Canada and Kenneth Eaton of the Finance Department, decided to offer $8,500 to the trustees of the Gilmour estate, with $3,500 down and a five-per-cent mortgage on the balance. This offer was low, Clark knew, but he was a canny negotiator and was prepared to go to $12,000 if necessary to secure the property.[30] To finance the deal Clark planned to collect a group of about twenty friends, each of whom would put up $200 for 'one share out of twenty shares representing the equity and the property. If we can limit ourselves to a $3,500 cash payment,' he said, 'that would give us a surplus of $500, which I hope will be sufficient to take care of various initial expenses and . . . operating charges for the balance of the year. . . . The annual membership fee,' he added, 'will run from $75 to $100 per year until the mortgage is paid off.'[31] That was a very clever way to get the property without much financial commitment from anyone, for most of the group had no capital to draw on.

The Gilmour trustees, however, broke off negotiations, and matters lapsed over the winter of 1939-40. For Clark, the Club idea was a necessity, particularly as the war presented new demands to tax his energy and nerves. Even before the war he had written to his former Queen's colleagues, W.A. Mackintosh and Bryce Stewart, that he was 'almost completely fagged out and must get away soon or bust . . . at noon today I did not think I could last through the afternoon.'[32] In February 1940, therefore, he renewed negotiations with the trustees, and these culminated successfully in June with a sale at $12,500.[33]

Now that there was a location for a fishing club, who was to belong? Clark's files include a number of lists showing those who were approached or considered. Despite being overworked that spring of 1940, he himself took on the task of contacting many of the possible members, aided by Bryce Stewart, now an industrial consultant in New York City, T.A. Stone of External Affairs, and Eaton and Bryce in Finance. At various points such men as Harold Innis, the great political economist at the University of Toronto, and B.K. Sandwell, the editor of *Saturday Night*, were considered, along with politicians such as Layton Ralston, Clark's minister, and Norman Rogers, the Minister of National Defence and a one-time Queen's professor of political science.[34]

On June 16, 1940, just at the time France was passing under Nazi domination, the Five Lakes Fishing Club came into being. At a meeting at Stone's house, fourteen of the prospective members came together and agreed to purchase the property for $12,500 and to pay an initial membership fee of $200. The regular annual dues, to begin the next year, were set at $75.[35] In all, thirty memberships were to be offered, although only 27 names were on the first list, a group that included Ralston as the only politician, Gratton O'Leary as the only journalist (although he in the end stayed out), and a fair selection of the mandarinate—Bryce, Clark, Gordon, Mackintosh, Robertson, Pickersgill, O.D. Skelton, and Wilgress. Others in the initial membership included Bryce Stewart, A.W. Rogers, the Secretary of the Canadian Bankers' Association, and Russell Smart, a well-known Ottawa lawyer.[36] By 1942 the full complement had been secured, and Pierrepont Moffat, the American Minister, Lester Pearson, Louis Rasminsky, John Deutsch, and others had joined, while some had dropped out. There were even very official-looking by-laws, regulations, and rules.[37]

The Club offered little luxury. The handsome property gave privacy, a chance to meet and talk with compatible friends about any subject, including government business. But its chief aim was to provide a relief valve, a place away from the East Block to let off pressure, to wear rough clothes, to eat and drink and sing, even to fish. All the mandarins—and their wives and children—loved it, and some, like Donald Gordon, partied vigorously there.[38] It didn't matter that the lakes turned out to be rather poor fishing territory, as an exhaustive biological survey in 1949 demonstrated.[39] Those who fished—a substantial number, including Gordon and Robertson, did not—came to be satisfied with the effort of trying, so long as it included the conversation and good times the Club offered. In 1952 nineteen of the original members still belonged, the best indication that the Club did provide something of what its founders had sought.[40]

The Fishing Club served a useful purpose. During the war and after, it helped to keep alive a group of men whose work was essential and wearying. In addition it served as one more meeting-place for the mandarins, where information, gossip, and shoptalk could be exchanged freely and without let. Essentially the Fishing Club welded the mandarins together and provided a much more casual meeting-place than the Château cafeteria, the Rideau Club, and The Dining Club. But the exclusivity of the Fishing Club, like that of all clubs, was a weakness as well as a strength: while fostering companionship among its members, it set them apart and aroused envy in outsiders. Nonetheless, by the 1950s membership was a sure sign of success in Ottawa. Twenty years later its cachet was sufficient to win mention in Peter Newman's *The Canadian Establishment* (1975),[41] but whether it was still a symbol of success by then was no longer clear.

In mid-century Ottawa the mandarins formed an identifiable species, and they personally, or the influence they exercised, continued well into the sixties. As Christina Newman put it in a reflective article written in 1968, the typical Ottawa mandarin 'was born of WASP parents in the early years of the century, very often in a small town in Ontario or Manitoba, received his undergraduate education at Oxford, often on a Rhodes scholarship, came strongly under the influence of Lord Keynes, was noticed by Clark or Skelton and induced to come to Ottawa in the thirties.' There is much truth in that description, as we have seen. In Newman's judgement one mandarin's life-style was much like any other's. 'He has lived for many years in a comfortable unpretentious house, often shabbily elegant but carrying a good address in

Rockcliffe or on three streets in the Glebe . . . he drives a non-descript car and lunches on oysters at the Rideau Club.' Ideologically, she adds, the mandarin is 'a drawing-room liberal who expresses considerable concern for the underprivileged over drinks . . . [and] fails to see the difference between good manners and compassion. In his office he is essentially a problem solver who turns an icy logic on every new suggestion, reacting to emotionalism of any kind with cold disdain. . . . His epitaph might read: HE SERVED HIS MINISTER WELL.'[42]

It's all true. Yet this description of a distinctive commonality is not quite the whole story. Within the mandarinate there were differences in policy, attitude, and personality; there was even one emotional mandarin who, in frustration and despair, wept before his startled minister. Still, these Ottawa Men shared more traits with each other than with the majority of their countrymen or, more significantly, with the civil servants who had preceded them in Ottawa. The study that follows will examine the personalities and policies that for some twenty years in the mid-century made the Canadian public service a model of policy innovation and efficiency—conceivably the very best in the western world.

THE EARLY CIVIL SERVICE

'Is there any inducement', the Royal Commissioner investigating the Canadian civil service asked a witness in 1907, 'for any brilliant boy to stay in the department?' The reply was quick and straight-forward. 'No. There is every inducement for him to go out. I think a young man is unwise to go into the Government service.' A decade later little had changed. A Member of Parliament told the House of Commons, and the country, that 'from my experi-ence, my advice to my friends and acquaintances has been to keep clear of the Civil Service above everything else. If you have any ambition; if you ever expect to make any headway in the world; if you place any value on your initiative, your freedom, then, for Heaven's sake, steer clear of the Civil Service. . . . If you want to become part of a machine by which you move along, without ex-ercising your initiative, then the Civil Service is the proper place for you.'[1] The Ottawa bureaucracy appeared to hold no prospects for an ambitious, bright young man of the Horatio Alger type, and certainly nothing for a woman.

Some of the complaints directed at the civil service in the early years of the century amounted to the kind of carping it has always elicited in every country, but most of them pointed to genuine flaws, to an endemic condition of incapacity that had made effi-cient administration impossible in Canada. Few believed that the civil service was working as it should or could; indeed almost no one had ever been happy with it. The government of the new Do-minion of Canada inherited its public servants almost wholly from the United Provinces of Upper and Lower Canada; only a very small number of Nova Scotia and New Brunswick men were added to the organization that had been operating in the Canadian capital of Ottawa for a decade before Confederation. The Admin-istration of the United Provinces was itself only little more than a quarter-century old. It was largely the creation of the Governor, Lord Sydenham, who had built on the ramshackle structure he had found at the beginning of the 1840s and had remodelled it into a relatively coherent system of departments that functioned in five areas: administration; revenue and finance; defence; education and welfare; and natural resources and development. That system, as Professor Hodgetts noted in his *Pioneer Public Service*, 'remained almost intact throughout the whole period of Union', and indeed formed the basis of the organization of the Dominion's public service.[2] It is striking that only a small number of men were involved in the pre-1867 service. Hodgetts sets the total at 437 in 1842, 880 in 1852, and at the time of Confederation 2,660, of which only 354 were in Ottawa, the remainder being scattered across the United Canadas.[3]

In the first years of the Dominion the departments it inherited from the Canadas were given legal status and some new ones were added. Customs, Inland Revenue, Agriculture, Public Works, Secretary of State, and the Post Office were established by statute in 1867; Justice and Marine and Fisheries in 1868; Finance in 1869; and Interior in 1873. Over the next decades Railways and Canals came into being in 1879, Trade and Commerce in 1892, Labour in 1900, and External Affairs in 1909,[4] by which time the basis of an effective governmental organization was in place.

But the civil service was stultified and stultifying. Some of its employees enjoyed their work only because they found in it, as Compton Mackenzie later wrote of the British service, 'a richer field for obstructive ingenuity.' He added that the 'temperament of the natural Civil Servant is not one that lends itself to adventure. . . .'[5] Most of the Ottawa public service was clogged with red tape, maintained an attitude to the general public that alternated between indifference and insolence, and employed people who lacked incentive and initiative. These conditions resulted in a Canadian government that was everywhere represented or served by men of little ability. The rot was present at bottom and top. For example, a parliamentary investigation of the government's printing bureau in 1919 found that it 'appears to have been used as a dumping ground for people who could not otherwise be placed', a group that included school teachers, lawyers, notaries, a doctor, a machinist, a baker, and a dry goods clerk, all employed as proof-readers. At least those employees worked, unlike the four individuals who drew their pay but were not required to appear at the printing plant at all.[6] Perhaps the salary levels contributed to the decay. An investigation in 1907 reported that employees were grossly underpaid and that salaries had remained virtually constant for thirty years. One man's salary had increased from $1,200 to $1,600 in twenty-six years, another's had remained the same for twenty-one years, and a third had been raised all of $100 in twenty-nine years. More striking still, salaries were notoriously inequitable, and sometimes an employee received more than his nominal superior,[7] a situation that was undoubtedly attributable to political patronage.

Abroad, the situation was not better. In Paris, for example, the representative of Trade and Commerce for much of the interwar period was Colonel Hercule Barré, a *boulevardier* who 'treated his appointment as a sinecure, a reward to French Canada in general, and he saw no reason to exert himself'—and didn't.[8] No one could force Barré to do his job or to leave the service if he would not. Equally troublesome and demoralizing to useful employees was the total failure to provide trade representatives and quasi-diplomats abroad with arrangements for home leave to help them keep in tune with their country.[9]

Both at home and abroad, while French- and English-speaking Canadians might sit in the same office, the 'two solitudes' remained resolutely unbreached. Whenever they communicated, English was almost always the language used; and this was invariably the rule in memoranda and reports. It was a habit that had been inherited from the pre-Confederation past. 'A standard complaint of the French group,' Professor Hodgetts wrote, 'was that the English-speaking race monopolized the bulk of the positions' in the civil service of the Canadas and 'that they tended to gravitate to all the key managerial posts.' In 1863 only 35 per cent of the headquarters staff were French-Canadian, and many of them held unimportant posts, as the salary records demonstrate.[10] The situation worsened for French Canadians after Confederation when the addition of new English-speaking provinces to the Dominion reduced them to a permanent minority position.[11]

The result, inevitably, was that bitter fights over promotions and places ensued. Each job, each promotion, became a test of the influence of a minister, and endless hours were wasted in deciding who was to get a post and at what level. And as there were more English Canadians than French in the cabinet and in the country, the latter were always defensive and unhappy. In the late 1920s relations were particularly hostile in External Affairs, despite its having only a handful of officers. 'There is bitterness and jockeying,' reported a British official at Earnscliffe, the High Commission in Ottawa, 'as well as one case, at least, of flat refusal on the part of an English Canadian to serve under a French Canadian, which bodes ill for the future of the Service. Perhaps in course of time this acrimonious feeling may be toned down,' he went on; 'otherwise we shall have Paris more or less stocked with French Canadians, London with English Canadians, and Washington, probably with those belonging to the nationality of each minister appointed.'[12] That unhappy state of affairs was not unique to External Affairs, and there was little doubt that French Canadians were seriously under-represented at senior levels throughout the civil service. In 1932, to cite only one example, five of fifty Trade Commissioners were French Canadian.[13] The government must have seemed virtually closed off to French-speaking Canadians.

Perhaps that is why Quebec politicians tried to mobilize the patronage system for their constituents and friends; but they were not alone in resorting to it. Patronage was the bane of effective administration, the evil singled out by every Royal Commission that examined the civil service. It may have been inevitable in a young country, with relatively few good jobs, in which strong party ties were among the few bonds that could link men together across the land. Still, the excesses were great. 'Politics enter every appointment,' the 1907 Royal Commission reported, 'and politicians on the spot interest themselves not only in the appointments but in subsequent promotions of officers. . . .'[14] *The Canadian Monthly* observed in 1876 that 'Appointments to the civil service are theoretically supposed to be based on individual competency; they are, in fact, the rewards of political subserviency.'[15] John A. Macdonald himself frankly told the House of Commons in 1878 that 'Every government selected for the civil service their own friends and no one could object to it.'[16] As usual Sir John was correct. The spoils system lasted well into the next century, affecting almost every position in Ottawa and across the country—the 'inside' and 'outside' services. For example, between 1922 and 1936, R. MacGregor Dawson noted, 'no less than 2,073 postmasters have been dismissed, or an average of 148 a year, the majority of them having lost their positions for alleged political partisanship.'[17] Both appointments and dismissals in the outside service were in the hands of the politicians.

Did this matter? Notwithstanding the occasional good man who was named to a job for which he was fitted, patronage inevitably led to poor appointments, and promoted the undeserving. It affected transfers, it hurt discipline and morale, and it sadly discouraged initiative and effort. 'Patronage', Dawson said, 'spells the death of efficiency in its largest and broadest sense; it invariably places the emphasis not only on the wrong factors but on the irrelevant ones. The skill and ability of the employee . . . may be considered but they will be incidental to the one outstanding merit, the party allegiance. . . .'[18]

The result of the excesses of patronage was that, as the historian W.L. Grant, one of the loudest voices for civil-service reform, wrote in 1934, 'we can all tell stories of the bankrupt tailor who was made a librarian, of the deputy minister who wanted a smart boy and was forced to take an elderly moron.'[19] In Ottawa where patronage extended to the office buildings rented or leased there, nepotism was rife. A non-partisan Senate committee reported in 1924 that 'the present housing of the Civil Service is due in large measure to political patronage and large rentals, and is so lacking in efficiency as to be little short of a national disgrace.'[20]

R.B. Bennett discovered in 1930, when he and his Conservative government took office, that the scandalous condition of the public service prevented the Prime Minister from being able to determine the financial situation of the government. 'It was impossible,' he told Parliament, 'to ascertain what sums of money we were obligated to pay at a given time,' for each department had its own accounting system of varying efficiency and there was, incredibly enough, no central control. Indeed, throughout the inter-war years little attention was paid to the Auditor-General's reports of waste, and there were actual cases of defalcation in the Finance Department itself.[21] The civil service was for the most part, a mess, a swamp of patronage, a refuge for the inefficient and the incompetent.

There were of course some able public servants in the technical branches of government. The land surveyors, geodeticists, agriculturists, entomologists, astronomers, foresters and the like were skilled and well-trained men, experts in their fields who made substantial and valuable contributions to the country.[22] And in more general areas of government there were some senior public servants of ability. The Department of Justice, for example, had some first-class men and Sir Joseph Pope—who established the

Department of External Affairs in 1909 and was Under Secretary until 1925—represented Canada in negotiations abroad with great skill; but, unfortunately, he had little interest in shaping policy.[23] Where, then, was policy advice to come from if not from a skilled public service? Did anyone believe that a harried cabinet minister, beset on every side by difficulties and facing election after election, was going to become an expert in foreign policy or agriculture or railways simply by virtue of taking the oath of office? Experts were essential to the government whatever its politics, but they would never come to Ottawa so long as patronage ruled.

Not that repeated and sincere efforts to cleanse the Augean stables had not been made. They had. Administration after administration from the earliest years of Confederation had promised reform, had created investigatory commissions and committees, all to no avail.[24] A 1912 report by a senior British official, Sir George Murray, found duplication of work by departments and a severe shortage of skilled technical personnel.[25] The inside service, those civil servants employed in Ottawa, had from 1908 been operating on a competitive, and allegedly patronage-free, basis, but the outside service—all those civil servants, on a thousand jobs, from rural postmasters to workers on the canal locks—was excluded from the competitive system and operated still on the spoils system.

Sir Robert Borden was among the politicians in Opposition who were most vociferous on the need for reform; and after the election of 1917, when his Union government was swept to victory, he proceeded to implement his promises. His goal, he wrote in his *Memoirs*, was 'to destroy every vestige of patronage in respect of the Civil Service', and he added that in this he had the support of 'all members of the Government' coalition. Borden pressed his measures for revising the Civil Service Act, and Parliament approved them in the spring of 1918. The Prime Minister remembered that his revised Act 'was not received with marked enthusiasm. In the minds of many members on each side of the House there was a natural reluctance to deprive themselves of the power or privilege of recommendation which was virtually the power of appointment to public office.'[26]

The results of Borden's measures were far-reaching. Almost all the outside civil service was removed from the sphere of patronage and brought under the system of competitive examinations. The Civil Service Commission, in existence since 1908, was strengthened, and a gigantic process of classification of government jobs was undertaken by an American firm, Arthur Young and Company. More than 50,000 positions were involved and the task was immense: classifying each position involved sixteen distinct steps. Though 800,000 operations now could readily be handled by computer, the task was likely too much for the American company, particularly because many of the civil servants, taking the opportunity to inflate the importance of their jobs, had attached an extra page to the form. The result was a mess, and when *The Classification of the Civil Service of Canada* was presented to Parliament in mid-1919, the cries of protest and scorn were loud.

The Young Report was called 'the joke book' or 'the best book of short stories in the English language',[27] and the Civil Service Commission was flooded with appeals as senior clerks found their titles—and salaries—altered. One senior member of Trade and Commerce, for example, was justly outraged: 'It is beyond understanding that I should be classified as a Senior Clerk with a salary from $1320.00 to $1680.00, a salary lower than that outlined by the Civil Service Commission for men supervising the work of a system of inspection and supervision which I planned and installed.' Another official in the same department, the superintendent of the exhibits and publicity bureau, came out of the classification process earning less than his chief clerk, his director of publicity, and his motion-picture editor.[28] Adam Shortt, a former Queen's University professor and Civil Service Commissioner who had attempted to model the Canadian public service on the British (and whose efforts had not met with much success), was terribly disheartened by the results of the *Classification*, and groaned to a friend about the 'trashy American model' that Arthur Young and Co. had foisted on Canadians.[29]

The protests brought about revisions that resulted in an amended scheme in the autumn of 1919; it established 1,729 standard classes of employees, further grouped into 34 occupational services. Everything was categorized, everything arranged. Each class had a title, a work definition, a statement of qualifications, a line of promotion, and a specified compensation range. Admission into the civil service was now to be by examination on special and more-or-less technical or practical subjects, and promotion was to proceed from the lowest to the highest positions within each class. Incredibly, no distinction was made between routine tasks and intellectual or policy-making work.[30]

Inevitably such a scheme discouraged the intelligent from applying. The whole idea of the classification, W.L. Grant wrote in 1934, 'seems to have been to bring into the service not young men and women of high general intelligence, who could soon learn the monkey-tricks which constitute the routine of office, but expert floor-cleaners, office-boys, typists, filing-clerks, *etc.*' The course of promotion, he went on, would see an 'egg-inspector of the second-grade . . . become an egg-inspector of the first grade. But if an egg-inspector of the second grade gives promise of having high administrative qualities of a more general type, it is extremely difficult to transfer him to a position where he may employ them in the service of his country.' Grant bemoaned the results of the 1918 Act, claiming that Canada once again had adopted an 'American practice just when the Americans themselves are outgrowing it.' In his view any educated man could be moved from department to department or position to position, his disciplined mind making him useful even if he had to pass some time in learning a new office routine. But a dullard, even if he had acquired some skill 'in some minute branch of floor-polishing or letter-filing, remains to the end only a polished dullard.'[31]

Polished dullards at the bottom. And at the top? The situation seemed little different in the rigid, heirarchical service—except that the age and pay were higher. In 1929 the average age of deputy ministers was sixty-two and all too often they had reached their posts only because of faithful, uninspired service in the ranks, or because they had served in high political office and were owed something by the party.[32] Something had to be done if Canada was ever to emerge as a modern state.

What was needed, in the words of Grant, were 'civil servants who can brief the over-worked minister; we need men who in these days of stress have leisure to think and brains with which to pursue the toilsome and difficult operation of thinking consecutively; men who can keep two or three jumps ahead of the game, instead of being overwhelmed with day-to-day routine.'[33] But in addition to able people who could function effectively within the complex structure of the civil service, there was a crying need for change in the structure itself. At the beginning of the Depression it was completely incapable of running the affairs of an aspiring nation. Monetary policy was made by guess and by god because there was no central bank to regulate credit. The Department of Finance had no firm grasp of spending in Ottawa's other government departments, and almost no officers capable of understanding the principles of economic policy. External Affairs was tiny and still dependent on the British for information about events abroad. There were no skilled ministers overseas and until 1927 no representation in the United States, except in commercial matters.

The problem was one of organization and people. Reorganization could be brought about whenever the government desired, but without able and properly qualified people to make it work, little would be accomplished. To get the right people, Ottawa's hoary traditions had to change. To effect such a change, the right man was needed.

3

THE FOUNDERS

The modern civil service had its creator in Oscar Douglas Skelton. When he left Queen's University in 1925 and became Under-Secretary of State for External Affairs, Skelton brought with him the conviction that the government of Canada could be improved only by regular infusions of bright, talented young university graduates. Over the course of the next fifteen years Skelton used his contacts with the universities to recruit staff and did this with great skill and success. His efforts made his own department into a pool of talent and, equally important, he attracted able men to other departments and encouraged some of the more hesitant deputy ministers to experiment and to recruit from the universities. Skelton changed Ottawa; he and his recruits changed Canada.

I

O.D. Skelton came from English-Irish Ulster stock. His family was Conservative, Presbyterian, and middle-class, his father being a school teacher in Orangeville, Ont., where the boy was born on July 13, 1878. Skelton was educated there and in Cornwall, Ont., to which his family moved and where his father became a public-school principal. In 1896 he won admission on scholarship to Queen's University at Kingston, that small but very good and very Presbyterian institution, and there he quickly established a reputation for himself. His academic results, as preserved on his transcript, were all first-class (except for a single third-class result in Philology in 1898), and he won prizes in Latin, Greek and Greek prose, a good scholarship, and his Master of Arts degree in 1899 for securing double firsts in the honours courses in both Latin and English.[1] Curiously, however, for one whose later academic work was to be in political economy, Skelton took not a single undergraduate politics course for credit, although in 1899 and 1900 he audited classes offered by Adam Shortt, perhaps Canada's first social scientist and one who tried objectively to consider social facts, not theories.[2] Nevertheless, Skelton impressed Shortt and the professor remained his mentor and benefactor ever after.

After receiving his M.A., Skelton spent another year at Queen's completing his work in Greek, and the following year, 1900-1, he went off to the new University of Chicago for graduate work in that subject. But he remained undecided about his future, and in the summer of 1901 he went to England, where he supported himself by selling 'stereopticon' slides,[3] while seeking entry to the Imperial civil service. He wrote the open examinations for the Home, Indian and Colonial services, competing, as one historian noted, 'against the cream of the public schools and ancient universities of England in an arduous and wide-ranging test of knowledge based on the school curriculum.'[4] Although he passed and qualified for the Indian service, for some reason, possibly inadequate eyesight, he withdrew his application.[5] His examination results, Skelton later told Shortt, were 'low in classics & high in pol. science'—an oddity, given his academic training at Queen's and Chicago, but a reflection of the new interests he was developing.[6]

Many Canadians of Skelton's generation looked to the United States for opportunity, and he found his as the assistant editor of *The Booklovers Magazine* in Philadelphia. In February 1902 he wrote Shortt to say that he enjoyed his work, that his 'financial prospects are satisfactory, but sometimes the vision of the future, always being dragged at the chariot wheels of the printer's devil, gives me pause.' His goal was to return to university, possibly to Columbia, for graduate work in political science. At Chicago, Greek had bored him; political science had not.[7] A week later Skelton told his old professor that 'I wish more and more I c'd have taken more work with you. My present stock of "polycon" [political economy] is rather too flimsy and chaotic to make a good foundation for graduate work. However that's the penalty I pay for not knowing what I wanted in time.' Then he unleashed his thoughts on Canada's place in the world:

I sh'd like to know what you think of the increasing agitation in Canada to secure preferential trade, both as to its honorableness and as to its practicality. I can't help thinking it is as mean and selfish as it w'd in the long run, if secured, be in-

jurious. The imperialist flood seems running high all thro'
the Empire tho' and it may sweep all theories away before it.
Every time I pick up a Canadian paper now and read the
enthusiastically Britisher speeches or editorials or Board of
Trade debates I wonder where I'm at and faint-hearted fears
trouble me that perhaps after all the ideal I've always
cherished, Canadian independence, is fated to be only an
ideal. However, it's some consolation that it can't be any
more impracticable than the policy of those who believe they
can afford to neglect the U.S. as a factor in Canada's future,
pile up tariff barriers & deepen national prejudices in a vain
attempt to deflect the current of destiny, and who believe
there can be any real or lasting community of interest between Canada and Australia or Timbuctoo, or whatever
other part of the map a Jingoistic spree may chance to paint
red.*[8]

This was the credo that governed all of Skelton's views for the rest
of his life: an ideal of Canadian independence, a skepticism about
the possibility of a community of interest between Canada and the
far-flung Empire, and a full awareness of the importance of the
United States to the Dominion.

But if Skelton in 1902 was a Canadian nationalist (a rare speci-
men, even if, as Laurier had proclaimed, the twentieth century belonged to Canada), he was not blind to the weaknesses and foibles
of his countrymen. 'Canada is a great country,' he wrote to his
friend W.L. Grant, 'Heaven bless it, but at present it's great chiefly
for the farmer & the shopkeeper. Another generation with its
more culture & leisure will offer opportunities for the writer & the
teacher. . . . Canada has had a fair crop of poets of second hand
inspiration & her full share of novelists but of men who can write
on literary or national subjects with applied culture & sane perspectives very few.'[9] Still and all, as he admitted, his 'incurable
Canadianism' could not be denied.[10]

---

* Almost thirty years later Skelton had changed his views scarcely at all. A
Northwestern University professor had written to propose a debate on the subject, 'Does the future of Canada lie with the United States or the United Kingdom?' 'It does not seem to have occurred to the gentleman,' Skelton wrote to his
friend Norman Rogers at Queen's, '. . . that the future of Canada might perhaps
lie with Canada.' (Queen's University Archives, Norman Rogers Papers, Box 1,
Skelton to Rogers, 28 Oct., 1931.)

Although Skelton thought several times of returning home, he remained in Philadelphia with *Booklovers*. In 1904 he married Isabel Murphy, like himself the product of a middle-class, small-town Ontario home, and a Queen's graduate,[11] and his marriage naturally complicated matters when the magazine changed hands and he lost his job. Although he was soon offered another magazine post in New York, Skelton wrote to Shortt that he had 'practically decided to go back into college work' with the intention of getting a doctorate in political science.[12]

By the fall of 1905, therefore, Skelton was back at Chicago with his now-pregnant wife, working on his doctorate, and this time thoroughly enjoying the university. Thorstein Veblen was one of his instructors—'a unique character . . . he has a stock of science and of philosophy & of first hand knowledge of business affairs unusual among the men here at least'—and became a life-long influence. Some of his other courses were on tariffs, a subject that spurred Skelton's interest in Canadian-American relations, international law, and American diplomatic history.[13] He worked hard at Chicago (including acting as a press agent in the President's Office and tutoring for $1 an hour in order to cover his fees),[14] but he did not neglect to keep in touch with Shortt. His cultivation of this connection yielded the offer of a fellowship at Queen's for 1906-7 and, when this proved impossible, for the following year. The stipend of $500 was rather small, but Queen's still attracted. There was also an offer of a post at Washington and Lee University at a much higher salary, although 'prospects', 'patriotism', and 'opportunity' combined to make Kingston the better choice. 'I should be very glad to take advantage of the opportunity you kindly offer,' Skelton told Shortt in the spring of 1906, '—both in order to do what little I can to ease the burden on your shoulders next session, and to keep in line for something better later on— one for you and two for myself.'[15] Skelton was nothing if not frank about his purposes and ambitions.

He taught at Queen's in 1907-8.[16] In 1908, when Shortt left the university to become a Civil Service Commissioner, the thirty-year-old Skelton, who had just received his doctorate *magna cum laude* and who had turned down a job offer from Chicago,[17] succeeded his mentor as the John A. Macdonald Professor of Political Science and Economics. 'It goes without saying that I should be very proud to be appointed to your chair,' Skelton had written to Shortt on August 31, 1908. 'I suppose that the shortness of the time before re-opening makes it more likely than otherwise that the man on the spot would have the best show; while the fact that you have so wholeheartedly recommended my choice will doubtless decide the matter.' It did. (Skelton was so confident of the chair that he turned down the offer of a position as Assistant Deputy Minister of Labour in Ottawa.)[18] But the university was not unaware that it had made a good catch. The Queen's *Journal* noted that Skelton was 'one of the youngest professors on the staff of any Canadian university . . . but for the excellence of the material which he has been giving in his lectures . . . the political science students are confident that the high standard maintained by the department will not be lowered in the slightest degree.'[19]

Skelton's worth became obvious immediately when he won a $1,000 prize for a manuscript—the product of a 'hasty summer's effort' in revising his doctoral dissertation[20]—that presented 'the case against socialism'. Skelton's book, published in February 1911, after substantial revision, as *Socialism: A Critical Analysis*, was a major piece of work. A staunch believer in liberalism and individualism, Skelton dissected the socialist case, countered it with some skill, and then subjected Marxism to a detailed critical analysis. In addition he rated the prospects for success of socialist movements around the world and dismissed Canadian socialists in less than a page as 'sporadic and quixotic'. Russia was scarcely mentioned at all and Lenin drew not a mention. Skelton was no prophet, but as a political scientist he was impressive, even if there is no evidence whatever for the still widespread belief that Lenin praised his book and had a copy entombed with him.[21]

By the time *Socialism* appeared, and while he was still in his early thirties, Skelton had already established a reputation as a writer and commentator on public affairs. His articles appeared widely in the United States and Canada, and he had contracted to write a general economic history of Canada for the multi-volume *Canada and its Provinces*, edited by Shortt. In 1911, when he did research for Mackenzie King, the Minister of Labour in Laurier's government, on the impact of reciprocity on Canada, he had his first direct exposure to parties and politics. Working in the Labour Department for the summer (at a salary that was 'less than that received for any work I have undertaken in the past eight years'),[22] Skelton put together a Liberal election pamphlet. He told King that he hoped some party official's name would be put to it because, though he had written strongly about what he saw as reciprocity's undoubted merits elsewhere, 'I do not however wish to be open to the criticism of preparing campaign material while in the pay of the public preparing official statistics.' King tried without success to persuade Skelton to accept extra payment for this work.[23] The election results—the defeat of Laurier's government and King's loss of his own seat—disturbed and depressed Skelton, who told King how appalled he had been by Borden's 'bloody shirt' campaign with its accusations that the Liberals wanted to sell Canada out to the Americans. 'It's a pity we in Ontario haven't yet got to the stage where our loyalty & independence can be taken for granted; apparently it must be demonstrated if need be by the sacrifice of undoubted economic advantage.'[24]

As Skelton's professional stature increased, so too did his popularity as a teacher. He attracted good students—Clifford Clark and W.A. Mackintosh among them—and in 1911 he was elected by the students as the honorary president of the Alma Mater Society, an extraordinary honour for such a recent appointee to the faculty.[25] He was beginning to press the university to modernize its curriculum[26] and was actively working to see that he and his colleagues spent their time studying Canada and Canadian issues.[27] At this time his salary began to reflect his worth to the university. In April 1913 it was raised to $2,500, and over the next several years it rose steadily until in 1924, just before he joined the Department of External Affairs, he received $4,000, plus $500 for his duties as Dean of Arts—a substantial professor's salary for that day.[28]

Skelton's personal connections with Liberals continued to intensify as well, although he never became an uncritical Grit. He wanted electoral reform and he called for changes in party financing. 'No one will deny', he wrote in 1913 in Queen's Quarterly, 'that the campaign chests of both parties have been very largely filled by contributions from subsidy-seeking railway companies.'[29] Skelton maintained his links to King, but more immediately important was a new contact with Sir Wilfrid Laurier, who was languishing in Opposition. The old man was flattered by Skelton's interest and attention, and long conversations led to his being named official biographer; he was given full access to Laurier's massive correspondence. This attachment to, and admiration for, Sir Wilfrid deepened as the Great War produced political storms in Canada. The issue of conscription in particular exercised Skelton, who wrote to a friend that 'I think conscription the fairest solution of our military tasks, but in the actual situation of Canada and in view of the method of its introduction, I think it most unfortunate that the issue has been raised. The real question was whether the additional military strength to be gained would outweigh the danger of national dissension and a consequent slackening of efficiency for war purposes as for everything else.' Quebec was the key, of course; Skelton did not acquit Laurier of playing politics by resisting compulsory military service; but he accepted his general argument 'that if he were to support conscription now it would simply mean handing over a solid Quebec to Bourassa and to still greater extremists. . . .' Skelton wrote, correctly, that the only certainty was 'the bitterest racial & religious scrap in our annals.'[30] After the December 1917 election Skelton said that 'the fanatics of Ontario & the fanatics of Quebec between them have done more to wreck Canadian unity in a few months than men of good will can do to heal the breach in a generation.'[31]

Skelton was no expert on Quebec and he had few close contacts there. But he was sympathetic to the problems faced by French Canadians and he had earlier worked to attempt to persuade Ontarians to allow French in the province's schools. In the spring of 1917 he had privately noted that Ontario sentiment was sharply against Quebec. 'I can't find any justification for it, in view of the plain fact that we went into the war wholly from racial sympathy with England. . . .' However, he continued, 'it's likely to lead to some precipitation of the discussion about imperial relations & perhaps matters will hereafter be put on a self-respecting national basis whereby we'll act as a nation, not as an echo, and can find room for every national element in our action.'[32] That was his goal, as it had been in 1902 and as it would be for the rest of his life.

To a great extent Skelton believed that this was Laurier's goal too. The drive for independence and pan-Canadianism, in the face of the opposition from the Imperial centralists, was one of the major themes of his *Life and Letters of Sir Wilfrid Laurier*,[33] which was published to substantial acclaim in 1921, two years after Laurier's death. The biography was a wholehearted defence of Laurier as a Gladstonian Liberal, and particularly of his role during the war. 'Unquestionably the chapters burn with a flaming loyalty,' wrote W.A. Mackintosh, 'for loyalties of sometimes quite unsuspected fervour and a generosity which rebelled fiercely

against all meanness and trickery were part of the essential spirit of
O.D. Skelton.'[34] The Laurier book, along with Skelton's massive
biography of Sir Alexander Galt, published in 1920, stand as Skelton's major academic achievements. Sixty years later, both are still
read for their analyses and pithy prose.

Now entering his middle forties, Skelton was a scholar of established reputation, a splendid teacher, and a commentator on public
affairs. Tall, balding, with a face not unlike Franklin Roosevelt's,
Skelton had charm, although he was reputed to be heavy-going at
dinner parties.[35] He was a nationalist, a believer in the future of his
own country, of its opportunities and possibilities. Britain held
some attraction for him, but he was convinced that the British
politicians and Imperialists had their own financial and political
well-being uppermost in their minds, and this deep and abiding
suspicion of English motives never left him. 'Try to get all you
can out of the year,' he wrote to his son Sandy, who was going to
school on the Isle of Wight for one year in 1922, '& don't bother
trying to convert Englishmen to new standpoints.' Five years
later, when his son returned to England as a Rhodes Scholar, Skelton secured letters of introduction for him from Sir Robert Borden, who had just returned from teaching at Oxford for a term.
'They will prove of much assistance . . . in breaking the ice which
sometimes is found there,' Skelton remarked in thanking the former Prime Minister.[36] He was well aware that the British were
different from Canadians.

He had put that view into an address on 'Canada and Foreign
Policy'—the product of much thought—that he made in January
1922 to the Ottawa Canadian Club, an audience that included the
new Prime Minister, Mackenzie King. Skelton said that if the Empire continued as a relationship of Mother Country and subordinate dominions, it would have no future. But if the Empire could
develop as a system of equals, bound only by allegiance to a common monarch, then it might last. The future did not, could not,
lie in centralization in London. He rejected a common foreign policy, calling for a Canadian foreign policy that was controlled in
Canada. To Skelton, foreign policy (particularly for Canada, with
its long border and substantial trade wtih the United States) was
essentially economic policy, and hence inseparable from domestic
policy. He was no isolationist, and he did not overstate Canada's
importance. 'Let us take our part,' he said, 'but let it be a modest
part and at the same time an intelligent part.' The path of security,

the path of safety, responsibility, honour, and duty lay in taking control of foreign policy, in following the course established by Macdonald and Laurier to its logical end.[37]

From that address sprang Skelton's career in the public service. King was impressed, and began to consider Skelton as a possible head of the fledgling Department of External Affairs. The next year King took him to the Imperial Conference, and the year after that he brought him into the Department as Counsellor, as the putative heir to the aged Sir Joseph Pope, who had been Under-Secretary since the Department's creation in 1909. At that time Skelton had described the post as 'a mighty desirable billet for somebody'.[38] Now it looked as though it was to be his.

II

In 1922 Mackenzie King was new to office, uncertain of his course, but convinced that a government led by him was better than one led by someone else, and certainly better than one led by any Tory. On Imperial questions King did not yet know where he wanted to head, but in at least one respect he was a nationalist: he was aware that in Canada, Imperial entanglements caused problems between French and English. But he was also a sentimental monarchist, and an imperialist, sure of the innate superiority of the English race—a contradiction that caused him few immediate difficulties. Still, Skelton's speech had touched a chord in him. His had been an 'excellent address', King wrote in his diary, 'pointing out that foreign policy was an extension of domestic policy & that as we had gained control of the one so we must gain control of the other as to matters affecting ourselves, & by conference & discussion co-operate with other parts of the league of Britannic Nations on the things we have in common.' Then the Prime Minister noted that Skelton's address 'would make an excellent foundation for Canadian policy on External Affairs, and Skelton himself would make an excellent man for that department. At the luncheon I told him that he might be wanted there some day. . . . He certainly has the knowledge & the right point of view.'[39]

Just as King assessed Skelton, so did the professor appraise the Prime Minister later in the year. During the Chanak crisis of September 1922, when Lloyd George's dying government sought to pressure the Dominions into pledging support for British actions in Turkey, King toughly refused to offer any men or promises. This action delighted Skelton. 'Never again', he wrote to King, 'will a Canadian government be stampeded against its better judgement into giving blank cheques to British diplomacy, now that your government has set this example of firm and self-respecting deliberation.'[40]

Thus Skelton was pleased to be invited by King to Ottawa for the summer of 1923 to work on preparations for the imminent Imperial Conference and to accompany the Prime Minister to London, and pleased too with his pay of $50 a day plus expenses, which was a far cry from his summer salary the last time he had worked for King.[41] The Prime Minister was determined that there be no more Chanaks; Skelton's memos and papers, toughly argued, took the same line. King's other major adviser at the Conference was John W. Dafoe, the editor of the *Manitoba Free Press* and another strong nationalist; but he was not entirely certain of King's *bona fides*. Of Skelton too he may have had some doubts, but when the professor showed him the papers he had produced for King (and that the Cabinet had unanimously endorsed), Dafoe noted that these were 'soundly Canadian in every respect and advanced'.[42]

Where was the Department of External Affairs in all this? Nowhere. In 1923 it had only three officers, and in fact one position was vacant. Sir Joseph Pope, the Under-Secretary, was a relic of Sir John A.'s day, and the Assistant Under-Secretary, W.H. Walker, did little work of a policy nature. That had been handled by the able Loring Christie, legal adviser to the Department under Borden and Meighen and under King to 1923. Unfortunately King considered Christie to be too much of a Tory imperialist centralizer to put much trust in him. By early 1923 Christie was so frustrated at being frozen out that he resigned and left for England to make his fortune in business.[43] In such circumstances the Department was incapable of producing the briefing papers King needed. Skelton, however, was a fast study. He quickly mastered the documentation London had sent the Dominions and prepared a coherent position for the Canadian delegation.*

In Skelton's view, 'The fundamental question before the Im-

---

* For the views on Skelton of A.J. Glazebrook, a Toronto member of the Empire-centralist organization, the Round Table, this sample from August 1923: 'The man who is going with [King to the Imperial Conference], namely Skelton of Kingston University, is a narrow-minded, extreme autonomist, whose time has been spent in hack writing and who is nervously jealous of what he suspects as English "superiority". I don't think King could have made a very must [sic] worse selection of a man to take over. . . .' (Bodleian Library, Oxford Univ., MSS. Eng. Hist. c.819, f.177, Glazebrook to Dove, 24 Aug., 1923.)

perial Conference of 1923 will be the control of foreign policy',
and Canada had to resist very strongly if it wanted to avoid a
united Empire policy. King had to insist that each component of
the Empire be allowed its own sphere of foreign policy and that no
part, not even Britain, should seek to influence the policy of another. Britain too, Skelton argued cleverly, was entitled to self-
government in foreign policy, and inter-imperial consultation on
foreign policy should be confined only to those areas where the interests of Empire governments genuinely overlapped. In Skelton's
opinion—one that, after Chanak, King accepted—a common Imperial foreign policy was nothing more than a blank cheque signed
by the Dominions, something that offered only the 'maximum of
responsibility and a minimum of control'.[44]

With Skelton's assistance and support, King pressed that view at
the Conference, crossing swords with the Foreign Secretary, Lord
Curzon, and drawing wholehearted support only from the com-
bative Irish. The climactic battle took place over the wording of
the Conference report. Skelton, Dafoe, and King all had a hand in
drafting the Canadian reservations to the centralist draft prepared
by Curzon, and 'Skelton's contribution', Dafoe wrote, 'was a perfectly clear declaration that it was desirable and necessary that the
Dominions should attend to their own foreign affairs recognizing
their powers to confer to-gether for the formulation of common
policies where this was in their interests.' King's additions were 'a
jumble of words from which it was hard to derive any clear meaning.' Skelton carried the Canadian draft off to a meeting with
Maurice Hankey, the Secretary to the Cabinet, who played a crucial role in the British government. Skelton's account, recorded by
Dafoe, stressed the difficulty of that encounter:

> . . . Hankey said they could not find out where Canada
> stood. Borden some years ago had asked for a share in
> foreign policy and last Conference [in 1921] Canada had
> agreed to uniform policy and common responsibility. Now
> Canada repudiated this policy. Skelton said the position of
> the present Government was that the decision of two years
> ago was a reversal of the policy which had been developing
> for fifty years and its intention was to see that the effects of
> this aberration were removed. The futility of any system of
> consultation involving a measure of control was stressed by
> Skelton.[45]

In addition, Skelton had successfully pressed King to resist attempts by the British government to establish a central body 'to give assistance in the formulation of tariffs and trade policies', telling the Prime Minister that such an agency would 'commit us to central review of every important economic activity', and 'would for example give good ground for intervention if we proposed a reciprocity arrangement with the U.S.'[46] Skelton's position at the Conference was consistent in every respect with the one he had held since the turn of the century. Mackenzie King was probably more timid, on occasion, than Skelton might have liked, but was more than satisfied with the advice he had received.

The result was that in 1924 Skelton was persuaded to take a one-year leave of absence from Queen's and join the Department of External Affairs as Counsellor. Promises were no doubt made that when Pope retired, Skelton was to be his successor, for that is what happened when Pope resigned on March 31, 1925. By order-in-council Skelton became Under-Secretary of State for External Affairs at a salary of $8,000, a substantial increase over his Queen's pay.[47] His connection with the university was severed for good.

If Skelton expected to be able to move quickly to create a genuine foreign office in Ottawa and a corps of diplomats abroad, he did not yet know his chief. King was not only Prime Minister but Secretary of State for External Affairs, the Minister responsible for Skelton's tiny department, and while he was ready and willing to use Skelton and his staff as aides on general government policy, he was hesitant, indeed fearful, about criticism in Parliament of expenditures for his own department. Thus only two appointments were made in 1925: that of Jean Désy as Counsellor and of Dr W.A. Riddell as Canadian Advisory Officer to the League of Nations in Geneva. Not until 1927, when King finally decided to open legations in Washington, Paris, and Tokyo, and when the High Commission in London was put on a quasi-diplomatic basis—not until then was there any further opportunity for expansion. The senior posts were filled with political appointees: Vincent Massey, a defeated Liberal candidate, as Minister in the Canadian Legation in Washington; Herbert Marler, another unsuccessful politician and, like Massey, a millionaire, as Minister to Japan; and Philippe Roy, the Commissioner General in France since 1911, in Paris.[48]

There were problems in all this for Skelton. Massey, for one, insisted on establishing a large corps of household servants at government expense in a $500,000 mansion in Washington, and he and Skelton argued bitterly over this. 'I am afraid I lost my temper over the telephone,' Skelton apologized to Massey, 'but I have been brought up in a thrifty school & sky high estimates of living needs irritate me. I'm open to conviction, however.'[49] Massey nonetheless received living allowances totalling $18,000 a year.[50] He was furious when Skelton arranged for the American representative to Canada to be received quite informally at Government House. The ceremony, Skelton told him, 'will be done decently and in order and with due impressiveness, even if we do have to omit the Marshal of the Diplomatic Corps and the Lord Equerry in Waiting and the other functionaries who lend solemnity to the affair in London.'[51] This was upsetting to Massey, who occupied himself by designing diplomatic dress for the Canadian foreign service, something that Skelton, an unshakable democrat, regarded as more than slightly silly. Should 'we seek some sartorial genius to devise a new one, or vary the British with some distinctive feature?' he asked. 'Or should we try the frock coat of the American gentleman, or the overalls of modern democracy?'[52] Massey nonetheless persisted and drove his staff to distraction with his insistence on diplomatic garb—and with what his chief officer, Hume Wrong, soon came to regard as his indifference to and incapacity for the work of the Legation.[53] For his part, Massey developed a deep dislike for the Under-Secretary and took to calling him 'Herr Doktor Skelton' in his diary.[54]

Massey did External Affairs at least one good turn, however, by bringing Hume Wrong into its service. There was no examination, no rigorous process of selection for Wrong. He was a family friend of the Masseys—indeed, he and Vincent had virtually grown up together in the Wrong family home, which was near the Masseys' on Toronto's Jarvis Street—and Massey chose him from the history department at the University of Toronto, where he had been teaching since his return from war service and Oxford. Others were soon appointed by similar informal methods: Laurent Beaudry, a Quebec journalist, went to Washington as Wrong's equal in rank, which caused subsequent bitterness between the two men; Pierre Dupuy, another Québécois, was sent to Paris; and Thomas Stone, a bright young man with a wealthy wife, went to Washington as well. Of that group, whose general level was quite good, Wrong became the Department's ablest officer.

The Civil Service Commission soon insisted that open competitive examinations be held for the Department's posts, something that Skelton probably welcomed. Appointments made by order-in-council had been subject to political pressures and cronyism, a method that did not guarantee that the right type of men could be found.[55] Thus in 1927 the Civil Service Commission advertised a competition for a 'Second Secretary (Male)' at $3,120. The duties were to consist of the preparation of reports on 'inter-imperial and international questions and communications with governments and Canadian representatives abroad'; the study and analysis of 'phases of the imperial and foreign relations work of the Department'; responsibility for a sub-division of the Department's work; and other duties. The qualifications were similarly grandiose. Besides an undergraduate degree and specialization in political economy or international law, the candidate was required to have knowledge of international law or diplomatic procedure, skill in modern office practice and a foreign language, ability to write memoranda, integrity, tact, perception, judgement, and 'good address'. If that failed to frighten off candidates, there was a written examination with questions on law and international affairs, the preparation of a précis, and a language test. Also important were the assessment of the candidate's record and an oral examination.[56] Thus the Commission attempted to define the qualifications of a diplomat.

What Skelton himself wanted—and got—were men of 'all-round ability, capable of performing in widely different assignments at short notice', not specialists.[57] He watched over the selection procedures personally, drafting the exam questions, reading the answers, and chairing the panel of oral examiners. His recommendations, not unnaturally, carried the most weight.[58]

The examinations in 1927 and those the next year, for first and third secretaries, essentially stocked the Department with its leaders for the next thirty years or more. Among those brought in were Lester Pearson, Norman Robertson, Hugh Keenleyside, and Scott Macdonald, all officers who served with distinction.[59] Skelton often feared that he would not outlast the Civil Service Commission's creaking machinery,[60] and he had repeated difficulties in persuading King to give him the staff he needed, but by July 1929 he could report that 'progress has been made. While the organization . . . is very small compared to the British Foreign Office or the State Department at Washington, it will provide for some measure of continuous and specialized attention to all sides of the Department's work and should prove adequate for the present.'[61] Skelton's staff the next year consisted of a Counsellor and a legal adviser and a first, second, and third secretary in Ottawa; in Paris a minister, a counsellor, and two second secretaries; in London a minister and a secretary; in Washington a minister, a counsellor, and a first, second, and third secretary; in Tokyo a minister, two first secretaries, and a second secretary; and in Geneva the Advisory Officer and a third secretary.[62]

For five years' work, that was not an unimpressive beginning. Most important and most striking was that for the first time Skelton had brought a group of broadly educated men into the civil service. And those recruits, to a notable extent, had common backgrounds, many of them sharing an Oxford education and almost all some postgraduate training. All could talk intelligently, most were affable and charming. Skelton generally had chosen well.

Norman Robertson, a Rhodes Scholar from British Columbia with graduate work at the Brookings Institute and a year's teaching at Harvard, enjoyed every aspect of his work, worshipped his chief, and told friends that he was getting paid for doing the work he would have wanted to do. But others, notably Hume Wrong, felt that Skelton's administration of the Department was so lax, believed that the work was so unimportant and the political leadership of the nation so timorous, that Canada's diplomatic service verged on farce.[*63] It couldn't even prevent some politicians from making policy as it suited them, one such occasion occurring at the League in 1932 when C.H. Cahan, the Secretary of State, embarrassed the government with a speech on Japan's aggression in Manchuria that seemed to thank the invaders for bringing stability and order to China.[64] But happy or not, very few of the men Skelton brought into the service left, although the Depression may have had something to do with that.

Certainly the Depression and its impact altered matters for Skelton. In 1929 he had been asked to return to Queen's as Principal,[65]

---

* Lester Pearson shared this view. In his diary on January 1, 1936 he wrote that 'I wish we had a chief who would add to Dr. Skelton's admirable personal qualities and remarkable brain, an interest in and aptitude for personnel & organization problems and a determination to fight for his men. Lord, how I would like to be given the job of pulling External Affairs & the Foreign Service apart & putting it together again, with a few of the pieces left out. Unfortunately, the Head, O.D.S. has apparently no inclination to do that. He is not ruthless enough; won't hurt people; won't fight for his subordinates.' (PAC, L.B. Pearson Papers, N8, vol. 1.)

and although he worried about the matter for some months, in the end he decided to remain in Ottawa, adding, as he told King, 'that my wife does not think very highly of my judgement in this matter.'[66] But having decided to remain, Skelton found himself in a difficult position when King lost the election of July 28, 1930 to R.B. Bennett and the Conservative Party with its promises of a cure for Canada's economic malaise. As King, in 1923, had driven out Loring Christie from External Affairs on the grounds that he was too close to the Tories, so might Bennett have forced Skelton to leave. Skelton feared this possibility, of course, but he decided to hold on to his post and not resign—to oblige the government to sack him if it chose.[67] Bennett, absorbed in setting up his administration, found himself, no doubt much to his surprise, increasingly reliant on Skelton for advice on a myriad of questions. Thus if Skelton had been intended for the axe, Bennett never swung it, and Skelton served his new master exactly as he had served the old.[68] The result confirmed the non-political character of the Department and its deputy, a principle that was of some importance to the country.

Skelton had transformed External Affairs into a department with able officers operating on the merit system, but this was virtually a unique situation in the civil service. In 1934 he wrote about this in a letter to W.D. Herridge, Bennett's appointee as Minister in Washington, answering his request for additional officers for the Legation:

> The number of really good men of the type you have in mind is deplorably small—not enough for the key positions which they ought to be occupying here. The whole question of filling the higher administrative posts is in a very unsatisfactory position in Ottawa. Many years ago Adam Shortt tried to meet it by providing for a Class I examination for university graduates, in much the same way as the higher ranks in the English Civil Service are recruited, but it was met by a storm of opposition, and his attempt failed. In the technical and scientific posts, many excellent men have been appointed and are doing first class work. There are, however, extremely few men in administrative posts with any breadth and flexibility of view. . . . I think we may fairly say that the endeavour of our Department to obtain men of this type through special examinations has started a number of

other Departments in the right direction. We have not always been fortunate in the men selected . . . but their superiority in general to the men obtained by other Departments through the ordinary Civil Service procedure, has been a matter of comment and envy, and I hope in time of emulation.[69]

Change had begun, but it was slow. Perhaps the quickest route was to begin at the top and to find good deputy ministers for the key departments. That, at any rate, seemed to be Skelton's idea.

III

In 1932 Ottawa was readying itself to play host to the Empire at the great Imperial Economic Conference. The main subject was trade, but the pall of economic depression hung over the world, and monetary policy had to be considered as well. Who could prepare the basic Canadian position paper on the subject? The Department of Finance was being directed by an executive committee of civil servants, and the Acting Deputy Minister, Watson Sellar, an accountant, was certainly not capable of preparing a complex brief on this subject; nor were any other members of the Department more qualified. Prime Minister Bennett asked Skelton for advice, and the Under-Secretary promptly suggested a former student and longtime friend, Clifford Clark, Professor of Economics at Queen's University. Clark wrote the memorandum on monetary policy, served Bennett as an adviser at the Conference, and soon after became Deputy Minister of Finance, a post he held for more than twenty years. No one, with the possible exception of O.D. Skelton himself, had more influence on the civil service and the country.

William Clifford Clark was born on April 18, 1889 at Glen Falloch near Martintown in Ontario's Glengarry County. His parents were farmers, operating a two-hundred-acre dairy spread in not very fertile country, and the boy was educated at the local one-room school house and at Martintown public school. He was sent to high school in nearby Williamstown where he boarded out—at $2 a month—for the school week, returning home to work on the farm on weekends. Clark was bright, so bright that one of his high-school teachers pressed his father to send the boy to Queen's, 'not merely because he was a brilliant student but because he was too small to be of much value on the farm'.[70] That he had also won an assortment of prizes and the Maclennan Glengarry Foundation entrance scholarship of $340 must have helped to persuade the father.[71]

Although Clifford Clark went to Queen's in 1906 to study mining engineering, it was not long before he decided that that choice of careers was a mistake. But he did not immediately opt for economics; he transferred to the honours program in Latin and French and proceeded to win all the prizes going. In 1907-8 he was first in Latin and French, second in English. Then he won the prize in senior Latin and came third in French and English, and in 1910 he received his Master of Arts, with double firsts in Latin and French.[72] But Clark did not stop there. He then enrolled in the honours courses in English (where he particularly enjoyed poetry), History, and Political and Economic Science, and over the next two years he took honours in all three programs. As W.A. Mackintosh noted, 'It is doubtful if any other student in the history of the University has completed the full honours courses in five subjects.'[73]

Clark was no Mr Gradgrind, however, A lively little man with dancing eyes and a kewpie-doll face, he wrestled and debated during his Queen's years and taught at summer schools on the Prairies and in northern Ontario. It was through the debating club that he came into contact with Skelton. 'There had never been before and there never was after', wrote a journalist some years later, 'a man for whose judgement, integrity and intellectual capacity [Clark] felt such great respect.'[74] Skelton stirred Clark, steered him into economics, and helped him win a good fellowship for graduate work at Harvard in 1912. He spent three years in Cambridge, working with Professor F.W. Taussig and greatly impressing the faculty there. In 1915, laden with honours, with a Harvard M.A. and all the requirements for his doctorate except the dissertation, he accepted Skelton's offer to return to his department to teach. Clark's starting salary, with effect from October 1, 1915, was $1,000 a year, which was not much even then.[75]

For the next eight years Clark taught at Queen's, his promotions coming quickly and his raises steadily.[76] He assisted in the special courses for bankers run by the university, became the first head of the Commerce program in 1919, and launched the correspondence courses through which Queen's trained chartered accountants in the province. And in this period, clearly under the influence of Skelton, he showed his leanings towards applied economics of a constructive sort.[77] At the same time he began to publish in *Queen's Quarterly* and the *Journal of the Canadian Bankers' Association* and to do long pieces for the *Bulletin* of his department, the first of which, in 1916, was 'The Country Elevator in the Canadian West'[78]—a subject that was not surprising, considering that his undergraduate summers on the Prairies had given him substantial practical knowledge. But current problems interested him too, and he began to write on inflation and prices during the Great War, explaining with much force the reasons behind the government's *laissez-faire* economic policy in the face of 'the working of powerful economic forces' over which it had 'little or no control'.[79] Later to become the architect of the Canadian economy in the Second World War—with its panoply of controls—Clark began as an orthodox economist.

In 1918 he left Queen's for a year and went to Ottawa to assist the Department of Labour's planning for, and establishment of, a national employment service. He worked on the statistical side, and he and a Queen's colleague, Bryce Stewart, established the first national statistical survey of unemployment trends in North America.[80]

Clark had married in 1916 and he and his wife, Margaret Smith from Martintown, had four children, one of whom was christened Kenneth Skelton Clark. The Queen's salary was too small to support so large a family, and when in 1921 an offer came from S.W. Strauss and Co., a Chicago firm of urban real-estate financiers, Clark leapt at the chance to abandon academe for Mammon, opting to become 'one of the earliest business economists in the United States, at a salary of $10,000'.[81] Until that moment, a reporter later noted, Clark 'had been talking about economics from behind ivy walls; now he got some practical experience in the hard-boiled Chicago Loop.'[82] He did indeed, and his rise was rapid as he grappled with detailed problems, applying his talent 'for balancing a promoter's zeal for what appears to be a constructive, imaginative project against a careful economic and financial analysis.' In 1926 he moved to New York as vice-president at a salary of $15,000 plus bonuses, buying a large and expensive house in Scarsdale and adopting a life-style to go with it. Although friends remember that the Clarks' income was always a little behind expenses, W.A. Mackintosh recollected that Clark was worried in the late 1920s by the effect a downturn in business might have on a company like Strauss, which was built on issuing

mortgage funds.[83] His warnings to the Strauss directors went un-
heeded and the company went under when the deluge of 1929
swept all before it. Clark went under too and was left with substantial debts that hung over him and blighted his family's finances
for the rest of his life.[84] He landed a position with President
Hoover's advisory committee on unemployment in 1930-1, but
soon his health broke under the weight of an osteo-arthritis attack
and in 1931, while his condition was still uncertain, Mackintosh
managed to get him his old job at Queen's. Clark came back to
Kingston as Professor of Commerce at $5,000, a good salary for
university work in 1931 but not a patch on his earnings in New
York and not enough to recoup his losses there.[85] His colleagues,
however, were an able group, with Mackintosh, C.A. Curtis, and
Norman Rogers all involved in public affairs, and that may have
provided some compensation.

Clark was destined to pass only one year in Kingston. In the
summer of 1932, at Skelton's instigation,[86] he worked on the preparations for the Imperial Economic Conference, producing a
long paper on monetary reconstruction. A later economic historian has called this 'a remarkable document for its careful weighing and proposed resolution of the conflict between external and
internal monetary objectives'.[87] Clark focused on the position that
the source of fluctuations in employment and production was the
instability of the general price level. This, he suggested, could be
stabilized chiefly through monetary policy. His proposal was for
ambitious international monetary reconstruction and co-ordinated
expansionary measures that would seek stability through acceptance of an international standard with a stabilized value—gold,
for example.[88] He advocated for Canada stable exchange rates
with other countries because of the critical role that trade and borrowing played in the economy; in addition, and most important,
he argued strongly for an independent financial policy and, to help
shape it, for the establishment of a central bank as the key to maintenance of the monetary control necessary for exchange stability.[89]

In its clarity of analysis and its sound policy prescriptions, this
paper was an impressive achievement, not least because the subject
had little to do with Clark's interests of the last decade. 'I did not
realize how far behind in monetary theory I actually was,' he told
Skelton as he wrestled with his memorandum,[90] and perhaps it
was on Skelton's advice that Bennett decided to send it for com-

ment to a baker's dozen of the leading economists in the land. The memorandum won their plaudits.[91]

Ironically, after all Clark's work monetary policy was hardly dealt with at the Imperial Economic Conference. The governor of the Bank of England, Montagu Norman, had warned his masters that a conference on trade in depression-poor Ottawa, with all the angry Dominions and dependencies jostling for advantage, was 'definitely *not* the place and the Ottawa atmosphere *not* the atmosphere for discussions', and his view largely prevailed.[92]

But that mattered not at all as far as Clark's own future was concerned. His name was made—as a result of a memorandum on a question that had little importance at the Conference for which it was prepared. Bennett, urged by Skelton, decided that Clark was the man to be Deputy Minister of Finance, and in his government Bennett's word was law. Bennett was usually adamant in opposing advice from long-haired academics,[93] but Clark seemed different. He had called up Charlotte Whitton—a Queen's graduate, an able social worker, and strong Tory—to ask, 'What can you tell me about this Queen's man of yours, this Dr. Clark? I know he's a Grit but I want him here.' Dr Whitton reassured the Prime Minister, who ended the conversation by saying 'I want him. He stood out head and shoulders above any but the tops of the U.K. delegation here [at the Imperial Economic Conference]. He's one of the few men in the country who think and talk their language.'[94] That was true enough, and by the fall of 1932 negotiations for Clark to come to Ottawa were in hand. On October 15, 1932, after getting his doctor's consent, Clark accepted the post of Deputy Minister in the Department of Finance, asking only that it be considered temporary for one year to suit the convenience of Queen's. The salary was $12,000 (less the ten-per-cent deduction that all civil servants submitted to as a Depression economy measure). In his letter of acceptance Clark told Bennett that, 'Having a good deal of Scottish blood in my veins I may be "slow on the start" but I hope to make up for this "on the home stretch".'[95] To what extent, if any, the Minister of Finance, E.N. Rhodes, had been consulted about the appointment is unclear, although the story spread through Ottawa that Rhodes had been summoned to Bennett's office and told to meet his new deputy.[96] In any case Clark's appointment marked the beginning of a new era in Canadian fiscal policy. Before Clark, Grattan O'Leary said, the running of the Finance Department had been largely a matter of wharves and post offices, and it didn't matter who the deputy minister was.[97] But with the Depression it did.

Thus Clifford Clark at forty-three was in the key position to influence Canadian policy. Clark had undoubtedly been helped along by Skelton, at least to the point where he was chosen to write the Conference memorandum. But after that he had been largely on his own, and his appointment as deputy minister owed everything to his ability.

IV

Clark's paper for the Imperial Conference called for the creation of a central bank as a necessary tool to maintain monetary control. There are undocumented suggestions that Clark sought and received a guarantee from the Prime Minister that a Bank of Canada was to be set up if he became deputy minister.[98] Certainly Clark acted as if he had such an understanding, and one of his early memoranda to his minister outlined the steps to set up a Royal Commission to investigate the necessity for such a bank and the ways to work out its organization. In February 1933 Clark suggested names of possible commissioners who could provide a unanimous report and make easier its acceptance by the country as a whole.[99]

The idea of a central bank had been bruited about for at least twenty years. It had been raised by farmer representatives, angry at mortgage foreclosures or the high interest rates charged by the commercial banks, and Clark himself had been in favour of the idea since 1918.[100] In 1923 he corresponded about the subject with W.C. Good, the Progressive Member of Parliament for Brant, Ont., and a farmer spokesman, and Clark expressed the need to surmount the opposition of the chartered banks; indeed, he thought—rather naively and optimistically—that with time he could even bring the Canadian Bankers' Association to sponsor the idea.[101] By the early 1930s others were taking up the cry, notably a young economist, A.F.W. Plumptre, who had just returned to Toronto from John Maynard Keynes's seminar at Cambridge. Plumptre, later the author of a long study of Commonwealth central banking, was already trying to incorporate Keynesian income-expenditure approaches into his arguments,[102] and he was working with a Liberal Party committee that was examining the idea of a central bank.[103] Pressure for a central bank was building both in the Opposition and in academe; and Plumptre later suggested that the Bank of England supported the idea of a chain of Dominion banks.[104]

Still, the new Deputy Minister was the key man. Clark privately told Floyd Chalmers of the *Financial Post* in January 1933: 'Canada is going to have a Central Bank anyway. The public wants it and if the government does not set one up the radicals will set one up some day. It would then be a dangerous institution. Under the present situation,' he went on, 'there is no one to initiate any policy of credit control; no one to say how the Finance Act is to be used. The government has handed over control of the country's monetary policy to the banks and the banks have not assumed that control with the result that it drops between two stools and often very menacing and dangerous things happen.' Clark added that he envisaged a bank that would be controlled jointly by government and the chartered banks.[105] Most important in Clark's view, a central bank was essential if effective financial and economic policies were to be carried out and if the government were to have the benefit of expert and impartial advice on fiscal matters.He persuaded Bennett to agree to set up a royal commission to examine the question.[106]

When Clark accompanied the Prime Minister to the World Economic Conference in London in the spring of 1933, he seized the opportunity to recruit as chairman to his Royal Commission on Banking and Currency, Lord Macmillan, the past chairman of the British Committee on Finance and Industry, and as a member, Sir Charles Addis, a one-time director of the Bank of England. The Canadian members, soon named, were Sir Thomas White, a senior banker and a former Minister of Finance; Beaudry Leman, General Manager of La Banque Canadienne Nationale; and Premier J.E. Brownlee of Alberta. The order-in-council establishing the Macmillan Commission was passed by Cabinet on July 31, 1933. On Clark's recommendation, Plumptre became assistant secretary to the Commission.[107]

The Macmillan Commission operated in haste. The British members arrived in Canada on August 4, met their Canadian colleagues four days later, and began hearings that concluded on September 11. At this point Macmillan announced that he was leaving in a few weeks and that the report was to be done before his departure. It was. The report arrived on the Prime Minister's desk on September 27 and the government made it public in early November; Bennett accepted the majority recommendation on

November 20. Not surprisingly, given Clark's influence over the personnel, the Commission members called for the establishment of a central bank, although White and Leman both dissented.[108] The Commissioners stated that the Bank of Canada should be privately owned—a form of management generally thought to be preferred by Clark, Bennett, and the Finance Minister—although this possibility had drawn no support in the testimony before the Commission.[109]

In their evidence to the Commission the chartered bankers had stood against the idea of a central bank. Their unanimity was broken only by the existence of a different view among some younger officials of the Royal Bank. The Canadian Bankers' Association had argued to Macmillan and his colleagues that a central bank was susceptible to political interference, particularly 'when years of unprecedented depression have brought dangerous currency theories into party politics.'[110] Clark, touching on that same point in his own evidence, argued the contrary position. He suggested that it was a burden on a political department to operate the Finance Act, thus delicately implying that a Bank of Canada should and could be free of political interference.[111] The chartered banks later opposed the government bill to set up the Bank of Canada, and Clark told Bennett that 'I am afraid our bankers have been spoiled by the Finance Act, which operated without requirements and without the possibility of control. . . . Mr Leman says that he is objecting to provisions which do not give the Central Bank adequate control. I fear that what he is really objecting to is that the Central Bank will have control for the first time in this country.'[112]*

When it came time to choose the Governor of the Bank of Canada, the government ruled that he had to be a Canadian and a banker. But Clark did not initially agree. The choice was too limited, he told Bennett, 'having in mind the very limited number of Canadian bankers who have, for instance, university training and a theoretical grasp of economic and monetary principles.'[113] But by September 1934 a suitable Canadian candidate had turned up in

---

* When the Liberals took power in 1935, Clark's attitude to bankers made him acceptable to Mackenzie King. King had asked the outgoing Prime Minister his view of Clark and was told, 'He's a good man and the bankers hate him.' 'I told him', King wrote in his diary, 'that I thought that was no fault.' (PAC, R. Finlayson Papers, draft memoirs, 113; King Diary, 27 Oct., 1935.)

the person of Graham Towers who, though only thirty-seven years old, was assistant general manager of the Royal Bank and a known proponent of the central-bank idea. To what extent Towers was Clark's choice is unclear (although Clark must have supported his selection), but there is no doubt that they knew each other, had visited each other, and had worked together in 1932, when the Royal Bank found itself in temporary difficulties, and on the executive of the Canadian Political Science Association, where both had supported the idea of establishing a Canadian academic journal in the field. O.D. Skelton too was heavily involved in the same Association and his acquaintance with Towers could not have hurt. The key factors in his appointment, however, were probably Towers' youth, his ability, and his support for central banking.[114]

Clark's great goal was accomplished when the Bank of Canada opened its doors on March 11, 1935. At last Canada had the means to control foreign exchange and the issuance of currency, and in Towers a central banker who was not afraid to exercise his power. Equally important, Clark and Towers, while never particularly close friends, could work together and trust each other, and both were absolutely convinced that able men had to be enticed to Ottawa if policy was to be made effectively. 'In those departments and agencies which could expand in the depressed thirties,' W.A. Mackintosh wrote, this was a great opportunity, 'for it was not difficult to recruit first-class people.'[115]

V

Graham Towers, the newest recruit to the top level of the civil service, was different from Skelton and Clark. His background, education, and career thus far were not similar to theirs. Only in his ability and his devotion to his work was he the same. Towers was a Montrealer born and bred, a product of the tightest, toughest, and most exclusive English-speaking community in the country. His family was well off, his connections were of the best, and he fitted right into the business community of St James Street as if to the manner born. And he was.

Towers was born on September 29, 1897 into a family of Loyalist and Scottish stock. On his mother's side he had a banker's lineage, extending back three generations to a founder of the Bank of Montreal, and that heritage must have been transmitted to Towers in his genes. He attended Montreal High School for a time and then was sent off in 1911 to St Andrew's College School, Toronto, where he was 'no marvel' in mathematics, the headmaster recollected. 'He was brilliant in his languages, French, English and Latin'—one similarity with Clark and Skelton. Towers won prizes for general proficiency at St Andrew's,[116] and when he left the school in 1913 it was to go to McGill University, where he stayed until the onset of the Great War. Like many of his generation (but unlike Skelton and Clark), Towers enlisted under age at seventeen, became a lieutenant in the Army Service Corps, and served overseas as a railway supply officer. His greatest danger during the war came not from enemy shells but from being stricken in the influenza epidemic of 1918, which he fortunately survived. After being demobilized he returned to McGill and to economics under Stephen Leacock. He graduated in 1919 with highest honours.

For a time it seemed that law attracted him and he enrolled in the McGill Law School. But when Leacock recommended him to Morris Wilson of the Royal Bank of Canada, who wanted a bright young man, his career was decided.[117] Initially hired by the Royal as an economist, Towers was shipped to Havana as an accountant in 1922, promoted to inspector of Cuban branches in 1923, and to inspector of all foreign branches in 1924. In that same year he married Mary Godfrey, a well-connected Montrealer whose father was vice-president and treasurer of the Montreal Steel Works. His career with the Royal was in no way hurt by his new connections and in 1929 he became Chief Inspector of the Bank, a title whose exact meaning was uncertain, but the position brought him into the rarefied atmosphere of the inner group on the second floor at Head Office. Two years later he became assistant to the General Manager and in 1933 Assistant General Manager of the Royal Bank.[118] His rise had been meteoric.

Towers' salary in 1933 was $25,000 and the Bank paid his income tax to boot.[119] Thus when the Bennett government decided on Towers for the Bank of Canada, it had at least to match that salary, a necessity that gave Bennett, away in England when the final decision was taken, acute heartburn. 'I am anxious that we do not pay more than the sum indicated for the first year,' the Prime Minister wired Ottawa, 'but am certain if service satisfactory during first year increase would follow.' That view was conveyed to Towers, but Sir George Perley, the acting Prime Minister, told Bennett that 'He states that salary you had in mind is less than he would receive under plan reorganization now contemplated by his present employer. Therefore thinks it should be somewhat higher. Minister Finance likes his appearance,' Perley continued, 'and we both favour giving him thirty and closing matter tomorrow. . . .' Bennett did not reply, so Perley wired once more that 'Thirty thousand subject to income tax is no better than Twenty-five not subject to Income Tax. . . . As appointment urgently necessary and Towers is considered specially qualified, Council decided put it through today.'[120] Towers had therefore been made Governor of the Bank of Canada at $30,000 a year, the highest salary in the gift of the government and three times that paid Skelton and Clark.* This stipend was publicly known;[121] however, there are no indications that it stirred resentment in the public service, although all of Tower's colleagues were well aware that he lived in Ottawa's Rockcliffe Village in a style to which they could not aspire. For example, Towers and his wife had four maids, expensive holidays each winter and summer, and the Prime Minister as a dinner guest. 'The Towers' house looks extraordinarily pretty,' Mackenzie King wrote after one such occasion in 1937, 'though very formal and a little cold. The table is exceedingly pretty, and the dinner most beautifully served.'[122]

Very formal and a little cold—these words fitted Towers himself. Only thirty-seven, he was already a formidable figure. He looked like the caricature of a young banker—prissy, precise, calm, and he peered out from behind his spectacles with a steady gaze. He was as cool as he looked. The *Financial Times* wrote on his appointment that he was the 'soul of discretion and rectitude' who could 'at need, give as good an impression of the Sphinx as Montagu Norman', the head of the Bank of England and a legendary figure.[123] Whether that was the real Towers was in some doubt. One Bank official who worked with him from the begin-

---

* Towers was as aware as anyone that his salary was out of line with those paid members of the civil service. But the Bank of Canada by design was not quite part of the civil service and he was not a civil servant. As he wrote in a memorandum for file in 1938, the position of the Governor was different from that of a civil servant or a chartered banker. The Governor was appointed for a certain term, not exceeding seven years, and there was no guarantee of reappointment. That presumably justified a higher salary than the Ottawa norm, but in any case, as he wrote, the salary paid to the Governor was lower than salaries earned by senior officials of the major Canadian banks. (Bank of Canada, Towers Papers, Memo #155, 11 Aug., 1938.)

ning thought that Towers deliberately cultivated a cold *persona* to camouflage a basic shyness; another believed that he yearned for friendship but could not draw it to him; and women who met him at Ottawa parties and heard him tell smutty schoolboy stories thought he did this to hide his unease.[124] A complicated man, Mr Towers, but he did his work with great professionalism, managed his Bank and his officers with skill, and treated his staff as adults.[125]

Towers proved as adept at recruiting good subordinates as Skelton. The men he chose—from names suggested by Mackintosh of Queen's and transmitted to him by Skelton and Clark—all had the advantages of a Queen's education (unlike Towers). Donald Gordon, for example, was Towers' choice for Secretary of the Bank. Though he had no university degree, he had taken the Queen's banker's course and had impressed Mackintosh—who spoke to Clark, who spoke to Towers. Gordon got the position.[126] Another product of the old-boy network was D. Alexander Skelton, O.D.'s son and a Rhodes Scholar. Towers made Sandy Skelton head of the Bank's research department, one of the very few offices in Ottawa devoted to applied research. Skelton was brilliant, and able enough to get the job on his own, but being Dr Skelton's son undoubtedly did him no harm. On the other hand, John Deutsch, who was appointed to the research department, had no influence in Ottawa or anywhere else; but the Kingston-to-Ottawa pipeline produced his name as well and launched another mandarin on an extraordinary career that had begun on a dirt-poor Saskatchewan farm. With a little help from his friends, Towers chose well.

VI

The Bank of Canada was a curious creation. When it was founded in 1935 it was a privately owned bank with 100,000 widely dispersed shares (no one could hold more than fifty), and seven directors. Together with the Governor, his deputy, and the Deputy Minister of Finance, who were to run the Bank, they were nominated from virtually every quarter of the country. Those elected by the shareholders ultimately were chosen from a slate put forward by the Canadian Chamber of Commerce, so that the directorship of the central bank of Canada was partly made up of names suggested by organized business and boosters—an extraordinary state of affairs. In 1936, however, the Mackenzie King government undertook a measure of nationalization, securing a bare minority of the stock and appointing six additional directors, each with two votes. Two years later it went the rest of the way, buying out the private shareholders (at $59.20 for each $50 share) and taking upon itself the right to appoint all the directors.[127]

The Bank had to struggle to become established. Its quarters were initially located in the Grand Central Hotel in Ottawa.[128] As Towers recollected, the government lent the Bank 'a desk and two chairs. At that point the number on the staff was one.'[129] Within two months there were ten, and when the Bank of Canada opened its doors for business on March 11, 1935, in the Victoria Building in downtown Ottawa, there were 213 employees, including 120 who had been transferred from the Department of Finance to the Currency Division of the Bank.[130]

The problems Towers faced were horrendous. The nation was staggering under the burden of economic collapse; provinces were near bankruptcy from soaring relief costs and stagnating revenues. These and other problems destroyed the Bennett government in October 1935 and returned Mackenzie King to power, but the change in administration did nothing to resolve the crisis, nor did the Bank of Canada's modest efforts to promote an easy-money policy ease the situation appreciably.[131]

Perhaps the most challenging problem was that posed by the plight of the provinces. In Saskatchewan, at the nadir of the Depression, two-thirds of the population were on relief,[132] wheat was selling below the cost of production, and crop failure had become the norm. In Manitoba, where substantial numbers in the labour force were dependent on Saskatchewan wheat for their work, the economic support was removed by 1933. Particularly hard-hit was Winnipeg, which absorbed over eighty per cent of the province's relief costs.[133] The result was that the Prairie Provinces were close to collapse and near a default on their bonds, a calamity that most in Ottawa feared could provoke a financial outflow, or lead to the curtailment of Canada's ability to borrow or attract investment.

In such circumstances Towers' role was crucial. One by one provincial premiers and ministers—not really understanding the Bank of Canada's role—came to him for help. In May 1935 Premier Pattullo of British Columbia sought a cash advance, a request Towers had to turn down. That was not the role of the Bank, he said. His task was to attempt to regulate credit through control of chartered-bank cash holdings: if the Bank could manage to create

stable conditions and a relatively favourable situation in the market for provincial securities, then it would have done a good day's
work.[134] The next month an Alberta minister visited Towers, bemoaning his inability to borrow $2 million for road-building from
the chartered banks except on ruinous terms. 'In stressing the
Province's need for the additional money,' Towers wrote, the
minister said 'that if they had to confess their inability to proceed
with the road programme Aberhart's campaign would be greatly
assisted.'[135] William Aberhart was leading the Social Credit forces
in the province, campaigning against the banks and the existing
monetary system, and promising a total alteration in the system
when Social Credit was implemented by his government. Towers
could give no assistance.

What was to be done about the provinces' financial plight? One
possibility was the creation of a loan council, which might allow
Ottawa to guarantee provincial debts, though the provinces
would have to pledge certain specified revenues as security for
their loans, and these loans would have to be approved by the loan
council—effectively by the Dominion Minister of Finance. This
possible solution was first considered by the Bank of Canada in
early 1935, when some of Towers' officials began to worry about
the rapid increase in public debt at all levels of government and to
fear that unwise borrowing by any one level affected the rest.[136]
The idea emerged again when the Liberals took power in the fall
of 1935, and when the Prairie provinces—including Alberta,
where Aberhart was now in office with a huge majority behind
him—seemed headed inexorably toward default.[137] With Towers'
urging and support, King's Minister of Finance, Charles Dunning, brought the loan-council idea to a Dominion-Provincial
Conference in Ottawa in January 1936. The provinces seemed receptive and the provincial treasurers decided to meet with Dunning to discuss it further. These talks produced an agreement on
the desirability of an amendment to the British North America
Act to permit a loan council, and in May a resolution for one was
introduced into the House of Commons.[138]

In the interim between the Conference and the resolution, the
provinces began to have second thoughts. A loan council was obviously going to authorize every provincial loan. What were the
implications of this? To some provinces the major one was the destruction of provincial autonomy, with Ottawa forcing higher
taxes and lower spending on them before granting approval to
borrow. The Premier of British Columbia was first to have

doubts. When he declared that he would accept the loan council only if his requests for loans were guaranteed approval, Dunning refused any such promise. Then Premier Aberhart sought to borrow enough from the federal government to meet the April 1 payment on $3 million worth of Alberta bonds. The King Cabinet was agreeable—but only if Aberhart accepted the loan council. Aberhart refused; Alberta defaulted on the bonds; and shortly after, the Alberta legislature passed an act arbitrarily cutting by half the interest rates on most outstanding provincial bonds.[139]

All this frightened Towers. Fortunately the Alberta default was seen by investors as a Social Credit aberration. So far—Towers noted on April 18, 1936—there had been no serious repercussions on other governmental borrowers. But if British Columbia, Saskatchewan, and Manitoba defaulted—Saskatchewan and British Columbia faced that prospect in May—he feared the slide might begin in earnest. Municipalities might join the rush to default, and this was certain to hurt the Dominion's credit. Towers stated that 'It is unnecessary to suggest panic conditions; we may rather anticipate an initial weakening in Dominion Government bond prices, followed by a continuous drag in the same direction over a period of years.' He added his fear that American investors, left holding substantial quantities of devalued Prairie paper, 'will change their attitude towards all Canadian obligations from general faith to general distrust.'[140]

But by this stage Mackenzie King himself had become convinced that a loan council was a mistake. If the provinces had begun to develop qualms, so had he, for King was notoriously cautious, and the loan-council idea threatened the federal treasury. King was much relieved, therefore, when the Tory majority in the Senate, led by former Prime Minister Arthur Meighen, refused to accept the necessary resolution to amend the BNA Act. The loan council was dead.[141]

However, the financial problems of the western provinces remained. The premier of Manitoba, John Bracken, carried the case for federal assistance to a December 1936 meeting of the National Finance Committee, which had been created the previous January by the Federal-Provincial Conference. The government of Manitoba (as well as that of neighbouring Saskatchewan) was close to bankruptcy, and out of that province's 1935-6 expenditures of $14,097,549, $5,934,402 had been paid in interest on outstanding debentures.[142] Bracken pleaded for help. Could the province reduce the interest on its bonds to ease matters temporarily? he asked Towers.[143] Could there be a review of the economic basis of Confederation to determine if the provinces had too many responsibilities and too few sources of revenue?[144] Towers was impressed with Bracken's case, and after the meetings he urged the Prime Minister not to allow the provinces to fall into bankruptcy. 'He thought', King wrote, 'that a loan of Seven hundred thousand dollars in one case, and a million in the other would tide over the situation. He thought there should be enquiry by Commission into the financial position of these provinces, and in their relation to provincial and federal services.'[145] But King was unwilling to supply funds to either Manitoba or Saskatchewan, and the two provinces continued to drift toward the rocks.

Thereupon Towers carried his case to the Minister, Charles Dunning, but he was not the one who needed to be convinced.[146] King was. Meanwhile Sandy Skelton urged that the Bank of Canada should recommend a cash grant and an immediate Royal Commission on the provinces' financial problems. He stressed that this would lead to the only satisfactory solution, and that this view should be put on record. 'Let the politicians take full responsibility for the selection of the alternatives if they will not follow our advice,' he said, 'and let us keep entirely free from supporting the Western arguments for the situation they adopt.'[147]

Whether or not that was good advice, Towers could not take it. The next day, January 21, 1937, when he saw King and Dunning to discuss the Finance Minister's proposal that the Bank investigate the financial situation of Manitoba, Towers objected that this was not a role for a central bank and was something 'that . . . might embarrass the Bank . . .' Towers then tried to argue for what King called 'the old idea of grants . . . with a Commission to investigate . . . .' King went on, 'I told him there was no chance of a Commission,' although he agreed that it was a mistake to put the Bank into a position 'where it might have to reflect on either the Dominion or the Provinces, and its purpose thereby being misconstrued.'* But a few hours later, after Towers had talked

---

* Towers had a clear idea of the proper role for a central bank. As he told C.D. Howe in May 1938, 'the relation of Central Bank to Government was a very special one . . . the name of the former should not be mentioned by the Government as the source of advice . . . we were not the makers of policy in relation to Government finances. The Government took certain decisions after receiving advice, but could not lay the responsibility for the decision on the advisor.' (Bank of Canada, Towers Papers, Memo #129, 3 May 1938.)

with Clifford Clark, he changed his mind, telling King 'that he will advise the Bank taking the step suggested; that he did not think it could do any harm. . . .' In those circumstances King changed his position too, and the Bank now was committed to investigating the financial situation of Manitoba.[148] (Later events led to investigations of Alberta and Saskatchewan as well.)

The *volte-face* of Towers was shrewdly timed, for it allowed him to achieve the Bank's objectives of both a grant and a Royal Commission. Within a few days Sandy Skelton was in Winnipeg beginning the Bank's investigation, and Towers followed soon after. On February 11, 1937 the report was ready. Towers and Skelton found that the Bracken government had run a tight ship, had tried to balance its budget, and had imposed taxes that were at least as high as those in any other province. What had put the province in trouble, Towers' report said, was that its revenues had increased by a smaller percentage over the previous ten years than those of all the other provinces but one. Manitoba needed more money to maintain its services, and only Ottawa could provide it. Moreover, Manitoba was not alone in its difficulties. Towers' report therefore recommended a Royal Commission on federal-provincial relations.[149] As he told the Minister of Finance, a decision to establish a Royal Commission was now necessary; if it did not come before February 18, Manitoba would be obliged to reduce the interest owing on its bonds.[150]

Faced with this report, the Prime Minister caved in—even noting in his diary, incredibly, that 'I have all along wanted a Commission on financial allocations. . . .' The Cabinet, probably startled by this, went along, approved the establishment of a Royal Commission, and Manitoba soon was given $750,000 in temporary assistance.[151] That was a victory for Premier Bracken who, desperate as he was, had argued a good case with skill. But it was also a victory for Towers. His flexibility and tenacity, good timing and judgement, had led to the creation of the most significant investigation of Canadian federalism: the Royal Commission on Dominion-Provincial Relations.

The Royal Commission was an achievement, even though its ultimate recommendations for a restructuring of federalism came in 1940 during the beginnings of the munitions-induced prosperity of the war and thus failed to win acceptance. In the history of the modern public service, however, it is significant that Towers in the Bank, and Clark in the Department of Finance, were providing innovative and carefully framed policy advice. Ten years earlier the Department of Finance had simply not had the capacity to give such counsel, and at that time monetary policy, which was lodged with the chartered banks, was not designed to serve the nation's needs or ends.

It was therefore in the middle and late thirties—the Depression years—that Ottawa acquired the basic tools for creating a sophisticated financial policy, and, in the Department of External Affairs, the beginnings of an able foreign office, one capable of representing the nation abroad and of advising the government at home.

The change from the immediate past was striking. Equally so was that the change had been brought about by only three men. Skelton, Clark, and Towers brought professionalism and competence to a public service that was sorely in need of both. They were the founders and builders of the modern civil service, and their impact on Canadian government was tremendous.

4

THE ISOLATIONIST
NATIONALISTS

The competence and professionalism that the founders brought to the public service was nowhere more evident than in the Department of External Affairs. In the 1930s Skelton's little department became widely known and admired for the extraordinarily able group it housed. Men such as Hume Wrong, Lester Pearson, Norman Robertson, and Loring Christie were all marked for the highest places in the bureaucracy, and the collective intellectual power they generated found no peer in Ottawa—or in London or Washington.

But intelligent and able as they were, the members of Skelton's band were as torn in their reaction to the dreadful events of the 1930s as most other thinking Canadians. The world was sliding inexorably towards war, and no one seemed to know how to stop it. Despite the lessons of the Great War, most ordinary Canadians still believed that they lived in 'a fire-proof house far from inflammable materials', and few took seriously the prospect of war. But a number of people were deeply concerned. The Canadian Institute of International Affairs, which had come into existence in the late 1920s with branches across the country, brought together interested laymen of all shades of opinion. On the left, the Co-operative Commonwealth Federation, founded in 1932, was creating a democratic-socialist forum for many who followed a neutralist line; and the League of Nations Society brought together many devotees of collective security. The Empire-minded, those who believed that Canada's place was 'at Britain's side whate'er betide', were less well organized because they were the majority, certainly among English-speaking opinion makers. Their view—the conventional wisdom—was that Canada would certainly do its duty and rally to the Empire if Britain and Germany went to war.[1]

The Canadian situation was also difficult because French Canadians were unhappy with any automatic commitment to the Imperial cause, whatever it might turn out to be. So too were many other Canadians who felt scant allegiance to Britain. Therefore the relatively few English-Canadian neutralists, because they were articulate and because they used their bases in the universities and churches as rostrums, had disproportionate influence and became a political factor to be weighed and considered.[2]

If the neutralist and isolationist case seemed credible in 1931, say, it appeared less so half-a-dozen years later. Hitler had been a middling German politician in 1931, but by 1937 he was the leader of a strong, aggressive Reich, apparently certain of its course and destiny. Events gradually began to alter public opinion in Canada, and this was as true within the Department of External Affairs as outside it. Nationalists and neutralists such as Skelton looked on heartsick as the road to war became clearer, altering their convictions only slightly as their political realism told them that Canada must fight if Britain did. Others saw the danger to the world more clearly and began to press for their country to adopt a firmer position.

These things are discussed in what follows. Lester Pearson, one of Canada's best-known public figures, is memorialized in his own autobiography and in a number of accounts that trace his diplomatic and political career, but relatively little is known about his attitudes during the 1930s when he wrestled with the ideas of isolationism, collective security, and resistance to Hitler. Loring Christie, on the other hand, is now remembered by only a few scholars. Like Pearson, he too grappled with the political and moral choices of the 1930s, but for this disillusioned and bitter man the decision in the end was different. Pearson and Christie, in their own ways, personify the difficulties that intelligent men of good will faced in that terrible decade.

I

Loring Christie had 'the keenest intellect of any of the people in External Affairs in my period',[3] according to his cousin John Read, the legal adviser in the Department of External Affairs. He was also—in the words of Hugh Keenleyside, another colleague—

'the handsomest member of the Canadian diplomatic service', and his charm was legendary.[4] With perhaps too fine an intellect, Christie was sometimes more than a little unstrung. His good looks also made difficulties: apparently his attractiveness to women contributed to the break-up of his first marriage.

He was born on January 21, 1885 in Amherst, N.S., into a well-off Baptist family of coffin and furniture makers. He attended the Amherst Academy and Acadia College, graduating with a Bachelor of Arts degree in 1905. The next year he went to the Harvard Law School and performed brilliantly there, winning a place as one of the *Harvard Law Review*'s editors in 1907 and becoming editor-in-chief the next year, the most prestigious position in the School. After graduation, and after failing to find a place with Toronto law firms unimpressed with his Harvard degree, he accepted a position with Winthrop and Stimson of New York City, a powerful firm headed by Henry Stimson and one that included among its juniors Felix Frankfurter, who had graduated from Harvard in 1906.

Frankfurter and Christie became friends and both soon gravitated towards public service in Washington. Although still a Canadian and British subject, Christie accepted a position with the Justice Department at $2,500, forgoing the opportunity to get rich in New York. 'Had good talk with Christie about our line of work,' Frankfurter wrote in his diary in 1911. 'Shared experience that our friends think us damn fools but agreed that there is going to be increasing opportunity for public work & the ordinary practice is spiritless without real service & mainly unfilled by money-making. . . .'[5] The two friends shared a modest house on 19th Street with some other idealistic young men—R.G. Valentine, Taft's Indian Commissioner, and Lord Eustace Percy of the British Embassy were two—and the talk was good, the sense of purpose clear, so clear that Mr Justice Oliver Wendell Holmes dubbed their residence 'The House of Truth'.[6]

But in April 1913, without consulting Sir Joseph Pope, the Under-Secretary of State for External Affairs, Sir Robert Borden brought Christie, a fellow Nova Scotian, back to Canada to act as legal adviser in the Department of External Affairs, which Borden headed. Christie's entry into the tiny department instantly raised its officer complement by a third and its competence by even more. Christie gradually became Borden's key adviser, and his influence stemmed from his ability to offer useful and sound politi-

cal advice or assistance when it was needed.[7] His advice had a
Tory cast to it, and with the war, conscription, and Union Government, Christie became if anything harder and more determined
than his Prime Minister, Borden. He did much of the legal research that underpinned the Military Service Act of 1917,[8] helped
draft the Union Government's platform, and after the election of
1917 was notably bloodyminded about Quebec. In a conversation
recorded by a fellow political aide, Christie said that he had liked
the Wartime Elections Act (the gerrymandering legislation that
had stripped the vote from the 'doubtful' immigrant electorate and
given it to the female relatives of soldiers) 'because it foiled the
schemes of the French, who . . . would have used the foreign vote
to buttress their own opposition to conscription and to the other
vigorous ideals of the rest of Canada.' His friend wrote that he was
'quite pessimistic' about the situation in the country at this critical
stage of the war. 'There was no essential unity between the French
and the English, he did not think there ever would be, and was inclined to think it was not worth trying to secure.' Borden agreed,
Christie said, adding that the Prime Minister had abandoned efforts to maintain unity 'and had not shrunk from actuality of dis-
union between Quebec and the other provinces, to secure the
great national ideal and duty of active, vigorous prosecution of the
war.'[9]

Though Christie's thinking was infected by the wartime
rhetoric of duty and ideals, he still retained a cool intelligence, one
that allowed him—forced him—to judge the political men with
whom he worked. Borden, he told Frankfurter, 'is not brilliant of
course, but his character has commanded a remarkable confidence
on the part of his country.'[10] Newton Rowell, the leading Ontario
Liberal in the coalition, 'has great ability, but he is not first class.
He talks too much & too righteously. He is an Ontario Methodist—a vicious breed—much worse than any Jesuit.'[11] Arthur
Meighen, Borden's successor, he described as 'a baffling study &
in some ways a fascinating one',[12] but Mackenzie King he dismissed as 'Babbitt Rex'.[13]

Babbitt Rex was as suspicious of Christie as Christie was of
him. Coming into office in 1921, King saw in Christie a civil servant who had been too close to Borden and Meighen to be trusted.
In fact that was probably unfair to Christie, who had told
Meighen when the former Prime Minister was in Opposition that
he could pass him nothing confidential because he was 'the servant

of the Cabinet and not of any party'.[14] That was quite proper, but King remained suspicious. Soon Christie found himself cut out, his salary frozen, his access to confidential files limited. During the Chanak crisis of 1922, as a reporter later noted, 'Christie saw none of the documents until the whole thing was finished. . . . He sat in his office with a bare desk—nothing to do.'[16] That was too much for a man of Christie's temperament, and in May 1923 he resigned. Christie later attributed King's antipathy to his first interview with the Liberal Premier:

> . . . he had talked about his political creed at great length, contrasting it with Mr. Meighen's and so on, and that at one or two appropriate pauses I had either been silent or had sought to talk about the Department. . . . I do not doubt, though I could not prove it, that it was simply a crude invitation to declare myself his faithful slave and what a wonderful time we would have together.

Christie's departure was an incalculable loss to the fledgling Department of External Affairs. Christie had accompanied Borden to the Imperial War Conferences of 1917 and 1918 and to the Versailles Conference of 1919. He had attended the first session of the League of Nations, the Imperial Conference of 1921, and the Washington Conference of 1921-2. More important, he had done more than merely attend; to a substantial extent Christie was the architect of the Canadian position at all these conferences, the drafter of the route to autonomy through a common Imperial policy, for which Borden and Meighen have received credit.[17]

Christie had a goal: to see Canada operating happily within a co-operative Empire and the Empire functioning within a universal League of Nations. This, to him, was the way to nationhood, the way to bid farewell to the impotent structure into which Canada had been locked at the onset of the war in 1914, when Britain alone shaped foreign policy, binding Canada and its sister Dominions to the course London determined. But the war had altered all this. The Imperial gatherings had held out the prospect of a common Empire foreign policy, jointly reached and mutually agreed upon, and the enhanced status Canada had won at the front seemed to have been confirmed by Canada's signing the peace treaty and by its admission to the League of Nations. The Imperial Conference of 1921, or so Christie firmly believed, had demonstrated the reality of a common foreign policy as well, for had Bri-

tain not ultimately agreed with Canada's opposition to the re-
newal of the Anglo–Japanese alliance?[18]

Christie was also persuaded that Canada should seek and take an
active role in the world. Under the Covenant of the League, the
Dominion had accepted responsibilities that effectively guaranteed
its status;[19] if the status was real, so too were the responsibilities.
For Christie, equality within the Empire led to equality within the
League, and that equality was the best guarantor of co-operation
and peace.[20]

But there were anomalies in all this, as Christie saw when Canada had to decide how to operate at the League sessions of 1920.
The British Empire was entitled to a delegate on the Council of
the League. What was the Canadian role in helping to select that
delegate? Christie had wondered how Canada could demand
representation as a lesser power while taking a part in the actions
of the greater powers, a situation that would result if Canada
sought to share in choosing the Imperial delegate. If it did, it
would inevitably be pulled into the larger sphere of British global
interests. The choices seemed clear: either an Empire representative would be rendered impotent by Dominion objections, or Dominion freedom would be eroded by Imperial initiatives. Equal
responsibilities within the British Empire could clash directly with
equal status in the world.[21] As it happened, Canada in the end did
not participate in choosing the delegate. Nonetheless, the problems raised by this issue were all too clear and all too difficult to
resolve. Christie's League experience in 1920 only compounded
his concerns. The world body was too exclusively associated with
Europe and too completely dominated by European votes to reflect the reality of global power. His process of disillusionment
had begun.

It accelerated after his resignation from External Affairs when
he went to England to make his fortune. His employer, Sir James
Dunn, was a Canadian millionaire with extensive business interests who was considered too flashy and shifty to be trusted in the
cool precincts of the City. Christie's interest in world affairs remained as strong as ever, however, and he soon found himself involved with the Royal Institute of International Affairs and the
Round Table. As his wife Jane wrote to her brother in November
1923, Christie had gone to a Round Table meeting

with fire in his eye and looking for a fight. His ideas on the

> Empire and foreign affairs, more particularly the League of
> Nations, have undergone some very radical changes in the
> past year, and now that he is a free agent, he gives vent to his
> views with vigour. . . . [He] looks on [the League] as a kind
> of League for minding other people's business. He is for get-
> ting out of European entanglements and only giving one's
> advice when it's asked for.

What had caused the shift? Jane Christie was frank: 'This has been
a hard year . . . full of shocks to his confidence in God—himself,
and his fellow men. His parents' deaths began it, MacKenzie [sic]
King's fair-speaking and evil-dealing with him aggravated it, and
what he sees under the surface in foreign policies finishes
it. . . .'[22]

Christie remained in England until 1927, his doubts about Imperial policy and the League hardening into convictions. 'The
Englishness of the English', he wrote to his wife in 1925, 'is an un-
failing phenomenon & for nationalism at its intensest they cannot
be beat. . . .'[23] That disturbed him, along with the British government's unconcern for the effect its actions might have in the
Dominions. 'No one, I feel, outside a Dominion,' he wrote to his
friend Philip Kerr (later Lord Lothian), 'can quite appreciate the
effects of Imperial controversy on the Dominions' internal development. It creates divisions that cut across what would otherwise
be party lines based on considerations of internal economics.'[24] By
the end of 1925, in part at least under the effect of what he perceived as a betrayal by Britain both of its policy of non-
involvement in Europe and of the idea of a consultative Empire at
Locarno,[25] Christie now concluded that all hopes of a common
foreign policy had been dashed. Canada had to shape its own
course, free of the apron strings of British policy. Soon he resigned from the Round Table,[26] and by 1927 he was back in Canada.

As Christie's wife suggested, he had suffered a series of emotional shocks through the 1920s, and to what extent these shaped
his altering views is unclear. When he had become engaged to Jane
Armstrong in 1914, he had written Frankfurter that 'she has
driven out a certain sense of loneliness that I have always been half
conscious of in myself. . . .'[27] For a decade the marriage seemed
happy, but in England troubles mounted. 'I am often hopelessly
inconsiderate', Christie apologized to Jane, and a few months later
he wrote that 'There is a mixture of devils and obtusities in me

that are simply intolerable; I blame no friend or enemy of mine who has concluded that he could no longer put up with them. . . .'[28] By 1928 the marriage had effectively collapsed. To continue to live with him, Jane told her brother, 'requires a kind of courtesy—in a situation like this, that I know Loring doesn't happen to possess. The disclosures of the past ten years culminating in his statement that he now *loves* someone else and not me—I just can't deal with yet. . . .'[29] The marriage could not be put back together.[30]

Thus by the end of the 1920s Christie had not only a shattered marriage but a shattered world to contemplate. From 1927 to 1929 he worked in Toronto as a special assistant to the chairman of the Ontario Hydro-Electric Power Commission, and from 1929 to April 1935 he laboured as legal officer and secretary-treasurer of the Beauharnois Power Company; but nothing was satisfying. Indeed, he got only a strong 'dose of disillusionment with Business and all that.'[31] Finally in 1935, just before the general election (and apparently with the concurrence of both Bennett and King),[32] Skelton brought him back to the Department of External Affairs as a Counsellor at a salary of $6,000. Nominally appointed by order-in-council to the Tokyo Legation,[33] Christie never went there but remained in Ottawa until the outbreak of war in 1939, serving as the Under-Secretary's closest colleague on questions of war and peace. As Christie wrote to John W. Dafoe of the *Winnipeg Free Press*, a wartime friend whom he favoured with his 'outbursts' of indignation on questions of public policy and world affairs, now that he had re-joined External Affairs he was 'scarcely entitled to outbursts any more. There will doubtless be times when I shall feel like a tart who has taken the veil!'[34] When Christie returned to the Department on September 1, 1935, Italy was increasing its pressure on Ethiopia, and the League of Nations was about to face its greatest challenge. Christie's neutralism would have the chance to be tested in action.

II

By 1935 Loring Christie's views were sophisticated, carefully formulated, and compelling, and prior to joining the Department he had had no qualms about putting them forward in public. In remarks he delivered to meetings of the Canadian Institute of International Affairs in Kingston in May 1935, he set himself the task of hitting the idea of collective security squarely on the head. The

League was more and more concerned with European matters to the exclusion of everything else, had become more and more a device for minding other people's business. What was Canada's role in all this? To Christie the answer was plain: 'In what sense and what degree can 10,000,000 Canadians enter successfully into a pooling of decision upon the problem of security with 300,000,000 Europeans 3,000 miles away? Must not our attitude toward the European process be radically different from that of a European state?' That was self-evident. But some must have quarreled with Christie's next point, that so far as the League was concerned,

> Canada can continue to regard it as a free, flexible conference method of diplomacy for world problems in which she is entitled to participate—at least she can take this line until such time as she might be forced out of the League; that she cannot consider special commitments until it becomes universal, including particularly the United States; and, as already said, that she cannot enter the special European regional system. Since the business today and for a long time to come is bound to be mainly European, all this means that Canada's true role is mainly that of an observer.[35]

Surprisingly, perhaps, some disparate men accepted Christie's line at Kingston. The National Secretary of the CIIA, Escott Reid, told him: 'After your paper . . . Colonel [Kenneth] Stuart [of National Defence Headquarters] and I turned to each other and said "Excellent. Agree with almost everything in it," and each was surprised at the other's attitude.'[36]

Christie, however, had been appalled at the general tenor of these 1935 meetings: 'As I listened and tried to envisage the real thing behind the facade of words,' he wrote to Lord Lothian, 'I had—never before so vividly—this kind of impression: that what they were really doing was sitting around the table as a General Staff planning for the next war.' Christie said that there were two distinct camps at Kingston, 'those who would from the outset plunge Canada into active participation in any war in which Great Britain became involved, assuming always that it took shape as a "League" or "Security" war against an "aggressor". And there were those who were for a declaration of neutrality at the outset, realizing that this would mean secession [from the Empire].'[37] Christie shared neither position, of course. As he told Lothian:

I asked the Conference to consider the position of people (like myself) who (a) believe that the orthodox notion of 'Collective Security' is a wholly unworkable or illusory notion and indeed disastrous and (b) recognize that when Britain is at war Canada is at war and that, having gone on with the Commonwealth, we cannot at the moment of danger simply say, 'Thank you very much, I have enjoyed your company, but now I have another engagement.' . . . it may be that I have done no more than express at great length and in a technical sense what is the instinctive or intuitive position of a good many Canadians. . . . If the war comes they will be in it, but not enthusiastically. . . .[38]

Christie's position, therefore, was by no means as extreme as that of some others. He recognized that Canada was almost certain to go into any British war; indeed, he seemed to suggest that it was legally bound to such a course. His concern, however, was to do what he could to minimize the dangers by arguing against what he saw as spurious collective security rationales for war. In this he was not very far from Dr Skelton. In a private note to Escott Reid, Skelton had argued that 'If it's automatic sanctions plus international legislation or chaos, the public will take its chance on chaos, in the trust that some other road will open in the multitudinous shiftings of the next ten years—at least on this continent.'[39]

By September 1935, then, when Christie rejoined the Department and while Canada was involved in the general election that would see Mackenzie King returned to office in October 1935, all these matters had passed from the theoretical to the practical. The heightening tension between Italy and Ethiopia turned to war at the beginning of October, and the League of Nations in Geneva was soon on the road to sanctions. For Skelton, this was a particularly difficult period. Prime Minister Bennett was distracted by the conduct of his disastrous election campaign, and his views wavered between isolationism today and support for collective security and economic sanctions against Italy tomorrow.[40] Pressures from the informed public were increasing as well. Yet to Skelton the matter was clear. Italy was an aggressor, but economic sanctions might lead to war. And if that happened, what was Canada to do in the face of the 'repeated and emphatic declarations of the necessity of prior approval by the Parliament of Canada', declarations that had been formalized on June 21, 1926 and that were impossible to implement when Parliament was in dissolution?[41] That legalistic argument had something to it, but it masked Skelton's antipathy to the League and to the very idea of economic sanctions. He and Christie were as one on this.

If anything Christie's views were bleaker still. Escott Reid had written him in early October to say that 'If we take part today in League sanctions against Italy it will be difficult for us to refuse to take part in one or two years' time in League sanctions against Germany. And I am afraid', Reid argued, that 'those sanctions will not be symbolic but will mean a first-class war.'[42] Christie replied that he was 'in complete agreement. We have no business gambling even on the accident that might happen today. We are fools to establish the precedent of intervening in all European crises, knowing full well they cannot bring aid to non-European crises and their present flurry is a bagatelle compared with the coming major crisis that today is in the back of all their minds.' To Christie a 'heavy responsibility' lay on all the League of Nations Societies, in Canada and elsewhere, that had propagandized for collective security and sanctions. 'They have propagated a set of phrases and generalities, and these phrases thus held out as a promise and an encouragement, have profoundly moved many people everywhere. . . . A primrose path to the promised land!'[43]

In the Department, Christie set out his views in a long memorandum of October 5 called 'Notes on the European Crisis'. A hurriedly drafted 32-page paper, it was embellished on his file copy with the handwritten addition ' "Sanctions" (Swiss for "War")'.

'What immediate, direct, vital Canadian interest is at stake?' he wrote:

> In what circumstances is it a Canadian interest to intervene in European affairs? Is the application of hostile Canadian pressure upon a part of Europe likely to be appeasing for Europe? Is it likely to be appeasing or useful from a worldwide point of view? Can we in any degree adopt the principle of Canadian intervention in European security arrangements and at the same time guarantee that Canadian energy will not be so exhausted or diminished as to leave us without hope of influence or defence in the fact of non-European developments? To what extent, if any, can we expend energy across the Atlantic without weakening our resistance to events im-

pinging from the south or from across the Pacific? . . . Is it possible to conceive the continued existence of a Canadian nation . . . on the basis of a principle under which . . . it is required (a) that Canada shall intervene [in European wars]; (b) that she shall do this alone from the outset as the representative of North America and carry on indefinitely, no matter whether the United States intervenes or not; and (c) that she shall so intervene whether or not all European countries themselves take up the cause? . . . On what basis do you estimate that 10,000,000 Canadians can undertake more than the holding of this seat and line of communication of civilization? If you propose more than this and yet recognise the absurdity of Canadian participation to the full in the European 'collective security' arrangements now going on, how—by what stipulations and limitations—are we to limit our intervention?[44]

That was a tough and clear piece of analysis, difficult to fault on logical grounds. It was also very similar to the arguments being made at the same time by American intellectuals. So too was Christie's later assessment, offered to Escott Reid in a confidential letter, that the supporters of collective security 'want and demand explicit automatism'. But, he argued, collective security worked only if the Great Powers wanted it to work, and if they did, that in effect would compel the small countries to participate once the machine began to roll, 'for by that time the alternative would look like revolution or desertion. So that, if the Great Powers start, you start; if they don't, you don't; where they go, you go; when they stop, you stop . . . the theory of our having a voice and control is eyewash.'[45] The logic was impeccable, and so was Skelton's comment that the 'significant trend in Canada is the willingness to face facts, our facts, not traditions or other people's facts or aspirations.'[46] Unfortunately, as both the senior men in the Department of External Affairs recognized, logic was as nothing when emotion was involved.

As it turned out, Canada's role in the sanctions question of 1935 was particularly inglorious. Acting without proper instructions, Dr W.A. Riddell, the Canadian representative at Geneva, proposed oil sanctions against Italy, and the Canadian government, under Mackenzie King once more, soon disavowed him.[47] Skelton—always the nationalist and isolationist—readily agreed with this, seeing in the repudiation of Riddell a possible end to 'our continuing to give blank cheque commitments to participate in every fresh trouble that may develop in Europe in the next twenty years.'[48]

Crisis followed on crisis, and by the time of Munich in September 1938, if not earlier, Christie and Skelton could no longer doubt that Canada would indeed go to war if Britain did. This pleased them not at all. Christie had told Felix Frankfurter in January 1937 that he feared Canada 'may have got into a position where she'll be hooked willy nilly' into the European mess,[49] but Skelton at the time of the Czech crisis in September 1938 told his colleague Norman Robertson that 'If Britain is in the war, I think there is little doubt that we will be in it soon after Parliament meets.'[50] Although both Skelton and Christie probably still hoped Canada could be a passive belligerent, they were prepared to face the facts of the situation—however much those facts displeased them.

Still, the prospect of war horrified Christie, whom Grant Dexter of the *Winnipeg Free Press* described privately as 'a very cynical, disillusioned man . . . ardently isolationist and anti-league'.[51] Cynical or not, Christie still struggled against fate. At the time of Munich he argued 'that there is no case whatever for Canada to participate in the sense of joining a European preventive war operation to beat Germany to her knees.' Perhaps; but Christie was well aware of the strength of 'the Imperialist party' in the country, and he appeared to believe that the least harmful outcome he could hope for was a war effort of 'the greatest caution and slowness', and a dawning public realization that Canada was not a belligerent like the others but 'an "Associate"—a North American Associate.' Only in a cautious war effort of this type was there any prospect of maintaining national unity, of preventing a split between French and English Canadians, and of 'managing to bring out of the catastrophe a Canadian community with a capacity for eventual self-healing and survival as a prosperous and not wholly negligible member of the North American homeland.'[52] That was a view that Skelton concurred with,[53] and it was shared by others in the Department, and in the country as well.

Even a limited participation disturbed Christie, but paradoxically he believed that Canada had to enter the coming war as a belligerent and 'at once'. There was, he said, 'the great danger that any attempt to improvise hurriedly a procedure designed to represent an "advance" in our position would in practical consequence represent a retrograde and even disastrous step . . . the safest course is that which allows the greatest flexibility and leaves the most doors open. . . .'[54] It was all too much for Christie, and by the summer of 1939, as he told Lester Pearson, who was in Ottawa on leave from his post in London, he expected to resign from External Affairs on the grounds that he was out of sympathy with participation in the approaching war.[55] His position was confusing—emotionally he wanted out, but intellectually he knew that Canada had to join in the war on at least a limited-liability basis.

When the war did come in September, Christie stayed in the service and even accepted the position of Minister to the United States, arguably the one he was best fitted for; it was also one of the most crucial positions in the gift of the country at that moment.[56] 'Strange business,' Pearson wrote.[57]

Christie himself was strange. With Skelton, he was the archetypal figure in the Canadian diplomacy of the interwar years, advocating neutralism and isolationism. The younger new men— Pearson, Wrong, Robertson *et al.*—may have agonized over neutrality versus a Canadian role in the world, but they actively sought involvement and they were less intellectual, less troubled, and more convinced that Hitler was an evil that had to be destroyed whatever the rights and wrongs of Canadian status and Canadian rights. Hume Wrong, from his post in Geneva, had written Pearson that one Christie memorandum in summer 1939 'might have been written by some superior being on Mars'. Pearson agreed—'it [Christie's prescription] was so superior and remote from reality as to be most irritating. It is characteristic of the stuff they are sending us from Ottawa these days. . . .'[58] That said it all. Christie and Skelton may have operated on the same facts as Pearson and Wrong, but their reality—a vision of an isolationist, nationalist Canada—seemed vastly different.

III

But on analysis this vision was not all that different from Lester Pearson's view of the nation and the world. Pearson was a complex man, careful in all his dealing with his friends and colleagues and unwilling to reveal what he truly thought. His views on the approach to war are worth study.

Lester Pearson was a product of the 'Vicwardian' era. He was born at Newtonbrook, Ont., on April 23, 1897, when to be born in Ontario of British stock meant that one inherited a belief in God and the Empire and an obligation to do one's duty to both without question. Because his father was a Methodist parson, who moved from charge to charge across Ontario, there could be no doubt about God. His grandparents and parents were of solid British stock, and there was as little doubt about Empire.

Pearson's upbringing was conventional—although, as he was named Lester and his brothers were named Marmaduke and Vaughan, there must have been something unconventional about the parents. The father was of the 'jolly churchman' type and had great charm. The family atmosphere was warm, and the children grew to be witty, amiable, and engaging. Lester's inherited and powerful charm would turn out to be his greatest weapon.

Equally important to Lester Pearson were connections. Some near relatives were beginning to rise to prominence; there were uncles prospering in the United States, and a web of influence was taking form. Those connections, as well as the ones Pearson formed on his own, were to be very important. As a product of a Methodist upbringing, one that made ambition a natural if sinful trait—to be camouflaged from others and from one's self—he attended Victoria College in the University of Toronto (an uncle on his mother's side was Chancellor), where Vincent Massey was dean of his residence. It was equally natural that when Lester's wartime ambulance service in Greece had begun to pall, Sir Sam Hughes, the former Minister of Militia and Defence, should be pressed into service as a family friend to have Pte Pearson transferred to England and commissioned.

There was nothing improper in these connections, or in the uses to which they were put. They were there to be used; everyone who had connections used them. But what is interesting is that fate always seemed to place the proper instrument close at hand where 'Mike' Pearson was concerned. If ever a man had God-given luck, it was he.

Even his nickname could be considered a sample of luck. No politician called Lester was likely to go far, but 'Mike' had the proper note of engaging informality. The nickname was given him by his squadron commander, the man charged with turning Pearson into a Great War fighter pilot. The route to the aerodrome was entirely conventional. In his two years at Victoria before the war, Pearson had led his class, but in the spring of 1915 he enlisted in the Army Medical Corps, and after training in

England his unit was sent to the Macedonian front. After almost two unglamorous years there, Hughes' string-pulling* got him back to Blighty, where, after four months' training at Oxford, he applied and was accepted into the Royal Flying Corps. His military career ended when he was hit by a bus during a London blackout—the luckiest stroke of all, as Pearson realized. 'I got hurt before I got a chance to get killed—that's about what it amounts to. Looking back now, there seems to be something that was protecting me. I didn't realize it. I never expected to come back from that war. You got to a point after a few years overseas where you just went on until you were killed.'[59]

After his war ended, Pearson resumed his interrupted university career, graduating third in his class with an honours B.A. in history.[60] What was he to do now? He tried articling with a law firm for a week, but disliked that and went instead to his parents' home in Guelph for a season of semi-pro baseball. Then he drew on his connections once more—an uncle was vice-president of Armour and Co., the Chicago meat-packing empire—to get a job with a Hamilton subsidiary. As a sausage stuffer he was no expert, but he was soon made a clerk in the Chicago offices of the fertilizer subsidiary—useful experience for a man whose prime ministerial career forced him to take an interest in the problems of branch plants and international conglomerates.

This spell in the United States convinced Pearson that business was not for him, and he decided to continue his education. The Vincent Massey connection proved helpful here in winning him a Massey Foundation Fellowship to Oxford in 1921, and he went to St John's College on the recommendation of a friend from the

---

* Pearson had quickly grasped the uses of influence in the army. As he wrote in his diary of the war years, 'The next week [in England in 1915] saw me installed in my new quarters and initiated into my new duties. By this time I had learned the efficacy of "pull" in army life and having a little in our unit I had no scruples in using it to the utmost to procure me exemption from ward duty and a congenial "job". I succeeded and never again did I have to play the part of "ministering angel", as one of my fond aunts put it, to the sick and wounded. My new position was in the quartermasters department the "cushiest" place in the hospital looking after supplies. I was the envy of all my less fortunate companions,' he continued, adding that he was able to supplement his rations 'with the odd hospital delicacy, having a feast with some of my cronies, and writing the missing articles off the books as lost in transit; and there are still some idealistic chaplains who claim the war purified the souls of our young men.' (PAC, Pearson Papers, N8, vol. 1, Diary of War 1914-19. I am greatly indebted to Prof. John English for this splendid reference.)

University of Toronto, J. Bartlett Brebner. Mike Pearson fitted right into the Oxford of the early 1920s. He was attractive, intelligent, athletic. He learned a great deal; he met many men—Malcolm MacDonald, Bonar Law's son Richard, Roland Michener; and he played every sport available, including hockey, tennis and lacrosse. 'Mike was a very delightful companion and personality,' Michener recalled. 'He was informal, approachable, not aged by his war experience particularly. He was sort of carefree. He didn't give the impression of being too much interested in his studies, you know, but he did them well and got a good degree.' That was a high second in history in 1923—but in hockey Pearson was outstanding. 'He was a good stick-handler', Michener remembered. 'He would swerve back and forth across the rink. . . . the Swiss in their sport columns called him Herr Zigzag. . . .'[61] This, perhaps, was the best training for politics and diplomacy.

After Oxford, it was back to the University of Toronto as a lecturer in G.M. Wrong's history department, at a salary of $2,000. As a teacher he was apparently an instant success, but he made his real mark coaching, gratifying his love for sport and earning a supplement to his tiny salary. Advancement was slow—Pearson remained a lecturer for four years and his salary in 1925-6 was only $2,450 (which must have impelled him to teach a correspondence course that year for $57).[62] He was not promoted to Assistant Professor until June 8, 1927.[63] Professor Wrong apparently told him that his chances of advancement were slim unless he got to work on a book. Pearson, whose capacities for abstract thought were limited, thereupon began research on the United Empire Loyalists.[64] It may have been this endeavour that led him to look elsewhere for employment—where there would be no pressure to publish. Or perhaps it was his marriage in 1925 to one of his students, Maryon Moody, a tart-tongued daughter of a Winnipeg doctor. There were soon two children and never enough money. Pearson had a meeting with O.D. Skelton, wrote examinations for First Secretary in the Department of External Affairs in May 1928, and soon thereafter became a civil servant. He ranked first in the competition (leading a group that included Norman Robertson and Hugh Keenleyside) and came to Ottawa with excellent letters of reference from, among others, Newton Rowell and W.P.M. Kennedy, the University of Toronto constitutional expert, who pronounced him a 'distinct success with his students . . . as an organiser' and 'outstanding in his knowledge on international affairs since 1870.' The chairman of the history department, George Smith, also noted that Pearson was a hard and loyal worker, but he added with perspicacity that 'As an office-man and administrator, I should place him below Mr. Hume Wrong'— Pearson's history department colleague who had already gone with Vincent Massey to open the Canadian Legation in Washington.[65] At the age of thirty-one, without quite realizing it, Mike Pearson had found his *métier*—at the good salary of $3,840.[66]

What kind of man was he? He was an anglophile—his Oxford experience had not changed this sympathy—and he was a nascent Canadian nationalist; a young veteran, very much affected by his war experiences, who was basically isolationist—he was very North American in that respect—and believed fervently that another war was unthinkable. He was also charming, very ambitious, and anxious to please, and a man whose great abilities were still untried. His constitution was strong, his capacity for work enormous, and he could write well and clearly and speak with clarity and force, despite his trace of a lisp. He also had the happy knack of being noticed, a trait that could be exercised more easily in the tiny world of well-educated civil servants who inhabited interwar Ottawa than it would be later.

Above all, Mike Pearson—a man who was a good judge of human nature—wanted to be helpful and to be liked; he wanted to co-operate. For example, when he crossed to England at the beginning of 1930 to attend the London Naval Conference as an adviser to Colonel J.L. Ralston, the Canadian delegate, an official in the British High Commission in Ottawa told the Dominions Office that Pearson deserved 'special kindness. A student at Oxford and one who has come away imbued with a great affection for Great Britain,* he has taken considerable risks on several occasions in order to impart to us information which otherwise would never have reached us.' Pearson, the official continued, was a man 'in whom our department can place implicit confidence and if you can succeed in obtaining for him free access not only to the Dominions Office but to other Government departments also we may . . . forge a new and very valuable link. . . .'[67] In other

---

* Later Pearson wrote in his diary that 'I have more than once been struck by the fact that some of our more ardent nationalists are Oxford graduates who find it quite easy to reconcile their Canadian nationalism with a devotion to Oxford. . . .' (PAC, Pearson Papers, Diary, 21 April, 1940.)

words Pearson already had made himself useful enough to the High Commission for that office to press London to assist him in return. And as early as 1932 an American Legation official was writing Washington about his informative conversations with 'Mike'.[68] That powerful charm and a judicious distribution of information was quickly opening doors.

Part of Pearson's charm was his ability to laugh at himself—at least in his dealings with friends and colleagues. In a letter written to a former colleague in Toronto shortly after he joined the Department, Pearson referred to his work on the now long-forgotten Sub-Committee on Territorial Waters. He admitted that the draft he had prepared was probably imperfect, 'but this is the first time I have ever had the honour of declaring the position of our country to the world, so naturally I was a bit overwhelmed.'[69] Later, during the Naval Conference in 1930, he wrote that 'The King had the honour of meeting me this afternoon at Buckingham Palace.'[70]

But behind the amiability was shrewdness and good judgement. His comment on the role of the Empire delegations at the Conference was exactly right: 'It got tiring. . . . It's a great thing to have 6 parts to one Empire but it's very exhausting when all six parts have to make a speech every time the Empire talks. No wonder the foreign delegations are a bit fed up with our peculiar constitutional structures.'[71] A few years later he wrote of a discussion during an international sugar conference: 'Of course no one here has any idea as to what the Canadian attitude toward this conference is, or even if there is a Canadian attitude. But I was reluctant to say this, so I chatted amiably for 15 minutes. . . . I kept carefully away from the sugar conference because I knew nothing about it; I kept even more carefully away from Canadian policy.'[72] The derision mingled self-mockery with more than a hint of annoyance at Ottawa's absence of policy.

Most important for his career was Pearson's growing reputation for efficiency and good sense. Like so many of the young civil servants brought into the public service by Skelton, Clark, and Towers, Pearson was completely devoted to his job and ready to put it before everything else, including his family. That capacity for service got him a position as secretary to the 1931 Stamp Royal Commission to Inquire into Trading in Grain Futures. It had its report ready in two months and cost under $12,000;[73] for both unusual accomplishments the secretary must surely have deserved the credit. Three years later Pearson was handed the politically sensitive Royal Commission on Price Spreads. It had sprung from the muckraking activities of H.H. Stevens, one of Bennett's more rambunctious ministers, and the job of administering and expediting was complicated not only by the Depression and the political sensitivity of prices and profits at a time of economic dislocation, but by the feuding between Prime Minister Bennett and Stevens.

Pearson's instructions were not to prolong the Commission, to wind it up as soon as possible and get the report out. 'Pearson made an impression on me at the time, and on everybody else, with the way he went at it,' Walter Gordon remembered. 'He showed his usual good humour. He worked very hard and he was extremely tactful, and he finished the job with a minimum of fuss. . . . it was a remarkably able piece of work on his part. . . .'[74] So it was, and the report remains a mine of information. The Commissioners all agreed, even writing Bennett to say that 'Since July last, all [Pearson's] time was devoted to the Commission. By "all" we mean on an average from 9 o'clock in the morning until midnight, Saturdays and Sundays included.'[75] His reward was an honorarium of $1,800 and the OBE.[76] To a friend who had sardonically congratulated him on the decoration, Pearson replied that 'I am fighting hard to maintain the democratic touch in spite of this amazing distinction. Possibly the law officers of the Crown will declare the whole thing unconstitutional.'[77]

Yet another reward was a posting in 1935 to Canada House in London. The High Commissioner was still G. Howard Ferguson, but when the Liberals won the 1935 election he was succeeded by Vincent Massey, who wrote Pearson to congratulate him. Pearson replied that 'For a time it looked as if I might not be able to make the change as I didn't see how I could live in England, bring up my family and do my job, as I thought it should be done, on the salary and allowance offered.'[78] In fact, the Department made a special effort for Pearson, increasing his $2,750 allowance by $750; this was in addition to his salary of some $4,000.[79] But money remained a constant concern to the Pearsons. His wife was notoriously unhappy about his low pay, and her complaints were continuous. Moreover, as Pearson told his friend Grant Dexter, he was 'thoroughly disheartened and disillusioned with respect to External Affairs department. Our foreign policy is "do nothing".'[80]

Thus Pearson was unusually receptive when, at the beginning

of 1937, he was approached to join the Canadian Broadcasting Corporation in a senior position in public relations. This episode is a fascinating demonstration of how Pearson could mobilize his forces, employ his allies, and bargain skilfully on his own behalf. It was Assistant Professor Pearson dealing with Dean O.D. Skelton and President Mackenzie King, and all seemed to have understood their roles.

The initial approach was made by Alan Plaunt, a bright and able young man with impressive connections, one of the stalwarts of the Canadian Radio League—a pressure group that had won the fight for the creation of a government radio network—and later a board member of the CBC. 'When I saw you in England,' Plaunt wrote on January 7,1937, 'I got the impression, perhaps mistakenly, that you would be willing to give up your diplomatic work and return to Canada if a sufficiently attractive opportunity arose.'[81] Hence Plaunt's suggestion of a job with the CBC, to which Pearson promptly replied, 'I am interested in the idea of going back to Ottawa in the capacity you mention, deeply interested. . . . I don't, and never have regarded my present work in London as permanent. Either it leads on to more important duties and greater responsibility in Canada's External Service or else I leave it and try something else. . . . But even the first alternative is conditional, in the sense that I would not hesitate to leave my present post, irrespective of glowing future prospects, for one where the work was even more interesting and the conditions even more satisfactory.'[82] In Pearson's view that meant that 'I wouldn't want to be tied to a Canadian Radio Corporation in 1941, which was in a similar position to the Canadian Broadcasting Commission of 1935, or even to the C.B.C. of 1936: to put it bluntly, the Corporation has to have a future.' That was sensible enough, and it demonstrated that Pearson had kept up to date on what was happening, and what was likely to happen, in Canada. Then he turned to money, setting out his prospects in the Department, the likely effects of these on his salary, and the unfavourable difference between his future diplomat's pay if things worked out as he hoped and the proposed maximum of $5,000 that Plaunt had suggested.[83]

Pearson outlined his interest frankly, implicitly inviting a higher salary offer from the CBC. But he did not cut his ties to External Affairs. Quite properly he informed the High Commissioner of the CBC's approach and Massey, who coincidentally had recom-

mended Pearson for promotion a month earlier,[84] promptly wrote
to Skelton. Pearson, he said, 'does not want to leave the Service—
nothing would be further from Pearson's intention than to use this
tentative approach as an argument for his promotion. . . .'[85] The
Under-Secretary did not take long to reply:

> It would be a great calamity to lose Pearson from our service.
> In addition to his intellectual capacity and a fine educational
> background, good judgment and ability to turn out first class
> work at high speed he has marked ability in getting on well
> with people and developing friendly relations with represen-
> tatives of other governments without losing his distinctive
> Canadian point of view. We are all both proud and very fond
> of him.

Still, there were difficulties in the way of doing anything for him.
Even if he was promoted to Counsellor, his salary would not rise
very much—Skelton's figures were different and lower than the
ones Pearson had used in writing to Plaunt—and Skelton, who recognized a bargaining situation when he saw one, did not even
promise a promotion. He did add that in 1935 he had not believed
Pearson yet ready to be a Counsellor.[86]

Matters rested there for some time. Gladstone Murray, the head
of the CBC, soon exchanged letters with Pearson, setting out the
scope of the job and raising the offer to $6,000 'or thereabouts'.[87]
But nothing happened that required a decision.[88] Finally on October 21 Skelton discussed Pearson's situation with the Prime
Minister, who noted in his diary that 'We reached an understanding on that matter which I conveyed to Massey over the 'phone at
night, indicating to him the possible changes that might be made
in the course of the next year, when the [departmental] estimates
will be before Parliament.'[89] Those possibilities included an increase in pay, promotion to Counsellor, and succession to the position of Secretary at Canada House if the present incumbent, Colonel Georges Vanier, was posted elsewhere. Massey told King
later that he thought this would do the trick, that Pearson was
pleased and likely to remain.[90]

Nonetheless Pearson, characteristically, was still playing his
cards carefully, fully aware that King's promises were qualified,
careful, and conditional—as always. When in November the CBC
formally offered him a 'Public Relations, Publicity, and Parliamentary' job at $6,000, with $1,000 allowance and the prospect of

a salary of $7,500 'within a reasonable time',[91] he now wrote, for the first time, directly to Skelton. 'I did not want to be put in the position of playing one organization off against another,' he wrote, doing just that, but he believed it was appropriate 'for me to find out, if possible, what the immediate future seemed to have in store both for the Service and for myself. . . .' Could Skelton reassure him that the prospects were still the same? 'I am genuinely attracted by the C.B.C.'s offer,' he added. 'It would, of course, put me in a much more comfortable position financially, as I have learnt that it costs at least twice as much to live in London as in Ottawa. . . . I am not under any illusions as to the difficulties of the job in question, but I rather like "tough jobs". In fact, in default of some—what shall I call them—"progressive developments" in my official career, I should be inclined to take it on.'[92] The unaccustomed bluntness must have shaken Skelton, and he was not pleased. In a memorandum to the Prime Minister of January 26, 1938, he set out Pearson's position, but his prose was noticeably cool.[93] Nevertheless he wired Pearson a month later that 'Can assure you definite and adequate promotion will be made this summer,'[94] and on March 3 he wrote to add that Vanier was to be transferred and Pearson would become Secretary of the Office of the High Commissioner at a salary of $5,760 with allowances of $4,000.[95] Thus the matter was settled, notwithstanding a new offer from the CBC of a post as deputy general manager for the West.[96] Pearson had received his promotion and the job he wanted—as Secretary he was effectively the number-two man in the High Commission responsible for the political reporting—and raises in pay and allowances totalling almost $2,000 a year. More important, he had achieved this without forfeiting Massey's good will and without alienating King or the Under-Secretary. He had, in fact, effectively demonstrated his marketability to them and increased his value to the Department at the same time. The outcome was a happy one all round. This was perhaps the first indication that Pearson was interested in a wider field than the somewhat constrained world of the diplomat.

IV

To handle his tasks as Secretary at the High Commission Pearson needed all those skills he had demonstrated in his job bargaining. Massey was much better at the social side of the work, hobnobbing with royalty, plutocrats, or the peerage, than he was at the daily grind of political reporting, calling on bureaucrats, and surveying public opinion. Nevertheless, Massey had strong views. For instance, he was convinced that Mackenzie King was a shifty character on Imperial questions, afraid to take a firm stand for fear of the political consequences. It was ironic that Massey himself regularly and religiously supported every shift in the Chamberlain government's line as it swung between appeasement and taking a hard line with Nazi Germany. He believed, however, that he was always consistent. For the more clear-headed Pearson, Massey was a problem that had to be coped with.

There was another problem. Pearson's letters and reports to the Department in Ottawa were read by Skelton, the unabashed nationalist and isolationist who was firmly convinced that British policy was vacillating in almost every respect but one—the desire to have Canada at its side in any war. How could he satisfy his two masters, Massey and Skelton, and his conscience? The problem was compounded by Skelton's fear that the officers of the High Commission would be seduced by the British into losing their Canadian good sense. Skelton knew well the predilections of Massey for everything English—he thought of him as a hopeless case—but as one of his earliest letters showed, he worried about Pearson. 'One of your main duties and most helpful services will of course be to keep in close contact with Whitehall, but not in the sense of undertaking any responsibility of communicating to Ottawa anything that the British Government wants communicated.'[97] The message—don't get too close—was clear; so was Pearson's reply that he, 'of course, never visualized my work of keeping in touch . . . as liaison in the sense of taking any responsibility in communicating to Ottawa anything that the British Government wants communicating. I did not think they would desire to use me in that capacity either. . . . By contact and liaison I merely visualize keeping in as close touch with the officials as is possible—getting their slant of things and figuring the nature of their views.'[98] It was curious that Skelton (who had never had a post abroad) seemed not to understand what a diplomat's work involved.

Initially at least, Skelton had no need to worry about Pearson's Canadianism. A strong believer in collective security at the beginning of the decade, Pearson became disillusioned with the League of Nations, and with Britain and France over the Hoare-Laval Pact, which attempted to sell out Ethiopia to Mussolini in 1935. A marked isolationism showed very clearly in a letter written in his first few months in London, probably late in that same year, when Pearson reviewed events in Europe—'a mad continent'—and took 'a pretty dark view of the future'.

> I hope my presumption will be pardoned if I say that if I were responsible for Canadian policy, I would assume that war in Europe is certain within five years, that this country [the U.K.], acting in my opinion more by instinct than by reason, will slide into the mess, and that, in view of the bloody chaos which will result, our chief interest now is to avoid being involved in any circumstances. I admit we may not be able to avoid it, but I feel infinitely more strongly than I did six months ago that the keynote of our policy should be such avoidance.
>
> . . . I wish I could talk as freely to those gentlemen whom one meets over here who take it for granted that, come what may, if the emergency arises Canada will rally to the support of the old land. I know we might in certain circumstances have to do so, and that, even, there might be occasions when we ought to do so, but it's time that people over here realised that there are other circumstances when we would be mad to become involved, and that we would owe it to ourselves to stand aloof.[99]

Dr Skelton or Loring Christie could not have phrased these sentiments better.

Pearson was also as nationalist as the Under-Secretary and the Counsellor. In the spring of 1936 he sat in on an Imperial Defence exercise at which the British participants assumed a centralized Empire with a common foreign policy. As Pearson wrote to Colonel Harry Crerar, a friend at National Defence Headquarters in Ottawa,

> we were asked to say if we really did assent to the principles and so I tossed my hat into the ring. I said that the principles as stated pictured a highly centralized Empire, such as I did not think existed. Indeed, I said, the inter-Imperial relation was directly opposed to the idea of centralization; it was, in fact, the last word in decentralization; that I could remember no Canadian Prime Minister ever having said anything that could lead me to believe that he . . . concurred in the view they expressed. . . .[100]

If Pearson was isolationist and nationalist, so too was he against British rearmament. In a letter to Skelton early in 1937, he remarked on the equanimity with which the British people seemed to be accepting the arms budget the government was foisting on them. 'It seems to me', he wrote, 'that one of the most significant features of the newspaper comment I have read is the frank and unabashed reversion to pre-War ideas that security can only be found in armaments. . . . All the talk now is about "arming for peace", relying on our good right arm, no war while Britain is strong, etc., etc. It is all very discouraging.'[101] When Hitler remilitarized the Rhineland, and an editor of the *Times* called on Massey to urge Mackenzie King to tell the British government that Canada would not support strong measures against Germany, Pearson agreed wholeheartedly.[102] Again, his position was much the same as Skelton's or Christie's.

Massey had agreed with that position too (although he failed to act upon it), but as the international crisis worsened it became harder for Pearson to maintain a balance between the views of Skelton and Massey. Pearson recounts in his memoirs how his own views began to change even before Hitler's annexation of Austria showed a determination to take more than Germany had lost in 1919. 'No longer was it possible for me to believe that Nazism was a temporary aberration in German politics . . . that the greater danger to peace was French over-reaction to Hitler's moves, with the United Kingdom supporting such reaction. This feeling was replaced by the fear of aggressive war brought about by the policy of a German regime which now must be considered as evil and savage and an immediate menace to freedom and to peace.' The Czech crisis added a new fear: if Britain and France came to terms with Hitler, this would mean 'the triumph of Nazism in Europe and beyond'. Nothing could be worse than a triumphant Hitler, Pearson wrote, and the only hope, 'however weak it might be, to avoid war without surrender was to arm; to unite the forces of freedom; to stand firm but without provocation. . . .'[103]

As the Czech crisis reached its apogee in September 1938, however, Massey believed that the abandonment of Czechoslovakia by Britain and France was statesmanship of the highest order, a view enthusiastically agreed with by King and accepted grudgingly by Skelton.[104] But to Pearson it was appalling. He told Grant Dexter, the *Winnipeg Free Press*'s London correspondent, that one British and French note to the Czech was 'the most brutal document he had ever read.'[105] Still, he neither wanted nor expected war: 'The Nazis are going to get 95% of their demands without difficulty. If they insist on 110% with difficulty,' he wrote to Ottawa, 'well, I still think France, & hence, G.B., will not fight them—The French are losing their nerve & the British are relieved. . . . But any rate', he concluded, 'we who have the misfortune to live by Trafalgar Square won't be dodging bombs—for a bit.'[106]

Six weeks later, after the 'resolution' of the Czech crisis, and after the Munich sell-out had been greeted with widespread relief, Pearson again wrote to Skelton. It is not known whether Pearson knew that on September 29, at the height of tension, Massey had told a High Commissioners' meeting at the Dominions Office that the Czechs were being 'deliberately dilatory' in acceding to the Anglo-French demands to surrender to Hitler.[107] Nonetheless he made no bones about his disagreement with his superior; indeed, he probably verged on the disloyal. 'If this were a High Commissioner's despatch,' he said, 'some of these ideas would possibly not appear because I take a more critical and pessimistic view of the situation than he does. Neither of us gets much comfort out of the Munich settlement, I none at all, as a solution of an immediate problem. But Mr. Massey feels, and I certainly hope he is right, that the unsatisfactory, to use a mild word, nature of the settlement and the way it was brought about, may well be more than balanced by a betterment of Anglo-German relations, possibly arising out of it. I think that view prevails in a good many influential quarters,' he went on, 'but my own impression is that public opinion generally gets no comfort out of Munich. . . .' Certainly he was pessimistic for the future. ' "Arm to the teeth" is the only slogan that gets much popular reaction now,' he said, 'Only very occasionally does some small voice point out that Germany will then arm beyond the teeth, and the race to the abyss will be on.' His opposition to an arms race clearly remained, but Pearson added that 'I am pessimistic enough to think that an armaments race is not necessary to cause trouble; the nature of the German state . . . should be enough to cause another crisis before long.' Nor did he have any faith left in the purity of Britain's motives: '. . . it is becoming more and more clear that if this country fights, it will be only in defence of her own imperial interests, defined by herself. Why should she expect any particular world support for that, unless it is because the defeat of her Imperial interests would mean the destruction of herself, and there are many overseas, I suppose, who would defend her against such destruction by a Nazi Germany.'

If Skelton appreciated that, he could not have been so pleased with Pearson's next point:

In any case, as a Canadian, having seen the disappearance of all post-war hopes of a new international order based on international co-operation and pacific settlement of disputes, largely because of England's negative and France's positive policy, I am not going to be impressed if next year I am asked to fight because of Tanganyika or Gibraltar.

My emotional reaction to the events of the last two months is to become an out and out Canadian isolationist, and yet when I begin to reason it out it isn't as simple as that. In short, I just can't find the answer to a lot of questions. For one thing, critical though I may feel of British policy leading up to the crisis, I can't sincerely quarrel with the decision as ultimately taken, not to fight. That being so, I have no right, I suppose, to assume that the present Government is not as aware of past mistakes and present dangers as I am. . . . In the second place, would our complete isolation from European events (if such a thing were possible) save us from the effects of a British defeat, and, finally, even if it did, could we stand by and watch the triumph of Nazidom . . .? I can't answer a single one of those questions. . . . But if I am tempted to become completely cynical and isolationist, I think of Hitler screeching into the microphone, Jewish women and children in ditches on the Polish border . . . and then, whatever the British side may represent, the other does indeed stand for savagery and barbarism. True, as Mr. Massey often tells me, there are seventy-five million decent Germans, who love peace and, apparently, revere Chamberlain!—That's a hope, I admit. But though I am on the side of the angels, in Germany the opposite spirits are hard at work. . . .

Pearson concluded by saying that he had heard little criticism from Britons of the cautious Canadian attitude during the Czech crisis. 'Only Canadians living in and visiting London, "plus Royalist que le Roi", have launched into tirades about our pusillanimous attitude.'[108] Presumably Massey was one such Canadian.

That letter put Pearson on record as having separated himself from Massey, while at the same time it hewed generally to a Skeltonian line—in every respect but in its implicit willingness to join a war against Hitler. Pearson had now moved to the point that Loring Christie (and Mackenzie King) had reached: if Britain were to go to war against Hitler, so too would Canada, no matter how shoddy British policy was.[109]

Pearson's belief that war was inevitable grew stronger in the winter of 1939 when Hitler violated the Munich accords and swallowed all that remained of Czechoslovakia. 'I don't believe in the inevitability of anything, except death and taxes,' he wrote to Skelton, 'but I do believe that if German policy or England's ultimate reaction to it is not changed, war here is about as certain as anything can be.'[110] The next week, after Chamberlain had begun to bury appeasement and offered guarantees to East European states that he had refused to the Czechs, Pearson wrote again to say that 'There are some here who are not quite happy at the manner of [appeasement's] killing, or at the efforts being made to put an alternative policy in its place. Both the Prime Minister and Halifax [the Foreign Minister] have, I think, rather overdone the "we have been deceived" thesis. Personally I'm not much impressed by this sudden and shattering revelation that Hitler has betrayed the old school tie of "Godesburg and Munich"; or by the argument, the fellow's a "cad", we can't now or ever again deal with "cads", so let's form a new club composed of gentlemen like Comrade Stalin and Colonel Beck [of Poland] and King Carol [of Romania].' Skelton and King would certainly have agreed. Pearson added that 'I have always felt that the first principle of the foreign policy of this country under present conditions should be to *ensure*, if possible, that any war with Germany should result *only* from a direct attack on England, or, what is more or less the same thing, France.'[111] Again, that was the Ottawa view. Skelton privately told a reporter that he could not understand Chamberlain's policy. 'If Chamberlain really meant to stop aggression why didn't he do it last fall when there were decent countries to be protected. Why not have done it for Czecho [sic]—the finest little country in Europe—or for the Spanish government which represented fine honest Spanish people[?] But having failed to do it then, why do it now for Poland and Rumania—the two worst countries in Europe[?]'[112]

Pearson's position had changed since he arrived in London. He had moved away from his isolationist attitude and by 1938 or 1939 apparently believed Canada should participate in a war against Hitler. But he was no enthusiast for war, and no firm supporter of British policies if his letters to Skelton are to be believed. He was a bit more forward than the Under-Secretary or Christie but not more ahead of them than the Prime Minister. In the final analysis Pearson, like King, was a typical Canadian in his attitudes. Like King, too, he was cautious and careful and concerned lest he be too far out in front. Mike Pearson's success as a mandarin—and a politician—was assured.

5

THE ROAD TO
FUNCTIONALISM

The challenges in the foreign-policy field that Canada faced during the war were far greater than those of the 1930s. The country entered the war with a fledgling foreign office and with a crew of able professionals in External Affairs, but whether it had a foreign policy was arguable—unless one considered Prime Minister King's dictum, 'Parliament will decide', to be a policy. As the war proceeded, however, there could be no doubt that Canada developed a new line of action and began to press it aggressively on its sometimes reluctant friends and allies. The key to this wartime shift was the *functional principle*, which argued that in certain specific fields Canada had legitimate claims to consideration from the great powers. In such 'functional' areas—the ability to produce food and raw materials, for example—Canada had world capacity and was, therefore, entitled to a share in decision-making and responsibility. The functional principle involved an equation of capacity and responsibility, power and influence, and was eminently suited to Canada. It was also, in its appropriate good sense, typically Canadian.

In the months following the fall of France in May and June 1940, Canada found itself raising vast armies, air forces, and navies, and giving away billions of dollars in gifts to Britain and the allies. What did it get in return, other than the important psychological satisfaction of assisting in a just cause? Pats on the head, bland assurances that a grateful Empire would never forget, occasional columns by Walter Lippmann, and regular friendly chats between Mackenzie King and Franklin Roosevelt.

Given the country's ineffectual record in foreign policy during the interwar years, Britain and the United States might be forgiven for taking Canada for granted. But the war changed Canada and Canadians, and this attitude was no longer acceptable. When Dr Skelton died in January 1941 he was succeeded as Under-Secretary of State for External Affairs by a very intelligent, able, and cautious man—one who did not suffer from his predecessor's suspicions of the British or his reluctance to see Canada involved in the world and taking positions. That was Norman Robertson. As he tried to guide Canada through the minefields of domestic and foreign policy and shape a coherent, reasonable policy to a divided France, he was to learn the difficulties that faced a small country. At Robertson's side throughout most of the war was Hume Wrong. Probably the ablest professional diplomat External ever had, Wrong had an intellect that was every bit the equal of Robertson's, a capacity to produce ideas, and the administrative and organizational skills necessary to implement them. The functional principle—the one distinctive position that Canada produced during the war and almost a declaration of nationhood—was his idea. The two friends complemented each other, and Canadian foreign policy was the beneficiary.

I

Norman Robertson was born in Vancouver on March 4, 1904, the son of Lemuel Robertson, a classics professor at Vancouver College, the predecessor of the University of British Columbia. Something of a prodigy, the boy was an omnivorous reader with an early interest in radical politics, a knack for doing well in school, and the ability to talk and argue brilliantly. These interests were sufficient to take him through public and high school with ease and to make him British Columbia's choice for a Rhodes Scholarship for 1923, despite an almost total lack of athletic skills.

At Oxford Robertson broadened his interests and developed a deep and abiding love for certain parts of the British Isles, as well as for the bookstores of London. He considered himself a socialist—a position that was shared by very few of his contemporaries at Oxford—and worked in support of the strikers during the great General Strike of 1926. The oddity of these sympathies at Oxford must have distressed him; so too did Balliol College, which Robertson considered to be at best second-rate intellectually and third-rate or worse in economics, the subject that interested him the most. His special field of study in his last year was the history of the Canadian tariff system, a subject that he continued to pursue—in 1927, after one year teaching economics at UBC—at the Robert Brookings Graduate School of Economics and Political Science in Washington, D.C.

The Brookings School was more enjoyable than Oxford—the students were better and he met his future wife there, Jetty, a Dutch girl studying on a Rockefeller scholarship. Robertson did well, but did not complete his dissertation. Instead, after spending 1928-9 tutoring at Harvard, he entered the Department of External Affairs as a Third Secretary, despite his having passed the examinations for First Secretary. He had tried those exams without much expectation of success in 1927, at the same time that Lester Pearson had written them, but despite his high placing on the list of qualified candidates, there was no spot available in the Department's tiny officer complement, except that of Third Secretary. Married now and in need of a job, not at all anxious to begin full-time university teaching, Robertson accepted the junior post when it was offered to him in 1929.

For two or three years he was the Department's odd-job man. He handled some League of Nations work, wrote economic studies, and even acted as secretary to Dr Skelton when he was President of the Canadian Political Science Association. There were opportunities to travel to Geneva with the Canadian delegation to the League of Nations and occasional bursts of high-pressure work. During the Imperial Economic Conference at Ottawa in 1932, Robertson played an important role, first in drafting a number of the Canadian conference papers and later when he was brought in to help negotiate a trade agreement with Britain. With his participation in that successful agreement behind him, Robertson began to be considered a trade expert and for the rest of the decade more and more of his time was spent working in this area. In 1935 he went to Washington to negotiate the first major trade agreement between Canada and the U.S. in more than eighty years. Then he travelled to England for discussions on ways to increase trade and relax the British preferences imposed at Ottawa that tended to strangle Canada's opportunities for commerce outside the Empire. Those talks produced the 1937 Anglo-Canadian agreement and led to the long negotiations in Washington the following year that culminated in a new Canadian-American treaty, which lowered tariffs further still. Robertson's skills as a negotiator were exemplary, his ability to move in step with the political leadership in Ottawa almost uncanny, and he found that he had the fortunate knack of being able to get on with King—surprisingly, for Robertson did not admire the Prime Minister and moved heaven and earth to be shifted out of his Office when he was posted there briefly in 1937.

Nonetheless King liked him, and when Skelton died he turned instantly to Robertson, passing over Pearson, who was in England; Wrong, whom he disliked intensely; Hugh Keenleyside, a First Secretary, who had blotted his copybook in the Prime Minister's view by supporting the Japanese Canadians too enthusiastically; John Read, the Department's Legal Adviser; Laurent Beaudry, the senior French-speaking officer; and Loring Christie, the Minister in Washington. Had Christie not been ill, it is possible that King might have turned to him, but in the circumstances Robertson was the choice. His skills as a trade negotiator had played their part in some of the Liberal leader's triumphs of the preceding half-dozen years: the trade treaties with the United States and the United Kingdom that had begun to move Canada toward freer trade and away from the high tariffs and Imperial preferences that the Bennett government had created. Then, too, King knew that Skelton had trusted Robertson implicitly and had the highest regard for his intellect; perhaps he also assumed that Robertson—whose most notable form of protest was a deep sigh—would be a pliant figure, an able man who could serve the Prime Minister's will effectively. That was true, but only partly true.

'The request to try & carry on in [Skelton's] shoes came . . . as rather staggering & frightening,' Robertson wrote to his parents in Vancouver, adding that 'The job is a big one & calls for a number of qualities I simply have not got. . . .'[1] In a sense that was so. Robertson was no organizer or administrator, and under his stewardship the Department was not as well run as it should have been. But he had the same qualities of mind that Skelton had had, he received Mackenzie King's trust, and possessed strong ideas about how Canada should be represented abroad—ideas that, as it proved, did not always square with Skelton's or King's.

II

One of the supremely political issues Norman Robertson had to deal with as Under-Secretary was the question of relations with France where, after the debacle of May-June 1940, there were the two contending parties: the Vichy régime under Marshal Pétain, and the Free French led by General Charles de Gaulle. Vichy had far more supporters in Quebec than Free France. It drew the admiration of those who liked Pétain's emphasis on family, church, country; those who saw Vichy as closer to God than the atheistic Third Republic it had replaced; and those who opposed the war as an imperialistic British struggle and rejected Canada's efforts to participate on a major scale. English Canadians, however, innocent of the subtleties, admired de Gaulle and Free France for their willingness to continue the struggle against Hitler, and many who were suspicious of Quebec avidly seized the opportunity to equate the province's sympathy with Pétain to disloyalty.

Thus the question of relations with France had major political implications for the King government as a whole and for its Department of External Affairs. The difficulties would be further complicated for Robertson by pressures exerted from London and Washington as Canada's senior partners struggled to shape a French policy of their own, by Mackenzie King's insistence on marching in step with the British and Americans (even when they followed their own individual drummers), and by a sharp dispute over the tiny islands of St Pierre and Miquelon off the Newfoundland coast. No series of interlocked problems was more vexing for Canada from 1940 to 1944; no issues were potentially more damaging to Canadian unity; no other subject so forcefully suggested Canada's need to develop the capacity for independent action.

Relations between Canada and France prior to the defeat of June 1940 were friendly but not close. There had been desultory prewar discussions about French aircraft purchases from Canada,[2] a visit to the front by Norman Rogers, the Minister of National Defence, in April 1940,[3] and talks about French purchases that began and ended in May 1940, after the opening of the blitzkrieg that destroyed the Republic.[4]

By the time Robertson succeeded Skelton in January 1941, the basic outline of policy had been determined. The Vichy government had retained its legation in Canada under René Ristelhueber, the Minister originally named by the Republic, and Canada, at the urging of London,[5] had sent Pierre Dupuy, the Chargé accredited to France, into Vichy to test the waters of Pétainist opinion about possible co-operation with Britain.[6] For a time the British believed Dupuy was producing useful information,[7] but London soon came to a different conclusion and formed the opinion that

Dupuy was a loose-tongued *naïf*.[8] Robertson and Mackenzie King shortly reached a similar conclusion.[9]

Robertson also found on taking office that plans for a Free French takeover of St Pierre and Miquelon were far advanced. In September 1940 they had received military approval in London but were shelved because of Canadian concerns that any action would produce an unfavourable response in Quebec, and perhaps for fear of American opinion.[10] The Monroe Doctrine, which stated that European powers or their surrogates should not expand or alter their possessions in the western hemisphere, had re-emerged as a credo in Washington; and there was concern, as Moffat told King, that a Canadian occupation of the islands, something that had not yet been suggested seriously, 'would give to Japan an excuse for occupying territory elsewhere. . . .'[11] This might have sounded far-fetched, but in the Far East, Japan was eyeing the territories still under the control of France and the Netherlands—countries occupied by its ally, Germany—and there was just enough sense in the American case to give reason for caution.

In the spring of 1941 the Newfoundland government expressed concern over the rising anti-British sentiment on the French islands and indicated its desire that Newfoundland, not Canada or the United States, should assume control.[12] The British, however, still favoured a Free French 'coup', but the military chiefs were now coming to believe that the islands were unimportant and, while they did not oppose Free French action, they had little enthusiasm for it. Desmond Morton, one of Churchill's close aides, wrote in June 1941 that if Admiral Muselier of the Free French navy, who wanted to seize the islands, could have gone ahead 'without saying anything to us', there probably would have been no objection from Canada and the United States, who might have acquiesced in a *fait accompli*. But once the British government had learned of Muselier's plan, 'it was impossible for us to connive at it without a warning to Canada and Newfoundland.'[13]

Word of these and other reflections must have reached Ottawa, for in May 1941 Pierrepont Moffat and Robertson began discussing St Pierre. The American reminded Robertson of an earlier Canadian agreement 'not to make any overt move in St. Pierre-Miquelon without full advance consultation',[14] and Robertson was soon urging King to send a Consul to the islands so that Canada would not be dependent on the Americans for information.[15]

In a further conversation between the Under-Secretary and the American Minister on May 28, Robertson expressed his fear that the St Pierre wireless could be used to endanger shipping. 'We talked a little bit about what might happen in the event some positive action . . . became necessary,' Moffat wrote, 'and Mr. Robertson gave it as his personal opinion that the idea of a trusteeship was not impossible if Canada were given the lion's share of the responsibility, but that in this case Canada would probably delegate as much authority as possible to a local Free French Government.'[16] Robertson was clearly not averse to action but, unlike some in his Department and in the Cabinet, he was sympathetic to de Gaulle.

The two did not discuss St Pierre again until July. Then Robertson indicated his doubts that the status quo could continue indefinitely. In a memo to the Prime Minister he wrote: 'I thought there was a growing interest and anxiety about their [the islands'] position in the minds of many people in Canada'; he worried about 'the use that might be made of the wireless facilities, etc., available in the islands.'[17] A few days later, after yet another discussion with Moffat, Robertson informed King that the Americans now feared overt action in St Pierre could cause difficulties in the French West Indies, where matters, thanks to co-operation between the Vichy French governor and the United States, were satisfactory. Robertson also added that he had told Moffat of a British request for Canadian views on permitting Muselier to sail to the islands 'in the hopes of . . . giving encouragement' to a declaration for Free France—Canada had been cool to this—and that he and Moffat had discussed *ad hoc* arrangements for the islands that might see the Administrator of St Pierre reach a satisfactory understanding with Canada on use of the wireless.[18]

In August, St Pierre came before the Cabinet War Committee, the government's key ministers, when a concerned Robertson reported growing RCMP fears about 'opportunities for espionage and sabotage'.[19] More than two months later an interdepartmental committee advised the War Committee of its view that Canadian personnel should be stationed on the islands to control radio communications. Increasingly anxious for action, Robertson then reported to the War Committee that on 'strategic grounds' the British Chiefs of Staff were now in favour of steps to 'remove Vichy influence' and supported action by Muselier as 'most appropriate'.[20] But the War Committee resisted this suggestion, deciding instead that the St Pierre authorities should be approached to see if they would accept Canadian troops.

When Moffat heard of this from Robertson he was worried. 'I asked what would happen if the Administrator . . . refused to allow these men into the wireless station. He said that this would create a very difficult situation . . . he recognized that there would be a large, if not predominant group in the Cabinet which would want Canada to take control of the island.' Moffat again reminded his friend of the Canadian promise of consultation and stressed that if the Canadian request for personnel on the islands were rejected, a difficult situation would result. Robertson said that London's preference was for a Free French seizure as a way of avoiding difficulty with the Monroe Doctrine, and Moffat asked whether Robertson agreed with that assessment. 'He said that there would be a division of opinion but that there were many people in the [Canadian] Government who would not even trust the Free French in so vital a strategic position with a wireless just a few miles removed from the convoy routes.'[21] That was an interesting commentary on the depth of Canadian suspicion of Frenchmen, whatever their politics.

Nonetheless by mid-November it seemed clear that a final decision on action had been delayed. Robertson had now begun to think of economic pressure as a way to force co-operation on the Administrator of the islands, which were dependent on Canada and Newfoundland for food, or for fomenting a popular revolt on the islands in favour of de Gaulle. Indeed, the next day Moffat came upon Hugh Keenleyside, who was drafting just such a recommendation for the Prime Minister.[22] On November 26 Robertson was able to tell the War Committee that the United States was prepared to acquiesce informally in the plan to send Canadian wireless personnel to the islands and to co-operate in economic pressure.[23] As a means of bringing those things about, the Cabinet War Committee thereupon agreed to send General Georges Vanier to St Pierre.

But before the next War Committee meeting on December 1, Robertson changed his position in a most uncharacteristic way. Without acquainting King with his plans, he put before the War Committee a proposal to send an officer from his department and military censors to the islands to control communications, this group being conveyed in a corvette that could seize St Pierre if immediate acquiescence was refused. Anxious and tired, frustrated at

the months of inaction, Robertson told the ministers that he did
not want to inform either the British or Americans of this scheme
in advance, and he added that he felt the chances were good that
the French governor would give in without the necessity for force.
Although the Committee seemed prepared to accept Robertson's
advice, Mackenzie King was not:

> . . . I said if war cabinet were determined to take the view
> that apparently the majority wished, that I would wish to
> have the minutes record that I was distinctly opposed, believ-
> ing that the course was entirely wrong. Once I took this posi-
> tion, the others came around to agreeing to have the pro-
> posed course submitted to the govts. of the U.S. and Britain,
> and awaiting their comments thereon before taking any ac-
> tion.

The Prime Minister added a few words to express his displeasure
with Robertson. 'I am even more distressed at finding Robertson
taking up these matters with other Ministers without discussing
all their implications with me first. His judgment is not anything
comparable to what S[kelton]'s was in matters of the kind.'[24]

Matters worsened the next day when Robertson submitted to
King a draft telegram he had written to Churchill asking his views
on the proposed course. King was angered by its phrasing and
tone[25] and called Robertson that evening:

> . . . I rang him up to tell him that I would not agree to a mes-
> sage of the kind being [sent] either . . . to Britain or the U.S.
> That I was to send a message to Churchill which would tell
> him the entire position and ask his views concerning it before
> any step were taken. I went on to say that I much resented
> having these matters brought before the War Committee
> without any discussion with myself in advance; that as P.M.
> and Secretary of State for E.A., I had responsibility to Parlia-
> ment for what was done, and I thought I was entitled to the
> full confidence of my staffs in all matters pertaining to my
> two officers [sic]. I resented very much matters being settled
> behind my back with other Departments. No consultation
> with myself in advance. I tried to restrain myself in the way I
> spoke but I could not help showing a very strong feeling of
> indignation at the persistent way in which in matters affect-
> ing peace and war, others were trying to settle policies for
> which I would have to take the responsibility. The trouble is

there is a little quota [sic] of men who are off by themselves, Robertson, Stone, and Keenleyside, Pearson, etc., a bureaucracy who are good enough men themselves but left to themselves without wide experience or political knowledge are liable to make many grave mistakes.[26]

Robertson deserved King's censure. Stubborn at times, he had again tried to get his own way. His tactics were bad and his advice was questionable. The modified telegram (unaccountably still suggesting use of a corvette and landing party if necessary) was finally sent off on December 3,[27] but not before Robertson had given the Prime Minister a rather formal memorandum, recapitulating the St Pierre question and essentially attacking King's belief that Canadian action on the island could serve as a pretext for Axis retaliation. 'This risk', Robertson argued, 'has to be set against the risk of information about fleet and convoy movements reaching enemy forces from St Pierre'.[28]

What was the explanation for Robertson's quite extraordinary and quite untypical behaviour on this occasion? First, he knew France well and loved it, and he was revolted at the thought that Paris should be under Hitler's control, that St Pierre, so close to Canada, should be in the power of the Vichy régime he despised. It also appalled him that so many French diplomats had stayed loyal to Pétain and that so few had rallied to de Gaulle. His frustration had been intensified by the long process of delay, of backing and filling, that had characterized policy towards St Pierre as Canada bounced helplessly back and forth between British and American plans, objections, and warnings. And he had undoubtedly been influenced by Thomas A. Stone, one of his officers who had served in the Paris Legation and who was a militant Gaullist, into favouring action against St Pierre, which was one area where Canada had the capacity—if not yet the will—to act. Nonetheless his recommendations to the War Committee and to King were so uncharacteristic that there had to be other reasons. Robertson was a bureaucrat, ordinarily patient and regularly long-suffering when it came to dealing with the Prime Minister. He must have anticipated the reaction he drew from King, but clearly it did not bother him this time. There was a war on, after all, and St Pierre could have been—and probably was—feeding information to the U-boats that were wreaking havoc on Allied convoys. In the circumstances—with men dying and supplies being lost—to hell with being cautious all the time; to hell with trying through tact and patient effort to persuade the Prime Minister to do something he should have done willingly; to hell with always worrying over London's and Washington's response. His was an emotional decision, and it was one of the few times Robertson allowed his heart to rule his head. That he did so suggests the self-discipline he imposed on himself to remain a calm and cautious bureaucrat: he was, after all, an ordinary man, subject to the usual pulls of sentiment and passion. That he reacted as he did is to his credit.

Meanwhile Minister-Counsellor Hume Wrong reported from Washington that State Department officials were 'strongly of the opinion' that economic pressure should be tried before 'the more drastic procedure' suggested in Robertson's telegram.[29] On December 15 Robertson spoke to Moffat about a Free French coup; he thought the Americans did not exclude that as a possibility but, Moffat wrote, 'I said that our thinking had been steadily moving away from that suggestion and that, on principle, if action were to be taken it would be preferable that an American rather than a non-American Government should take it.' Robertson, digressing somewhat, then said, 'we should all have to think about recognizing General de Gaulle and the Free French movement as an alternative to being forced into war with France,' a real possibility if Vichy drew much closer to Hitler. Moffat wondered what Robertson knew of de Gaulle's leadership abilities, an enquiry that sounds more curious now than it did in 1941. While there were problems in de Gaulle's view of himself as the embodiment of a redeemed France, Robertson stated that he had sound advisers around him. The meeting ended with Robertson announcing his departure to have lunch with Admiral Muselier, who was then on a visit to Ottawa.[30]

Churchill's reply was finally received late on December 15, and the British leader indicated that his government favoured a Free French seizure of the island. 'Free French headquarters', the Cabinet War Committee learned the next day, 'were being advised that the United Kingdom would have no objection.'[31] But Muselier had seen not only Robertson but also Moffat, who advised the Admiral that the United States strongly disapproved of any Free French action. Muselier had told Moffat that, although his orders from de Gaulle were to take the island, he was not going to act until he had the support of Canada, the United States, and Newfoundland.[32] Robertson had been impressed with the Admiral, but at another meeting with Moffat[33] he too learned how the

Americans now felt and he informed the War Committee accordingly. As a result the Committee decided that any action taken should be by Canada, not Muselier.[34] A few days later, however, the cautious Prime Minister and War Committee decided to do nothing until the British and American positions were in accord.[35]

Thus everything remained in stasis. Moffat recorded that the general view in Ottawa now was 'that the St. Pierre show has been hashed. It has been talked over so much and so often, and so much time has elapsed since it was first proposed in early November that it is becoming progressively harder to justify as an emergency measure.' Worse, Muselier had told the Canadians that all France would resent the posting of Canadian radio technicians on the island as an infringement of French sovereignty. Moffat added that 'Robertson, Pearson [back in Ottawa as Assistant Under-Secretary] and Stone are definitely among those who think that we have made a tactical mistake. Tommy Stone was all for saying, "To hell with consulting the United States. This is a war measure. . . ." '[36] A few days later Robertson told Moffat—with the great sigh that was his trademark (as well as a sign of his exhaustion and exasperation)—that 'it was terribly hard for Canada to keep in step with both the United States and Great Britain, particularly when the two big powers chose to walk in diametrically opposite directions.'[37] The frustration continued, tearing Robertson apart.

This was the situation on December 24, when Muselier arrived at St Pierre, with three Free French ships and one submarine, and seized control. He then announced plans for a plebiscite.[38]

The next day, Christmas, Robertson was to leave Ottawa with the Prime Minister for Washington meetings with Roosevelt and Churchill. 'During the afternoon,' King wrote in his diary, 'word came that Mr. Hull was very disturbed at what had happened . . . and wished Canada to order the Free French forces away and reinstate the Governor.' King's response, entirely in keeping with his position so far, was that the British and Americans should talk and decide what to do and then Canada would act. King added that 'what had been done at St. Pierre was by the Free French not only without instructions from our part but in direct opposition to our policy.'[39]

Nonetheless Moffat was under terrific pressure from the State Department and was suspicious of his Canadian friends. He first learned that Tommy Stone thought Muselier's action embarrassing but 'a good thing'. He then called Robertson

> who repeated Stone's expression of surprise and embarrassment. He said he had not telephoned me last night as he had been in a personal jam which he had to straighten out before anything else. Yesterday afternoon, Mr. Ristelhueber, the Vichy Minister, had called on him and said that he had heard two rumours: the first, that Admiral Muselier was going to take over the islands, the second that the Canadians were going to take over the islands or the communications. Mr. Robertson had taken the occasion to talk to him more frankly than he had for a long time past. He said it was not true that Admiral Muselier was going to take over the islands but pointed out the constant potential menace to Allied security of the wireless station . . . it seemed that when Mr. Robertson had given the assurances that the Free French would not take over the islands, they were already in occupation. Mr. Robertson had accordingly gone right around to call on Mr. Ristelhueber to explain that Admiral Muselier's action was a complete surprise. . . .

Those conversations apparently satisfied Moffat 'that there was no possible collusion between the Canadians and Admiral Muselier, a conclusion that seems correct.'[40] But Secretary of State Hull was still angry and peremptorily told his Minister that he wanted the Canadians to remove Muselier forthwith.

Moffat next located Robertson at Stone's house, just sitting down to Christmas dinner, and quickly ruined the meal. The Under-Secretary, who must have been relieved and almost delighted at the Gaullist coup, spent the rest of the afternoon on the telephone trying, as Moffat put it, 'to find a formula that would save de Gaulle's face. He appreciated all the dangers. . . . On the other hand, he felt that we must think twice before taking any step to disavow him or his Movement, as the repercussions of this disavowal might be most unfortunate in France.'[41] Robertson's position, the epitome of good sense, carefully focused on the main issue; the American response on the other hand, shaped by Hull's distrust of de Gaulle and his open-line policy to Vichy, was slightly hysterical, as well as unrealistic and silly. A statement was immediately released in Washington in which Hull noted that 'This Government has inquired of the Canadian Government as to the steps that Government is prepared to take to restore the *status quo* of these islands' and to expel the 'so-called Free French.'[42]

Now it was Robertson's turn to be furious at this incredibly inept public comment. 'In a word', Moffat wrote, Robertson's 'whole attitude had changed from one of helpful cooperation to one of most reluctant cooperation.'[43] Why Hull seemed to feel that Canada should resolve matters was anyone's guess, but Moffat was in the middle, trying to explain matters to the uncomprehending in Foggy Bottom while simultaneously trying to press the Canadian government to do what Hull wanted.

By this point Robertson and King had boarded the train for Washington. At Montreal, Robertson talked with Pearson on the telephone and learned that Moffat had presented 'an ultimatum', or so King described it. According to the Prime Minister's secretary, J.W. Pickersgill, the Prime Minister, left to himself, might have done what the Americans wanted, 'but Norman and I were so opposed to the American attitude, as were most of the Ministers concerned [the three Defence ministers were aboard]. We all said that Canada cannot disturb the occupation by the Free French. It has happened and that is that.'[44] King's diary is stronger in its response to the American threats than Pickersgill recollects, but the Prime Minister did write that he had 'the same concern that Mr. Hull does' about de Gaulle's actions. In King's view the crisis proved that, as usual, he had been right when he advocated doing nothing at all.[45] Nonetheless a message was soon drafted for Washington: 'Canada is in no way responsible for the Free French action. . . . We decline to commit ourselves to any action or to take any action . . . until we have had an opportunity of considering action with the President and Mr. Churchill, the Canadian Government cannot take the steps requested to expel the Free French.'[46]

Curiously, the crisis was almost over: Canada was soon off the hook, and when de Gaulle refused to budge, St Pierre remained under his control. There was still to be much shouting, however, from Hull, who was suspicious of the Canadians and the British, suspecting their connivance with the Free French.[47] But Hull's anger created only confusion at the State Department; Hull failed to keep his staff informed and the American side dissolved in confusion.[48] Much time was wasted in Hull's offices drafting and redrafting position papers, but by February 1942 the issue was as 'dead as a doornail'.[49]

There were no winners. Canada had dithered too long initially, although it had little choice, given King's cautious insistence on Anglo-American agreement before Canada moved. The Americans had behaved with appalling stupidity, while the British had probably failed to keep the Americans as fully informed about Free French activities and plans as they should have. And de Gaulle's Christmas surprise had caused problems and sharply increased American enmity to his movement.[50]

For Norman Robertson the issue was important. This was his first major political crisis as Under-Secretary, and in general he had managed it well from Christmas onward, keeping the Canadian interest clearly in view and preventing any acquiescence to Washington's ultimatum. But earlier he had tried too hard to push King toward action of a sort for which he was not attuned, and had been severely and justly rebuked for this. Robertson could learn from experience; henceforth he would be more skilful in dealing with the Prime Minister.

As for King himself, he had no hard feelings at all. Moffat had dinner with the Prime Minister on January 9, 1942 and recorded afterwards that the St Pierre affair was 'the only problem on which [King] and Robertson materially differed. Robertson and Stone had cooked up a plan of sending Stone to the islands in a corvette to take over the radio. [King] had approved Stone's going but had absolutely vetoed the corvette. He felt that if Robertson and Stone had had their way they, rather than Admiral Muselier, might have upset the equilibrium with repercussions all over the world. He thought that the realization of this had sobered them and that they had learned a valuable lesson without cost.' This was likely true, and Robertson was never so rash—or so human—again.

King also told Moffat that 'He thought that the group in the Department of External Affairs was peculiarly able and deserving of praise. Robertson and Pearson were obviously his two favorites. He said, however, that they always wanted to go a little too fast.'[51] King was a wily old fox who knew that young men were always in a hurry.

More important and more dangerous than St Pierre was the larger question of Canada's relations with Pétain and de Gaulle, a subject that was not only of interest to Ottawa but to London, which was concerned with the large questions of strategy. In May 1941 Mackenzie King sought Churchill's advice on breaking relations with the Pétainist régime. Such a step, he knew, had much appeal to English Canada, which was ready to brand Vichy as 'enemy', but it was certain to provoke an unhappy response from French Canada, which was still sympathetic to Marshal Pétain's government. Opinion in Whitehall was divided too,[52] but Churchill told King that 'I think, myself, that there may be even now advantages in maintaining some contact with Vichy for a while.'[53] The Canadian government accepted the Churchill view—quite properly, since this was a case with ramifications greater than the relations between France and Canada—but in fact Robertson and his colleagues were trying to persuade Ristelhueber to resign his post and close the Vichy Legation in Ottawa, thus ending the problem indirectly. Robertson told Moffat this on May 17, adding that he 'and the whole Department of External Affairs will be much happier when the Vichy Legation is no longer functioning in Ottawa.'[54] In the end Ottawa decided to maintain relations with Vichy, but shortly before this decision was reached Robertson learned that all of Ristelhueber's bank balances had been converted to cash, and noted that if it had been done by anyone less honourable than the French diplomat, 'it would look like a contemplated flight'.[55] Once again, in August, the Canadians tried to cut the tie with Pétain; and again the British suggested delay,[56] and did so again in November when King tried a third time.[57] There seemed little doubt that Ottawa assessed the situation differently from London, while acceding to London's strategy.

What of de Gaulle's Free French? In February 1941 the Canadian government had permitted an official envoy of the General to come to Canada for a visit,[58] and soon afterwards a permanent representative was accepted. In addition, an information office was set up under Elisabeth de Miribel, a close friend of Robertson who would soon be an influential figure in Ottawa.[59] But if this shift in attitude was more in the direction of Robertson's inclination, he was not yet ready to advocate recognition of Free France as France. As one historian noted, Robertson wanted to delay defining the relationship with de Gaulle so as to be able to adapt to changes in the 'general French position'.[60]

By the early stages of the St Pierre situation Robertson had convinced himself that the general trend could best be served by straight recognition of Free France. That was a tenable position until December 24, 1941 and Muselier's coup; afterwards the idea of recognition infuriated the United States government. Robertson said in February 1942 that 'The Canadians were having to carry water on two shoulders . . . they did not wish to do anything that would drive Vichy further along a path toward collaboration. They also did not wish to do anything that would disorganize or discredit the Free French movement.' Moffat, the recipient of these truisms, added that 'It was by no means easy to keep on carrying water on both shoulders, particularly with the amount of tension throughout Canada.'[61]

The tension was great. The resurrected leader of the Conservative party, Senator Arthur Meighen, was preaching conscription and total war. A plebiscite on the question of releasing the government from its promises of no compulsory military service overseas had been announced for April 1942 in the Speech from the Throne in January, and the War Committee itself was badly split on the subject of conscription. In the circumstances anything that upset Quebec opinion further could not be tolerated by the government, so the need to tote water on both shoulders continued.[62]

The government's difficulties were compounded in April by the recall of the United States Minister in Vichy. This was curiously accompanied by advice from Washington that Canada should not follow suit.[63] The United States and Britain were both anxious to keep some links with Pétain if possible, and if Canada could persist (and keep some of the heat off its allies) that was all to the good. At the end of April, however, Mackenzie King came close to making the break with Vichy—which was now clearly cooperating with the Germans—this time at London's urging.[64] Robertson told Moffat that he thought the action could come within days, in all likelihood immediately after the plebiscite, though his own preference was for the breach to take place before the vote on conscription.[65]

But once again the break was postponed, the Americans pressing Ottawa not to take the ultimate step that would consign Vichy wholly into the Nazi darkness.[66] All that Robertson could get was to have Ottawa demand the recall of the Vichy consuls in Quebec City and Montreal who were using their offices as distribution centres for propaganda and disaffection.[67] There matters rested uneasily until November 1942, when the Anglo-Americans made an assault on North Africa and when the Vichyard defenders fired on the invading allies. Those shots forced action on Ottawa. But how to make the break in a way that minimized Quebec's hurt?

'Norman sat in his room and brooded,' his colleague George Glazebrook remembered, '—he didn't want to talk to us very much and then he announced that the only solution was to terminate relations.'[68] That was more or less the situation, but he also had conversations with King, Moffat, and Pickersgill. With assistance from Pickersgill and some, probably, from Arnold Heeney, the Secretary to the Cabinet, Robertson produced a statement that justified the new Canadian policy and incorporated the idea, as Robertson told Moffat that night, 'that Vichy no longer represented the French people and that, accordingly, they had no recognized representation abroad.' In other words, Canada was not breaking relations with Vichy: Vichy for all practical purposes had ceased to exist.[69] Pickersgill later recollected the situation:

> Norman and I discussed this problem and I don't recall which of us first suggested the formula which the government accepted. The Prime Minister announced that the French Government had ceased to exist . . . there was no diplomatic precedent for such an attitude. Norman realized that if we broke off relations it would mean we recognized that the Vichy government was still in existence and we might well have found ourselves manoeuvered in[to] a state of technical war with France. . . . We couldn't be at war with a government that didn't exist.[70]

That interpretation was based on Robertson's fear of the consequences for Canada if the country found itself at war with France.[71] As Pickersgill said, Robertson believed that treating France in a way that minimized hostility between English- and French-Canadians was 'the most important single controversial thing about the conduct of that war . . . [the] very existence of Canada depended on our maintaining the right kind of attitude.'[72]

Robertson's clever inspiration did not win ready acceptance. Moffat thought it 'unnecessarily subtle',[73] and Cordell Hull found it a 'metaphysical point'.[74] But the fertile mind of President Roosevelt grasped the idea, telling King that 'In other words, [Vichy] ain't.' Exactly, King said.[75] Thus the Canadian position was as Robertson formulated it.[76] Relations with Vichy ceased, and poor Ristelhueber, more concerned about his pension than anything else, finally got his walking papers.[77] However, not until August 1943 did Canada recognize Free France 'as administering the

French overseas territories which acknowledge its authority and as the body best qualified to ensure the conduct of the French effort in the war within the framework of inter-Allied cooperation.'[78] In October 1944, some months after the liberation of Paris, a day that Jetty Robertson remembered as the most exciting and happy of the war for her husband,[79] Canada finally recognized Free France as the provisional government of France. It had been a long road for France, for de Gaulle, and for Norman Robertson, and the hazards of the journey left scars on General de Gaulle, who did not forget Canada's lack of haste.

The difficulties over Canada's relations with the two competing French régimes had shown the delicacy of the relationship between domestic and foreign policies. They had also demonstrated how important it was to Canada that the United States and Britain move in the same direction; if the two great powers disagreed, as over St Pierre and Vichy, then problems of the most serious kind arose in Ottawa. That was understandable when global matters— the fate of France—were at stake, and few observers could have objected to Mackenzie King's caution in the circumstances, or to the constraints he placed on his sometimes precipitate foreign-service officers. Small states, after all, had to be cautious in a world of great powers; they had to know their place. But what was Canada's place to be? The nation had burgeoned during the war, and Canada's acquisition of military and economic power gradually convinced the mandarins, and the government they served, that Canada's place could no longer be passive. How was this strength to be used? How could the nation carve out a role for itself that recognized the new reality? In creating Canada's functional principle, Hume Wrong was to play the crucial role in answering those questions.

III

Hume Wrong was born on September 10, 1894, the son of Professor George M. Wrong and Sophia Hume Blake. His father, ordained an Anglican clergyman at Wycliffe College, was to become the first professor of Canadian history in the country, the creator of the Department of History in the University of Toronto, and the dean of the profession. His mother was the only surviving daughter of Edward Blake (1833-1912), the mercurial and brilliant Liberal politician who had served briefly as Premier of Ontario, as

Minister of Justice in the Mackenzie administration, and as Leader of the Opposition in Ottawa for long and contentious years. The Wrongs were comfortably off, well established in Toronto society, and from their home, 'Humewood', on Jarvis Street[80] (now The Red Lion, an undistinguished pub), they mingled with the Masseys and only rarely with the masses. Indeed, young Vincent Massey spent as much time in the gayer surroundings of 'Humewood' as he did in his family mansion up the street, and Professor Wrong apparently played an instrumental part in getting Vincent admitted to Balliol College, Oxford, at the same time as he sent his second son Murray and daughter Marga there in 1911.[81]

Hume Wrong too was destined for Balliol. But this intelligent though troubled boy had difficulties on the way. At five he lost an eye to a childhood accident, a circumstance that contributed to making his time at Upper Canada College and Bishop Ridley College in St Catharines a hell. His sister still remembers his detestation of Ridley—even though he eventually became head boy.[82] At the University of Toronto he read Classics—notably with Maurice Hutton, Principal of University College, a family friend and one of the great men of the university[83]—and he did well. Hutton's letter of recommendation, sent to Balliol in the spring of 1914, observed that 'The simplest and most illuminating description I can offer of the boy is that he is very much a replica of his brother Murray whom you know; he may not write quite as well perhaps; per contra his classics are stronger.' Hutton added that Wrong's class work had suffered that year: 'In this gay place a boy who knows everyone & whose people know everyone is beset with distractions & is apt to hand over the headship of the class lists to the students from the back townships & the concession lines or to those who live at least on those lines metaphorically.' In other words, Hume Wrong, though 'extremely attractive, absolutely trustworthy & honourable and distinctly clever', was unlikely to earn better than a second-class degree.[84] Hutton said this without irony. Eight years later he cheerfully married off his daughter Joyce to Hume Wrong.

In fact Wrong's entry to Balliol had to be delayed. An operation for appendicitis weakened him and forced him to accept *aegrotat* standing in 1914.[85] Then the Great War began. Wrong, who completed his B.A. at Toronto in 1915 and failed in his efforts to join the Canadian Expeditionary Force because of his blind eye, crossed to England on his own. His intention was to join the British Army (its standards were already markedly lower than those of the Canadian Army) or, if he was balked again, to attend Balliol. The Oxford and Buckinghamshire Light Infantry, however, accepted him, commissioned him in July 1915 as a second lieutenant, gave him a modicum of training, and shipped him to France in November and to the trenches in January 1916.

The war marked him ever after. As Anglophilic as all his family—his eldest brother Harold was killed on the first day of the Somme offensive, July 1, 1916, while serving in the BEF, and his brother Murray remained at Oxford for the rest of his life—Hume Wrong at no time seemed to feel out of place as a Canadian in the British Army. His letters home tried to be cheerful, but the horror showed through. On September 3, 1916, he told his brother that 'our general loves fighting', a remark offered with no enthusiasm whatever, and other letters dwelt on the lice, the mud, and the problems involved in commanding a company, a chore that fell to him as a lieutenant when casualties had wiped out his seniors. 'I can't pretend I'm happy or even cheerful', Wrong told his sister in a bleak letter on July 22, 1916, during the dreadful Somme battles. 'My great desire is to get out of it honourably, and I don't mind what the end may be. I've seen too much death to be afraid of it anymore.'[86] A fragment of poetry written a few months earlier said much the same thing: 'It's Sunday morning in Flanders but we must work today/Although our work be slaughter . . .'[87]

Yet despite the slaughter Wrong could see some of the 'glamour of war'. In a letter written in February 1918, after his return to Canada with trench fever and a weak heart, and after his transfer to service with the Royal Air Force at training bases in Ontario, he observed that 'Even this muddy, sordid sort of fighting has a sort of glamour. That's why I don't believe wars will ever stop. Today I feel as though I could ask nothing better than to hear a big army coming over, to see the half circle of flares going up all along the horizon, and to smell the stench of mingled H.E. and dead things. . . . I know if there is another war before I die, I shall have to go if I can get there. . . .'[88]

Perhaps those remnants of romanticism helped shape Wrong's attitude to those who shirked the fighting. In March 1917 he wrote of his extreme irritation with an American who had asked what the British Army thought of the United States and how that had provoked him into writing a poem: 'Our best are lost; 'twere better lose the whole/For you, great nation, you have lost a soul.' 'In very truth,' he added, 'I prefer Germany to the U.S. in many ways; while I fear the one as a nation, I despise the other.'[89] Much the same animus infected Wrong's view of French Canada, which was reluctant to participate in what was widely seen as an Imperialist war. 'It really looks now as though there was going to be something approaching a rebellion in Quebec', he wrote in May 1917. 'In any case, there is bound to be bloodshed, in rioting if not in organized revolt. I would welcome a little military activity in Quebec. My C.O. and I have arranged a little punitive expedition to consist of a string of cars armoured with boiler plate and armed with Lewis guns. It would be the greatest sport in the world to fight against an enemy which was without artillery or machine-guns. And I should delight in catching Lavergne or Bourassa [the *nationaliste* leaders]. Still let us hope for peace—and conscription.'[90]

Fortunately this mad plan was unnecessary—although it was a near run thing, and Wrong's war petered out in boredom. As soon as he was able, he crossed to England, still a Captain on active service, reapplied to Balliol, and began to read history. From 1919 to 1921 he took the 'Shortened Course' designed for 'demobbed' servicemen and he graduated with a B.Litt. 'with distinction', roughly equivalent to a first-class degree.[91] His solid and polished B.Litt. paper, *The Government of the West Indies*, was eventually published in 1923; four years later his popular biography, *Sir Alexander Mackenzie, Explorer and Fur Trader* (1927), was published in the 'Canadian Men of Action' series.

The Oxford experience removed some of the rough edges the war had left on Wrong, as it probably also reinforced some of the snobbishness he was given to as a young man. But another result of his experience abroad was that for the first time he began to think about international problems, and about Canada's role and position in the world. In early 1920 he wrote home from Oxford that, although he no longer knew many people in Canada, still 'I regard Canada as the place I ought to return to. . . .'[92] He was a Canadian—this was something that his service with the BEF and his Oxford education could not change—and he wanted his country to have its due place.

Thus in 1919, when Sir Robert Borden was troubling the Great

Powers at Versailles with his demands for a seat in the League of Nations, Wrong sent his father in Toronto his views. 'The Assembly' of the League, he wrote,

> is little more than a talking shop . . .
>
> . . . the legal interpretation of Imperial sovereignty is against us . . . [but] the question of status in the league is of minor importance compared with its getting to work . . .
>
> . . . [Canada's] position would be much stronger if there was a Canadian statesman (there isn't so far as I know) who would and could state that our membership in the League implies a new responsibility and a new duty in carrying out the work of the League, and that Canadian brains and Canadian money will have to be used in a new field.[93]

In other words, Canada had to assume responsiblities, not simply talk of status. That conception, formed when he was twenty-five years old and after he had watched his generation destroyed by war, was to be the guiding principle of his career in his country's service.

But that career was still in the future. In 1920 George Wrong, as head of the department at the University of Toronto, offered his son a position teaching history. Such out-and-out nepotism troubled Hume. 'I am not a historian,' he wrote his father and prospective employer, 'I know no history before the middle of the 18th Century and very little after that.'[94] But the father, arguing a shortage of qualified men, prevailed over the son's qualms and the objections of President Falconer of the University. Hume Wrong became a lecturer in history in the fall of 1921.

That job lasted six years. Wrong taught long hours and large classes, at least by this day's standards. Records of that period of his life are fragmentary, but it seems clear that he tried to argue against the tutorial system that had been imposed on the department by his father[95] and, particularly after his marriage to Joyce Hutton in 1922, that he scrambled to make ends meet, offering summer courses (for $300 in 1925) and extension classes (in 1924 for $150).[96] He found the work uninspiring. 'I am getting fed up with teaching history . . .' he told his brother, 'and I think I won't get acclimatized. But one can't take so many chances with a wife attached. . . .' The students were dullards, the academic years seemed interminable, and he could simply not see teaching as his life work.[97] But for all his constant complaints, at least one student remembered Wrong warmly. Paul Martin, later a Liberal Party warhorse and distinguished political figure, remembered attending meetings of the History Club to watch Wrong in action; in particular, and with some glee, he long savoured Wrong's devastation of a paper presented by another young Department lecturer, one Lester Pearson.[98]

What did interest Wrong during his time at the university was his work with the imperialist Round Table movement and with its journal, *The Round Table*, published in England. From 1922 he played a leading role in Canada for the organization as its secretary and as chairman of its educational committee; in addition he coordinated the preparation of the Canadian articles that appeared in the journal, occasionally writing them himself. If the journal thrived, however, and to some extent it did, the organization in Canada was virtually defunct, and by 1923 Wrong knew that the very name carried unfortunate connotations in Canada: '. . . the Round Table has achieved an unfortunate and undeserved reputation in Canada as a propagandist organization directed from London against Canadian democracy.'[99]

That was not yet his own view, but as his nationalism developed it became so. In 1924, still an imperialist, he worried about Mackenzie King's foreign policy, telling his brother that the problem with King's stand on the Lausanne Treaty 'is that we'll have to be consulted in some way or other on all important treaties, and this may act in the same way on Br. foreign policy as the Senate does on the U.S.A.—to impose inaction.' Ill-informed Dominion statesmen with an eye on their voters could block British action.[100] But by 1926 Wrong had swung round, telling his father of his work on an article that took 'the general line that the navy defends British interests (as contrasted with Canadian or Australian), that it isn't our business to pay for it, and that the absence of a naval contribution does not therefore invalidate our claim to an "adequate voice" in foreign policy. . . .' It was, he argued, important to stop the British 'talking of sharing the burden of naval defence . . . as though we were cowering for protection behind a navy we won't help support.'[101] And the next month he said that he had become unpopular with the Round Tablers because he attacked their conceptions so sharply. 'They will *preach*, and the burden of their sermon is: Agree with us and you'll save your soul; disagree and be damned.'[102] That was a fair-enough assessment of the whole Imperial unity crew in England and Canada, and after

Wrong concluded that Viscount Byng had 'been a fool' in the great King-Byng crisis of 1926, there was no doubt that he believed that he was soon to be cast into the outer darkness by his erstwhile Round Table colleagues.[103]

The opportunity to escape the boredom of the university and the righteousness of the Round Table came suddenly. At the beginning of February 1927 Vincent Massey raised the possibility of Wrong's joining the staff of the Canadian Legation in Washington. Mackenzie King had asked Massey to open the Legation in 1926, and early the next year Massey was beginning to gather a staff. As an old family friend—as a *quondam* Round Tabler, as an educated, cultivated young man with an attractive wife—Wrong seemed an ideal choice to the wealthy aesthete.[104] He himself relished this opportunity to do useful work for his country—and to start at the top of the fledgling Canadian diplomatic service as a First Secretary with a salary of $5,000, substantially more than he had been earning at the University.[105] He accepted the position and moved to Washington in April 1927.

But in fact his links with Vincent Massey and his wife Alice soon began to dissolve as the Massey duo showed far more concern for the social side of their diplomatic role in Washington than for the work. Wrong's letters home began to reflect his bitterness. In October 1928 he wrote: 'V. and A. returned on Monday, & left, as usual, for N.Y. on Wed. They can't stay put here for a week on end, and V. has no real conception of the business which goes on. I don't mind much because I know I'm much more competent to handle it than he is!' A month later he wrote that 'A new episode is added daily to the Massey saga. I must never be tempted to writing a novel, as I would be moved to use this obvious material.' Or again: 'V. and A. are growing more and more like spoiled children; some of their actions and remarks are positively incredible. I'm afraid they will come a bad cropper soon, because they are bound to make themselves strikingly unpopular in Canada, though these Americans will stand a lot of swank.'[106]

Wrong was never adept at hiding his disdain for 'accomplished dilettantes' like Massey, and the Minister in turn soon formed a dark opinion of his First Secretary. He had no doubt of Wrong's ability, he wrote in his diary, but 'the difficulties inherent to his temperament become more and more evident . . . I suppose it is natural that Edward Blake's grandson should be both a selfish colleague & disloyal subordinate. . . . Jealousy of myself I believe was the key to his bearing in part. . . .' Massey then gave vent to his feelings about Wrong by listing a string of adjectives to describe him: 'pompous, self important, arrogant, selfish, sycophantic, obstinate, vindictive, priggish, perverse, ungenerous, overbearing, uncivil, dictatorial, officious, surly, inquisitive, calculating, disloyal! Now I feel better,' he concluded.

The Masseys were a difficult, flighty couple, more comfortable when travelling in the grand manner and entertaining with a panoply of liveried servants at their beck and call than in doing the dull day-to-day work of the Legation. Massey was lazy, none too bright, and all too willing to leave the chores to Wrong. But there can be little doubt that Wrong was a difficult colleague, however great his abilities. At this time of his life, and for a dozen years after, he was unhappy with his work for the Department of External Affairs and often contemptuous of those of lesser talents. It was probably inevitable that Wrong's intellectual arrogance would clash with Massey's social pretensions—the Blake in Wrong was too strong to prevent this. Fortunately, as he grew older, his Wrong inheritance—friendliness and humanity—showed through more and more.

But that was in the future. Wrong's work in Washington did not seem very important or stimulating. His first comments in 1927 told of his being initiated into the problems of rum-running from Canada into the U.S. and the extradition of criminals; he next spoke of being 'appallingly ignorant of it all'; and then, expressing his boredom, referred to the 'usual flock of deportations, lunatics, criminals, and harassed enquirers' that were his daily lot.[108] Within a few months he wrote that 'The qualifications for a successful diplomat in Washington were:

(1) a good head for liquor, which I possess as long as I don't mix my drinks;
(2) a manner successful with the ladies—in this I am deficient but I am rapidly progressing . . .
(3) ability to get along on about five hours sleep . . .
(4) common sense—everyone thinks they have this quality . . .
(5) an orderly and methodical mind . . .
(6) cynicism about governments and pessimism about human nature, with both of which I am amply provided;
(7) a capacity for producing orally and on paper, polite guff at a moment's notice . . . this is becoming mechanical. . . .[109]

Of the United States and of Americans, he took a dark view.

'This is a most unintellectual life,' he wrote. 'A great many of the younger Americans in society seem to find their only stimuli in drink and sex.'[110] 'I won't start on U.S. politics,' he told his sister Marga who was a missionary in Africa, 'but it is a barbarous country. Why don't you civilize them instead of hankering after naked and happy Africans? They need it more. . . .' In January 1929 he added that 'Politics in this country naturally make one cynical; in politics the U.S. has achieved less civilization than in any other aspect of its life. This is largely because gov't is so much less important to the community than in any European country or even in Canada; also because the constitution is designed to foster insincerity and guff. . . .' Wrong added of the new President, Herbert Hoover, that he was 'elected by soggy contentment & virulent prejudice.'[111]

The onset of the Depression did away soon enough with any contentment in the U.S., and Wrong's perceptions became gloomier. 'This country is more profoundly unsettled than ever. . . .' he wrote in January 1933, adding that he expected President-elect Roosevelt to be an improvement on Hoover. His initial impression of the new President was also favourable: he 'has done a very good job,' he wrote on April 2, 1933, 'and will remain top-dog for the present . . . with an admirable expression of calm serenity & self-confidence.'[112] But within months Wrong was anticipating 'some sort of social revolution',[113] and blaming the mess on the President. His main source of information, and his closest friend in the Capital, was Dean Acheson, the son of his father's classmate at Wycliffe College. Acheson had served briefly, before resigning, as Roosevelt's Under-Secretary of the Treasury, and the two unhappy friends went on long walks together, watching birds and bemoaning the conditions of the world and their respective countries.[114] On November 1, 1933, Wrong wrote:

> The President's fundamental weakness & incompetence are being more clearly revealed every day. I am afraid that he is not a big enough man to admit mistakes, that he will blame his failures on malignance of others, and that he has a belief in his own omniscience. . . .
>
> A friend of mine said to me a few days ago [he wrote on November 23, clearly referring to Acheson]: 'I have worked with the President for six months, sometimes very closely, and I can only describe my feeling for him as contempt . . . no guts and extreme obstinacy. . . .'[115]

Obviously, then, Wrong had little innate regard for most Americans or for their President. The country was barbarous and uncouth, the politics unpleasant in the extreme, and the leaders tossed up by the system were spineless or worse. And yet, when Wrong attended a meeting of the Royal Institute of International Affairs, he was 'appalled', as a typical Canadian, by the Englishmen's 'savage pleasure in applauding anything at all critical in tone' of the United States.[116] The United States and Americans were facts of life for Canadians, forces of nature that had to be dealt with in some way or other. As the representatives of a Canada desperate for trade and investment in the 1930s and for some years later, Wrong sought American largesse without fear of economic continentalism.[117] But if this aspect of the Canada-U.S. relationship did not frighten him, he always worried over what he once described as the 'Materialism & the aggressive & dangerous chauvinism which now infects the country under the guise of patriotism. . . .'[118] In some respects he was not very different from a long line of Canadian nationalists who feared the United States. But by the 1930s the British connection had lost much of its emotive power for Wrong. And if he was always aware of being an Anglo-Canadian, what he sought was an independent Canadian policy, within a British Commonwealth for the time being, or a policy that at least recognized that Canada had interests of its own, responsibilities it owed, and could seize opportunities to express its nationhood in the world.

Unfortunately for Hume Wrong the Canadian governments of the 1930s looked inward to the nation's domestic problems, deliberately turning a blind eye to the world. If he could be scathing in his description of American government, he was doubly so in his comments on that of Canada, and on his own Department of External Affairs. He considered Mackenzie King to be a dangerous incompetent, and he made no secret of his feelings, even in conversations with the Prime Minister.[119]* His Department, he be-

---

* Mackenzie King talked with Wrong on August 6, 1936, about the possibility of his being posted to Tokyo as Minister to Japan. King recorded in his diary that Wrong said: 'he will not go to Japan. . . . Would consider Geneva later on. . . . Had not wanted to succeed Herridge [Bennett's Minister to the U.S.], & thought it unwise to succeed to a position where one had been a subordinate & finally he thought no one could succeed in Canadian Service who was not a French Canadian. He would like Beaudry's post—second-in-command to Skelton. It was really unlimited presumption on his part to talk that way, was critical even of Skelton, etc. I was patient with him, and felt like telling him to go to blazes. I, however, advised him to take a holiday. . . .' (PAC, King Diary.)

lieved with some justice, was woefully inefficient and rife with incompetents, not least Dr Skelton. 'The Dep't of External Affairs,' he said in 1934, 'is lousy, & will remain so while Skelton is at its head, in spite of his great intellectual capacity. I have two near morons to assist me [at the Legation], of whom I can't get rid [because of Civil Service Commission regulations] and whose work I do for the most part.'[120] The French Canadians in the Department, he believed, intrigued with politicians for promotion and place and were incapable of doing the work.[121] Most of the officer staff—he excluded only his Toronto friend Lester Pearson, Norman Robertson, Charles Ritchie, and one or two others—were of no account. The ministerial positions in the service were worse yet, filled by political appointees of the Massey stamp. At one point, for example, Wrong characterized the Minister in Paris, Philippe Roy, the Minister in Washington, Sir Herbert Marler, under whom he was obliged to serve, and the Minister in Tokyo, Randolph Bruce, as the 'deaf, the dumb, and the blind'—a cruel comment on Roy's hearing problem and Bruce's blindness.[122] Unhappy, frustrated, bored, Wrong again and again contemplated leaving 'the service of my singularly stupid government'.[123] But except for some unattractive university offers,[124] no other position offered itself that was interesting or challenging enough. So he hung on and remained in Washington until 1937.

In that year, after a decade in Washington doing the pick-and-shovel work of diplomacy—Wrong called his routine chores 'dishwashing'[125]—he was posted to Geneva as Canadian representative to the League of Nations. A year or two earlier that post had been important when Dr W.A. Riddell, Wrong's predecessor, had put his government into difficulties because of his too-enthusiastic support for sanctions against Italy. But by 1937 the League was almost moribund, and Wrong's frustrations mounted while war drew nearer.[126] He was appalled by the inaction of the Canadian government, and the posturing of its politicians, as the Mackenzie King Liberals manoeuvered to keep Canadians as unconcerned with international events as possible—and hence as united as they could possibly remain.

To Wrong it was horrifying to be sent to meetings and conferences with instructions to 'Say nothing & do nothing. . . .'[127] And even before he left Washington he had become concerned by the implications of Mackenzie King's continuous blathering about status and equally continuous and conscious avoidance of policy.

He wrote to Skelton in December 1935 that Canada was certain to be involved in any major British war no matter what disclaimers issued from Ottawa. 'The loyalties of too large a number of our people are deeply engaged,' he said correctly. But he was not unaware of London's tendency to act first and then advise the Dominion after the fact. Canada was going to be pushed 'out on a limb, and we either have to sit there uncomfortably or drop off ignominiously and precipitate a domestic row. . . .' The choices were difficult so long as Canada shirked its duty of formulating its own policy—'accepting a new sort of colonial status or of asserting our independence of judgment after the occurrence of an event which has profoundly compromised that independence in fact.'[128] That was no choice at all.

Wrong had put his finger precisely on the flaw in the line Mackenzie King had been following since the Chanak crisis in 1922. King had created a spurious freedom of action for Canada, but he had done so only by abdicating his government's right to participate meaningfully in the formulation of policy. Even after the Munich 'nightmare' of 1938,[129] there was little chance of that policy's being altered because of the domestic benefits it conferred on the government. Nonetheless Wrong tried to persuade Skelton yet again, writing the Under-Secretary that the 'startling feature of the [Munich] crisis was the evidence that, if war had come, Canada would have been immediately involved as a belligerent, although the Canadian Government had played no part in the negotiations. . . . Canadian self-government,' he said, 'obviously is incomplete so long as the most vital decision which can arise in the life of a nation is not taken in fact as well as in form by the leaders of the Canadian people.' Wrong's suggestion was that a 'revision of the ends and the means of Canadian foreign policy . . . be begun at once, with the object of insuring that eventually all vital decisions, whether these are to stand shoulder to shoulder with the United Kingdon or to pursue a separate road, should be taken in Ottawa.'[130] While there was no doubt that Wrong supported the idea that Canada should join in a British war against Hitler if it came, there was equally no doubt that he was almost ashamed at the way Canada was being made to back into war.

Skelton bleakly conceded the correctness of Wrong's analysis. 'There would have been a good deal of dissension and bitter feeling' if Canada had had to go to war at the time of Munich, that good man wrote, 'but I have myself not much doubt of what the immediate outcome would have been.' Wrong had urged the desirability of greater consultation with London, but Skelton scouted that idea. 'Aside from the technical difficulties of consultation in times of crises,' he said, 'my conclusions after a good many years of observation have been that the United Kingdom would accept our advice only when they wanted it and would then state that they were adopting this policy' only because the Dominions wanted it. What he meant by this statement was that blame might be fixed on Canada as a consequence of consultation.[131] Thus Canada in the 1930s remained paralysed. Certain to be involved in any major British war, whatever its cause, it was unable or unwilling to proffer advice, both for fear that Whitehall would pin any unfortunate consequences on Ottawa, and because of the disruptice effects any advice might have on public opinion in a divided Canada.

The war came in September 1939 when Hitler invaded Poland and Britain honoured its commitments that had been made without any consultation whatever with Ottawa.[132] As Skelton and Wrong had expected, Canada became a belligerent in almost as colonial a fashion as in 1914. For Hume Wrong, and for those in the Department of External Affairs who thought as he did, this was shameful, another in the 'series of defeats', as his colleague Escott Reid later characterized them, that Wrong had witnessed in his career thus far.[133] The war was necessary, the cause just, but Canada had backed into it ignominiously, and it was Wrong's profound belief that this situation could not be permitted to recur. Canada's relations with Britain, with the world, had to be put on a new basis.

The war did not immediately alter Wrong's personal fortunes or those of his country. The Canadian mission to the League stayed in business all through September 1939 while Wrong fumed. 'Almost my most serious inconvenience to date,' he told Pearson in London on September 11, 'was to find today that my barber had been mobilized. That brings it home to one!'[134] But when the government finally ordered him to close up shop in Geneva, it sent him to London as a Special Economic Advisor. Ordinarily that might have been an ideal job, but Vincent Massey was the High Commissioner, and the old feelings remained as strong as ever in both men.[135] Also Pearson, technically subordinate to Wrong in rank, was in fact ahead of him in the Canada House pecking order.[136] Worse still, Wrong's assigned work, while important, was limited initially by the British reluctance to place orders in Canada. Then, after the collapse of France, and the defeat of most of the nations whose trade with Canada had been his special charge, his duties evaporated.[137]

Skelton knew Wrong's ability and tried to get him to Ottawa, suggesting a number of posts, but the Prime Minister refused to have him close at hand: he rejected the idea that Wrong should work on the newly-established Permanent Joint Board on Defence (PJBD),[138] and offered no encouragement to Skelton's idea that he should run internment operations in Canada.[139] Other suggestions followed—ministerial posts in Japan, Argentina, or Brazil, all of which Wrong refused because they seemed inconsequential to him in wartime and because he was concerned about the effects on his family of another foreign posting, his children having spent most of their lives away from their native country.[140] He complained that at one point, when his children were enrolled in boarding schools in Canada, he and his wife were in London and their furniture was in Geneva.[141]

Wrong was not brought back to Ottawa from limbo in London until the beginning of 1941, and when he arrived he found that his proposed responsibilities had been assigned elsewhere. 'I expressed my disappointment to Skelton,' he said of an interview on January 25, 'who was friendly & sympathetic and promised remedial action within a month. Two hours later he was dead.'[142] This forced far-reaching changes on External Affairs.

First, as we have seen, Mackenzie King selected Norman Robertson to be the new Under-Secretary. Robertson was extremely able, but he was technically the most junior of the potential candidates for the succession, a fact that soon aroused Wrong's ire at being passed over.[143] Skelton's death, however, also precipitated a long overdue reorganization of the Department, and this helped ease the problems of inefficiency that had driven Wrong and others to distraction.[144] Things altered again a few months later when Loring Christie, the Minister to the United States since the outbreak of war, became ill and had to be replaced. General Harry Crerar wrote to Pearson: 'I am sure that Hume . . . would be glad to take over Loring's job, but I don't think poor Hume stands very high with the P.M. these days.'[145] That was true enough, but when King chose Leighton McCarthy, an elderly Toronto lawyer who was friendly with President Roosevelt, to replace Christie,

McCarthy insisted on taking Wrong with him.[146] After some resistance to returning to Washington in the same rank he had held
when he left for Geneva in 1937, Wrong agreed to go, but once in
Washington he did not take long to realize that McCarthy was incapable of doing the work. 'Leighton is very little use as Minister',
he complained. 'He's a nice chap, but too ignorant & too old to
learn. A foolish appointment. The British retire their diplomats at
60; we appoint ours at 71!' Later he added that 'A six hour day in a
four day working week is about all he can manage . . . the whole
thing is rather grotesque.'[147]

But if he had serious doubts about his Minister's capacity, the
querulous note, the griping and bitching that had characterized his
correspondence for years, soon disappeared, never to return. The
reason was simple. Wrong at last was in an important post doing
vital work as the *de facto* head of the Canadian legation to the
United States at a time when the relations between the two nations
were particularly important. The Ogdensburg Agreement and the
Hyde Park Declaration had begun the process of linking the two
nations militarily and economically. And so long as the United
States was neutral, concerned above all with keeping the Western
hemisphere free from Nazi contagion, Canada remained of great
importance to the U.S. as its closest economic and strategic ally.

Canadian-American relations were close and friendly, and
Wrong, after his earlier years in Washington, had contacts at every
level. Even so, Ottawa was not always able to secure its aims. In
the summer of 1941, for example, Canada began to press for the
right to create a military mission in Washington, an idea that could
have been seen as a logical extension of the closer military co-
operation symbolized by the PJBD. But the American generals—
prompted by the British, who were already engaged in secret
planning with the U.S. Chiefs of Staff—were reluctant to approve
such a mission, and Wrong spent months in a fruitless effort to
carry out the desires of the Canadian military.[148] Soon after Pearl
Harbor and the U.S. declaration of war, Wrong found himself in
the middle of the mighty furore over the Free French seizure of St
Pierre and Miquelon on Christmas Day 1941.[149] The affair blew
over, but as Washington began to gear up to lead the Anglo-
American coalition against the Axis Powers, Canada's position in
Washington would inevitably be diminished.

Matters were no easier for Wrong in his relations with the British in Washington. Before the United States entered the war Can-

ada had a special entrée to the President and the British had been co-operative with Wrong and his officials. But the new world war changed all this, as Wrong discovered in a conversation with Lord Halifax, the British Ambassador, on December 12, 1941. 'I got into an argument with him on the possible need for a consultative political body in Washington to thrash out . . . difficulties and differences between the staff', Wrong wrote in a diary memorandum. 'I fear that Halifax thinks of the war now as a U.S.-U.K. affair, with Russia as a distant partner. . . . He leaves Canada out as a principal. We deserve this, but it irritates me.'[150] Others in Ottawa were also becoming irritated. On December 29 Mackenzie King complained to Winston Churchill, who was present at a Cabinet War Committee meeting, that Canada was being left out of the direction of the war, that 'while we had been in during two and a quarter years, things would be so arranged [as a result of American entry into the war] that the U.S. and Britain would settle everything between themselves. . . .' Churchill replied that Canada should certainly be consulted on matters involving its interests, but he added that where 'joint U.K.-Canadian matters were concerned, it was his responsibility to see that the Canadian government were fully informed.'[151] Churchill's paternal, not to say imperial, attitude applied to other areas as well.

This became apparent on January 26, 1942, when Churchill and Roosevelt announced the creation of a number of Combined Boards designed to co-ordinate the war efforts of their two countries—and their allies. There were to be Boards to control shipping, raw materials, and the assignment of munitions; Boards were later set up to deal with food and production matters; in addition, a Combined Chiefs of Staff Committee was formed to direct war strategy. All this had obvious importance to Canada, but there had been no consultation with Ottawa and no thought of how to integrate Canada's war production with that of the coalition.

Wrong struggled to get any information he could. He had learned something of Anglo-American planning before the January 26 announcements,[152] and was already looking at the implications for Canada:

> The principal question causing me concern [he wrote to Norman Robertson on January 20] is the nature of the Canadian representation which should be sought and the status with respect to their British and U.S. colleagues which

should be claimed for Canadian representatives on any of the combined organizations. There are now 26 governments at war with the Axis Powers, and there are also the Free French to take into account. . . . Any allied war organization which gave full representation to all the belligerents would be like the Assembly of the League of Nations and would inevitably be so ineffective that it could not exercise real control. . . .

How far, then, is Canada entitled to go in pressing a claim to participate in inter-Allied bodies which are designed to co-ordinate the war effort? It is easy to state the general principle, but remarkably difficult to apply it. The principle, I think, is that each member of the grand alliance should have a voice in the conduct of the war proportionate to its contribution to the general war effort. A subsidiary principle is that the influence of the various countries should be greatest in connection with those matters with which they are most directly concerned. Among suppliers of war materials . . . Canada ranks third. In her direct military contribution of trained fighting men . . . perhaps fifth or sixth. . . .[153]

Wrong then went on to list some of the possible courses Canada might follow in seeking representation on the Boards that were about to be formed. He knew there was little chance to get a seat on all of them, but he seemed to believe that it might be possible to work through the British, a tactic that was unlikely to win acceptance from Mackenzie King, who was always wary of British intentions. The best among his suggestions was to 'seek representation only on those combined bodies . . . with whose activities Canada is most vitally concerned.'[154]

In this letter Wrong had begun to conceive the Canadian idea of the functional principle. Although a few Canadians, notably Loring Christie, had flirted with this conception some years earlier, Wrong almost certainly knew nothing of this. Nor was the concept being bruited around Washington. Most likely the idea had come to him as one that fitted the needs of the moment.[155]

The politicians in the Cabinet War Committee were slow to react to the problems posed for Canada by the new Anglo-American coalition,[156] but in the Department of External Affairs there was a growing concern that Canada's place in the grand alliance was negligible, that Canadian interests were being overlooked by the British and the Americans. Wrong wrote a long and very frank personal letter on the situation to Pearson, who had been in Ottawa since the spring of 1941 as Assistant Under-Secretary. He knew of Ottawa's resentment, Wrong said, and recognized that it was 'possible to make a strong case' for it. 'Resentment, however, is not a useful emotion in winning a war.' The first duty of Roosevelt and Churchill was to co-ordinate their war efforts, and the structures they had put in place had so far not been used in a way inimical to Canadian interests (indeed, had scarcely been used at all). Secondly, Wrong argued,

> the business of running a grand alliance in wartime is too difficult to combine efficiency with constant respect for the status of each of the members of the alliance. . . .
>
> Thirdly, what has happened so far with regard to Canadian participation in these bodies does not seem to me to be at variance with the position hitherto taken by the Canadian Government. You and I know of a hundred instances since the war began in which Canada has refused to take responsibility for decisions of policy with which we were not immediately concerned. One difference now is that these decisions tend to be joint decisions of the United Kingdom and the United States in place of decisions by the United Kingdom alone. If Canada had been satisfied before . . . should this change cause dissatisfaction now?

Wrong continued by saying that he advanced his irrefutable points only to argue against the growth of a spirit of resentment in Ottawa. Certainly, he affirmed, 'I am not for a moment satisfied with the part which we have played in the conduct of the war. . . .' In his view, and he was writing very freely now, 'the Government has hitherto adopted in these matters what may unkindly be called a semi-colonial position. With the entry of the United States into the war we are not as well placed to influence the conduct of the war as we were when the United States was neutral. . . . Now we become only a junior member of the partnership. If we had sought earlier to undertake more extensive political responsibilities, it would be easier now to maintain our status. We have tended to be satisfied with the form rather than the substance.' Did the ill-feeling in Ottawa over the Combined Boards mean that the situation there had changed? he asked; 'are we actually seeking to exert greater influence on the conduct of the alliance?'[157]

The answer to Wrong's question was yes. From the beginning

of 1942 Canada began to press its claims for a share in the decision-making with great vigour and skill. Wrong's arguments, tentatively advanced in January, quickly persuaded Robertson and Pearson, and all three argued their case in memoranda and papers without cease. By the summer of 1942 the politicians had largely been persuaded too, a development that was helped by circumstances. For the first seven months of 1942 the Cabinet was absorbed almost wholly by the long debate over conscription, and King in particular had his hands full in trying to keep caucus, Cabinet, and country together. By the time the Prime Minister had the breathing-space to pay attention to other matters, the Canadian policy was effectively in place. Then some of the stronger ministers—C.D. Howe and J.L. Ralston, for example—had axes of their own to grind about the Combined Boards structure, and this also hurried matters along. Furthermore, and perhaps most important of all, the Department of External Affairs itself had changed over the past year. Until January 1941 Skelton had largely directed matters himself, in consultation only with Mackenzie King, and both men, with their deep distrust of Whitehall and their almost obsessive fear of plots against Canadian autonomy, had tended to prefer disengagement where delicate matters of policy were concerned. But once Robertson took charge, and acted almost as a minister of a department (King, the Secretary of State for External Affairs, was wholly occupied elsewhere), External Affairs assumed an active role. Robertson was assisted by the two ablest members of the service, Wrong and Pearson (who switched posts in May 1942). All three were relatively young, untroubled by the shibboleth phrases of the past, and confident of their country's worth and potential.

It was inevitable that the direction should change when the generations did; that it changed so much was a tribute to the ability of the great triumvirate that led the Department. Wrong was probably the best intellect, cool and quick, a polished technician and a supremely organized man, but Robertson also had a deep and splendid mind, even if he was no administrator. After a learning period (the St Pierre affair was important in this respect), he became superb at working with Mackenzie King, who learned to trust him implicity and to allow himself to be led by Robertson to positions he might never have contemplated formerly. Pearson was ambitious and charming, adept with the press. His abilities suffered only in comparison with those of Wrong and Robertson.

The three friends reinforced each others' strengths and compensated for their weaknesses; together they changed their country's course.

Back in Ottawa as Assistant Under-Secretary, Wrong and Robertson began to put the functionalist case into practice. As realists they saw no point in seeking a place on the Combined Chiefs of Staff. The Canadian generals were probably not high-powered enough to merit a seat on the supreme strategy board, even if Canada's military contribution might have justified such representation. But the Combined Boards that Roosevelt and Churchill had created were a different matter, as was the United Nations Relief and Rehabilitation Administration, which had been created to administer postwar relief and to which Canada was expected to be a heavy contributor. The Combined Production and Resources Board [CPRB], the Combined Food Board [CFB], and UNRRA were to be the testing grounds for the functional principle.

Wrong directed the battle, working closely with Robertson in the East Block and in close and constant communication with Pearson at the Washington Legation. His tactics were constrained by his determination to be reasonable. 'We appreciate the difficulties inherent in the operation of multi-national boards,' he wrote at one point, 'and we have throughout considered the Canadian relationship to the Combined Boards with these difficulties in mind.'[158] But 'you can't expect total effort and heavy sacrifice unless you allow people to feel that they are party to the decisions from which these consequences flow.'[159] The line between obstruction and responsibility may have been a fine one, but Wrong pressed vigorously for Canada's place in the sun.

The British balked at Canada's request for a seat on the CPRB or CFB, arguing that if Canada got a seat other countries would ask for one too. The Canadians argued with uncharacteristic toughness, coolly advising London that if other countries produced as much military equipment and food as Canada did, their claims should be considered too. Furthermore, Canada was giving the United Kingdom billions of dollars in military and food supplies without charge. Such largesse was unlikely to be continued if Canada's concerns over representation on the directing bodies of the Combined Boards went unrecognized.[160] This was an unusual negotiating stance for Canada, and its toughness, orchestrated by Wrong, struck responsive chords in Clifford Clark in Finance. The country and its diplomats had changed. The war had produced a new nationalism in Ottawa, and the functional principle was its outward manifestation. Canadian seats on the CPRB and the CFB were the rewards for Wrong's efforts.

There was less immediate success with UNRRA. The relief agency brought together all the great powers, not the Anglo-Americans alone, and the problems of securing Russian and Chinese recognition for Canadian claims were more complicated, more difficult. The British initially advanced their standard arguments that if Canada won a place, other countries would feel left out; but again the Canadian threats about cuts in financial aid swung London around. But none of the other powers were interested in expanding UNRRA's directing council, and Wrong and Robertson feared that the four-power pattern of control was to be replicated over the entire area of postwar organization. This could not be tolerated, and the Canadian government delivered a note to the British and Americans in February 1943 that was as toughly worded as any the Canadians had ever written: 'so far as Canada was concerned we believed that it would be very difficult after the war for us to play our expected part unless we could satisfy Parliament and the public that we had a fair share in the direction of [UNRRA].'[161] When the British then suggested that Canada might take their seat on the UNRRA directorate and act as a Commonwealth representative, that proposal was flatly rejected. 'This [offer] amounts to a revival of the old concept of the diplomatic unity of the Commonwealth,' Wrong wrote, 'and is an unexpected consequence of our attempts to secure a proper place for Canada in the Relief Administration. . . .' The diplomatic unity of the Empire was gone now, and Canada, Australia, New Zealand, and South Africa were effectively independent. 'If in one context we were to agree to speak for the whole Commonwealth,' Wrong argued, 'undoubtedly in other contexts the assumption would be made that the U.K. would speak for us when we were not present.'[162] Britain had to speak for itself, the message went, and so too did Canada.

This same approach was also evident at the great conference on civil air transportation that was held in Chicago in late 1944. The United States and Britain were jockeying for postwar advantages and profitable routes, grandly proposing competing charters to control aviation and specifying 'freedoms' of the air. The Canadian government, convinced that Canada was at the crossroads of the postwar air routes, crept up the middle, produced its own charter, and saw most of it accepted as a compromise between the British and American positions. The key figures in this instance were Escott Reid and Robertson, but it was clear that the functional principle had been their guide.[163] That principle had been stated in Parliament on July 9, 1943 by Mackenzie King. His words were almost certainly drafted by Hume Wrong:

> . . . authority in international affairs must not be concentrated exclusively in the largest powers. . . . A number of new international organizations are likely to be set up as a result of the war. In the view of the government, effective representations on these bodies should neither be restricted to the largest states nor necessarily extended to all states. Representation should be determined on a functional basis which will admit to full membership those countries, large or small, which have the greatest contribution to make to the particular object in question. . . .[164]

The functional principle made clear that Canada was a middle power, one with special capacities in certain areas. In such areas— air transportation was only one example—Canada demanded the right to full representation on the directing agencies.

Other countries had always bargained and negotiated in this manner, threatening action against friendly states that operated in ways they disliked, striking compromises, and protecting their independence and freedom of action. In the past Canada had functioned in this way only when negotiating trade treaties; but now, startlingly, Canada was acting like other states, making threats and possibly even meaning them, in order to secure a share in decisions and to assume the responsibility for carrying them out. In accepting the necessity for any nation-state to speak for itself and to employ all the power it had at its disposal, Canada had begun to grow up.

That was all Hume Wrong had ever desired; he had said as much in his letter to his father in 1919. In March 1943 he set down in a concise, clear, and markedly non-utopian form the current state of his thinking on functionalism and its role in the planning for post-war organizations then underway:

> We are, of course, deeply concerned with both the form and the substance of international post-war planning. As to the substance, a good deal of preliminary study has been given here to some of the economic questions, notably in the

monetary field. . . . As to the form, we have hitherto advanced, in our approaches over the Relief Administration and to some extent in connection with the Combined Boards the principle that representation on international bodies should be determined on a functional basis so as to permit the participation of those countries which have the greatest stake in the particular subject under examination. We have used this principle both to combat the argument that the four largest powers should have a special responsibility in all the fields of planning and organization and to avoid the other extreme which would allow each member of the United Nations to be represented on a basis of nominal equality. I think we should stick to the functional principle. If we can secure its general acceptance, it would permit the representation of Canada on most of the bodies in which we are deeply interested.[165]

The general acceptance Wrong hoped for was difficult to secure from the great powers. But tough bargaining did make Canada the sole country outside the Anglo-American duality to get direct representation on the Combined Food Board and the Combined Production and Resources Board. Negotiation also secured for Canada a seat on the Supplies Committee of UNRRA in 1943 and two years later a place on the directing committee. In 1945 the Canadians also managed to secure the inclusion of a few functionalist phrases in the Charter of the United Nations Organization. These were all small victories—the Combined Boards did not amount to much in the end, UNRRA remained fully under the great powers' control, and the clauses Canada won in the UN Charter proved unworkable in practice. Canada regrettably never received the type of representation on postwar agencies that its wartime efforts had earned for it. But such things are ultimately irrelevant. What is important about these wartime assertions of Canadian status is that with them Canada, for the first time, fought for its right to share in the power exercised by its allies and also sought to share in the responsibilities that went with power. The seats on the Combined Boards, the share in directing UNRRA, the success at the Chicago Conference—these were demonstrable proof that Canada had won the grudging acquiescence of Britain and the United States for its aspirations. Furthermore, the functional principle became the touchstone of status and responsibility not only for Canada but for middle powers such as

Belgium and The Netherlands, giving voice to their insistent demands to be consulted on all issues that affected them.

Hume Wrong had been the architect of the Canadian position. His prewar experience in Washington and Geneva had convinced him that Canada had to have a policy of its own if the nation was ever to emerge from colonialism. The war gave him his chance to make his case, and the fortuitous circumstances of the day allowed him and Robertson the opportunity to carry out their plans. There could be little doubt that Canada's massive war effort, coupled with its tough advocacy of the functional principle, made it one of the leaders of the middle powers for a few years during and after the war. And if, as Michael Howard later noted, 'Prestige remains the coin of the realm of international politics . . .'[166] then Canada's coinage was of purest gold. Hume Wrong and Norman Robertson deserve much of the credit for that. Their efforts had given Canada a foreign policy at last.

6

NEW MEN, NEW IDEAS

If Canadian foreign policy had been changed by the Second World War, so too had the Canadian public service. The war brought new men and women to Ottawa to staff the great bureaucracies created by the Departments of National Defence and Munitions and Supply, the Wartime Prices and Trade Board and other new agencies, and to make possible the expansion of established government departments such as Finance and External Affairs. The marked change in Canada's power and influence, and in the Canadian economy, gave many senior civil servants not only important challenges to deal with at home but the opportunity to spread their wings and perform on a larger stage. Abroad and at home the bureaucrats won a high reputation for the skilful way they had managed the war economy and reconstruction, raised and spent billions of dollars, and controlled inflation through wage and price controls. On the larger world stage, mutual aid, the creation of new political and economic structures for the world, and the questions of international monetary policy were some of the problems that absorbed the attention of the top civil servants in the 1940s. Two of them—Louis Rasminsky, one of the architects of the new monetary system that was established at the Bretton Woods Conference, and W.A. Mackintosh, a key economist and adviser—rose to great prominence as a result of handling brilliantly their responsibilities during the war and in planning for its aftermath.

I

Born in Montreal in 1908, Louis Rasminsky grew up in Toronto. His father, who had a wholesale electrical-products distributing business, was not poor, but there was never enough money, and when his son won all the prizes at Harbord Collegiate, including a tuition scholarship to the University of Toronto, there was as much relief as pride.

Rasminsky blossomed at university. He took courses in economics and battled for standing with his good friend, A.F.W. Plumptre, who would later be a colleague. The class of 1928 in economics was exceptional, one of its professors, V.W. Bladen, recalled; the best students met regularly and informally in the Plumptre house to argue with and learn from each other.[1] The competition was fierce but friendly. In 1926 Plumptre placed first in the group (or 1.1) while Rasminsky was second (or 1.2); the next year Rasminsky was 1.1 and Plumptre 1.2; and in 1928, when they graduated, both tied at 1.1. The Massey Scholarship in Economics, however, went to Plumptre, who proceeded to Cambridge University to study under John Maynard Keynes. For Rasminsky there was nothing.

At this point, one account has it, Professor Gilbert Jackson of Toronto's Department of Political Economy called on a Toronto rabbi to say that if Rasminsky had been an Anglican, he would have made this call on the Anglican Bishop of Toronto. But, 'as he is a Jew, I come to you. It would be a disgrace if your community didn't give this boy the opportunity for graduate study.' Within days, so this story goes, enough money to provide a fellowship for a student of the Department's choice had been donated to the university. According to the same source, the money was provided by the man who subsequently became Rasminsky's father-in-law.[2]

Whatever the circumstances and whatever the source of his fellowship, a grateful Rasminsky left Toronto to attend the London School of Economics, intending to take a doctorate. He had chosen LSE because of its interesting reputation and because it was in London; but also because, with Allyn Young there as a Visiting Professor, it seemed strong in Money and Banking, the area that interested Rasminsky after his Toronto work under Bladen, Harold Innis, and Jackson. But when Young died soon after his arrival, Rasminsky was left high and dry until he attached himself to Harold Laski, with whom he soon became friendly. In a letter he sent to Innis in Toronto shortly after his arrival in London, Rasminsky talked about 'The School', pronouncing his amazement at the wide choice of interpretations it offered: 'one can worship at the shrine of Marx, Mill or Edmund Burke as one chooses. But this form of expression is rather unfair: one worships nothing

at the London School of Economics, or perhaps better one constantly changes the object of one's worship.' He was not attending
many lectures, he added, that being incompatible with serious
work.[3] His interest was in post-war commercial policy, and his
choice of thesis topic was 'The Quest for Non-Discrimination in
Trade Relations'—in effect an examination of the most-favoured-
nation concept.

But that thesis was not to be completed. Early in 1930 the LSE's
director of graduate studies mentioned to Rasminsky that there
was a job going at the League of Nations in Geneva. Friends at
Toronto had also suggested that he apply,[4] and he did so, partly
because he wanted to spend more time—two years more—in
Europe before returning home; partly because the League had an
idealistic attraction for him. 'It is easy to be cynical,' Rasminsky
wrote to Norman MacKenzie, a law professor at the University of
Toronto,

> but it has struck me that those who are loudest in their cyni-
> cism generally, have an eye single to the political work of the
> League and completely neglect the work of its technical orga-
> nizations. I feel that it is precisely the technical work of the
> League that, removed as it is from political controversy and
> dispute, is best able to be conducted along scientific lines and
> to achieve results immediately useful.[5]

That attitude presumably impressed the League selection committee, or perhaps it was what Rasminsky later called his 'sheer ef-
frontery' in applying, for he won the post.[6] He was only twenty-
two.

His first desire, however, was to get married. According to
Rasminsky's own (probably apocryphal) account, he wired Lyla
Rotenberg in Toronto: 'Have accepted job League of Nations at
13,700 Swiss francs. Will you marry me?' She allegedly replied:
'What is exchange rate on Swiss francs?' However, her reply was
also affirmative. The marriage soon followed, on July 15, 1930,
produced two children, and a warm, close relationship. Lyla Rasminsky is remembered today, among other things, for her interest
in music and for the good care she took of her overworked husband, refusing invitations when she thought his load too great.[7]
This was presumably a rare wifely attitude in the Ottawa mandarinate and its circle, since it has stayed in people's minds.

But it was ten years before Rasminsky joined the Canadian public service. His Geneva position was a junior one. He was on the professional staff of the League's Economic and Financial Section and his initial task was to work on League publications in the Economic Intelligence Service. Each year a volume on banking was published, as well as a world economic survey. One study discussed whether scarcity of gold was exerting a worldwide influence, and there was a study of silver prepared for the World Economic Conference of 1933 in London. This work, along with regular visits to Geneva paid by the stars of the economics profession and opportunities to meet visiting statesmen and diplomats, provided much excitement for the young man. In 1936-7 Rasminsky took charge of a major study for the 'Mixed Committees on the Relation of Nutrition to Health, Agriculture and Economic Policy', whose findings anticipated the later creation of the United Nations Food and Agricultural Organization.

As Hitler's shadow spread over Europe, Rasminsky continued his work for the League in ever more responsible roles. In 1938 he examined European exchange controls and worked as secretary-economist to the Financial Committee, particularly on its 'Delegation on Economic Depressions', a major examination of the measures that might be employed to prevent or mitigate economic depressions.[8] But the next year, convinced that war was coming, Rasminsky sent his family home to Toronto, and in August 1939 he too went home on leave, intending to return.

With the outbreak of war, however, he was ordered to remain in North America. From a base in Canada, Rasminsky was dispatched by the now-moribund League to report on the economic and financial situation in Bolivia (whose tin was vital) and Argentina, and to run Fiscal Committee meetings in Mexico and Nutrition meetings in Buenos Aires. Most important, perhaps, he helped in the negotiations that saw the League's Economic Intelligence Service transferred intact to the Institute for Advanced Study at Princeton.[9] Rasminsky joined the Bank of Canada in 1940, but not until 1943 did he formally sever his connection with the League;[10] indeed, at the League's last meetings in 1945 he represented Canada on the Economic and Financial Committees.[11]

Early in his Geneva years Rasminsky had attracted the attention of Clifford Clark and O.D. Skelton, the two senior mandarins, the creators of the Canadian civil service, who were always on the lookout for bright young men. After watching Rasminsky perform at the 1933 World Economic Conference, Clark offered him a job shortly after but was turned down. Skelton, too, thought highly of him. There were difficulties, however, as Dr Skelton wrote to his friend, W.L. Grant in 1934:

> . . . the difficulties which our unavowed but quite effective Canadian anti-semitism places in the way of such men. When last in Geneva I was much impressed by a young Canadian of Jewish extraction named Rasminiski [sic], a Toronto University graduate, now in the Economic Section of the League Secretariat. He struck me as having about the most vigorous and clear-cut intellectual equipment I had met in a young man for years. Clark, Deputy of Minister of Finance, was also impressed . . . and made efforts to secure him for a minor post. . . . As it happened Rasminiski was not prepared to take the post. . . . Even if he had been willing there would probably have been difficulties because of the prejudice in question. . . .[12]

Under the pressures of war, however, those prejudices had eased, and when Rasminsky and Clifford Clark, who had kept in contact through the 1930s, met at the meetings of the American Economic Association in Philadelphia in December 1939, Clark again invited him to Ottawa. Rasminsky had commitments to the League, but Clark unrolled the red carpet, even staging a dinner for the prospective recruit, a gathering attended by all the senior financial officials in the capital—including Graham Towers, Governor of the Bank of Canada—many of whom he already knew. Rasminsky may not have realized just how unusual this elaborate form of wooing was, but he was pleased and flattered and decided to join the Bank of Canada and its 'wholly-owned subsidiary', the Foreign Exchange Control Board, on April 1, 1940, as head of the Board's research and statistical section.[13]

The Bank and the Finance Department had a number of sophisticated, even brilliant economists in its employ, a group that included Alex Skelton, John Deutsch, W.A. Mackintosh, R.B. Bryce, and others, to say nothing of Clark and Towers themselves. But among them, Rasminsky had more experience of international financial questions, more interest in and knowledge of exchange rates and controls, and probably more understanding of the flaws in the world monetary structure that had led to the Depression and war. In a very real sense the expert had found his niche, and Rasminsky was in a perfect position to influence, even shape, Canadian policy at a time when events placed Canada in something approximating a mediating role between Britain and the United States.

II

The telegram from London to Ottawa, dated May 22, 1942, was straightforward in its language. 'There is a great need for a new or improved system of organisation for the settlement of international balances on current account.' Such a system, the message from the Secretary of State for Dominion Affairs said, 'would not of itself rectify the disequilibria from which the world is likely to suffer at the end of the war, but it would provide a medium which, in conjunction with other agencies and actions, would give the best chance of a prosperous world.' Canada was advised that the Treasury had drawn up an outline plan 'for a new organisation which aims at substituting an expansionist for a contractionist pressure on world trade generally and which might be styled for short an International Clearing Union. Its object would be to provide in the international sphere an organisation which would perform for participating States the functions performed for individuals by the ordinary banking system i.e., the clearing of accounts debit and credit, between different customers and the provision of overdrafts for those who need them.' The aim of the plan—which had been prepared by John Maynard Keynes, the great economist who was acting as a wartime adviser to the Chancellor of the Exchequer—was to have the principal countries of the world adhere to the Union, 'which would have the function of settling international balances of payments by credits and debits in a new international monetary unit having a specified gold equivalent.'[14]

This proposal suggested a radical change in the way nations traded with each other. Prior to the war, if a company in country X wanted to trade with one in country Y, the two had to settle their accounts with each other's currency at a fixed rate of exchange. But if the company in X wanted to buy more than an agreed amount of the company in Y's exports, it had to make up the difference, ordinarily either in dollars or gold. This bilateral system was unwieldy and the war had worsened matters. It also, as The Economist noted long after, 'threatened to put a brake on international trade, since individual countries could easily find themselves unable to increase their deficits with some partners even though they had surpluses with others. . . .'[15]

That was a problem of which Canadians were fully aware. Canada was a trading nation, dependent on exports far more than most countries, and the Depression had laid waste the Dominion precisely because its trade had collapsed.[16] Various expedients had been sought as a way out of the dilemmas of the 1930s. The Ottawa Conference of 1932 had entrenched the system of preferential Empire tariffs. This hung like a millstone around the country's neck ever after, and the Mackenzie King government had worked to circumvent or supersede it from the moment it took office in 1935. Trade agreements with the United States and Britain had chipped away at the preferential system with some success. But Canadian officials were convinced that only a multilateral trading world could ever truly restore prosperity. For Canada, multilateralism in its simplest terms meant that the surplus Canada built up in its trade with Britain could be used to cover the habitual Canadian trade deficit with the United States—'in other words,' as Rasminsky said, 'we must be able to use our exports to the United Kingdom and Europe to pay for our imports from the United States.'[17] Keynes's plan, coming as it did from the country that was widely perceived to be the least enthusiastic about multilateralism, seemed a hopeful sign.[18]

The British suggestions, however, had not come to Ottawa as a bolt from the blue. Similar proposals had been raised in the United States on unofficial and semi-official levels and, indeed, a few Canadians had touched on the need for some kind of clearing union as a way of facilitating trade. Rasminsky, for one, had distributed a personal memorandum to senior members of the bureaucracy in July 1941 in which he argued that 'the prospects of post-war stability and reconstruction would be improved if the arrangements could be made between the United Kingdom and allied and friendly governments which enabled the United Kingdom to introduce a higher degree of multilateralism into the operation of its exchange control.'[19] And Robert Bryce, once one of Keynes's students and one of the first to bring his theories to the United States,[20] and now a rising power in the Department of Finance, had offered roughly similar comments in a paper printed in the *American Economic Review* at the beginning of 1942.[21] Thus, when Britain in August 1942 invited Canada to send a delegation to London in October to discuss the Clearing Union and other financial subjects, there was substantial enthusiasm in Ottawa.

Although the Canadian High Commission in London (with no

one on its staff 'who is particularly conversant with general economic and financial policy', Norman Robertson remarked acidly[22]) seemed to believe it could handle the talks, the senior civil servants in External Affairs, Finance, and the Bank disagreed. The Prime Minister accepted the need for a delegation from Ottawa,[23] and for some six weeks the Canadians prepared for the meetings. Involved in the preparations were Hume Wrong ('primarily for educational reasons,' he said); Clark; W.A. Mackintosh, the Queen's University economist who had come to Ottawa to work as Special Assistant to Clark, his old friend and former colleague; Graham Towers; and much the most junior member, Rasminsky.[24] Nevertheless Rasminsky was far from unversed in the subject, and he was perhaps the best-informed member of the group about the complex subjects under discussion. Others must have agreed with that judgement for Rasminsky, Wrong, and Mackintosh formed the Canadian delegation sent to London for the discussions that lasted from October 23 to November 9.

Those talks were 'the high spot intellectually in the discussions that preceded Bretton Woods,' Rasminsky later said;[25] he described them as a first-rate graduate-school seminar. Keynes was the professor, no doubt of that. But around him were his students, a group that included Sir Frederick Phillips, Sir Wilfred Eady, and Professor Dennis Robertson on the British side; representatives from Australia, New Zealand, South Africa, and India; and the Canadians, who were the only representatives to enter into the discussions fully. The Canadian case was largely put by Rasminsky, who 'did most of the talking for us,' Hume Wrong wrote, 'and did it very well.'[26] Keynes's proposal for the International Clearing Union was discussed in six meetings, and the Keynes-Rasminsky contributions were the highlight.

Keynes presided amicably—he 'has been rude only once,' Rasminsky wrote[27]—setting out his intentions for his Union. International trade was of great importance to all those countries represented, he said, and the maintenance of full employment depended on keeping trade at a high level. Because of 'the maldistribution of the world's monetary gold reserves,' according to the Canadian summary of Keynes's remarks, 'there was great danger that countries would be obliged to resort to beggar-my-neighbour policies after the war unless action to forestall this were taken on an international plane. The alternative was bilateralism, which should be avoided at all costs.' Hence his proposals aimed 'to achieve balance in international payments and so facilitate full employment. . . .'[28]

Most of the delegations, except the Canadian, were quiet, though even Ottawa's team were cautious. 'We began by stressing the informal and non-committal character of our representations,' the Canadians said, but they did indicate that the minds of those in Ottawa concerned with such matters 'had been moving in the same general direction.' Canada was 'obliged to recognize the necessity for international action in dealing with most post-war problems', and Ottawa's view was that a consensus was building in the United States as well for multilateralism. Indeed, that consensus seemed to include the other Dominions too. As the delegation's report made clear, no one at the meeting initially attacked the idea of a Clearing Union 'and there seemed to be general agreement that the idea was sound and should be given a trial.' That was progress, a step away from the closed world of protective tariffs and Imperial preferences created by the 1932 Ottawa Conference.

After the preliminary session, detailed paragraph-by-paragraph consideration of the Keynes plan followed, and here Rasminsky shone. The Canadians had been impressed by what Clifford Clark later called Keynes's 'simple and elegant application of banking principles to international transactions',[29] but they argued that it would be an error to load too many extraneous functions onto the Clearing Union. Rasminsky wrote Towers that the Union should be regarded only 'as a piece of machinery for the clearing of international balances and for the initial extension of foreign currency credits within certain limits; it should not be regarded as a panacea which would cure all post-war economic ills. . . .' He went on to say that the success of the Clearing Union 'might be jeopardized if it were cluttered up with other functions which led to a large extension in the volume of bancor [Keynes's name for his proposed international currency] outstanding.' 'Charity', Rasminsky said, 'should be recognized as such and not give rise to International obligations even in the form of bancor.'[30] In other words, as the delegation's report made clear, 'the debit and credit balances in the Union should not be swollen by items for which there was in fact no ultimate hope of repayment.' Rasminsky argued his case effectively here, and as he told Towers, 'I believe that the British have come round to this way of thinking though we have been careful not to press the point too hard.'[31]

Keynes's scheme also called for sanctions against countries that exceeded the debit or credit limits set by the Union. Rasminsky queried this, arguing that the bancor position of a country might not necessarily reflect its true international position, which would actually be based on its entire short-term assets and liabilities. His real intent was to query the British attitude on the relationship between the sterling area and the International Clearing Union, but he received only dusty answers. Keynes, it seemed clear, had no particular sympathy with the idea of the sterling area, but he was up against the Bank of England here and had only limited flexibility on that point.[32]

The discussions also focused on the position of creditor countries—in effect the United States, the country that all could see was certain to emerge from the war with most of the world in its debt (in more ways than one). On several occasions, the Canadian report noted, 'we found ourselves in the somewhat curious position of expressing views which might have come from representatives of a creditor country', a reflection of the Canadian understanding of the American situation, of conversations Rasminsky had had with the American Ambassador to Great Britain,[33] and also of the fact that Canada itself was likely to emerge from the war in a vastly stronger position financially, vis-à-vis Britain, than had been the case in 1939. The Canadians could not support an open-ended financial commitment to Keynes's Union, therefore, and they alone of the conferees showed an understanding of the 'special factors which make it difficult for the U.S.A. to fail to run a surplus.' Rasminsky and his colleagues sharply noted that 'It is naturally difficult to say to what extent this stress on the responsibility of the creditor countries reflects a strikingly rapid progress of economic thought in the U.K. during the past few years and to what extent it reflects the loss of foreign assets.' The Canadians succeeded in amending the draft plan to reflect their concerns, having spotted the fatal flaw in Keynes's scheme, and had substantial impact on the discussions.

The British had listened to the Canadians 'with attention', and Keynes had generously deferred to Rasminsky on discussions of the operation of foreign-exchange markets.[34] 'Indeed they were so anxious to meet our views', the delegation reported, 'that we were at pains to make it clear to them that we had no way of knowing that by doing so they would be coming any closer to the views which the Canadian government would ultimately take. . . .'[35] That was true, but there could be no doubt that Rasminsky and Mackintosh were pleased with the results and certain to play key roles in the Ottawa discussions to come. Both had won their international spurs in London. For Rasminsky, still just thirty-four years old, the experience had been exhilarating. As he told Towers, 'On the whole I feel in duty bound to say that I am having a very good time and enjoying the discussions, though I add in self defence that it is quite hard work.'[36]

The hard work now was devoted to the Canadian attempt to reconcile Keynes's plan with that prepared simultaneously in the United States by Dr Harry Dexter White of the Department of the Treasury. In contrast to Keynes's 'overdraft' scheme, White proposed an international stabilization fund, designed to expand trade and stimulate loans in an accelerated fashion, to which member nations would subscribe gold, government securities, and their own currencies up to a total of $5 billion. Each national contribution was to be determined through a complicated system utilizing factors such as fluctuations in, and holdings of, foreign exchange and gold, the magnitude of fluctuations in national income, and other related indices. White went further than Keynes in providing for international controls: countries might see their exchange rates set by the fund initially, and the management of the fund could require them to alter those rates as circumstances dictated. This detailed and carefully worked-out plan was far more managerial than Keynes's, and White had clearly drafted his ideas in the full expectation that the United States was certain to be *the* economic power in the postwar world. The dollar was to rule.

Canada did not become privy to White's early drafts until the beginning of 1943,[37] although visits back and forth between Washington and Ottawa had provided some inklings of the American trend of thought. In the following months, too, there were informal consultations with British and American officials as both Great Powers tried to rally Canadian support and reconcile the differences between the two proposals.[38] Intellectually the Canadians seemed closer to Keynes than to White, but they understood, as the British did not fully, the changes that the war had forced on the world economy. In particular they were sensitive to the American desire for a fund with a limited liability. They had to be, for increasingly there was every likelihood that Canada too would emerge from the war as a creditor in current account. The civil servants in Ottawa were also worried by the unpredictability—even the bloody-mindedness—of the United States Congress. Could that flighty body be expected to approve any scheme at all for international co-operation in finance?

Rasminsky's doubts and fears about the prospects for benevolent American involvement in the post-war world strengthened after he attended a conference held by the Institute of Pacific Relations at Mont Tremblant, Quebec, in December 1942. The topics did not deal with international finance, but the conflicting attitudes expressed by American and British participants were frightening, and Rasminsky returned to his desk 'in a pretty gloomy frame of mind . . . due to the obvious lack of understanding between the British and Americans. . . .' The British were adamantly opposed to the Americans on most issues. The Americans in turn had 'provided their fair proportion of grounds for pessimism by taking a very gloomy view regarding the prospects of American participation in a world order post-war. . . .' About all they had agreed upon, Rasminksy wrote, 'was to run the world between them.' For Rasminsky the only achievement of the conference was to bring to light how great was the gulf between the U.S. and Britain and how urgent was the need for their co-operation. Above all, he saw an arduous role for Canada in bringing this co-operation about.[39] He resolved to seek a mediating position for Canada between the White and Keynes plans.

The first person to suggest that Canada might consider drafting its own plan for an international clearing union or stabilization fund was A.F.W. Plumptre, Rasminsky's friend from university days. Plumptre, the financial attaché at the Canadian legation in Washington, was 'very troubled' by White's plan, particularly its intensive treatment of virtually all aspects of international finance. 'I feel strongly . . . that we are a very long way from the time when we ought to be discussing such details,' Plumptre wrote to Clifford Clark. In his view, 'It seems essential to reach a broad agreement amongst the more important countries concerned regarding the general approach,' and an early meeting with the Americans alone to discuss their plan would not serve this end. Instead, and to avoid the necessity of having to choose either the U.S. or the U.K. plans, Plumptre suggested 'an alternative proposal for discussion', a Canadian plan that 'would resemble the

British rather than the American', but 'differing from the British on as many points as seemed reasonably possible.' If there were three plans, he argued, attention might shift from the details to the broad principles. That was Plumptre's goal.[40]

All aspects of Plumptre's argument did not win acceptance from his colleagues in the Department of Finance, but Mackintosh nonetheless found much to like in the idea of a Canadian plan. To this end he proposed setting up a small planning group made up of Rasminsky, Bryce, and himself to consider the idea and then to report to the same informal group of mandarins who had first considered the Keynes scheme in October.[41] No record of the trio's work seems to have survived, but it must have received the go-ahead because it began to put suggestions on paper.

The idea of a Canadian plan, initially at least, seemed attractive to the few British officials to whom it was mentioned, men who had objected strongly to White's plan.[42] Some opportunistic Canadians saw that if the British and Americans remained in their fixed positions, as seemed likely, then a Canadian plan that combined aspects of both the other plans might slide up the middle and win approval. John Deutsch, another of the brilliant economists in Ottawa, suggested that at the very least a Canadian plan could help 'to crystallize the Canadian views and might also be useful to have in reserve.'[43] Deutsch also told Norman Robertson that Rasminsky had been working on a plan of his own for some time. In fact by March 11, around the time the Keynes and White plans were made public, Rasminsky told a subcommittee of the Economic Advisory Committee, the key group of economic officials, that his plan was ready 'as a basis of discussion in Canada and from which suggestions may be evolved for the amendment of the United Kingdom or United States plans if one of these was accepted as the basis of discussions between our three countries.'[44] By March 24 Rasminsky had distributed copies of his plan to Mackintosh and Bryce.[45]

Rasminsky's plan was an amalgam of the White and Keynes approaches. It rejected Keynes's closed system of bancor—although Rasminsky believed then and after that it was a 'beautiful creation'—and adopted White's idea of a fund with a bundle of currencies. The determining factor in Rasminsky's decision to adapt the American plan was an expedient one. He feared that Congress would not accept any plan that suggested U.S. involvement in a new financial organization—however much one was needed to achieve a world stabilization of currencies—without knowing how much the American contribution would be. Given his assessment of the American mood, which was shared by all in Ottawa involved with the Keynes-White plans, Rasminsky had concluded that something other than Keynes's open-ended American commitment was necessary. White's plan, however, with its fund limited to $5 billion for all members, was far too small *in toto* and equally skimpy as an American contribution to the reconstruction of the world. Therefore in his draft Rasminsky doubled the size of the fund to $10 billion, to be raised from each member—'having regards to the volume of the external trade, the fluctuations in the balance of international payments, its gold and foreign exchange holdings and the size of its national income.'[46]

Rasminsky's draft was subjected to the examination and cross-questioning of his Canadian colleagues in a number of sessions in April and after. No mention of this was made to the British or Americans, although Rasminsky had drafted a series of questions that he, with Deutsch and Mackintosh, would put to White's officials about the American plan on April 21.[47] Still, there was enough public interest in the Canadian government's reaction to the White and Keynes plans for the Department of External Affairs to hold a press conference on them on April 8, 1943, attended by Rasminsky, Mackintosh, and Deutsch, none of whom breathed a word of a Canadian plan.[48] Nor was there any direct hint of one at a small dinner in late April attended by Towers, Clark, Robertson, and Floyd Chalmers of the *Financial Post*, the weekly paper with very good links to the financial bureaucrats. The mandarins talked freely about the American and British schemes and seemed, Chalmers noted, to favour the British. 'Canada's position', he wrote, 'was that it wanted a common plan. We want a simple way in which we will be able to turn our surplus pounds into U.S. dollars. . . . If we have any influence we'll seek to bring Britain and the United States together on a common plan.'[49] That was a clue to the Ottawa intention: if the only way to get a common plan was for it to be drafted in Canada, so be it.

That certainly was Rasminsky's conclusion. In a formal memorandum drafted on April 30 he said that 'It seems to me very desirable that Canada should formulate a plan, either to be put forward as a Canadian project, or . . . treated as a revised plan which we had worked up with the United States. I think such a plan should be completed at an early date, and that it should be accompanied by an explanatory memorandum or preamble . . . something which would be designed to show the weaknesses in the U.S. approach without specifically criticizing White's proposals.'[50]

That view found favour with the economic mandarins (all of whom knew that Rasminsky had his draft almost ready), and it must have been reinforced by a letter of May 19 from Keynes to Hume Wrong at the Department of External Affairs, written just after the new Lord Keynes had delivered his maiden speech in the House of Lords. 'I hope I have not overstated the opportunities and possibilities for a synthesis of the two [U.S. and U.K.] proposals,' the great economist wrote. 'I am convinced that such a synthesis is possible, and very possibly you in Canada might use your good offices to put something forward on these lines at the right time. But the question when the right time will have arrived needs some thought.'[51] Keynes's caution, while not forgotten, fell victim to his encouragement, and soon the Minister of Finance, J.L. Ilsley, was urged in a memorandum by his officials to sponsor a Canadian plan and to permit its presentation to an international meeting scheduled in mid-June in Washington. It was argued that a Canadian plan could bring the British and Americans together and make clear that Canada, sharing a continent with the United States though part of the Commonwealth, was 'neither pro-London nor pro-Washington'. A Canadian plan might also let other countries avoid making a hard choice between the British and American plans and 'bring discussion into the open and probably establish some merger of the two plans as the desirable model.' Moreover, as the U.S. Treasury Department was viewed with great suspicion in the Congress and in financial circles in the United States, and as Canada's success with war finance had 'an almost embarrassingly high position' in those circles, a Canadian plan might find support, which White's plan would not likely do and Keynes's plan certainly would not because of the 'instinctive opposition' in the U.S. to things British.[52] A few days earlier Prime Minister Mackenzie King had heard for the first time about the possibility of a Canadian plan. Norman Robertson told him that 'Our experts in this field are really very good . . . ,' adding that 'I think there is a good deal to be said for them now trying to work out a new and synthetic scheme which might, if the Government approved of it, be put forward for confidential consideration by other Governments as a distinctively Canadian contribution. . . .'[53]

In fact Robertson and key officials had already received the final version of Rasminsky's plan and Rasminsky had called a meeting on May 25 to consider it.[54] It was not for the first time that the government was being asked, in effect, to give retroactive sanction to the work its officials had done.

The Rasminsky plan had undergone some modification since March. Rasminsky still favoured the adoption of the American idea of a fund, but one larger than that proposed by White. His suggestion now was for a fund of $8 billion and for an additional borrowing capacity equal to half that sum. He proposed a method of eliminating the American suggestions for a veto power for the United States, coming up with proposals that modified the rigidity inherent in the White plan without accepting the total flexibility of Keynes's.[55] As Rasminsky wrote to Keynes on June 3, when he sent him a copy of his plan, 'I think it would be accurate to say that while we have adopted the American form, our purposes have been to propose an institution with adequate resources to modify the rigidities of the American plan, to achieve a truly multilateral monetary organization and to make the operative sections workable.'[56]

Rasminsky added that his plan had yet to be adopted by the government (although, as he may not yet have learned, the Cabinet War Committee had agreed to it the day before[57]), and there was no assurance that his plan might not be revised or that it would even be put forward officially at Washington. Indeed, the official and quick British response to the Rasminsky plan was sharp. The High Commissioner in Ottawa told Clark and Robertson 'on instructions from his Government' that the United Kingdom was 'very anxious' that the proposals not be circulated at Washington. Keynes himself objected to some provisions, and in particular, as Robertson informed Mackenzie King, 'felt that if it were submitted for consideration the United States would refuse to examine the British scheme.' Robertson and Clark urged King to let the Canadian plan be circulated,[58] and King assented, although it was apparently at his insistence that the plan was timidly labelled as the 'Tentative Draft Proposals of Canadian Experts'. The British continued to complain, telling Mackintosh, who was in London at another conference, that the 'finality and finished quality (flattery) of our plan' undercut the chances for full consideration of the Keynes draft. That *was* flattery; but before the Canadians could consider withdrawing their plan, they were forestalled by White's inadvertently listing it for discussion on the agenda of the Washington talks. The Canadian delegation thus had no option but to release it on a 'confidential basis'.[59]

Thus for the first time in the war—and in all likelihood for the first time ever—Canada had taken a distinctive position on a subject of major international importance, one that involved the two great powers with which Canada was most closely associated. This is not to suggest that Canada had never before proposed ideas; it had, and the functional principle was only the most recent. But Canada had not previously intervened in quite this way: seeing an opportunity to be helpful, preparing a broad, far-reaching, and carefully worked-out proposal, and then putting it forward. That had never been the Canadian style, and it was not Mackenzie King's style at all. But this time Canada had something truly significant to offer.

How had this come about? The Canadian plan, while not wholly the product of one mind or one man, was undoubtedly Rasminsky's. He had seized on the idea for a distinctive compromise plan, he had prepared the first draft, and after discussion with his colleagues he had completed the revised final version. It was a Rasminsky plan just as much as it was a White or Keynes plan. Rasminsky, an undoubted expert in the subject, was in Ottawa doing work that required him to remain on top of questions of international trade and foreign exchange. In 1943 it was still a novelty for the Canadian government to have in its employ a man who could develop a synthesis of plans proposed by Keynes and White.

It would be ideal from the point of view of this book if one could say that the Canadian plan—Rasminsky's plan—swept all before it, reconciling Britain and the United States and earning the gratitude of other nations. Regrettably it did not, for the Americans insisted on their own plan and had the financial clout to make sure that its broad outlines survived intact. Nonetheless, there were changes that could be made to White's scheme, and Rasminsky's plan had very substantial influence in persuading the Americans and others to support modifications. Equally important, Rasminsky himself had established a reputation as a thinker and a skilled technician, and this became apparent again at the great Bretton Woods Conference in New Hampshire in July 1944 that created the International Monetary Fund.

His influence, as Rasminsky later recalled, primarily lay in helping to speed up the process of international agreement. Rasminsky's plan (inevitably dubbed 'off-White' by the British[60]) played a considerable role in creating a widespread recognition that Keynes's bancor idea was dead, that given the realities of American public opinion, in fact, it had never had a chance.[61] After those Washington meetings in June 1943 and after bilateral Anglo-American discussions in September, even the British were coming to realize this. As Keynes wrote to Rasminsky in that latter month, with just a touch of annoyance showing through, the Canadian plan had seemed to him a bit premature in its timing, and although 'your draft was an improvement on the Stabilisation Fund and more logical in clearing up doubtful matters, it did not, so far as we were concerned, go far enough in certain directions to form any certain basis for a compromise.'[62] Rasminsky had chosen to go in White's direction rather than Keynes's, and this choice made the British critical and their position more difficult. It also helped ensure that the major outlines of the American plan were the ones that were followed.

By the beginning of 1944 the British had conceded the crucial points. The 'Joint Statement by Experts on the Establishment of an International Monetary Fund', published simultaneously in several capitals, including Ottawa, in April 1944 made this clear.[63] And by July 1944, when the allies convened at Bretton Woods to adopt rules and regulations for the International Monetary Fund, the broad outline was clear.[64]

The Canadian delegation at Bretton Woods was headed by Mackintosh and included as members Towers, Deutsch, Plumptre, and Rasminsky. But of these Canadians, the most important at the conference unquestionably was Rasminsky. He was the rapporteur to the plenary conference on Commission I, the committee working on the Fund that included White and Keynes as members; he was also a delegate on two committees under that Commission and the chairman of the crucial drafting committee. More than that he was, as A.F.W. Plumptre wrote his wife, one of the key people doing a 'magnificent back-stage job at this conference . . . at meetings lasting until 2 and 3 a.m. night after night.'[65]* His influence was enhanced by the largely fortuitous

---

* Plumptre also wrote that on one occasion the Canadian delegation, minus Rasminsky, had its photograph taken. 'Afterwards, of course [the photographer] took down all our names in order. Just at that time a small Russian, bewhiskered and goggled, passed by. Towers immediately remarked, "We should have pulled him into the picture and given in his name as Rasminsky!" ' (Mrs A.F.W. Plumptre Papers (Ottawa), Plumptre to Mrs Plumptre, 4 July, 1944.)

publication of an article by him in the July issue of *Foreign Affairs* that received wide circulation at Bretton Woods. Rasminsky had aimed his arguments at Americans doubtful of the merits of, or the need for, international financial institutions, and his cogent text was much appreciated by the American and other delegations.[66]

To Rasminsky fell the task of delivering the Report of Commission I to the Bretton Woods Conference as a whole, and in it he referred to the process of consultation, extending over eighteen months, that had produced agreement on the Fund. That process had resulted in a wide area of agreement on principles 'and this having been ascertained, there was no great difficulty in reaching a satisfactory accommodation as regards the secondary questions relating to techniques and amounts.'[67] That was true enough, even though some of the fighting for position and place had been fierce.[68]

There was no doubt that the Canadians had made a large contribution in pushing the British and Americans toward agreement. On a visit to Ottawa, Keynes said magnanimously that Canada 'played a very distinguished and dignified part all through at Bretton Woods . . . not from any narrow self-interest [but] because Canada was very keen for monetary stabilization plans. . . . Your Mr. Rasminsky . . . rendered most trojan service as chairman of the most important technical committee and his tremendous assistance in that connection brought results which satisfied all concerned.'[69] Other British officials seemed to agree, one from the Dominions Office informing London that 'The Canadian Delegation contained some of the most competent technicians at the Conference. Mr. Rasminsky, Dr. Mackintosh, Mr. Plumptre and Mr. Deutsch distinguished themselves and earned the highest praise from all sides.' The official continued by noting that Bretton Woods 'served once again to demonstrate that Canada is fully alive to the responsibilities of her newly-found status as an almost-great Power, and that she possesses officials with breadth of vision and intellectual equipment equal to the role which she is assuming.'[70]

In all the complex discussions that led to the creation of the Fund, Louis Rasminsky had been the right man at the right place at the precisely right moment. Before the war his talents may not have been wanted in Ottawa, but by 1940 there was a place for him, and in all his activities throughout the large series of international financial negotiations he demonstrated that he and his country merited a place at the table of the great powers.

Another man who was in the right place at this time was the economist W.A. Mackintosh, Special Assistant to Clifford Clark, the Deputy Minister of Finance. He was on leave from Queen's University, the only mandarin who was not a permanent member of the civil service, but there could be no doubt whatever that he was a mandarin. Indeed, because Mackintosh was the first to spot so many of the bright young men who became mandarins, in a sense he deserves to rank with Skelton, Clark, and Towers as a founder of the club. It was Mackintosh—like Skelton and Clark, his former teachers and university colleagues—who created the idea that Queen's University was and should be the nursery of the civil service. But it was also he, in his own right, who played an important role on advisory boards, on royal commissions, and during the war as a full-time member of the Departments of Finance and Reconstruction; for a time in 1945 when Clark collapsed under the strain of his work, Mackintosh acted as Deputy Minister of Finance, very likely the pre-eminent post in the bureaucracy. Yet when the emergency passed, Mackintosh happily returned to the university, soon becoming its Vice-Principal, then its Principal, and to the end remained a revered figure—notably at Queen's, but also among economists and within the public service.

III

William Archibald Mackintosh was born on May 21, 1895 in Madoc, Ont., where his father was a school inspector. 'I think of your father,' John W. Dafoe wrote to Mackintosh in 1941, in a reminiscent mood about his schooling in North Hastings. 'I can see him yet, a brisk, eager, valiant man, hopping into the schoolroom on his crutches, and putting us through our paces. That he should have made a lifelong impression on a youngster is a testimony to his personality.'[71] That personality also had to impress itself on the young Mackintosh, the junior member in a family of seven, a family rich in Scots-Presbyterian beliefs (although little of its religiosity remained with this son). His education took place locally and at St Andrew's College, Toronto. When he was only seventeen, Mackintosh—who had, as a long-time colleague put it, 'chosen to be born in Queen's country'—went to the university at Kingston.[72]

There he did brilliantly in every aspect of college life. His instructors—Skelton for his whole period at Queen's and, at the end
of his undergraduate work, Clark—recognized him instantly as a
brilliant student, and he won prizes in history and political science,
became president of his class, college fencing champion, and a par-
ticipant in rugby and soccer. In 1916 he graduated with an M.A.
degree, his thesis being a study of the political and social ideas of
Leo Tolstoy, a subject that indicated there was some breadth to
the young man. In the summers, like other Queen's men before
him, he went west to instruct in prairie schools, developing a life-
long interest in the agricultural problems of the region and in the
organizational methods the farmers were employing to cope with
them. When he went to Harvard University in 1916 to work on
his doctorate, he chose agricultural co-operation in western Canada as his dissertation subject.

His thesis was not handed in until 1922. By that time Mackin-
tosh had taught for two years at Brandon College, from which
Skelton hired him in 1920 to be an assistant professor at Queen's at
$2,300 a year.[73] Thereafter his rise was speedy. When Clifford
Clark left the university to try his luck at business in the United
States, Mackintosh was promoted to associate professor, and two
years later, when Skelton departed for the Department of External
Affairs in 1924, Mackintosh was promoted again to professor, a
very senior rank for a man who was just thirty years old. In that
year, however, the ambitious Mackintosh came close to resigning,
so infuriated was he at the way the Principal had appointed a new
head for the Department of Political and Economic Science. He
had expected the position for himself and believed it had been
promised to him, and in a long letter to the Principal he set out his
grievance: 'Quality of work rather than length of experience
seemed to me the essential factor,' he said, 'but after seven years of
reasonably successful and not unvaried experience in University
work, I did not consider myself altogether a novice.'[74] To Skelton
in Ottawa, Mackintosh added that 'I have never had a great deal of
sympathy with a person who knew his subject but couldn't get it
down [on paper] . . . my present very strong inclination is to
quit.'[75]

Whatever the reasons, however, Mackintosh stayed, and two
years later he became head of his department. The next year he
married Jean Easton of Renfrew, Ont., a 1926 Queen's graduate in
Commerce and one of his former students. Gradually his respon-

sibilities, his areas of teaching, and his salary increased. By 1937, for example, his pay of $4,500 was being charged to four different departments: Economics, Commerce, Banking, and Accounting.[76]

Teaching was only part of his life; he was obsessed by scholarly research and publication. Mackintosh never found it difficult to get his ideas down on paper. His thesis was published in 1924; he became editor of the Queen's University 'business studies'; the director of research for the 'Canadian Pioneer Problems Committee'; and co-editor of its *Canadian Frontiers of Settlement* series, as well as author of one of the volumes and co-author of another. This series he liked and justified because it combined a detached scholarship with a relevance to contemporary problems—ideal concerns for an economist, he believed.[77] In addition, he produced a flood of articles in scholarly journals and a number of pieces of popular comment in such publications as *Queen's Quarterly*. By the time he was forty Mackintosh was undoubtedly a leading Canadian scholar.

While a student of Skelton and Clark, Mackintosh had become convinced that he had a duty to devote himself to the study of his native country. But when he worked at Harvard he became familiar with the writings of Frederick Jackson Turner on the American frontier and with the work of G.S. Callender, the American economic historian whose writings stressed the importance of staples exports in developing frontier areas. As a teacher in the West, Mackintosh had gained experience to which this theory could be related, and by the time he had returned to Queen's he had become convinced that for a new country, 'one problem takes precedence over all others—the problem of discovering a staple product with a ready market. The world makes a path to the door of those regions fortunate enough to possess such a product. . . . So well do young communities understand this fact, that it is almost possible to write the history of the settlement of North America in terms of the search for new vendible products. . . .'[78] This theme was soon picked up and developed by Harold Innis.

One of his *Canadian Frontiers of Settlement* volumes was on *The Economic Problems of the Prairie Provinces* (1935), in which Mackintosh wrote extensively on the wheat pools and on broader questions of foreign exchange and trade.[79] In a sense this was a preparation for his most important work, *The Economic Background of Dominion-Provincial Relations* (1939). This economic history of

Canada from Confederation was prepared as a research study for the Royal Commission on Dominion-Provincial Relations and completed in the summer of 1938, and then revised for publication. It was not only the first detailed history of the Canadian economy (since that by Skelton in *Canada and its Provinces*), but the first full study of the effects of the tariff on the different regions* and a concise and clear examination of the effects the National Policy had—and had not—had. As J.H. Dales observed some years later, Mackintosh's analysis spared few sacred cows. For example, to those who argued hotly that the West had been victimized by the National Policy, Mackintosh noted that the tariff did not reduce the income of prairie farmers 'because [in the words of Dales] the West was settled after the tariff had been adopted, so that the cost of the tariff was discounted in the original price paid for the land.'[80] To Mackintosh, it was fitting and proper for economists to remain aloof from the political passions of the day, for their discipline 'prescribes no policy and enunciates no doctrine apart from the analysis of the particular facts of the moment.' That was what he had always tried to do. To him the only bias of economics was to remain 'unalterably opposed to all programmes based on unreason'.[81] A good economist, in other words, could play an active role in public policy while still preserving the integrity of his discipline. Perhaps some in his profession could not; Mackintosh could.

Mackintosh's influential research study for the Royal Commission had not been his first government-commissioned project. In the mid-1920s he had worked on an investigation of an alleged combine of wholesale and retail druggists under the Combines Investigation Act, and from 1926 to 1929 he was a member of the Advisory Board on Tariff and Taxation. Most important, however, was his work from 1936 to 1939 on the National Employment Commission, a body established by the Mackenzie King government, and responsible to the Minister of Labour, Norman Rogers (a member of Mackintosh's department at Queen's until his election to Parliament in 1935), to study the unemployment that was then wracking the country. When Rogers was seeking the Liberal nomination in Kingston, Mackintosh was on sabbatical in Europe, but he sent advice on organizing the town, on the ne-

---

* Curiously, Norman Robertson had chosen this subject for his Brookings' dissertation, which he did not complete.

cessity of building a machine 'of several hundred people of all classes gossiping on the street corners for you and feeling that they have enough knowledge of you to deny confidently any anti-Rogers gossip. . . . I have always had a hunch that I knew how a campaign in Kingston ought to be organized. However,' he added, 'I know I could not be elected poundkeeper in any place and perhaps I could not get any one else elected. I only hope that we are back in time to cast two votes for you.'[82] Rogers' recommendation, no doubt supported by Skelton and Clark, had secured Mackintosh's spot on the National Employment Commission, and he played a key role.

Initially Mackintosh opposed any idea that public investment could resolve the crisis of the Depression. In that respect he sounded little different from orthodox economists, politicians, and commentators. But in the area of housing, for example, Mackintosh believed that the government could spend without fear of competing with private interests, a conflict that in 1936 he was still concerned to avoid. There was a substantial shortage of housing in the country, and thirteen per cent of all employable men who were on relief had previously worked in construction, while a further thirty-two per cent were general labourers. Thus housing was one area where unemployment could be tackled, and Mackintosh proposed a three-pronged assault: assistance for renovations, slum clearance, and increased federal money for mortgages.[83] With this recommendation the seeds of the National Housing Act of 1938 were planted.

Mackintosh was also the leading member of the NEC who took part in its decision to recommend that Ottawa establish a system of unemployment insurance and take over the responsibility for employment assistance for 'the employable unemployed', a measure with significant implications for both federal powers and the finances of the country. The result of this recommendation was a terrific struggle between the Prime Minister on one side and the Minister of Labour and a majority of NEC members on the other. Inevitably King won, but not before he denounced in his diary 'these men, all of whom are Queen's University, Department of Economics'—the reference was to Rogers, Skelton, Clark, and Mackintosh—who 'have been working jointly to seek to bring about a change in constitutional relations which will lead to a centralization of powers and away from the present order of things.'[84] That was January 1938. Two years later King had persuaded himself that he was the father of unemployment insurance, the man who had pressed it forward despite the opposition of powerful groups.

For his part Mackintosh by 1938 had reached the conclusion that the days of limited federal power were gone forever. He had also begun to move towards a partial acceptance of the ideas of John Maynard Keynes, whose views on deficit spending as a way out of the Depression were still seen by the orthodox as heresy. Mackintosh did not march the whole way with Keynes. To Mackintosh public investment could be used only to keep the level of public and private investment stable: in other words, the government should not contract its spending when the economy was in a downswing, something that Bennett and King had attempted.[85]

Thus W.A. Mackintosh revealed himself as a sensible economist, a man with what Professor Vincent Bladen described as 'a good constructive feel for the right answers'. Whether his answers on the NEC were correct—or advanced enough—might be argued; certainly he was ahead of the politicians and most of the economists.[86] That he was also a good and humane man needs saying, and in support of this view Bladen provided an example. In 1937, at a time when Harold Innis was a candidate for the chairmanship in political economy at the University of Toronto, Mackintosh was scheduled to become president of the Canadian Political Science Association. But because he hoped to see Innis become chairman of his department, Mackintosh 'urged us to select Innis as President as a form of manifesto directed at the Board of Governors [of the University of Toronto]. He, Mackintosh, could wait for election at a later date. Innis was elected.' As Bladen noted, he did not know if Innis's CPSA presidency helped clinch his eventual chairmanship, 'But the generosity and good judgement of Bill Mackintosh deserves to be recorded.'[87]

IV

With the outbreak of war Mackintosh was summoned to Ottawa and to the Department of Finance by his old teacher and friend, Clifford Clark. As Special Assistant to the Deputy Minister he played a major role in a number of capacities in Finance over the next five years before he transferred to the Department of Reconstruction in late 1944. The change from professor to bureaucrat was not an easy one. Initially Mackintosh had to find someone to teach his courses at Queen's, and one class at least was taught by

John Deutsch, who commuted from his post with the Rowell-Sirois Commission in Ottawa to Kingston for that purpose. There were also some financial problems. Although Mackintosh entered Finance with the same salary Queen's paid him, $5,000 a year,[88] working in Ottawa meant that there were no opportunities to supplement that stipend with summer work, and rents were higher; the Mackintoshes had to cut back. The work was also much more taxing; the intensity and strain of the bureaucracy were infinitely greater than in academe. But there were compensations. The Department and the mandarinate in general brought together some of the ablest men in the country: the opportunity to work, on what he saw as a noble task, with Clark, Bryce, Towers, Skelton, Robertson, and Wrong was exhilarating. Mackintosh did not take long to decide that it was in wartime Ottawa that he could best fulfil himself. As he and Clark lived side by side in Rockcliffe and saw much of each other socially, their relationship became especially close. Everything considered, the war for Mackintosh was the best of times.[89]

As Clark's right hand Mackintosh moved instantly into the inner circle of Finance, and of the bureaucracy. The key centre of action was the Advisory Committee on Economic Policy—or, as it was usually known, the Economic Advisory Committee. It had been suggested by Clark even before the declaration of war and was a product of discussions with Skelton and Robertson.[90] But it was Skelton who passed the idea to the Prime Minister, along with a draft order-in-council, telling King that because of 'the important and close inter-relation of financial and economic measures' the EAC could be of 'material help for primary surveys to make sure that all necessary points are being examined and measures co-ordinated.'[91] The draft order added that the EAC was to facilitate the work of Cabinet committees responsible for supervising policy in supply and war finance, that it was to help avoid duplication of effort by departments and agencies, and that it was to ensure effective co-ordination of economic and financial policy.[92]

The suggestion ran into heavy weather in Cabinet, in part because the draft order noted that the EAC had been suggested with the concurrence of both the Prime Minister and the Minister of Finance, Colonel J.L. Ralston. But, as King wrote in his diary, 'Ralston, to my surprise, said he had not seen the order. That', King ruminated, 'is one of the mistakes our bureaucracy continually makes, taking for granted Ministers will simply follow what they suggest.' The Prime Minister also grumbled that 'we have far too many committees already, and the staff will be attending to committees instead of to their more immediate duties.'[93] Nonetheless, King signed the order,[94] and the EAC came into being. It was potentially the most powerful grouping of civil servants, a body ideally suited to integrating financial policy and economic controls, and it brought to the same table Clark, Graham Towers, Robertson, Dana Wilgress of Trade and Commerce, the Commissioner of Customs, the Chairman of the Wartime Prices and Trade Board, the Deputy Ministers of Agriculture and Mines and Resources, the Dominion Statistician, and Lt.-Col. H. DesRosiers, the Associate Deputy Minister of National Defence and the only French Canadian in the group.[95]

The work of the EAC, initially at least, was concerned with the problem of settling the terms and arrangements for Canadian food exports to Britain—a particularly difficult question, given London's unwillingness to pay the prices the Canadians thought adequate.[96] But by December 1939, about the time Mackintosh began attending the EAC meetings (which were usually held in the evenings so that members' regular duties were not affected), the EAC was looking at wage policy and unemployment, an area in which Mackintosh, because of experience with the National Employment Commission, was an undoubted expert.[97] That work led inexorably to the draft of an Unemployment Insurance Bill, which the Prime Minister was at last prepared to bring forward, the war seemingly guaranteeing a diminution—if not a complete end—to unemployment, and thus an opportunity for workers' and employers' contributions to build up the insurance fund as a cushion for expected postwar joblessness.[98] In May 1940 Mackintosh also put together a report on relief policy for the EAC.[99]

These were not the only areas Mackintosh was studying, however. He had also become the EAC expert (with Robertson and Towers) on the growing crisis in foreign exchange that had begun to face Canada in 1940 because imports and exports were increasing.[100] By the beginning of 1941, if Clark for any reason was absent from the EAC, Mackintosh—who was technically still not a member of the Committee—took the chair. As Clark's aide he was accorded a substantial status, but he had easily built a reputation on his own.[101]

By 1942 a host of agencies had sprung up—the Wartime Prices

and Trade Board was probably the largest one—carving out whole empires for themselves and aggressively seeking out expanded mandates and defending their turfs, and the EAC had begun to seem a committee without a role. Was the co-ordination that the EAC could provide still a necessity? Some had begun to doubt the need for a large EAC, to suggest that perhaps the Privy Council Office—itself one of the expanding bureaucratic empires in the capital—could handle the job of co-ordination.[102] At this point, apparently by coincidence, events conspired to renew the EAC's life and give it a major role in Canada's war.

The Committee on Reconstruction, a body headed by Principal F. Cyril James of McGill University, had been created in March 1941 to study the problems Canada was expected to face after the war.[103] Responsible to the Minister of Pensions and Health, Ian Mackenzie, the James Committee created a small staff to work for its blue-ribbon panel of members, a group that included J.S. McLean of Canada Packers; Percy Bengough, the President of the Trades and Labour Congress; and R.C. Wallace, the Principal of Queen's University. In October 1942 the Committee presented an interim report that suggested new structures within the government to handle reconstruction, including the appointment of a minister to handle all economic matters or, alternatively, a co-ordinating minister without portfolio. These proposals stung the Economic Advisory Committee into action.

It was not the suggestions themselves that upset the mandarins—although the ideas were viewed as impractical, and too much of a departure from the norm to stand much chance with the politicians—but the very idea that a non-governmental body was proffering them. Clifford Clark's suggestion, the EAC minutes of November 10 noted, was

> that the main work in preparation for post-war action would have to be done in the Departments, and could only be properly done there by those familiar with the problems and with the views of the Government, and able to advise the various Ministers concerned. He suggested that the Economic Advisory Committee or some sub-committee of it should be the main agency responsible at the official level for the development of plans for dealing with post-war questions. . . . He said that the Committee on Reconstruction could fit into such an organization; that there were important parts of the

work which it could do. . . . This subject was discussed at some length [the minutes continue] and there seemed to be a feeling that while the Committee on Reconstruction could be fitted into such an arrangement, there would be difficulties in it. . . .[104]

After that meeting the EAC produced a report for the Cabinet War Committee on November 30, pointing out the urgent need for postwar planning and particularly for measures to meet domestic unemployment after demobilization and the closing-down of war industry, and, predictably, finding itself unable to accept the James Committee's recommendations for ministerial control of the process. Instead it recommended that 'planning must be the responsibility of the Government itself and that the bulk of the preparatory and advisory work must be done within the ordinary Government Departments and agencies.' To do this work, the EAC proposed itself:

> The Economic Advisory Committee should be asked to plan the work of investigating and reporting upon post-war problems, to allocate responsibility for studying specific problems to the various departments and agencies in order to assure that the field will be adequately covered, to follow up the work being done, to receive reports and discuss them with a view to assuring co-ordination of the various programs and policies proposed, and to prepare the necessary documentary material for consideration of the Cabinet.

The EAC proposed to establish a subcommittee, under Mackintosh, to perform this task, and to neuter the competing Committee. It suggested that the James Committee report to Cabinet through the President of the Privy Council under a new designation: the *Advisory* Committee on Reconstruction. As the Prime Minister was also President of the Privy Council, this recommendation meant that in effect James would deal with Arnold Heeney, the Clerk of the Privy Council, who was also a member of the EAC and one of the major drafters of its recommendations.[105]

This was a bureaucratic coup. The EAC had watched the James Committee horn in on spheres that it saw as the bureaucracy's, not those of an outside, appointed, advisory group that reported to Mackenzie, a weak minister, and did not, could not, understand how Ottawa truly worked. But the coup did not seek to destroy the James Committee. It was left intact, but was made to function in a limbo where Heeney could readily control its access to Cabinet, where the EAC could make use of the Committee's advice at its discretion, and where Mackintosh's subcommittee would have total charge of planning for peace. The EAC's skill in bringing about this transfer of power was impressive—even though the change was justifiable. Reconstruction *was* too important to be left to outsiders; there did have to be detailed and co-ordinated work; and the regular departments did have to be involved.

Heeney presented the EAC recommendations to King on December 10, the Cabinet War Committee accepted them on December 23, and James surrendered on December 28.[106] 'Lunched at the [Rideau] Club and talked to Cliff Clark re Reconstruction,' Senator Norman Lambert wrote in his diary a few days later. 'He explained that the P.M. was taking matter out of Ian McK's hands and Economic Council would deal with it.' Two days later Ian Mackenzie, the minister, told the ubiquitous Lambert that he did not mind losing Reconstruction to the Prime Minister. 'Thinks James not liked by P.M. due to professional jealousy of others.'[107] Thus the EAC had done its work well, even to persuading the minister concerned that the Prime Minister, always one to worry about 'planners' and their desires to go too far too fast, had dispensed with James.

The Economic Advisory Committee was somewhat less successful in hiding its hand when it had to deal with the proposal for a scheme of national health insurance that Ian Mackenzie's department presented a few weeks later. The idea had been produced by Dr J.J. Heagerty, the Director of Public Health Services in the Department of Pensions and National Health (and, incidentally, John Deutsch's father-in-law), and was the product of several years' work. But the EAC, after receiving the Minister and his officials in audience on January 16, was not impressed. Clark and others argued that the costs of the plan were very high and probably insupportable for some provinces. Moreover,

> The Chairman said that it was his belief that it would be desirable for the Dominion to propose a comprehensive scheme of social security, if it could be given the constitutional and financial powers to carry it into effect. He thought that the public and Parliament would support proposals to give the Dominion the necessary powers to this end. He said he

> would be very loath to see this health insurance measure put forward as a separate, independent proposal at this time. . . .[108]

That conclusion, which formed the basis of the EAC's report to the War Committee,[109] provoked a raging Ian Mackenzie into denouncing the 'stalling, by a financial group, of two years' work in the Health Department' and into hinting at resignation if the EAC was upheld.[110] The Cabinet considered the question on January 22, but when Clark appeared to attack the scheme, Mackenzie's plan was effectively scuttled.[111]

Again the EAC had emerged victorious, this time against a minister. The struggle had been with a weak department and a lacklustre politician, of course, but for a committee of bureaucrats to take on a minister in a straight-out fight was still unusual; even more unusual was the speed of the victory. Reconstruction and social-security planning were now in the EAC's hands—in Mackintosh's hands. Again, this was almost certainly the proper result. Mackenzie had been pushed aside because he was pressing for piecemeal solutions where co-ordinated treatment was required. Nonetheless the EAC had confirmed its status as the most powerful group of civil servants: it was the only body in Ottawa to rival the Cabinet War Committee itself.

And by January 1943 Mackintosh was the EAC's only full-time member. At the committee meeting on January 7, 1943, the Cabinet War Committee's decisions on reconstruction planning were discussed and the EAC members suggested 'that it would be highly desirable if Dr. Mackintosh could devote his full time to the work of the Committee and particularly its sub-committee. . . . Mackintosh said he believed it would be possible for him to devote practically his full time to this work now.'[112]

Mackintosh's subcommittee soon became a minor growth industry. The initial members were Alex Skelton from the Bank of Canada, Louis Rasminsky from the Foreign Exchange Control Board, John Deutsch from External Affairs, R.B. Bryce from Finance, J.R. Baldwin from the Privy Council Office, and Jean Chapdelaine, a young External Affairs officer, as secretary. That was an extraordinarily high-powered group of men, all of whom were then just below the top ranks—but all of whom would reach them. The subcommittee work was organized around two basic themes: the practical problems to be faced in peacetime and the constitutional alterations necessary so that Ottawa would have the powers to resolve them.[113] In effect, the EAC was beginning to take a comprehensive look at the powers that the federal and provincial governments had, or needed, to create what amounted to a new country. Mackintosh and his subcommittee members had come to the conclusion that co-ordination was necessary, that economic policy and social-welfare planning had to be accomplished at one and the same time if the expectations that the Canadian people had for the postwar years were to be met. After the Great War there had been massive labour unrest and a botched effort at re-integrating the returning veterans into society; Mackintosh believed that after this war the people of Canada would accept nothing less than a new society. This meant a greater degree of state intervention than had been the case before 1939; it meant applying Keynesian principles to federal budgeting; and it meant the creation of social programs designed to establish a national minimum standard of living. As a direct corollary of these things, there must also be a far greater centralization of power in Ottawa.

The subcommittee—created, directed, and staffed by Mackintosh—charted a course of action for the government. Not until the summer of 1943—by which time the CCF and the Conservatives were beginning to rack up gains in the opinion polls, in by-elections, and in the provinces—did the Liberal Party, as opposed to the government, begin to respond positively to the proposals that were working their way through the subcommittee. The key figure in interpreting them to the Prime Minister was King's secretary, J.W. Pickersgill, who respected the EAC's work and, as a pragmatist, believed as strongly as Mackintosh in the necessity of social security and strengthened powers for the federal government. Pickersgill sold the package to Mackenzie King, and at the beginning of 1944 its inclusion in the Speech from the Throne gave governmental sanction to the reconstruction program.[114] Soon new departments were being created and legislation began to move through Parliament on family allowances, generous veterans' benefits, and a revised and strengthened National Housing Act, among other enlightened social measures. Preparations were also in hand for a Dominion-Provincial Conference, and a Cabinet committee was created with an advisory committee under Alex Skelton to draft proposals and plans for the new division of constitutional powers that would permit the government to shape and direct the new society.[115]

The work of Mackintosh's subcommittee was almost done. Its responsibility for reconstruction planning was handed over by the EAC to the new Department of Reconstruction in the autumn of 1944, and the EAC itself soon faded away.[116] Mackintosh, as the expert on reconstruction, joined the new department as Director-General of Economic Research; C.D. Howe, a very powerful minister indeed, was the head. The main responsibility of the new department was to ensure that the transition from war to peace went as smoothly as possible. However, Mackintosh took upon himself the personal goal of seeing that the federal government fulfilled the commitment it had finally begun to make to a minimum standard of living for all Canadians.

The Reconstruction Department under Howe was a mixed blessing to Mackintosh. It was possibly the most important place to be in 1944-5, but Mackintosh told Grant Dexter, the *Winnipeg Free Press* reporter who was a personal friend, that he was 'Fed up with being a civil servant. Has no bump for organization and no temperament for the rough and bruising career of a civil servant. Prefers educating young men with open minds to trying to split open the solid craniums of cabinet ministers in order to get ideas in. Is convinced that there is no such thing as an open-minded minister. All hopeless.' Howe in particular was a hard nut: Mackintosh 'essays daily an intellectual form of volleyball—bouncing ideas off Mr. Howe's battleship steel headpiece. Some of them bounce pretty far. . . . He finds that Howe agrees but does not know what he is agreeing with.'[117]

That was probably unfair to Howe, for whether he understood or not, Howe ultimately encouraged one of Mackintosh's ideas: a white paper on the reconstruction program setting out the government's intentions in an understandable form—that might also, Howe saw, be useful in the coming elections. That was not Mackintosh's concern, however. What he sought was government support for the two principles that his and Skelton's subcommittees had championed: a strong government that stressed the common national interests; and an interventionist role for the state, one that could employ economic tools such as tax relief, subsidies, and public works to keep employment up when times were hard. 'Though the battle over Keynesianism had been pretty well conceded' by that time, Mackintosh recalled, 'I had some interest in seeing how far some of the elements of Keynesianism could be presented as the most ordinary of common sense.'[118]

His initial efforts to sell the white-paper idea to Howe met with a cool response, but early in March the minister authorized a draft, which was produced over a weekend. 'His attitude,' Mackintosh said, 'though short of enthusiasm, was favourable enough' to permit a full-length treatment.[119] Mackintosh showed this draft to most of the economic mandarins and incorporated their suggestions,[120] while Howe tried it out on friends and associates and allowed himself to be influenced. The amended paper then went to a Cabinet committee of Howe, Louis St Laurent, the Minister of Justice, and J.L. Ilsley, the Minister of Finance—the three strongest ministers in a strong Cabinet. Mackintosh spent a day briefing them, using a text 'in which I had underlined in different colours the specific commitments, the general statements of policy, the implied commitments and all statements in the name of the Government. I required specific approval to each. . . .' By the end of the day, after 'my schoolmasterish drill', Mackintosh had it.[121] The Cabinet accepted its committee's recommendation, and on April 12, 1945, the momentous day when President Roosevelt died and a federal election was announced, the *White Paper on Employment and Income* was tabled in Parliament.[122]

It stated that 'the maintenance of a high and stable level of employment and income' was 'a major aim of government policy', 'a great national objective'. Depression could not be allowed to return, and to this end, 'The Government will be prepared, in periods when unemployment threatens, to incur deficits and increases in the national debt resulting from its employment and income policy, whether that policy in the circumstances is best applied through increased expenditures or reduced taxation. In periods of buoyant employment and income, budget plans will call for surpluses. The Government's policy will be to keep the national debt within manageable proportions and maintain a proper balance in its budget over a period longer than a single year.' That was Keynesianism presented as the most ordinary of common sense, just as Mackintosh had desired.

The *White Paper* also listed all the projects Howe's department was pursuing, their basic aim being to maintain a high level of economic activity. There were programs for promoting trade through multilateral tariff cuts and through an Export Credits Insurance Act; there were tax breaks and special depreciation allowances for industry; there was even a pledge 'not only to reduce taxation as rapidly as possible' but for government to 'develop its fiscal policy so as to encourage the increase of private investment to a high and stable level.' The *White Paper* also pledged the ending of wartime controls, as well as the disposal of wartime Crown Corporations where practicable. It was an elaborate expression of free-enterprise Keynesianism, as well as a shrewd political document.[123]

'The White Paper did not invent a policy,' Mackintosh said, 'it simply recognized that the responsibility for employment policy, which the Dominion had rejected in 1937-38, it could not avoid in 1945. . . .'[124] The war obviously had changed many things. Not least was Mackintosh's own shift. Having rejected Keynes throughout most of the Depression, he had come round to adhering to the British economist's doctrines as the most efficacious way of dealing with Canada's problems. He had also helped to bring along Howe and others, and that was no mean achievement.[125]

Canada had come a long way in a few years. In the 1930s fiscal policy was closer to that of 1867, when negativism was the order of the day, than to that of the next decade. Now in 1945, thanks to the hothouse effect of the war, bold thinking had replaced negativism, and this was as true of ministers as of officials. But it was the officials who seemed to have the upper hand, for at the beginning of the postwar era, matters concerning the economy and finance were all-important, and those who understood their mysteries had power thrust upon them. Clark, Bryce, Mackintosh, and Skelton were among the few who understood Keynes; they were the keepers of the secrets, the wielders of power. Contrary to almost all predictions, the potency of the new economics these men fashioned for Canada was confirmed by a postwar boom, and with prosperity their influence was assured. The economists ruled in Ottawa.

1. *(Above)* The Department of Political Economy, Queen's University, Kingston, about 1915. O.D. Skelton is third from the left and Clifford Clark stands above him on his left.

2. *(Left)* Clifford Clark in the late 1940s.

3. O.D. Skelton in the 1930s.

4. Prime Minister Mackenzie King and Graham Towers,
Governor of the Bank of Canada, at the laying of the
cornerstone of the Bank building in August 1937.

5. Graham Towers about 1937.

6. Loring Christie about 1940.

7. O.D. Skelton and Lester Pearson on board
the *Berengaria*, en route to Canada, in the mid-1930s.

8. Lester Pearson at his desk in the Canadian High Commission, London, 1939.

9. Norman Robertson in the 1940s.

10. Hume Wrong, Canadian Ambassador to the United States, speaking in front of the United Nations building, New York, September 1947.

11. Louis Rasminsky in the 1940s.

12. W.A. Mackintosh *(left)* and Health and Welfare Minister
Brooke Claxton at the United Nations, May 1946.

13. Arnold Heeney in the late 1930s.

14. Jack Pickersgill at his desk in the Prime Minister's Office, September 1948.

15. Escott Reid *(right)* giving a newspaper interview at the United Nations, September 1947.

16. Dana Wilgress, Canadian Ambassador to the USSR, in Moscow, about 1944.

17. R.B. Bryce as Clerk of the Privy Council, August 1959.

18. Donald Gordon with his two sons in the 1940s.

19. Mitchell Sharp, April 1952.

20. A.F.W. Plumptre, September 1954.   21. John J. Deutsch, September 1953.

22. Alex Skelton in the 1940s.

ORGANIZATION AND POLITICS

Reporting in his diary on a long discussion with Skelton in March 1937, a tired Mackenzie King noted that 'we got into question of staff appointments'. He had spoken 'very plainly' to the Under-Secretary about the difficulties he suffered as a result of inadequate staff in the Prime Minister's Office and the 'little help I have received in getting it organized—also effect this was having on my usefulness—the objections that Skelton raised to suggestions generally & particularly to many matters, e.g. apptmts. whereby my own efficiency could be increased. . . .' King reflected that he might have gone further than he should have in his conversation with Skelton—'certainly further than was good for myself as it brought on anew the depression I feel. . .'[1]

That was not an unusual refrain for King, who was both the Prime Minister and Secretary of State for External Affairs. He was forever complaining about the difficulties of organizing his office and facilitating his work. In truth, the problems were real. The slapdash methods that had sufficed in the 1920s were no longer acceptable, for the role of government had expanded during the Depression, the complexity of issues had increased, and the demands on the Prime Minister's time and energy had escalated dramatically. Skelton, who had handled everything—or so it seemed—after his appointment as Under-Secretary of State for External Affairs in 1925, no longer had the time. His responsibilities in External Affairs had increased as the number of Canadian legations abroad mounted, and the gravity of the world crisis filled his days. He could still help King on special problems, but he could no longer give him his undivided attention. And, as King's biographer has noted, 'there was nobody to take his place.'[2]

After King's return to power in 1935 his office staff consisted of a private secretary, H.R.L. Henry, an assistant private secretary, E.A. Pickering, and a number of clerks and messengers. Other staff members, such as Edouard Handy and Walter Turnbull, were borrowed from government departments, and occasionally an officer from External Affairs was seconded to King's office, as happened briefly with Hugh Keenleyside and Norman Robertson. The disadvantages of a tiny staff were compounded by King's reluctance to delegate work, by his constant demands for the total attention of his staff to the problem of the moment, and by his own lack of punctuality and aversion to routine. The long hours King worked were irregular at best, and he simply failed to accept that his staff had lives and homes of their own and could not serve him at any hour on a moment's notice.[3]

King's office establishment did have provision for a Principal Secretary, someone who ideally could take over the operation and set it to rights. But King had never been able to find the right person. In fact he had not really tried. In May 1927, for example, he had approached Burgon Bickersteth, the Warden of Hart House at the University of Toronto, about 'building up a Cabinet office' and becoming 'secretary of the Cabinet'. Writing to Lord Tweedsmuir in January 1936, he told the Governor-General that 'From the first I saw great difficulties, not the least being the fact that I am English. . . . There were the further difficulties that the P.M. had not consulted the Opposition nor had he discussed the matter, except very cursorily, with the French Canadians in his own Government.' Those omissions frightened Bickersteth. He also knew the British situation well, and he knew Sir Maurice Hankey, the Royal Marine officer who had moved from a relatively unimportant job on the Committee of Imperial Defence into the Cabinet Office and who, during the Great War, had brought organizational efficiency and command of the files to a Cabinet and government desperately in need of both. Bickersteth had talked to Hankey about the Canadian problem and he also discussed it with Tom Jones, a long-time aide to a succession of United Kingdom prime ministers. After these conversations he wrote a memorandum to King about introducing certain features of the Jones-Hankey systems into Canada, but Bickersteth decided in the end not to accept the offer to join King's staff. He commented to Tweedsmuir that 'The fact that the P.M. . . . should have as his assistants merely Pickering and HRL Henry seems pathetic. Both these men are good in their own particular line, but neither is of the type to control the P.M.'s office still less to undertake the work of a cabinet office.' He concluded that 'the failure of our public men in Canada to surround themselves with really able assistants is notorious. . . . It would almost seem as if the P.M. & Cabinet Ministers were suspicious of brains in this capacity.'[4]

Tweedsmuir had already given King some advice of his own. 'Here', he wrote, 'you have no Hankey as a permanent reservoir of knowledge, and you have not a sufficiently developed Civil Service to make it easy to second the right people when you want them.' What was needed, the Governor-General said, was a permanent principal assistant to head the Prime Minister's Office, to serve as an 'intelligence officer' ready to advise the Prime Minister on anything he deemed important, and to serve as a liaison officer with the departments of the government.[5]

All this was good advice, but King still did nothing—beyond complaining—about his unhappy situation. In December 1937, while he and Skelton were on holiday in Florida, the Prime Minister observed that his Under-Secretary 'has built up a large staff & wants to increase it—with good reason perhaps. I wish, however, my own staff could be equally well organized in the first instance. Had I the equivalent in the P.M.'s Office, life would be a joy.'[6] King was particularly gloomy because Skelton had just persuaded him to release Norman Robertson from his office to permit him to return to trade-negotiation work in External Affairs, a transfer for which Robertson, no expert administrator and no admirer of King or his methods, was truly grateful. His replacement might have been expected to be a junior officer from Skelton's department, someone who would be worse than useless.

But in fact King's troubles were about to be resolved (although his complaints never ceased). The Department of External Affairs dispatched J.W. Pickersgill, one of its newest third secretaries, to fill Robertson's slot in the office,[7] and Pickersgill took to the work with an avidity that soon guaranteed him a post there for as long as he wanted it. And within six months King had found his Principal Secretary in Arnold Heeney, a Montreal lawyer, who brought organization at last to King's office and eventually to the functioning of the Cabinet as well. Just in time, too, for with the beginning of the war in September 1939 organizational efficiency became critical.

I

In some respects Arnold Heeney fitted the concept of a perfect civil-service mandarin. Tall and slender, he was extraordinarily handsome, and always dressed in expensive well-made clothes; his wife was stunningly attractive; his two children were good-looking and well behaved. There was a clergyman father, the author of several books; there was his education at Oxford on a Rhodes Scholarship, a law degree from McGill, and a blossoming career in one of the best law firms on St James Street. The background and training were perfect; Heeney seemed to the manner born and made. Yet underneath the gloss and patina provided by his upbringing and training, Arnold Heeney was both more and less than he seemed. The confident face he showed the world belied insecurities; the iron control he exercised in his dealings with his political masters masked a man who worried and fretted; and the organization that he provided to a bureaucracy desperately in need of it was matched by an almost obsessive preoccupation with planning for his own career, a characteristic that occasionally troubled his colleagues.

Arnold Danford Heeney was born on April 5, 1902 in Montreal, the son of Bertal Heeney, an Anglican priest from a modest Irish-Canadian background.[8] His father had been born at Danford Lake in the Gatineau Hills of Quebec (and had named his son after his birthplace), but rose out of his background of rural poverty by dint of intelligence and hard work; and the Anglican Church gave him a living, as well as the opportunity for frequent moves. The Heeneys travelled to Belleville and Barrie, Ont., and to Newport, Rhode Island, before they finally settled in Winnipeg, where in 1909 Heeney took charge of St Luke's Church, a new building in the Fort Rouge area. There was little money, however, and the need to keep up appearances; but somehow enough money was found to send Arnold, after his public schooling (where Maryon Moody, the future wife of Lester Pearson, was a classmate), to St John's College School in 1911. The boy fitted right into that pious and athletic atmosphere and did exceedingly well. In fourth form he won prizes in Latin and French and stood third overall; the next year he won medals in Latin, French, English, and Mathematics, and led his year. He was also a star on the playing fields as gradually his 'fear of exhibiting embarrassing incompetence diminished with experience.' It was a brilliant beginning, even if St

John's filled Heeney with too much of the *Tom Brown's Schooldays* ethos.[9]

At the University of Manitoba, where he started classes at the very end of the Great War, Heeney continued his pattern of success. Again there were prizes in French (he soon became almost bilingual) and in English, honours on the field as captain of the football team, and selection as Valedictorian of the Class of '21.[10] There was even some militia service during the Winnipeg General Strike in the summer of 1919, the subject of one of the earliest surviving letters in the Heeney Papers:

> The strike's over at last [Heeney wrote his mother at the cottage] and it can't be long now before I 'get my ticket' (probably in less than a week). I am certainly 'fed up' with the soldier's life and with guards in particular. If the strike had gone on a few days longer I would have had two stripes. . . .
>
> Last Saturday was quite exciting when the fight came off downtown I was detailed to a machine gun as a covering party. The gun (a Lewis) was mounted on a truck. We tore down town on orders about 3 p.m. at a fierce lick. The fighting was practically over and we didn't open up at all. The Mounties got all the fighting and several were badly battered up. I was down town on picket [i.e., patrol] until 11 p.m. in the pouring rain. Very exciting. Hundreds of troops, filling the main streets between the City Hall and the Post Office. . . . Mounted Police in their wonderful scarlet Mounted Rifles, Infantry with fixed bayonets, Fort Garry Horse, Ambulances, Machine Guns and Crews, 2 armoured cars . . . and even Winnipeg's only aeroplane overhead. Very grim in appearance. This display of force has broken the opposition.[11]

We can forgive the seventeen-year-old Arnold Heeney his unthinking support for constituted authority and his almost complete unawareness of the issues involved in the General Strike. But it is significant that his first involvement in public affairs was in behalf of the maintenance of order.

In his third year of university, and again in his fourth, Heeney tried unsuccessfully to win nomination as Manitoba's Rhodes Scholar. He then took a job in 1921 as a junior master at St John's, while simultaneously working for a Master's degree in English with a thesis on Rupert Brooke.[12] The next year he tried again for a Rhodes Scholarship and his persistence paid off. As he wrote his mother, this was 'an ever memorable day in which my fate was decided and when I became famous.'[13] Without the Scholarship's stipend, Heeney could not have afforded Oxford, and in a real sense his fate *was* decided—and he did become famous.

At Oxford Heeney attended St John's College and created a highly favourable reputation for himself as an athlete and club-man.[14] He studied modern history, rowed for St John's and eventually became Captain of his College's Boat Club, played rugby and hockey, became President of the Amalgam Club, chairman of the College smoker, and a member of the Junior Common Room Committee, the King Charles Dining Club, the Ralegh Club, the Colonial Club, and the Irish Society.[15] As that last membership might suggest, Heeney's Irishness blossomed at Oxford, where he became known as 'Pat' to his friends. In 1925, much to his father's horror, he even added the name Patrick to his two Christian names, and it was as Arnold Danford Patrick Heeney that he was ever afterwards known.[16]

His Oxford years were grand for Heeney. Girls aplenty flocked around the handsome athlete. There were close friends such as Norman Young, who would become Lester Pearson's brother-in-law; Norman Robertson, a British Columbia Rhodes Scholar and the son of a McGill friend of Heeney's father; and Graham Spry, soon to be the leading public-interest lobbyist in Canada. There were parties and carousing—'Cocktails before dinner at the George,' Heeney wrote in his diary,—17!'[17], and there was even some work. '. . . I like my work when I'm at it; it's the initial effort that causes all the trouble.'[18] Worrying about his grades troubled Heeney, as did his continuing doubts over his public image and self-worth. 'As usual,' he scribbled, 'I played the genial, weak ass at tea—people must think me both vacant & conceited.'[19] Worst of all was his terrible fear of failure. 'I don't see at the moment how I can possibly avoid showing myself a complete slacker and ignoramus in the Schools,' he wrote on May 30, 1925, and it was with 'Hands sticky, brow damp, desk wriggly and close by a man who walks up for his second book at half time' that he sat his examinations.[20] In the end he received a good second class—an enormous relief. 'All that worry and sweat for two years. . . .'[21] His third and final year at Oxford, during which he and Norman

His third and final year at Oxford, during which he and Norman Robertson shared 'digs', was pleasantly spent reading Roman and English law and building a reputation. (During the General Strike of 1926 that wracked England, the two took different sides, Heeney actively working in support of the government.) The confidential report on Heeney prepared by Rhodes House noted that he was 'Excellent all round. A manly fellow of good wits & sound character. Will do well.'[22] It was all true.

Heeney learned something about himself and his country at Oxford. 'No fear that I have turned Englander,' he wrote in July 1925. 'I am as much a Canadian as ever whether this is to my credit or no.' Later he added that 'I am very much of a Colonial—we can never be English if we would.'[23] Reminiscing about his former colleague, Jack Pickersgill once observed that Heeney developed his Canadianism at Oxford, 'that greatest of all schools of English Canadian nationalism.'[24]

Oxford also provided the opportunity to listen to and meet the great men of British government. In March 1925, for example, Heeney went off to the Ralegh Club to 'hear Sir Maurice Hankey on "Cabinet Procedure". Extraordinarily good and first hand.'[25] The fates must have been at play that evening: fifteen years later Heeney would be the Canadian Hankey.

Back in Canada he landed on his feet. He was accepted as an articling student by Meredith, Holden, Heward & Holden, one of Montreal's most powerful law firms, and he began attending law school at McGill. 'Very strange', he wrote his sister, 'to be a college lad again though I'm not as anxious as I used to be to produce the complete college hero from the ashes of a former self.'[26] To his mother he wrote that 'my chief delight in my new work' was 'to feel that one has some essential part to play in getting things done. . . . Without some practical outlet for my energies I am apt to become much too introspective. . . .'[27] A very revealing comment, that, on his need to organize and do things. Heeney buried himself in his texts, working late in his office, and getting involved with a group of bright young nationalists in the Canadian League that was gathering around Brooke Claxton, Eugene Forsey, and F.R. Scott.[28] He even found time to teach an American-history course at McGill, where one of his first students was Margaret Yuile, who became his wife in 1931.[29] In 1929 he graduated with his BCL and joined Meredith, Holden full time.

Heeney's career seemed to be set on a straight line to wealth and prominence. In 1931 he became president of the Montreal Junior Board of Trade; in 1934 he began to lecture in law at McGill; and later he was named counsel and secretary to the Quebec Protestant Education Survey, which was undertaking a full-scale appraisal of the minority educational system in the province. There were important clients—although these had to be competed for against other able lawyers in the firm—and a rising income that insulated the Heeneys and their boy and girl from the effects of the Depression. 'People call me lucky,' he wrote to his father on one occasion, '—but it's not luck. I thank God mightily for you my father to whom I owe and shall always owe so much more than I can ever express. . . . The greatest thing you have ever given me is the foundation of sound mental process. Pray that I may develop them in the directions you have taught me.'[30]

There was something else that Canon Heeney gave his son. He had formed a friendship with Mackenzie King, who had been impressed by his writing and came to believe that the Anglican clergyman's thinking was much the same as his own as it had been expressed in King's *Industry and Humanity* (1919).[31] Attending the Liberal Party's Summer School at Port Hope in September 1933, Heeney and his wife met King, then Leader of the Opposition, for the first time. King spoke warmly of Canon Heeney, of the 'divine guidance' there had been in their earlier meeting, and of the comfort and support the Canon had given him.[32] Over the next five years the relationship of the Heeneys, father and son, with the Liberal chief grew warmer. Canon Heeney sent King a copy of *Place and Power*, his newest book, in 1934, a gift that elicited the reply from King that he hoped 'you will continue to be indifferent to place and power. . . .'[33] Arnold, while working for the Liberal Party in Montreal St Lawrence-St George in the 1935 election, wrote about the campaign to the certain-to-be-victorious King, who replied in part: 'I hope the future may afford us many years of continued and, if possible, increasing friendship.'[34]

In 1936 King recorded in his diary: 'Had Arnold Heeney to dinner. He is a very fine looking man and I much enjoyed the talk we had together. He was most appreciative of the house. Spoke to me about his desire to enter public life or the public service notwithstanding he is making fine headway in his profession. . . . I have a great mind to bring him into my own office.'[35] But if that was King's idea, it slipped away, along with his plans for improving the organization and operation of his office.

Both Heeneys worked assiduously to keep Arnold's name before the Prime Minister. At Christmas 1936 the Canon sent his
friend a framed photograph of Arnold and his sister, and in the late
summer of 1937, when the Royal Commission on Dominion-
Provincial Relations was organizing, Canon Heeney wrote King
suggesting that his son be considered for a position with the Commission. King replied that he would put Arnold's name forward,
but with characteristic caution he said that the Commission's appointments were out of his hands.[36] Although Arnold wrote to
King to apologize for his father's request, he added that there was
'no work in which I would sooner be engaged.'[37] To his father
Arnold wrote simply that 'I have written [King] a line of thanks
myself to keep my name fresh in his mind.'[38]

Those efforts—a combined and masterfully co-ordinated operation if ever there was one—paid off handsomely in July 1938 when
Heeney visited the Prime Minister at Kingsmere on a Sunday afternoon. King later wrote to him that 'you repeated to me your
desire to become engaged in some form of public service work,
should opportunity in that direction be afforded. From what you
told me I gather you had, at one time, in mind, the possibility of
entering the diplomatic service, and that what you have more immediately in mind, at present, is the possibility of becoming a
Member of Parliament.' Clearly Heeney had been fishing, looking
for something different and more challenging than commercial
law. On that visit to King he also met Dr Skelton and talked about
his prospects, again trolling the waters to see if any fish would
take his lure.

The Prime Minister bit. After consulting Skelton, who had
been charmed by Heeney, King offered the young lawyer a plum:
the position of Principal Secretary to the Prime Minister, 'which
position would correspond in a way to that of a Deputy Head of a
Government Department . . . in immediate touch with the Prime
Minister . . . act as a liaison with other Ministers of the Crown
and exercise a general supervision over the work of the Prime
Minister's Office.' King added that he had considered Heeney for
the post some years before but had wanted to see if his present secretaries would develop and grow. 'Quite frankly, I have been disappointed in the hopes . . . I had entertained.' He finally offered
Heeney the job at a salary of $7,000, a very substantial sum for
that day. While frankly admitting that there was no guarantee of
tenure, King wrote to Heeney that Skelton believed 'we would be

justified in undertaking, should you so desire, to appoint you, prior to any general election, to a position of First Secretary in the diplomatic service.' He also pointed out that there was the prospect of becoming Ottawa's Hankey. 'I see no reason why a similar post might not be developed in Canada . . . it is the man who makes the position, not the position which makes the man.'[39]

This was exactly the kind of job for which the well-organized and well-disciplined Heeney was suited. He was attracted but also frightened, and it took him more than a month to decide. King's letter, he said to his father, was 'most flattering, extraordinarily attractive, and somewhat disturbing.'[40] What worried him was the political nature of the job. In a handwritten memorandum that was almost a military appreciation of a problem—it was the product of wide consultation with his friends—he set out his views:

> As I see it, the position should not involve participation in the activities of the Liberal or Conservative (or other) parties as such. Irrespective of the secretary's personal sympathies or previous allegiance he should, upon being appointed, discontinue connection with any political party and should thereafter be called upon to perform no duties of a partisan character.
>
> He should, therefore have no association with party whips, caucuses or officials of national or local party organizations. . . . contact [with the Prime Minister] should be clearly an association in the conduct of the business of the Cabinet and the administration of the country's affairs; it should not in any sense relate to the management of the party nor should the position constitute an adjunct to the P.M.'s personal staff. The future of the position will depend upon this distinction.[41]

Thus Heeney was thinking of a non-political civil-service role that would guarantee him tenure. But such a position was far from King's mind. What the Prime Minister wanted was someone to organize his affairs and to do his bidding; someone to travel with him on business—public, political, and personal; someone to deal with everything.

After another meeting with King on July 27, and after again consulting friends, Heeney finally wrote to King on August 24 accepting the post. He interpreted the details in a rather extraordinary and brash letter to the Prime Minister. The position was to be called Principal Secretary and the stipend to be $7,000, but since King's first offer the 'conditions have been developed and altered somewhat in the talks we have had together.'

> As soon as I am able to leave my present position I will be appointed Principal Secretary. . . . As such I will act as a liaison between the Prime Minister and the other Ministers of the Crown, assist the Prime Minister in general and particularly with the business of the Cabinet, and exercise a general supervision over the work of the Prime Minister's Office. . . .
>
> Prior to any general election I will be given the alternative of regular appointment to the permanent Civil Service either as Clerk of the Privy Council or First Secretary in the Department of External Affairs. . . . The choice between these two posts will be determined according to their suitability to the performance of those functions which you have in mind.
>
> It will be the intention to develop in Canada the kind of post formerly held in the United Kingdom by Sir Maurice Hankey namely that of Secretary to the Cabinet. While it is understood that such a position could not be brought into being at once, this objective will be kept in mind and in the event of my proving suitable, the post will be created and I will be appointed.[42]

Thus Heeney expanded the guarantees he sought. Once King accepted these terms and conditions, he was close to committing himself to the creation of a Cabinet Secretariat. In addition, Heeney had created for himself the option of becoming Clerk of the Privy Council, nominally the senior position in the public service. All that remained undefined were Heeney's duties in connection with King's political activities. This area would eventually cause problems for both master and servant.

Heeney received very soberly some advice from his father a few days after he had accepted the appointment. 'The damnation of many a politician's life', the Canon wrote, 'and the destruction of his character is the substituting of expediency for honesty. The moment a young man begins to speak half truths and to act with expediency rather than honesty he begins to tamper with his character. Your new position will expose you to the most subtle and powerful temptations on these points. But if you are as I think you are no man whatever his position or influence will suggest twice in your presence these devious and crooked ways to reach a goal.' The Canon added that his son had once told him that he had a second-class mind. He disagreed, but he told Arnold that his strength lay in his character. That was a wise letter. Arnold Heeney's strength did lie in his character, and he needed all that strength to resist the temptations his father had forewarned him of. The Canon knew Mackenzie King well.[43]

Thus Arnold Heeney became Principal Secretary to the Prime Minister. The order-in-council naming him to the post was passed on September 8, 1938 and Heeney took up his position on October 1, 1938.[44]

II

'Nothing could be more to my taste than the work I shall be called upon to do & to direct,' Heeney wrote shortly after he came to the East Block in the fall of 1938. 'By contrast the practice of law appears arid & remote from the stream of living & doing. I made no mistake in my decision. I continue to be the most fortunate of men.'[45]

That was Heeney's true opinion of his new post. On October 4, Mackenzie King took him around the office,[46] and shortly afterwards Jack Pickersgill, who had been in the Prime Minister's Office for eight or nine months as secretary, began to show his new boss the ropes. 'My salary was $2,280,' Pickersgill remembered, 'but Mackenzie King found no incongruity in asking me to initiate Heeney into his new duties.'[47] Heeney himself wrote his parents that he had spent the first two weeks getting to know how the office functioned and acquainting himself with the staff who 'have been kindness itself, which considering my introduction to their midst as their untried chief, has been very gratifying.' He added that 'The variety of work . . . is astounding from the selection & clipping of important items from the whole Canadian (& much of the non-Canadian) press & its circulation to the secretaries to the drafting of correspondence for Mr King's signature to Provincial Premiers and others. . . . The preparation of messages upon national occasions, correspondence with the departments of government, drafting of addresses, arrangements for hearing deputations, and many minor tasks keep the staff in almost continuous activity. My own work', he went on, 'will consist first of organization or reorganization of the office & its subsequent supervision (it is already clear to me that a "head" has long been lacking), second my own particular work will be the preparation for Cabinet

meetings (by briefing the P.M. on subjects to be on the agenda) &
subsequent carrying out of decisions reached (by correspondence
with depts. involved etc).'[48]

In fact, as Heeney wrote in 1946, matters were more complicated, particularly insofar as the work of the Cabinet was concerned. There was no fixed or written agenda other than the order
of business the Prime Minister kept in his head and altered to suit
his convenience. There were no minutes, there were no officials in
the Cabinet room, except on rare occasions, and there was no record of conclusions, except as King told Heeney of them. In short,
the business of the nation was handled with an inefficiency that
would discredit the meanest parish-pump council.[49] In 1935 the
electorate had been told that the choice was 'King or chaos'; in the
conduct of government, it had got both.

Heeney was unable to alter matters immediately. The Prime
Minister worried, naturally enough, that by changing and sys-
tematizing the procedures he was accustomed to, his and his predecessors' methods might be destroyed and his own power to
direct and shape the policy of his government minimized. Nonetheless Heeney was usually brought into the meetings of the Cabinet Sub-Committee on Defence from November 14, 1938 as
Canada struggled to prepare for a war that all could see was approaching but that all still hoped might be averted.[50] It fascinated
Heeney to be situated at 'the ever-rotating hub of a wheel which
never stops',[51] but occasional exasperation with King—who
blocked the reforms that he could see were essential—crept in.
'. . . Mr. King,' he wrote to his father, 'by long habit' is not 'the
easiest person for whom to work. . . .'[52]

Quite apart from his well-known lack of consideration for his
staff, Mackenzie King was exerting pressure on Heeney to involve
himself in Liberal affairs. Party officials probably were unaware
that Heeney wanted to deal with public business only. Thus, in
April 1939, Norman Lambert, the head of the National Liberal
Federation and the effective director of the party's organization
and election campaigns, talked with Heeney about the political situation in Ontario, where the maverick Liberal premier, Mitchell
Hepburn, was causing political and organizational chaos. A few
months later Lambert wrote in his diary that he 'Told Heeney the
implications of the Trinity [a Toronto constituency] patronage situation; and said that I could not be responsible for Toronto organization under these circumstances.'[53]

Patronage questions involved greasing the wheels of the Liberal party and had little to do with such questions as, for example, the determination of a grain policy for Canada. The difference was clear, and Heeney's concern over the way party matters impinged upon him may be why he launched a campaign to remind King that he had promised him the position of Clerk of the Privy Council before the general election that was fast approaching. If the Liberals lost, Heeney must have feared, that promise—and his present job—would be worthless. On June 23, 1939, the Prime Minister noted that he had talked over Heeney's claim with Ernest Lapointe, the Minister of Justice and his closest colleague. 'I found him greatly taken by surprise and inclined to be strongly opposed. He wanted a French Canadian . . . I told him frankly that I must select my own deputy, and think the office had to be differently managed, that I had secured Heeney on promise of this post, could not have got along without him, & needed him to manage Council affairs. . . .' That was flattering to Heeney, even though his campaign had irritated King, who did not like being pushed: 'What annoyed me today was Arnold's pressing to be appointed at once & Lemaire [the then Clerk of the Privy Council—an efficient clerk with little interest in policy] wishing his retirement announced July 1. They have been working together, without my ever having said to Lemaire who I had in mind to succeed him. . . .'[54]

Heeney returned to the charge in a long memorandum to King on July 25 in which he argued that the intention to make him Clerk necessitated a reorganization of the Prime Minister's Office. 'The Prime Minister', he wrote, 'has remarked that a substantial proportion of the work at present done by the Prime Minister's secretariat might quite properly be carried on by the Clerk of the Privy Council, or under his direction.' He agreed, Heeney wrote, citing the preparation of material for the Prime Minister and Cabinet, the receipt and passing on of instructions after Cabinet meetings, official correspondence, and the like. 'In fact, the Office of the Clerk of the Privy Council now provides the legal machinery which, by practise and use under the proper guidance and as time goes on, might quite well develop a secretariat for the Cabinet which would be able to take over much that now occupies such a considerable amount of the time and energy of the members of the Prime Minister's staff. The Prime Minister's staff', Heeney argued cleverly, 'would thus be relieved for other work' of a political nature.[55] Although Heeney later gave credit for suggesting the development of the Cabinet secretariat to Dr Skelton, the idea was probably his.[56]

On August 22, after a 'bronzed' Heeney returned from a holiday, he was as anxious as ever to secure his position as Clerk of the Privy Council and even decided to modify his opposition to doing party work. He told King, as the Prime Minister later recorded, 'that he had been thinking over the talk I had with him before he went away. . . . Was quite prepared to do anything I wished in the matter of the political tour or anything else. . . . He revealed a fine spirit.'[57] Heeney had apparently expressed his willingness, just before the beginning of the war, to assist in political activities. The Prime Minister had seemingly extracted a *quid* for his *quo*.

The war saved Heeney from dirtying his hands with politics because it increased his workload massively. The Cabinet seemed to sit continuously, the special session of Parliament called early in September ate into his time, correspondence multiplied, and a number of Cabinet committees were struck of which one was crucial. Initially called the 'Emergency Council' but soon to be reconstituted (on December 5, 1939) as the Cabinet War Committee, this group of powerful ministers gradually assumed effective control of Canada's war and, over the course of its 343 meetings,[58] of the operations of the government of Canada. From the beginning Heeney usually attended these meetings, sometimes with Dr Skelton. If Skelton was present and Heeney not, then he informed Heeney of decisions. If neither attended, then King told his Principal Secretary what had taken place—or as much as he wanted him to know.[59]

That makeshift procedure was roughly similar to the pre-war Cabinet practice, but now it was completely unacceptable as a way of handling government business. Indeed, even before the War Committee had taken form Heeney had begun to press for more organization and co-ordination. 'One method that might be followed', he wrote, 'would be to require Ministers to give notice of their intention to bring a subject up, and the preparation, as a result of notice, of an agenda which could be put into the hands of all Ministers at the beginning of each meeting.' It was important to keep a careful record of decisions made, which should be supplemented by 'an adequate system of follow up which will give a reasonable assurance that appropriate action is being taken.' Heeney also suggested that the positions of Principal Secretary and Clerk of the Privy Council be combined so he would be in a 'much better position to keep himself informed of what the government were actually doing from day to day. . . . ' This arrangement might lead to the development of an administrative organization that could better handle the work.[60]

Again events conspired to delay any major alterations in organization and procedure. This time it was King's decision to call a snap election. On January 19, 1940, King wrote that 'I told Arnold I had decided to bring on the elections at once. He seemed dumbfounded. . . .'[61] Well he might have, for the election raised anew the question of political work. Precisely what followed remains unclear. Certainly Norman Lambert continued to discuss political questions with the Principal Secretary,[62] but somehow Heeney managed to avoid travelling with King on the campaign trail. He told his parents that 'I'd as soon avoid any overt campaign activities and remain in charge of the office . . .' Instead Pickersgill, although he was every bit as much a civil servant as Heeney—indeed more so, for he had been seconded from External Affairs and had entered that department via examination—happily took on the chore and did it well.[63]

Heeney continued to fret and worry about his future. However, to the Prime Minister's credit and to Heeney's great relief, King lived up to his pledge to make him Clerk of the Privy Council. It was not until March 13, less than two weeks before election day, March 26, that King told him that he proposed to make the appointment on March 22.[64] On that day King recorded his annoyance at the way Heeney had drafted the order-in-council for his appointment and he was annoyed again by Heeney's attitude that 'party politics is something with which it is not well to have oneself too closely identified. . . . He is an exceedingly lucky man to get this post,' King wrote, 'though I believe exceptionally well qualified for it. . . .'*[65] The order went through, appointing Heeney Clerk of the Privy Council and Secretary to the Cabinet at a salary of $9,000.[66] The latter post was a bonus, a chance to become in fact what Heeney had wanted to be: Canada's Hankey. After King's electoral triumph, however, the Prime Minister took the gloss off this appointment:

---

* General Maurice Pope, who worked closely with Heeney during the war, later said that 'Arnold came into the Prime Minister's Office as a Crown Prince and he'd never served that apprenticeship and to my mind that always showed in Arnold's attitude, opinions and work.' (Department of External Affairs, Pope interview, 28-9 June, 1977).

I told him that he must regard his appointment as Secretary of the Cabinet as simply additional duties to those of Clerk of the Council, not as a creation of some new post. I told him later tonight, in Skelton's presence, that the feeling of Cabinet was against having any Secretary of the Cabinet and that the feeling was that he should have started at the same salary . . . $7000. . . . Ralston [Minister] of Finance had helped me out in getting for him [$9000] by suggesting the insertion on the Order of the additional duties of Secretary of the Cabinet, which I had spoken of as involving additional work etc. I am a little disappointed in Heeney's emphasis upon position, appearances, etc., and desire to rush everything at once. Quite the opposite of the kind of true greatness one sees exemplified in a man like Skelton.[67]

Nonetheless both Heeney and his parents were delighted. Canon Heeney wrote to say he was 'so thankful for the permanency of your post and the scope for your . . . efforts & service. Also for the increase in salary, . . .'[68] And despite King's caution about the additional post as Secretary of the Cabinet, Heeney was now in a position to bring order to the operations of the War Committee. This he set to with a will.

Heeney began to take minutes of the War Committee meetings.[69] As he told his father soon after his appointment, 'I have been dictating draft minutes . . . all afternoon. To-morrow they will be revised, sent to the P.M. and letters written to Ministers and others concerned in decisions to be taken. Yesterday the whole afternoon was taken up in the meeting itself. To a greater & greater extent the War Committee absorbs my time.'[70] As the drafter (and keeper) of the minutes, Heeney became the War Committee's memory. Pierrepont Moffat, the American Minister to Canada, was told by Heeney that 'with growing frequency he had to intervene in the debate and point out that some decision just taken was contrary to previous recorded decisions on policy.'[71] These occasions were caused by the pressure of events, for the most part, but they were also due to King's lack of, and aversion to, system. Heeney wrote that Mackenzie King 'continues to rely on instinct and gets very tired—he is infinitely less systematic than Brian'—Heeney's son, who was not yet in his teens.[72]

Heeney's reorganization of the work of the Cabinet was essential and he pressed ahead. The new Secretary of the Cabinet in Britain, Sir Edward Bridges, offered advice, as did Lord Hankey.[73]

After King made his first wartime visit to Britain in September 1941, he told the War Committee how Churchill's War Cabinet functioned. A printed agenda, along with relevant papers, was circulated before each meeting and the Prime Minister conferred with ministers about matters they wished to raise. A record of 'conclusions' was maintained.[74]

That system was almost completely in operation in Ottawa. Reluctantly King had agreed to an agenda in the spring of 1940; he also agreed, but with trepidation, that it might be circulated in advance. Eventually memoranda, telegrams, and papers were attached to the agenda to provide necessary detail. Heeney had the minutes indexed and filed by his first Cabinet Secretariat assistant, James Conacher;[75] the papers that helped shape decisions were also kept on file. But not until April 1940, when Heeney began to be present at every meeting by right, was there any certainty that the conclusions of the War Committee were understood by all; and not until then could anyone check that decisions had been implemented. The development of these practices, Heeney wrote later, 'was essentially a pragmatic process, involving much trial and error, particularly at first. The objective was an uncomplicated practical régime of procedure combining flexibility and precision and capable of enabling Ministers to deal with a heavy volume of important business promptly and efficiently.'[76]

The war increased the government's—and Heeney's—work, and his staff began to grow. Initially Heeney seems to have served as secretary to all Cabinet committees. He also participated in a number of officials' committees—including the Economic Advisory Committee, the key advisers' group in Ottawa—as a member in his own right.[77] His time and strength were not infinite, however, and gradually he added officers to the Cabinet secretariat, including a deputy Secretary to the Cabinet who could attend War Committee meetings and take minutes in his absence. As Heeney told an American team (including the political scientist V.O. Key) investigating the organization of the Canadian war effort in 1943, he had a staff of forty or fifty, with six or eight officers, including such able men as John Baldwin and Jean Chapdelaine. Few of Heeney's officers were formally associated with the Cabinet secretariat or the Privy Council Office; most were simply seconded from government departments.[78] 'The "professional" members of the staff serve as secretaries of some, but not all, of the interdepartmental committees', the American investigators noted.[79] They set and prepared agendas, gathered information from departments, prepared reports and memoranda for circulation, and kept minutes and records of conclusions. The Americans learned that 'In the selection of his staff Mr Heeney has chosen "Generalists" with historical and economic training rather than technical experts. He has sought persons with personal characteristics enabling them to sit in with the top level committee . . . with broad analytical ability rather than persons with operating proclivities or particular technical backgrounds.' The Americans also found that 'He will not assign a man solely to deal with particular agencies; rather a man is assigned to deal primarily with a particular subject-matter field, no matter where it leads him within the government structure.' By 1944 the military secretariat of the Chiefs of Staff Committee had been integrated with Heeney's secretariat, giving him virtual control over the funnelling upward to the Cabinet War Committee of policy and military advice.

Thus Heeney's role and power had increased substantially. As his men played indispensable roles as secretaries of the key committees of officials and ministers, he became the government's helpful fixer, able to spot difficulties at an early stage and overcome them. There was opportunity to facilitate meetings between representatives of warring departments, or to advise a minister that his department's policy was causing problems for another department. He could take the initiative in advising a department or agency of the need for action in a certain area; and he could help kill bureaucratic (or even ministerial) initiatives that seemed to him unlikely to prove useful.[80] Of course the exercise of this role required tact and care, for ministers were notoriously jealous of their prerogatives—none more so than the Prime Minister. For example, in February 1941 an angry King blasted Heeney:

Before the meeting of Council, I spoke with Heeney about having taken in hand this morning the swearing in of deCarteret [as Deputy Minister of National Defence (Air)] and going to the Chateau [Laurier] for the purpose without conferring with me. In other words, taking instructions from Power [Minister of National Defence (Air)] instead of myself on a matter for which I was responsible and concerning which I would have adopted a different course. I also expressed surprise at his having, as my Deputy, let an order go before the Cabinet respecting the appointment of Deputy Minister of Transport which was in the nature of a recom-

mendation from myself without my being present, and
which had resulted in conflict in Council. . . .

I also expressed surprise that he had never spoken to me
about the intention of the Minister of Justice to have him
[Heeney] made K.C. and presenting the order to the Cabinet
which he, himself, must have prepared without ever letting
me know of its existence. I said I thought he had meant well
in all these things but that clearly it was not the kind of a
thing that could continue if I was to be held responsible for
these matters. . . .[81]

Such conflicts were not abnormal. Heeney's task was to make
King's work easier, and occasionally he overstepped King's
bounds. As for Heeney's designation as a King's Counsel, this
tended to confirm the Prime Minister's view that 'Arnold's character discloses a defect which one regrets to see. He is very selfish
and ambitious in ways that one is sorry to notice in so fine a type
of man.'[82] King, of course, spotted defects in others faster than in
himself, but he had correctly assessed Heeney's self-interest and
ambition. Later, at the time of the great conscription crisis in the
fall of 1944, in which Heeney worked tirelessly to serve the Prime
Minister, King again complained about the way Heeney had interpreted the minutes of the Cabinet War Committee, 'far too often
keeping out the vigour of my protests against courses being taken
. . . soft-pedalled anything by way of criticism on my part of the
action of some of the Ministers to the lengths to which they were
going. I am sure Heeney must now see wherein it would have
been much wiser and more helpful to have given always the
proper emphasis.'[83] Perhaps, but had such emphasis been present
in other ministers' remarks, it was just as likely that King could
have objected on the opposite grounds.

Nonetheless, however much he complained, King realized the
value of Heeney's organized and efficient work. And in February
1946, as Heeney recorded in his memoirs, the Prime Minister
staged an elaborate dinner at Laurier House to honour him and
Norman Robertson, Heeney's friend at Oxford and the Under-
Secretary of State for External Affairs. In the presence of the two
senior officials' parents and wives, King 'rose to his feet and em-
barked upon an extravagant and lengthy paean of praise for Norman and me. . . . "Never," he finally concluded, "would I have
been able to endure the heavy burdens of office at a time of war

had it not been for Norman and Arnold".' The wives, aware how King had abused their husbands, were not impressed, but the parents beamed. Heeney thought the praise was perfectly genuine. So it should have been, for Heeney's disciplined efforts at organizing the business of government had made the difference between efficiency and confusion at the top.[84]

Fortunately Heeney was able to persuade King that the methods established for the War Committee should be carried over to the peacetime Cabinet.[85] Major questions now were to come to the whole Cabinet at its regular weekly meeting; there was to be an agenda, the circulation of papers, and records made of Cabinet conclusions. In addition, deputy ministers or expert officials were permitted to attend Cabinet meetings when necessary, as well as Cabinet committees.[86]

Almost single-handedly Heeney had carried the Canadian government into the modern era. On Heeney's death in 1970, Gordon Robertson, the Clerk of the Privy Council, wrote: 'It was he who designed the machine that co-ordinates all the vital decisions of government . . . the basic design is unchanged because he designed it so well.'[87] In the process of doing this, Heeney had converted the Privy Council Office from a minor functionary's post into an executive secretaryship that handled the whole range of government business. He made the Clerk of the Privy Council and the Secretary to the Cabinet the invaluable servant of Prime Ministers, ministers, and the government, as well as an official with significant power in his own right. And Heeney established the non-partisan nature of the joint post, making its incumbent a civil servant like the others. While he dealt with policy, associated closely with politicians, and served the government of the day to the best of his ability, he himself remained strictly non-political. This characteristic of the Secretary's role was absolutely critical (even if it did not prove to be permanent) and enabled Heeney—who had become the government's organizational expert and continued to serve in senior posts well into the 1960s—to work smoothly with Canadian politicians whatever their political coloration.

III

Although he was as much a civil servant as Heeney, no one would have said that John Whitney Pickersgill was not political or partisan. Assigned temporarily to the Prime Minister's Office from the Department of External Affairs at the end of 1937, Pickersgill provided the benefits of his very great intelligence and knowledge, a facile mind, and an abiding interest in matters political to both Mackenzie King and Louis St Laurent from that time until 1952, when he became Clerk of the Privy Council. After holding that post, the pre-eminent one in the public service, for only a brief period, Pickersgill entered the Cabinet and active politics. In the process, he probably dealt the concept of a non-partisan, non-political civil service a body blow as severe as any it had suffered since Lester Pearson left the Department of External Affairs to enter the Cabinet in 1948.

One of the most engaging and able men of his time in Ottawa, Jack Pickersgill was born in Wyecombe, Ont., in 1905, the eldest son in a family of English and Loyalist stock. His parents moved to Manitoba in 1907, first to Cartwright on the Prairies six miles from the United States border, where his father's parents and brothers had already settled, then in 1911 to the bush country between Lake Winnipeg and Lake Manitoba, in an area that had been opened up for homesteading only the year before. The Pickersgill property was adjacent to the railway station at Ashern where Pickersgill's father and a partner started a country store and where his father served as postmaster while the family simultaneously tried to create a farm out of bush. In 1916 his father enlisted in the army and served in France with the 16th Canadian Scottish. He was invalided home in 1918, his health broken, and he died a too-early death in 1920. His wife, a trained nurse and one-time school teacher, was left with five children. This tough and frugal woman kept the family together and managed, with the help of her eldest son, Jack, to encourage all her children to get through university at a time when only a tiny percentage of high-school students proceeded to tertiary education. Naturally enough his mother had the greatest influence on Pickersgill. 'The most impressive lesson she taught me', he remembered later, 'was to accept nothing on faith, but to prove all things. . . .'[88] Eventually that made Pickersgill an agnostic; by the time he was twenty he had also begun to move away from the Tory traditions on which he had been bred.

His schooling took place initially in Ashern's one-room schoolhouse, and while that system stultified some students, Pickersgill thrived on it, aided and abetted by his mother's encouragement. Pickersgill's mother sold milk in the village and Jack delivered it in the evening. But since no French was taught in the one-room school, and since Pickersgill had to pass his first two years of high school there, his mother arranged for an Acadian woman who had been a teacher in New Brunswick to tutor the boy in French each evening in return for free milk. This grounding in French served Pickersgill well. Like Heeney, he eventually became reasonably fluent in the language.

After high school Pickersgill went to the University of Manitoba in Winnipeg where, predictably, he did well. After history courses from Chester Martin, and daily exposure to John W. Dafoe's editorials in the *Free Press*, he took his B.A. in 1926. The class yearbook saluted him by noting that 'Even though vanquished he could argue still,' a comment applicable to his whole career. So too was this appraisal from *The Brown and Gold* of the University of Manitoba: 'The power behind the throne has been felt in the many activities of our four-year term.'[89]

Pickersgill took his Master's degree in history at Manitoba in 1927 under Martin, and that year he won an IODE fellowship that allowed him to go to New College, Oxford, for two years. There he read history and developed his interest in France, particularly in the politics of the Second Empire. The opportunity to visit France on his 'vacs' also appealed, and Pickersgill developed an abiding love for the country, something that he communicated to his younger brother Frank. But although he qualified for his B.A. and B.Litt. at Oxford, Pickersgill did not take his degrees—he could not afford to pay the fees. Not until 1953, in fact, did Pickersgill pay the £9 12s. for his B.Litt.: it was covered by £10 caution money that he learned from the Warden had been on the books of his College for a quarter-century.[90] That must have amused the tight-fisted Clerk of the Privy Council. He refused, however, to pay the same fee for his B.A.

That combination of frugality and need persisted after Pickersgill found a teaching job in the history department at Wesley College, Winnipeg, in 1929. He was hired as the second member of a two-man department, the other instructor being Arthur R.M. Lower, who was taken on at the same time. Pickersgill's appointment was something in the nature of a compromise between factions on the College Board, particularly as one Board member had insisted on the post's going to his son. In the end, Pickersgill got the nod. Wesley's president, the Reverend J.H. Riddell, told Lower that he was 'a very bright young fellow and has given a

splendid account of himself in his studies. His whole background
of training is such as will, I think, make an efficient lecturer. . . . The adjustment of your work will rest between the
two of you.' Riddell added that if Pickersgill failed to work out, he
could be let go, 'for Pickersgill is a young man with no definite at-
tachments or burdens.'[91]

In fact Lower and his young colleague became fast friends, sharing their office and all their courses and students. They offered
courses in seven different fields of history and instructed between
270 and 365 students each year through the mid-thirties, an extraordinary teaching load and range by today's more effete standards.[92] By Lower's account Pickersgill was a good teacher, who
was popular with his students and colleagues, and who took an active part in the life of the college and city. Indeed, because the
Pickersgill family house—their mother having moved to the city
in 1926—served as a Wesley meeting place, he probably knew
more students socially than most instructors.[93] In 1936 Pickersgill
and Lower helped their students organize a foreign-policy ballot,
which demonstrated that a majority favoured severing Canada's
tie with the Empire if that was the only way to keep Canada out of
war.[94] Certainly this was Pickersgill's own view, for the youthful
Tory had turned into an ardent nationalist (although Lower
grumpily remembered that, by comparison with him, Pickersgill
was still soft on the Empire).[95] In April 1936, for example, Pickersgill wrote tartly to Frank Underhill, the University of Toronto
historian and nationalist-neutralist, to complain about an article
Underhill had published in the *Canadian Forum*. 'Why', Pickersgill
wrote, 'must you destroy the usefulness of your argument by saying "of course, if we try to stay out of Europe, we shall drift into
the orbit of the United States." ' That upset Pickersgill, who
found such an attitude 'despicable'. 'Why can't we stand on our
own feet for a change? I can see no disgrace or dishonour in being
a small nation without any real international responsibilities, and
enjoying the considerable advantages which the frank acceptance
of that position would give us both practically and psychologi-
cally.' Pickersgill said he rebelled against being forced to be imperialist or internationalist or pacifist or continentalist. 'I merely
want to be a Canadian and I don't see why it is impossible.'[96] He
expressed similar views in the Winnipeg-branch meetings of the
Canadian Institute of International Affairs, where he met Dafoe of
the *Free Press* and the group of able men that great editor had attracted to him.

The young professor continued to work on French history, but his scholarly writing—not very extensive—focused on more contemporary subjects. In 1931 he published an article in the *Dalhousie Review* on French foreign policy;[97] and in 1939, after he had left Wesley, his article on 'The Front Populaire and the French Elections of 1936' appeared in the *Political Science Quarterly* (New York).[98] But he was increasingly drawn to Canadian affairs and politics, and his first article on that subject appeared in the *Canadian Forum* in April 1935, when that journal was briefly under Liberal control. 'The Decay of Liberalism' looked at the decline of that creed throughout the world, but its message was aimed directly at Canadians. Liberalism, Pickersgill argued, had survived in North America only because 'it is the only type of conservatism to which North Americans can turn. But', he said, 'when Liberalism ceases to be radical, it ceases to be vital.' Pickersgill clearly saw himself as a radical and a Liberal, one who sought a society in which the 'socialist aspiration after individual and social security may be, somehow, combined with the Liberal devotion to the preservation of sufficient liberty to permit of genuine individuality.'[99]

Pickersgill had personal reasons for being concerned about security. In 1932 President Riddell had informed his young history instructor that he wanted his post for his son Gerry, a former student of Pickersgill, who had sent him to New College, Oxford, with strong recommendations.[100] To his great credit Pickersgill resisted the attempt to drive him out to satisfy Riddell's nepotism. In tough interviews and in a brilliant letter he outfaced Riddell. The President had speciously argued that the appointment of his son would serve the interests of the College and said that 'the welfare of an institution was greater than that of its members'. Pickersgill countered this self-serving twaddle with the respectful argument that he doubted 'whether the principle of reasonable security of tenure for its staff could be compensated for by an incidental advantage.' The President was forced to concede that the historian need not in fact look for another position. Lower marvelled at Pickersgill's courage, particularly as there was no way of blocking the President from bringing his son (who knew nothing of this, and who, during the war and after, had a distinguished career in the Department of External Affairs) into the College if he chose.[101]

This incident made Pickersgill realize that he had little future at Wesley, although he hung on for five years more during the Depression. His salary was only $2,300 by 1937, but even that was a purely nominal figure because the college deficit was pro-rated and faculty salaries were reduced accordingly[102]—although his take-home pay permitted a car and a cottage at Lake of the Woods.[103] In the circumstances—and particularly as he had married Beatrice Young, the daughter of a Winnipeg doctor, in the summer of 1936—other work looked attractive. On the advice of Dafoe (and presumably with his support and strong recommendation),[104] he wrote the examinations for the Department of External Affairs in the fall of 1936, though he did so a shade reluctantly: 'there's no question in my mind', he said later, 'that my true vocation was teaching and I would never have left the University if the salaries had been decent.'[105]

In April 1937, unaware of how well he had done on the written examinations, Pickersgill went to Ottawa to sit for the Department's orals. As he wrote Lower on April 22, he had learned unofficially from James Stitt, a Civil Service Commissioner and a former Manitoba Conservative M.P. who had become a friend, that he had placed first on the written papers with 82.33 per cent and had 'made the best impression in the interviews', not least on the French-speaking member of the panel who had been pleased with Pickersgill's fluency in French.[106] Pickersgill wrote Lower to say that he would not return to Wesley in September. But he did not want to resign without formal assurance of the government post, which was delayed for months by Skelton's attendance at the Coronation and the Imperial Conference of 1937, by the snail-like procedures of the Department and the Civil Service Commission, and finally by Skelton's serious illness in the early fall of 1937. Meanwhile his friend Lower was unable to proceed with a new appointment and President Riddell fulminated at Pickersgill's planned desertion of Wesley.[107] By September the College had to secure a replacement and Pickersgill was cut adrift, still uncertain of his future. This was a serious difficulty because he had travelled to France with his wife during the summer and the Pickersgills had neither money nor a place to live. The Acting Under-Secretary in Skelton's absence, Laurent Beaudry, was indecisive; Norman Robertson was sympathetic (he offered Pickersgill a loan) but powerless; and the Pickersgills struggled to avert destitution. Finally on October 14, 1937, a year after he had written External Affairs' examinations, Pickersgill was hired as a Third Secretary in the Department and reported for work in the East

Block.[108] His salary was $2,280. As Pickersgill later recollected, it was a long time before he recovered financially from that trip to France and that uncomfortable period between jobs. But as his wife died suddenly in January 1938, he never begrudged the trip or the enjoyable if penurious days in Ottawa he had shared with her.[109]

IV

In the fall of 1937 the Department of External Affairs was still tiny. It employed fewer than twenty officers in Ottawa, and while some of them—O.D. Skelton, Loring Christie, and Norman Robertson, for example—worked extraordinarily long hours wrestling with intractable problems, others—either because Skelton believed them less able, or because fate had assigned them more manageable subjects—were far from overworked. Pickersgill was introduced to an easy-going Department. He remembered that soon after he arrived, one senior colleague advised him to read the *New York Times* before settling down to decode the night's cable traffic. Most of the cables, he said casually, found their way into the paper.[110] Pickersgill's first area of responsibility had to do with a mundane question involving shipping with New Zealand. Perhaps because his assignments lacked urgency, and he did not want to arrive at the office before the secretarial staff, he never reported for work before 10 a.m.

But the soft life soon ended. In December John Read, the Department's Legal Adviser and the Acting Under-Secretary while Skelton was in Florida on holiday with Mackenzie King, came into Pickersgill's office to tell him that he had been assigned to the Prime Minister's Office as a Secretary in place of Norman Robertson, whose skills Skelton needed to handle trade negotiations with the British and Americans. Read told the new recruit that he 'had been chosen as a sacrifice'. 'But,' he added, 'you won't last six weeks; no one does.'[111]

Pickersgill went to the Prime Minister's Office at a time when, as we have seen, King was unhappy with his staff and with the organization of his work; there was a place for an industrious hand. Although Pickersgill began with relatively simple tasks—keeping watch on the hearings of the Royal Commission on Dominion-Provincial Relations—he was already a bear for work. He dug in, but he felt he was almost invisible; his contacts with the Prime Minister were minimal. He did not meet him until the day after his wife died, when King offered condolences; the next meeting was three months later. But in the summer of 1938 E.A. Pickering, the number two in the office, left. King summoned Pickersgill, told him that he knew he had been doing most of the work in the Office, and asked him to take over the second position in the Office 'until I can get a competent secretary.'[112] Pickersgill accepted and continued as second-in-command after Heeney arrived as Principal Secretary in the fall of 1938. The new régime ran a happier office, without the Byzantine plotting that had characterized earlier years.

So Pickersgill became established in the Prime Minister's Office. As a recent widower—he remained so until June 1939 when he married Margaret Beattie, the sister of his old Winnipeg friend J.R. Beattie who had come to Ottawa with the Bank of Canada—he had almost no social life (although his roommate, James Coyne of the Bank of Canada, also from Winnipeg, tried to prevent him from becoming a recluse), and until Heeney became head of the office Pickersgill immersed himself in work. He thrived on the load that was dumped on him and he proved unusually capable of withstanding King's assaults on his patience and time. Pickersgill was even able to become involved in a host of extraneous issues and to make friends across higher levels of the public service. One friend was Loring Christie, the Counsellor in External Affairs and by this time as strong a nationalist and neutralist as Pickersgill himself. An acquaintance was Clifford Clark, the Deputy Minister of Finance, who found himself obliged to produce a four-page response to a lengthy memorandum of Pickersgill's advocating federal government responsibility for unemployment relief.[113] Occasionally Pickersgill had to take on chores for Skelton as well as King.[114]

The Prime Minister quickly discovered that he had found a man who shared many of his own opinions about Canadian policy and had few qualms about expressing disagreement if required. 'Discussed with Heeney and Pickersgill statement re Canada being at war when Britain at war', King wrote in his diary of one typical discussion on January 20, 1939. 'Pickersgill thought it an "appalling" statement. Returned to point of view declared by Laurier which he thought represented a colonial attitude.'[115] Such a response to the Prime Minister's views could never have come from Heeney, who was smoother, more tactful, and less definite in his nationalist views than Pickersgill. Surprisingly King did not fly into a rage at the young man's temerity. He soon came to rely on Pickersgill more and more, particularly as Heeney continued to balk at handling political matters. On August 11, 1939, for example, the Prime Minister discussed the coming election campaign with Pickersgill. 'I found him very willing to do anything that he could do, and would fit in anywhere. He has first-class ability,' King purred. 'He told me of the Committee of the Cabinet [working on election preparations] wanting to have him join them in preparing statement of party policy, but I told him that was a thing I did not expect or want him to do. I want him to devote his time exclusively to me and the needs of my office.' King added that Pickersgill 'has come into a close confidential relationship, and I feel a good deal of confidence in his judgment as a young man . . .'[116] King no doubt concluded that as Heeney was unwilling to undertake political work, he could fall back on Pickersgill to do it.

Initially Pickersgill had some qualms about working on political questions, but he checked with Skelton, who told him that it was his duty to do whatever the Prime Minister wanted, 'so long as it did not involve making public speeches or statements on my own.'[117] Pickersgill later argued that in Canada the private secretary fills a unique position 'in the never-never land between the worlds of politicians and proper bureaucrats',[118] but it was the circumstance of his willingness to respond to King's needs on the political front—as well as the advice of his Deputy Minister—that put Pickersgill into this never-never land. He saw that the political work had to be done, did it well, and quickly became the Jack of all trades and master of most.

Pickersgill's capacity for work and his talents as an adviser made him invaluable to King once the war began. Pickersgill suffered over Canada's decision to enter the war.[119] As a civil servant he had to remain silent—he referred to himself as one of the 'castrati' in a private letter to Frank Underhill, adding that 'the essential Peace Aim of Canada should be to get completely free of the British connection!'[120] But he did his job nonetheless, helping King keep tabs on the Quebec election of 1939 and above all helping the Prime Minister with almost every aspect of the election campaign of 1940. King should have been pleased. But when, after election day, and after Heeney had become Clerk of the Privy Council, Pickersgill left for a week's holiday, the Prime Minister viewed this brief absence almost as a personal affront and made Walter

Turnbull, an officer on loan from the Post Office Department, the Principal Secretary, leaving Pickersgill as the assistant. Turnbull remembered that Pickersgill was white-faced and tight-lipped when he learned of this change on his return. However, Pickersgill said that he could work for Turnbull, though he could never have worked for any other. Turnbull also remembered King's having remarked that Pickersgill was too irresponsible to be placed in charge of the office.[121] Pickersgill later recalled that 'I just went on doing the work I had been doing and always communicated directly with Mackenzie King never through Turnbull.' Then he amended this statement: 'That's not totally true because he would telephone Turnbull in the morning and say would you ask Pickersgill to do so and so but about my work there was no question of Turnbull being an intermediary the way Pickering had been or even the way Arnold was.' Pickersgill soon came to feel fortunate that he had not become head of the office: 'I dealt with Mackenzie King direct but I didn't have all the day-to-day irritations.' If he had had the title, he probably could not have survived the war and King's demands; without it, he was able to remain in the backrooms and do the work.[122]

His activities touched on almost every aspect of domestic politics and war policy. Little stands out because Pickersgill worked day-by-day with King, suggesting a change of phrase in a statement today, arguing for a specific action tomorrow, and urging delay the next day. It was not glamorous work, but it was essential, and the Prime Minister came increasingly to rely on Pickersgill's judgement. For example, when Germany declared war on the United States after Pearl Harbor, Pickersgill helped King draft the government's statement welcoming the Americans as an ally in the war against Germany.[123] He worked closely with the Prime Minister on all matters concerning conscription, the subject that preoccupied King more than any other throughout the war and one on which Pickersgill held strong anti-conscriptionist views. Occasionally he tried too hard to press his nationalism on King and his concern that French Canada not be unfairly treated. In June 1942, for instance, at a time when the debate over Bill 80 took every minute of the Prime Minister's time, Pickersgill tried to secure the inclusion of a phrase in a statement that amounted, in King's view, to 'an out-and-out attack on the conscriptionists. Some lecturing as to how Quebec should be treated and above all an appeal on strictly Canadian lines. . . . He is excessively nation-

alistic,' King complained in his diary.[124] Pickersgill was also concerned about civil liberties throughout the war. In a letter to a Liberal M.P. in 1943, he said that he had not approved of the use of
the War Measures Act to proscribe the Communist Party and the
Jehovah's Witnesses 'because it seemed to me that it [proscription]
was contrary to the very fundamentals of liberalism . . .' Nonetheless, he ended his letter with the hope that 'the Liberal Party
will become liberal once more. . . .'[125] He told his brother Tom,
who had been asked to take on the job of dispersing Japanese
Canadians across the country after the war, that it was better to
have someone who disagreed with such a policy in charge of it.
That person, unlike an anti-Japanese zealot, would at least do a
distasteful job fairly.[126]

The confidential relationship between Prime Minister and Secretary was such that King ordinarily felt free to discuss any subject
with the 'very helpful' Pickersgill,[127] although occasionally a seed
of doubt might germinate. 'There is a great need of having some
outside mind to discuss some of these aspects with,' King wrote
after a talk with Pickersgill on one potentially explosive question.
'Found P. helpful, but am always fearful that he does not keep
matters strictly confidential. There is a danger of his talking with
members of the press, Claxton and others.' King's worries were
probably founded on Pickersgill's well-known friendship with re-
porters such as Bruce Hutchison, Grant Dexter, and others (although Pickersgill usually offered them opinions, not secrets.)[128]
He was particularly close to Brooke Claxton, King's Parliamentary Secretary and the M.P. for St Lawrence-St George and after
1944 the Minister of National Health and Welfare.

In a period of a few years the civil servant who had worried in
1939 that he might be overstepping the bounds of propriety by
helping King in an election had turned from a civil servant into the
prime-ministerial aide, with a finger in every pie, whatever its political content. As an aide who was expected to offer advice on
policy, he certainly did his job properly and well. When King was
wavering about the baby bonus in 1943, he asked Pickersgill why
he was such a strong advocate of family allowances. Pickersgill
said that if his mother had not received a pension as the widow of a
veteran, he would have had to help support his family and could
not have attended university. He was later told that this reply had
been instrumental in converting the Prime Minister into a supporter of the great social-security measure.[129] But in 1943, at

Brooke Claxton's invitation, he helped Claxton draft the resolutions to be placed before the National Liberal Federation, and the two friends virtually ran and directed the Liberal publicity campaign in the election of 1945.[130] Unquestionably Pickersgill was meeting the wishes of the Prime Minister in so acting; whether he ought to have done so is another question entirely.

How can we account for Pickersgill's behaviour? The work of drafting political resolutions and running campaigns fascinated him and engaged his full attention. He had become convinced that the policies of the King government were in part his own—after all, he had drafted some of them, or persuaded the Prime Minister to act here and not act there. Above all, he did whatever he was asked to do, justifying his actions by persuading himself that he was carrying out Skelton's orders to do what the Prime Minister wanted done. Finally, he developed a genuine dislike for the Conservative Opposition, whom he saw as playing a deliberately divisive game on such subjects as conscription. In a letter to Arthur Lower after the great conscription crisis of 1944, he said: 'I think we have come through . . . much less damaged than I would have expected. The Tories are totally discredited in Parliament, and it should be the business of every patriotic Canadian to see that they are equally discredited outside.'[131]

But if he was a partisan, he was still a civil servant, and he began to develop a healthy concern for his own fate should the Liberals fall from power. In 1944, after the Department of External Affairs re-classified all its officers, he went to the Prime Minister to argue that he had not been ranked as high as he would have been had he not come to Mackenzie King's office. Pickersgill was worried, King noted, that he had not received 'what he thought is needed to protect him in the future. . . .' The Prime Minister obliged by asking the Under-Secretary of State for External Affairs to reconsider the matter, 'in the light particularly of the fact that the services P. had rendered in the P.M.'s Office not only to myself personally but to the Cabinet, were much beyond those which other members of the diplomatic service could possibly have rendered.'[132] A few months later, in 1945, Pickersgill finally became the head of the Prime Minister's office.[133]

In 1948 King retired, to be succeeded by Louis St Laurent, the Quebec lawyer who had come into the Cabinet in late 1941 as Lapointe's successor in the Justice Department and who had been a highly successful Secretary of State for External Affairs from 1946 to 1948. St Laurent's courtesy, honesty, and ability had impressed Pickersgill from the beginning of 1942, and he was convinced that a French-Canadian Prime Minister was needed in the interests of national unity. As a result Pickersgill once again involved himself politically by drafting St Laurent's speeches for the Liberal convention in August 1948.[134] The next month, when King, still Prime Minister despite the convention so that he could make one last trip to Europe in style, wanted to take Pickersgill with him, it took the negotiating skills of Lester Pearson to keep him in Ottawa. King lamented in his diary: 'I learned from Pearson that [St Laurent] was terribly disappointed at the possibility of my taking Pickersgill to Europe. He feels P. is one person who knows the Dept. [i.e., the Office]. Knows where my papers are and knows the line that I would probably wish to have taken on different measures, and also how the business of a new session is to be made ready.'[135] Pickersgill stayed in Ottawa, the indispensable head of the Office (and the head of a staff of about 35).[136]

He was involved in every aspect of the new régime. Stuart Garson, the Premier of Manitoba and St Laurent's choice for Minister of Justice in his government, happened to have been a longtime friend of Pickersgill's, so Pickersgill went to Winnipeg at the Prime Minister's behest to negotiate the terms of Garson's entry into the federal government and to help decide the constituency Garson would run in.[137] Similarly Pickersgill was at the heart of discussions about the creation of new departments of government and the planned shifts in responsibilities between departments.[138] And when a shuffle of positions among the senior mandarins became both possible and necessary after Pearson joined the government as Secretary of State for External Affairs, Pickersgill, as St Laurent's man, was at the centre of the operation. After negotiating with Norman Robertson, the High Commissioner in London, and with Arnold Heeney, the Clerk of the Privy Council, he helped to shape the ultimate decision that Robertson should take Heeney's post and Heeney should succeed Pearson as Under-Secretary of State for External Affairs.[139] Pickersgill had hoped that Robertson could serve as another adviser to St Laurent, for the Prime Minister 'had begun to rely too exclusively on my advice.'[140] As it turned out, Robertson and St Laurent, while cordial enough, did not develop a close, confidential relationship, and Pickersgill remained the sole aide to whom the Prime Minister gave his full confidence.

St Laurent had little interest in the details of party organization, but Pickersgill was an expert on the subject after a decade of working for Mackenzie King. In 1949, when the Prime Minister went to the people for the first time, Pickersgill travelled with him, living in the same railway car as the St Laurents. He soon became 'accepted almost as one of the family.'[141] The extent of Pickersgill's control of the Prime Minister's national tour is striking:

> He gave me full responsibility to decide what places he would visit and how often he would speak. It was understood that I would make no commitments without his express approval, and that he would make no commitments on his own and would refer all requests for changes in his programme to me. I persuaded him that when he had someone else to do it for him, a Prime Minister should never put himself in the position of having to say 'no' to a friend or supporter. . . .
>
> We agreed St Laurent would not start his campaign until 10 May. . . .
>
> I attached the greatest importance to making a strong impression in Toronto. . . .[142]

No wonder the watchword in Ottawa was 'Clear it with Jack'. One reporter said that Pickersgill knew the winner in each constituency in every federal election since the turn of the century. 'Some would say this is idle knowledge. Yet it is such "idle knowledge" which keeps political parties in power. Pickersgill would be able to forewarn Prime Minister St. Laurent, for instance, that when he got to St. Joseph in Huron County he could expect to speak a few words of French.'[143] That kind of advice won votes. So did Pickersgill's shrewd advice to Claxton, now Minister of National Defence and the effective campaign manager, on the broader strategy of the election. Senator Tom Crerar wrote a friend 'that Jack is quite an influential man and probably has as much to do with determining policy in many matters as most of the Ministers have. Scarcely a day passes that he is not with some Minister at lunch in the restaurant.'[144] And Mike Pearson told Bruce Hutchison, of the Sifton newspapers, that 'When Jack takes [a] view you may be sure it will be the P.M.'s. Jack will sell it to him.'[145] Even Pickersgill himself said that 'I had a very great influence on Mr. St. Laurent. He had more confidence in me than in any cabinet minister or anyone else.'[146]

Though this much was true, it would be wrong to assume that Pickersgill controlled the Prime Minister. St Laurent was as able as any man who had held the top office in the land. He knew his own mind and enjoyed getting his own way. Pickersgill was important to him, perhaps even indispensable, but his reign would last only so long as the head of the Prime Minister's Office knew his place and kept to it. For a civil servant who was still on the books of External Affairs as a Foreign Service Officer Grade 7 (while Heeney and Robertson were Grade 10) at a nominal salary of $7,800 (though as head of the PMO his income was increased to $12,000),[147] he had risen to astonishing heights of position and power. But he had done this on his own skills; he was indispensable because he was so able. He was also, in the eyes of the Opposition, increasingly a marked man.

In the spring of 1952 Pickersgill was appointed Clerk of the Privy Council in place of Norman Robertson (who went back to London for a second term as High Commissioner) and became a public figure. Why had he left the Prime Minister's Office for the Privy Council Office? Naively, perhaps, Pickersgill was attracted by the 'security it offered my family and I thought for my own future',[148] particularly in the event that St Laurent retired. Unfortunately the appointment was seen by the Opposition, as well as by the press and academics, as confirmation of their growing concern that the civil service had become an adjunct of the Liberal Party.[149]

The new post, first in precedence in the civil service, had been treated as a non-partisan and non-political one by Heeney and Robertson, and Pickersgill understood this: 'We knew I would have to give up all partisan activities but I could continue as adviser to the Prime Minister on government policy as well in one office as the other.' It was extremely difficult, however, for Pickersgill to be non-partisan. On a trip to British Columbia with the Prime Minister in late August 1952 he avoided attending Liberal gatherings but was unsuccessful in escaping political discussions with local Liberal leaders who had grown used to 'clearing it with Jack' when he had been in the Prime Minister's Office. Rumours of this type of activity, though not necessarily of these B.C. meetings, must have spread, for in November 1952 a backbench Conservative member—Frank Lennard of Wentworth, Ont.—placed a series of questions on the order paper seeking information on the duties of the Clerk of the Privy Council and on how they squared with Pickersgill's activities since his appointment.[150] These queries were brushed aside, the House being told that Pickersgill had accompanied the Prime Minister because he had been asked to do so and because some official had to keep the Prime Minister in touch with Ottawa. Pickersgill admitted in his memoirs that it had been hard for him to separate the advisory role he had previously played from the new one.[151] Had he made it at the time, the confession would not have surprised the Tories, who continued to chivvy Pickersgill.

The Opposition became even more upset in 1953 when Pickersgill left his position as Clerk of the Privy Council to enter the Cabinet as Secretary of State; he intended to run in the election of August 10, 1953 in the not-entirely-secure Newfoundland constituency of Bonavista-Twillingate. His decision to enter the government seemed to some to have been prompted by a *contretemps* in the House over a relatively trivial incident. The manager of the Fort Garry in Winnipeg was transferred to a lesser post after Pickersgill arrived at the CN hotel with a Cabinet minister to find no reservation and no one on hand the next day to greet the Prime Minister when he checked in. The Clerk of the Privy Council, infuriated at sloppy service, raised the matter with Donald Gordon, the president of the CNR, and Gordon acted. The incident was brought up in Parliament, and in April 1953 St Laurent responded to questions about the propriety of his making political trips with the Clerk of the Privy Council by stating the principle of the separation of the civil service from politics and assuring the House of his future adherence to it (without admitting any transgressions in the past): 'When I am engaged in political campaigning and political tours, I do not take the Clerk of the Privy Council with me. I recognize that it would not be proper to do so, and I do not intend to do so.'[152] The next day, April 28, Pickersgill sent the Prime Minister a letter of resignation to take effect after the Coronation of Elizabeth II in June 1953. 'After this experience,' Pickersgill later wrote, 'I realized I would never be acceptable to a Conservative government as Secretary to the Cabinet, nor would I want to serve one.'[153]

In fact Pickersgill's decision to enter politics had been made much earlier, primarily because he wanted to be free to manage St Laurent's election campaign, but also because he wished to escape the false position he was in as Clerk of the Privy Council. In December 1952 he discussed his prospects with his friend Norman

Robertson in London. One option then seemed to be to enter the Senate as Government Leader, an idea that did not pan out.[154] By the end of January 1953, however, Pickersgill found in Joey Small-wood, the Premier of Newfoundland and a friend since the days when Pickersgill had worked with him to bring the island into Confederation, a powerful figure who was prepared to guarantee him a seat (as much as a seat in Parliament could ever be guaranteed), and to support him once he became the minister representing Newfoundland in the Cabinet. This was an odd solution to Pickersgill's desire to escape from the Clerk's office, but not an ineffective one, and St Laurent readily agreed to it.[155] Pickersgill entered the Cabinet on June 12, 1953, and two months later he won his first election to Parliament. He wrote to a Conservative friend that 'I have taken the plunge into the icy waters of the Atlantic',[156] abandoning the security of a civil-service pension for the risks of politics.

His friends in the press were not surprised by Pickersgill's transformation from Clerk to Minister, but they had reservations. Grant Dexter of the *Winnipeg Free Press* wrote privately that Pickersgill 'will now become an honest man, possessing power properly but in due course . . . will land on his face in the street. His constituency is a pocket borough and will go Liberal only so long as the Liberals are in office.'[157] George Ferguson of the *Montreal Star* told a friend that Pickersgill had ceased being 'an informed source' and become only 'a cabinet leak', adding that 'The Privy Council job had really run out on him, he was so blatantly political, and the Cabinet is the place for him.'[158] Ferguson later added that while Clerk, Pickersgill had told him 'that we appreciate yr. 79 p.c. support', a reference to the occasionally tepid attitude of the *Star* to the government. That was, he said, 'a fine remark for the Sec. of the Privy Council! I am glad he jumped the fence.'[159]

Pickersgill himself seemed immune to any suggestion of criticism, although he was said to have resented the way a few civil servants cut him socially. He set out his views on the proper conduct of the civil servant in a letter he sent in September 1953 to J.M. Macdonnell, a Conservative Member of Parliament whom he thought of as a good and upright man:

> I have no doubt you will continue to consider that I have, as you put it, 'committed a gross breach' of my duty as a civil servant in continuing, as you put it, to do party chores after I became Clerk of the Privy Council.

I state categorically that I did not take any part at all in party activities even *as a spectator* after I became Clerk, and no one that I know of has ever given any concrete evidence to support the charges that were made to that effect.

. . . It seems to me that there is a fundamental difference between a civil servant and a judge. The latter is expected to be independent of the government and is denied a vote. The former is the servant of the properly constituted *government*—not of Parliament or of the Opposition and it is his duty to carry out loyally and zealously the policies of the government. Once you get civil servants setting themselves up as independent of the government of the day, and doing it successfully, you have a real bureaucracy. It is in that sense that I believe the civil servant is properly the 'chore boy' of the politician in office under our system. Of course, when the people change the government it is the duty of the civil servant to serve the new govt. with equal zeal and loyalty, whatever his private views.

But the civil servant is permitted to have private views, to express them in private and to his friends, and to vote . . . he retains all the rights of a citizen except the right to take an active part in party politics.

Through the period I was Secretary to the Cabinet I acted in that way, and I confess I found the restraint very irksome. . . .[160]

This description of the role and duty of a civil servant is a correct one. Pickersgill tried, as Clerk, to remain aloof from party concerns, but what happens is not always more important than what people think is happening. Pickersgill's transition from the number-one civil servant to a Minister of the Crown, coming only five years after Pearson's entry into politics, confirmed the growing opinion that the civil service had become the handmaiden of the Liberal party. The concept of an impartial civil service suffered grievously. When, four years later, John Diefenbaker led the Conservative party to office, the whole public service felt the repercussions.

That Pickersgill ran into difficulty as Clerk of the Privy Council is, in a sense, the clearest proof of Arnold Heeney's success in making the senior post a non-partisan one. Heeney had greatly expanded the functions of the office, making the Clerk's post truly the most important one in the bureaucracy. He became the gate-keeper of the Cabinet, the man with the capacity to decide what the Cabinet saw and when it saw it, and his officers tended to control Cabinet committees and officials' committees in much the same way. This was power, but it was not used for partisan purposes.

The partisan work resided in the Prime Minister's Office, and Jack Pickersgill in 1952-3 paid the price of his success in his former post. He served King and St Laurent faithfully and assiduously, advising on matters political, national, and international. But over time the line between a non-partisan civil servant and a party supporter tended to blur, if not disappear completely. Probably if Pickersgill had been less open in expressing his opinions on the follies of the Opposition's positions he might have continued as a civil servant, and as one whose vast knowledge would be of use to a new administration. But if he had not been so open he would not have been Pickersgill, and it was certain that an incoming Tory government would have replaced him as Secretary to the Cabinet.

The role of the civil servant who is obliged to associate on a daily basis with prime ministers and cabinet ministers is of necessity a delicate one. Ties of friendship and understanding often build up, and there is a natural tendency to believe that the opposition are wilfully stupid in opposing policies that in all likelihood emerged full-blown from within the bureaucracy. Of the men and women in the public service who had difficulty in keeping the proper distance from their political masters, Pickersgill has to stand as a prime example. Others, notably Arnold Heeney, resisted the tug of party and confined themselves, although with great difficulty, to a proper public-servant's role.

8

THE RUSSIANS, THE
AMERICANS, AND US

Well before the victorious conclusion to the Second World War in 1945, the great powers had begun to fall out with one another. The Soviet Union remained as darkly suspicious as ever of the motives of the capitalist nations, and in the United States there were planners and politicians who pointed to the results of wartime summit conferences as justification for distrusting Moscow's intentions in every part of the world. For Canadians, anxious for peace, the building tensions between the two super-powers raised serious questions. What were the implications of Soviet-American hostility for Canadian defence? Did such tension oblige Canada to grant peacetime facilities in the North to the U.S. armed forces? Would a cold war require Canada to maintain larger forces than it had in the interwar years? No one in Ottawa had any doubt that, in the event of a showdown, Canada would stand with the United States and Britain against the Soviet Union; but the new world balance of power demanded that difficult questions such as these be thought about.

But to project Canada's role in the postwar world, policy-makers needed information. During the war, in 1943, Canada had established its first diplomatic mission in the USSR. The minister, to become Canada's first Ambassador to the Soviet Union in 1944, was Dana Wilgress, a knowledgeable expert on Russia and a close student of Soviet behaviour. His reports and dispatches posited one conception of the Russians: he saw them as desperate for security and uninterested in exporting revolution. But others took a different view. Escott Reid, a rising young officer in External Affairs, had observed Soviet behaviour at the 1945 San Francisco conference that created the United Nations, and at the first session of the new world organization, and he brought a powerful and moralistic mind to bear on the problem of shaping Canadian policy in the postwar era. Moreover, Reid had served in Washington before and during the war, and he was one of the first officers in the department to become concerned about the United States and its impact on Canada, in the light of the new postwar constellation of power.

From their differing perspectives and posts, Wilgress and Reid tried to assess the motives and aims of the Russians and Americans, seeking to calculate a course that best served Canada's national interests. Sometimes their views coincided: sometimes they differed. But all their memoranda and dispatches were grist for the policy mills in the East Block. Wilgress preached caution and moderation, urging Ottawa to try to understand the reasons for the USSR's actions, while Reid took a harder line that envisaged Canada as part of a great Western coalition. Inevitably—perhaps partly because he was in Ottawa after 1946 and Wilgress was not—Reid's perceptions became those of External Affairs, and ultimately of the government. His tough position eventually led to Canada's playing a major role in the creation of the North Atlantic Treaty and the military alliance of North America and Western Europe.

I

All the mandarins did not join the public service as a result of the recruiting efforts of Skelton, Clark, and Towers, nor did all have extensive post-graduate training. Dana Wilgress joined the civil service well before Skelton came to Ottawa in 1924, did so with only a Bachelor of Arts degree, and spent his first twenty-nine years in Trade and Commerce. He was not a typical mandarin.

Born in Vancouver, B.C., in 1892, Leolyn Dana Wilgress was the son of the provincial paymaster of the Canadian Pacific Railway. The family was relatively well off—his father had the use of a railway car—and Wilgress grew up in a comfortable home full of servants. When he was still young, his father moved to Hong Kong to work with a shipping company and then to Japan, where the boy quickly picked up Japanese from his *amah*. His formal education took place in the English-language schools in Yokohama, but he returned to Canada for university. He first attended the Vancouver college that had been established by McGill University—he read classics there under Lemuel Robertson, the father of Norman Robertson—then moved to Montreal, his mother's home, in 1910, to go to McGill itself, where he studied political science and economics and stood high in his class. (His competitor as head of his year was Jacob Viner, who became a distinguished economist at Princeton and Chicago.) The chairman of the department was Stephen Leacock, whose books of humour had been appearing almost annually since 1910 and had brought him a degree of international fame and entrée to the highest circles in the land. In the spring of 1914 the Minister of Trade and Commerce told Leacock that he wanted to hire two university-trained recruits for the Trade Commissioner Service, which sought business for Canadian firms abroad. Before 1914 the Service had been staffed by bankers, businessmen, or former commercial travellers; but now the minister, George Foster, wanted to put the Trade Commissioner Service on a sound and permanent basis by bringing in intelligent young men and training them properly to represent Canadian trade abroad.[1] Leacock pressed Wilgress on Foster, telling him that he was 'an excellent choice . . . a student of great ability'; he added that he had already sold an article by Wilgress to the *Journal of the Canadian Bankers' Association*. Foster interviewed Wilgress and passed him on to the Commissioner of Commerce, to whom Leacock wrote: 'Between you & me, one sentence is better than many words. Wilgress is just the man you want.' Leacock sent along another paper of Wilgress's on 'Canada and the Pacific', a 35-page handwritten essay that ended dramatically: 'As the nineteenth century was for the United States and the Atlantic, so will the twentieth century be for Canada and the Pacific.' The Commissioner read the paper—an 'awful job because of his appalling handwriting'—and pronounced himself 'much taken' with it. Wilgress was duly appointed, and two weeks after his graduation from McGill, on June 1, 1914, he became a sub-Trade Commissioner at $1,500 a year.[2]

He began his training in Ottawa, where he learned how the Department functioned. The next year, though the Great War had begun, he was sent east to survey industry in Quebec and Nova Scotia,[3] and in 1916 he received his first posting abroad as Trade Commissioner—to Omsk in Russia. Wilgress was a little stunned by this: 'I left Sir George Foster's office in a daze and went back to our room,' he wrote. A friend asked where he was going. 'I replied that I would tell him in a moment. When I had found Omsk on the map I pointed it out to him and said: "There, to Omsk." '[4] Omsk, in western Siberia, was a provincial town of no particular importance, but after he arrived there in mid-1916 Wilgress plunged quickly into learning the language and travelling through as much of Siberia as he could reach. There seemed relatively little business to do, and he did not know enough Russian to become involved in complicated negotiations in any case.[5] That he was one of the few Canadians to be living in a nation wracked by war and revolution appeared to have little significance for him. At this time Omsk was not much affected by the upheavals. The revolution made itself felt, Wilgress wrote in his memoirs, only in long debates in the town council: 'Instead of considering matters of urgent local importance, such as the state of the Omsk streets . . . the town council became embroiled in endless debates about such questions as whether or not independence should be granted to Finland.'[6] In 1918 he was transferred further east, to Vladivostok. There he attempted to acquire for Canada a share of any economic opportunities that might be going in the area; he was also present to watch the folly of Canadian troops, sent to Siberia as part of an Allied force, assisting in attempts to destroy the Bolshevik revolution. That military effort came to naught, as did Wilgress's attempts to seek out trade. The sole practical result of his time in Vladivostok was his marriage. His new wife, Olga Buergin, was the daughter of a Swiss engineer and a Russian mother. Wilgress had boarded in the Buergin home—'The food was good but the room I was given was very bare and uncomfortable'—and he had courted Olga through the turmoil of Red revolution, White reaction to it, and ineffectual foreign intervention.[7]

For the next dozen years Wilgress continued his job of expanding Canadian trade—in Bucharest, London, and Hamburg. The work was sufficiently interesting to keep him happily in the government's employ, contented enough that after the Great War, when he was approached by the Royal Bank, he turned down the offer and recommended instead Graham Towers, a distant relative on his mother's side.[8] By 1932 he was back in Ottawa, after sixteen years of foreign service, as Director of the Commercial Intelligence Service of the Department of Trade and Commerce, a senior post. And it was logical enough that during the Imperial Economic Conference of 1932 Wilgress should be called in—along with Norman Robertson of External Affairs and Hector McKinnon, the Commissioner of Tariff—to handle the detailed and difficult negotiations with the British that broke a political deadlock and allowed the Ottawa Conference to close with an Anglo-

Canadian trade pact. The next year Wilgress, Clifford Clark, and Norman Robertson accompanied Prime Minister Bennett to the World Economic Conference in London. He was becoming well known in Ottawa now, and O.D. Skelton could write in 1934 lamenting that 'There are . . . extremely few men in administrative posts with any breadth and flexibility of view—men say of the Wilgress or McKinnon type.'[9] Wilgress did more trade negotiation work in 1935, again in harness with Robertson and McKinnon, as the Liberal government of Mackenzie King began to work at lowering tariffs and attempted to restore trade with the United States. That 1935 agreement drew him favourably to King's attention, and also led the Americans to think highly of him. The Minister in Ottawa, Norman Armour, noted that Wilgress was 'outstanding . . . one with whom you can talk very frankly and from whom you can expect equally frank replies . . . a great friend of us all . . . he has played ball with us consistently since the [trade] agreement went into effect.'[10] Wilgress added to his reputation, both with the Americans and with his own service, during the lengthy negotiations of 1937-8 that produced Anglo-Canadian and Canadian-American trade agreements, a process that kept him, Robertson, and McKinnon—the three were now seen by all as the 'ace' Canadian negotiators—in Washington almost continuously for ten months.[11] W.A. Mackintosh, an acute observer, noted in 1939 that Wilgress had become 'one of the ablest government officials',[12] and he was the natural choice to become Deputy Minister of Trade and Commerce in 1940.

The difficulty with that post was that, as the Nazis were swallowing nations wholesale, the work of the department had greatly diminished. Trade and Commerce, as Wilgress knew, had never been the strongest or happiest department in Ottawa, and he had always disliked committee work and administration.[13] Too much of his time as deputy minister was taken up with the newly established National Film Board, which had been placed in his department's charge, and its rule-breaking founder and genius, John Grierson. In a letter written early in 1941, Grant Dexter of the *Winnipeg Free Press* characterized Wilgress and described his worried preoccupation with Grierson and the NFB:

> He is the perfect civil servant with a due respect for rules and regulations and red tape. I could not help but think, as I talked with him, how utterly impossible it would be for either John or Dana ever to understand each other. . . .

> Dana would love if John and his Film Board could be removed the hell out of Trade and Commerce. But of this, he says, he sees no hope. . . . And he is equally clear that he isn't going to be roasted alive by all the treasury blood hounds and the auditor general's torturers for the incredible things John does, without consulting anyone.[14]

The 'perfect civil servant' was an unusual one who wanted to *give up* a part of his empire!

More striking yet was Wilgress's desire to have the Department of External Affairs take over the global network of the Trade Commissioner Service lock, stock, and barrel so that it would form the basis of a Canadian consular system, and to create in its place in Trade and Commerce 'a strong Bureau of Foreign and Domestic Commerce with a liaison officer in External Affairs to expedite the transmission of commercial information.'[15] The idea—an attempt to hand over his entire domain to another department—did not come to fruition, but it was clear that its defeated exponent could not remain happily in Trade and Commerce as it was structured.[16]

Fortuitously Canada required a representative in the Soviet Union. The need for such a position became apparent once Hitler invaded Russia, and with his years of service in Omsk and Vladivostock, Wilgress was unquestionably the best-qualified man in the civil service for the post. Besides, he spoke Russian, and his wife was half-Russian; and an appointment to the USSR would take him out of his unhappy situation in Trade and Commerce. The appointment was arranged in the casual manner that was common in those days. On the way to lunch in the Château Laurier cafeteria, Norman Robertson asked Wilgress if he would like to have it. Wilgress said he would and the matter was settled. The announcement was made early in November 1942, and after celebratory dinners in his honour, including one thrown by all the deputy ministers and featuring 'gushing' toasts, the new minister to the Soviet Union was on his way.[17]

The journey to Russia was long and roundabout during the war.[18] The initial site of the Canadian mission was Kuibyshev, a provincial town located well to the east of Moscow, which was still not totally secure in March 1943. Wilgress, however, quickly settled in, and before long his reports were arriving in Ottawa. As he told External Affairs, his duty was to seek to interpret Soviet actions, and to understand the Russian point of view.

This is not an easy task. On the contrary it is a most difficult and thankless one, but it is a task that must be faced if anything constructive is to be gained from an analysis of Soviet policy. It is so much easier and so much more productive of cheap applause to condemn the Soviet Government out of hand and to attribute the worst motives to all their actions. But this sort of approach gets us nowhere.[19]

In his view, Western perceptions of the USSR were as distorted as Soviet perceptions of the West.[20] However, Wilgress was not in any way soft on Communism, or unmindful of the differences in attitude and approach between East and West. His task was to understand and analyse, not to condemn. Copies of his dispatches circulated regularly to the U.S. State Department and the Foreign Office and Dominions Office in London, and Wilgress's views drew praise initially. 'The quality of the despatch', the Dominions Office patronizingly noted of one in 1945, 'is up to the standards of the F.O.,' and a Foreign Office official on the Russian desk called others 'intensely interesting'[21]—though one officer was unhappy with some harsh words from Wilgress on British policy and complained that those comments illustrated the Canadian *'mentalité petite puissance'*.[22] In any case Wilgress the Russian commentator was taken seriously by London, Washington, and Ottawa.

He, of course, like other diplomats in the Soviet Union during and after the war, secured only irregular access to Russian officials and ordinary citizens, and his reporting had to be based on the press, official documents, occasional closely shepherded excursions, and discussions with his colleagues in the diplomatic corps. Wilgress's training as a trade commissioner made him particularly interested in the prospects of Canadian-Soviet trade—not very substantial, he concluded—and he proved quite expert in reading between the lines of Soviet production statistics to determine how the USSR was faring in its attempts to meet the norms set out in the latest Five Year Plan. 'There is a grave danger of a let-down after the war if the Soviet Government is not capable of applying the proper psychological methods required by the circumstances,' he wrote home in June 1944. 'Any suggestion of further five-year plans brings a shudder to the average Soviet citizen.'[23] Other dispatches dealt carefully and intelligently with the emergence of a new privileged class of officials and party functionaries; with the sources of news in the Soviet press, and its operations; and with

the way the government dealt with, and kept pacified, the auton-
omous nations of the Soviet Union.[24] But it was his comments on
Soviet foreign policy, and the motives behind it, that drew the
most interest.

In Wilgress's view, Soviet foreign policy was simply the newest
expression of the age-old spirit of Russian nationalism. Its aims
were fourfold: to secure strategic frontiers and a buffer-zone
between the motherland and Germany, which had moved east
with brutal force twice in the twentieth century, and now had to
be left permanently weakened; to ensure its security by gaining a
free hand in eastern Europe; to rebuild its vast devastated areas
under peaceful conditions; and to prevent any anti-Soviet alliance
in Western Europe, possibly through the creation of a strong
Anglo-Soviet or Franco-Soviet link. Clearly Wilgress was making every effort to understand the Russians' point of view.[25] In
July 1943, for example, a dispatch set out his support for the
Communist-dominated Polish government-in-exile rather than
the rival conservative one that was based in London and that had
the support of the Western nations:

> since cooperation with the Soviet Union is the only policy
> which will assure their continuance as a government, it is not
> asking too much that a Polish government in London be
> formed capable of carrying out such a policy. Moreover this
> is essential in the interests of future world peace and of con-
> tinued cooperation between the Soviet Union and the West-
> ern Allies after the war. The world has suffered already too
> much from the past actions of reactionary Polish govern-
> ments and in a war of this magnitude we all have a right to
> demand that the government of any participant be represen-
> tative of the ideals for which we are fighting.[26]

This was strong stuff. So was Wilgress's later insistence that 'it is
not the Soviet Union alone that has brought about the division of
Europe into zones of influence',[27] and that the Russian demands
for an advantageous border with Poland and for a government
there that was not anti-Soviet were correct. 'Both of these objectives', he said of Soviet Polish policy, 'should have been recognized as reasonable from the point of view of a country that had
prevented the Germans from permanently retaining control over
Eastern Europe. Who now would venture to affirm that without
the Red Army we could have beaten the Germans?'[28]

That may have been a truism, but few in the West—and few Western ambassadors in Moscow—were admitting any such thing in early 1945. Wilgress's views in fact were beginning to mark him as an almost unique Western observer of the Soviet Union, who had become convinced that the USSR was now a country much like others—motivated by a desire for security. To Wilgress, the Leninist creed of a universal and permanent revolution had disappeared, to be replaced by Stalin's proclaimed ideal of 'Socialism in one country'.[29] Here there was an opportunity for a long-lasting peace if a satisfactory and workable system of general international security could be established.

At the United Nations Conference on International Organization at San Francisco, in the spring of 1945, there was a chance to create a new world order. Wilgress had been summoned back from Moscow to attend the Conference as a Canadian adviser, and he returned to North America full of hope. This did not last long, for at San Francisco the Russians seemed to be deliberately obstructive. Wilgress became 'depressed about the way the USSR is behaving', Escott Reid wrote to his wife. 'He feels he has misled the government by his prophecies about the moderate line which they were likely to adopt after the war.'[30]

If in 1945 Wilgress could be seen as representing a 'soft'—or pro-Russian, if by no means a pro-Soviet—approach, a 'hard' one already existed in Ottawa before the San Francisco Conference, and it became entrenched after the Gouzenko spy revelations of September 1945 provided new evidence of Soviet methods and aims. The major initial interpreter of the hard-line was Arnold Smith, a young officer on Wilgress's Moscow staff who viewed matters from a different perspective than the Ambassador. Taking advantage of Wilgress's absence in the spring of 1945, Smith prepared a series of papers on Soviet policy in the form of dispatches. But because the Chargé, Leon Mayrand, refused to sign them, they went to Ottawa only as memoranda.[31] In Smith's view the Russians were attempting to create a *cordon sanitaire* in reverse, in which their influence was to be exclusive and through which the 'corruption' of the West could not gain entrance. Although Smith saw no signs of immediate Soviet aggressiveness, he argued that the Western powers had to create a bloc, in which British and American influence would be paramount, with a view to inducing the USSR to integrate its economy and policies with those of the West.[32] Smith's memoranda were read with great interest, and the young officer was brought back to Canada, soon to find himself acting as an adviser to the Gouzenko spy-case investigators, and to Norman Robertson and Hume Wrong, the two key policy-makers in External Affairs. At this point the Ottawa line began to toughen.

Wilgress's position had also altered. In early 1946, from Moscow, he watched the Soviet attempt to retain a large portion of Iran and became deeply troubled. His advice to Ottawa then was that the West should seek neither to appease 'Stalin's dictator mentality' nor to over-react to it. The West had to treat the Russians' opportunistic aggression with firmness and flexibility—he had little patience with those 'who preached toughness'. To Wilgress it was the Anglo-American alliance that was 'so essential to the maintenance of peace and security. . . . Not that policy of toughness which . . . means treating the Soviet Union as an inferior or as a pariah, but a policy of firmness based on a coalescing of American and British policies on a high moral plane. . . . There should be no more compromising with these principles for the sake of brief vodka honeymoons in Moscow.'[33]

When the Gouzenko affair became public in February 1946, Wilgress's position in Moscow became almost untenable, and in July 1946 he left the USSR. For the next several years Canada's representation in Moscow would be handled by a Chargé d'affaires, a mark of Ottawa's disapproval of Russian espionage. For Wilgress the next months were spent working at the opening sessions of the United Nations in London. In 1947 he was made Minister to Switzerland, his primary task being to represent Canada on trade negotiations that were under way. (He also undertook graduate work at the Université de Genève and in 1949 completed a doctoral thesis on trade policy called 'A New Attempt at Internationalism'.)[34]

But he continued to comment on Soviet policy and the Western response to it. His view remained generally constant: the Soviet Union did not want war. The mixture of firmness and flexibility Wilgress had called for earlier was still his goal, and he continued to suggest that the Russians would lose their revolutionary zeal and possibly 'return to isolationism'. Under all circumstances, Wilgress argued, 'we must keep our heads. I think the most important need is to maintain an attitude of being more or less indifferent to what is taking place in the Soviet Union and its sphere, provided that what they are doing does not overflow into the sphere of the Western powers.' He worried that a tough American policy might goad the Russians unnecessarily. 'Recent visitors to Moscow must have been impressed by the unreasoning hostility shown by some of the United States representatives on the spot. Our detestation of totalitarianism and all that it stands for', he wrote in April 1947, 'should not lead us into treating the Russians differently to the manner with which we would treat any other country with which we were not on particularly friendly terms.' The chief danger of the hard-line American policy that was encompassed in the Truman doctrine of 1947 was 'that some of the proponents of that policy seem so bent on humiliating the Soviet Union that before long a feeling of sympathy may gain support and this may lead to another of those marked reversals of United States policy that are such a danger to the world.'[35]

But he was never blind to the dangers Russian policy posed in the long run.[36] In 1948 he told Lester Pearson, then Under-Secretary of State for External Affairs, that he did not see a major war as an immediate possibility 'because (1) it would not suit the Russians to start a war unless they knew for sure that they would win, and (2) it is not possible for the democratic countries to secure the necessary popular support to wage a preventive war.' But he agreed with those who saw Stalin preparing for an inevitable struggle. The Russians' 'whole policy is to prepare for this struggle', and the West had to keep its guard up and consistently 'bear in mind the possibility of a major clash between the two great powers some ten, fifteen or twenty-five years hence.' Wilgress then turned to a paper written by Arnold Smith, 'The Russians and the Rest of Us'. Betraying some resentment towards one of the leading Department hard-liners and his former officer, Wilgress said the paper was simply wrong-headed. What could be gained by forcing the Soviet Union out of the United Nations, as Smith had suggested, other than to secure sympathy for the Russians 'among peace circles in Western countries'?[37]

By 1948, however, External Affairs had already launched itself on a crusade for the establishment of a North Atlantic alliance, and Wilgress's softer views were out of favour in Ottawa. What is striking, however, is that no attempt was ever made to punish Wilgress for his position. (In the U.S. State Department, those officers who had reported the corruption of Chiang and the coming victory of Mao were driven from the Foreign Service.) That tolerance is much to the credit of External Affairs. But there is equally no doubt that Wilgress was never a member of the Department's inner circle, made up of Robertson, Wrong, Pearson, Heeney, and Charles Ritchie (not coincidentally, all Oxford men). Arnold Heeney, a good friend of Wilgress, later noted that this was partly because he was 'very reserved and has never in any sense been one of the boys with NAR[obertson], LBP[earson] etc. I wonder what the basis of his unpopularity with certain of my senior colleagues really is.'[38] Wilgress did have a stuffy manner and he was not a good administrator; but we might wonder if his variant attitudes to, and assessments of, Soviet policy during and after the war did not contribute to his absence from the inner circles.

That absence was only relative, however, for Wilgress served as High Commissioner in London after his time in Switzerland; and in 1952-3 he was Under-Secretary of State for External Affairs, the senior professional post in the Department. From 1953 until his retirement in 1958 he was the Canadian permanent representative at NATO headquarters. His career was distinguished and worthy, yet he did not quite receive the rewards to which he was entitled. Dissident views were not punished overtly in Ottawa, but they were responded to nevertheless—negatively.

II

If Dana Wilgress had tried and failed to interpret the Soviet Union to Ottawa, Escott Reid, before and during the war, had the job of explaining American policy to External Affairs. He was the mandarin who seemed to see furthest ahead, who detected coming trends before his colleagues had a glimmer of them. And he always had a long memorandum ready and waiting. That he was brilliant and hard-working none doubted; that he was often difficult to get on with and overfilled with nervous energy was also true. Reid was therefore looked on with a touch of dismay. His judgement was not always trusted, and as a result his career in the Department was not crowned with the Under-Secretary's post he wanted.

Escott Reid was born in Campbellford, Ont., on January 21, 1905, the son of an Anglican clergyman who had immigrated to Canada from England in 1885. After serving in a number of Ontario parishes and in Toronto at St Mark's, the Reverend A.J. Reid in 1918 was made first Rector of St Chad's Church in Earlscourt, a largely Anglo-Saxon working-class area of Toronto, and remained there until his retirement.[39] Thus it was in Earlscourt that Escott Reid grew up, attending the Toronto Model School and Oakwood Collegiate Institute, then a new school but a good one. If the speeches he made at Oakwood are any indication, the young Reid was very much the product of the Toronto of his day: patriotic, somewhat narrow, and Anglocentric. 'Immigration flowing into the country', he said in a speaking contest in 1921, 'must be such that the nation remain predominantly British. For it is unthinkable that our country should ever be inhabited by a polyglot race, speaking a babble of tongues, and not possessing British ideas.'[40]

Surprisingly Reid did not graduate from Oakwood. For lack of money he was forced to leave school to work for two years as a clerk for the provincial government, and he took his senior-matriculation courses at night at Harbord and Jarvis Collegiates. But by 1923 he had saved enough money to enter Trinity College, University of Toronto, where he excelled, standing 1.1 in political science in each of his four years there. He participated in College affairs, wrote for student publications, and spoke out on any and all subjects. By this time he had moved away from the juvenile xenophobia of his high-school days. He tried to organize a branch of the socialist League for Industrial Democracy at the university, an attempt blocked by the President, and joined the quasi-pacifist and internationalist Student Christian Movement; a few years later, like many students after him, he became involved in a controversy over the meaning of Remembrance Day.[41] His iconoclasm, however, did not prevent him from being selected as one of the two Rhodes Scholars for Ontario in 1927.

His Oxford college was Christ Church, his field of study Politics, Philosophy and Economics (PPE). Slender, very erect, and extremely good looking (he resembled a more vigorous Edward, Prince of Wales), Reid made his mark at Oxford, scoring a First. A student politician of sorts, he was a member of the Labour Party and treasurer of its club at Oxford, President of the English Club, and an unsuccessful candidate—twice—for the presidency of the Oxford Union. As he told a Toronto friend, he was a centre-lining socialist now, a difficult course in both Oxford and Toronto. 'If the police continue their practices [in Toronto, where they had been busting up socialist meetings], I shall be afraid to return . . . I had rather face the prospect of being stoned by the left-wing in England for being a moderate, than be kicked by the police in Toronto for being a socialist.'[42]

After graduating in 1930, Reid decided to work for the degree of Doctor of Philosophy at Oxford and chose the Canadian party system as the subject of his dissertation.[43] His inclinations, however, were already tending toward some idea of public service. 'I am still enthusiastic about doing something for international peace,' he wrote a bit grandly to a friend in Toronto, and asked for advice on how he could get a job with the League of Nations, which in his view was the best hope for peace.[44] That idea went nowhere; instead Reid took a Rockefeller Foundation Fellowship in the fall of 1930 to allow him to study at Harvard University and to do research for his thesis at the Public Archives of Canada and across the country. That year he also married Ruth Herriot, a Winnipeg girl he had met at Oxford. The next two years were devoted to research, in the course of which he conducted extensive interviews with active and retired politicians—this was the first systematic oral-history project by a Canadian scholar.[45] His work at Harvard impressed its Government Department, and he was offered a job there in 1932. But Reid had already accepted the post of national secretary of the Canadian Institute of International Affairs in Toronto and turned Harvard down (the position was eventually given for one year to Norman Robertson of the Department of External Affairs).[46] Unfortunately Reid's CIIA job forced the virtual abandonment of his research.[47] This was a great loss to scholarship because the essays he wrote and published over the next few years—'The Rise of National Parties in Canada', 'Canadian Political Parties: A Study of the Economics and Racial Bases of Conservatism and Liberalism in 1930', the first statistical study of voting in Canada, and 'The Saskatchewan Liberal Machine Before 1929'—were brilliant examples of political analysis to which students, half a century later, are still referred.[48]

Reid did not stop writing when he joined the CIIA, although his interest quickly switched to problems of Canadian foreign policy. The Institute had been formed in 1928 by a blue-ribbon group of notables—including Sir Robert Borden, Newton Rowell, and John W. Dafoe—to encourage interest in foreign affairs, and its charter defined it as non-political, non-partisan, and non-official. Reid's task as the first national secretary was to make the organization function effectively. A man of his immense energy was just what the CIIA needed, and the Institute's records are full of memoranda and reports demonstrating just how effective he was.[49] At the same time the difficult and outspoken Reid, whose sympathies embraced socialism, neutralism, and nationalism, and whose ability with the pen secured him outlets for his articles across the country, caused the more conservative CIIA elders great pain. In 1936 Brooke Claxton, the Montreal lawyer and Liberal activist who was generally sympathetic to Reid's outlook, wrote that

> after a discussion with him, I found him obdurate, obstinate and obtuse. As he is also a fanatic and completely spoiled and undisciplined, it makes ordinary human relations, not to speak of business relations, rather difficult. . . . He called us all the emissaries of Dafoe and Rowell. He refused to admit that anything he had done had injured or could injure the Institute. He said that he was serving the purpose for which he was hired. Alternatively, he was free to use his spare time as he liked. . . .
>
> I am not going to talk to Escott any more about this. If he insists on hanging himself, that is his own lookout, but it will be hard on his family as he will find it very difficult to get a similar job in Canada.[50]

Reid refused to be bridled, continued to write and speak freely, and soon was pressing for an overhaul of the CIIA's structure and practices. John W. Dafoe in 1937 lamented to a friend that 'I stepped into a bit of trouble that Escott Reid has precipitated—he is not a judicious young man.'[51]

What had Reid done to offend his masters? First, he had become an active member of the League for Social Reconstruction and the CCF, an early draftsman of the Regina Manifesto, and helped to write the chapter on foreign policy for *Social Planning for Canada*, the book of the decade for CCF supporters. 'The internationalist must be a socialist,' Reid wrote in his draft of the chapter, 'just as the true socialist must be an internationalist.'[52] That kind of rhetoric did not sit well with the Bordens, Rowells, and Dafoes of the CIIA. Nor could they have been pleased by Reid's draft of 'A Foreign Policy for the CCF', prepared in June 1934, in which Reid argued, much like intellectuals in the United States, that 'never again, under any circumstances' should Canada 'send armed forces over seas to take part in hostilities of any sort, whether or not the purpose of these hostilities is said to be the defence of Canada or the British Empire or the League of Nations or democracy or freedom.'[53] This deliberately all-encompassing statement suggested world-weary cynicism, but Reid was no cynic. At another point in the draft, italicized for emphasis, he called for a 'World

Commonwealth . . . which will ensure Permanent Peace founded upon International and Social Justice. A reformed and strengthened League of Nations can form the basis of this Commonwealth.'

What bothered the executive most was Reid's advocacy of neutralism for Canada. In articles, speeches, lectures, and letters Reid argued that Canada had to secure for itself the legal right to neutrality in any future war. He recognized that this was in effect a call for the right of secession from the British Empire, but as a Canadian nationalist he was not at all bothered by this. As he put it in 1935:

> If Canada wants to remain neutral in the next great war in which Great Britain is involved, the Canadian government should as soon as possible, issue a declaration approved of by her parliament, stating that Canada is resolved to maintain her neutrality in all future wars whoever the belligerents may be. . . . There should be passed through parliament a stringent neutrality act, the enforcement of which should be mandatory upon the government. . . . The existing machinery for consultation with Great Britain on matters of defence should be scrapped, and we should either reorganize our defence policy and arrangements, or disarm completely. Finally we should attempt so to reorganize our national economic life that our trans-oceanic trade shall become relatively less and less important.
>
> These measures, if supported by a strong public opinion which is prepared to face their implications may make it possible for us to preserve our neutrality in a British war. If the United States gets involved in a major war . . . we should recognize that if the United States wants to infringe our neutrality, there is nothing we can do about it except to send a note to Washington.[54]

That concern about the influence and power of the United States was to become one of Escott Reid's recurring themes.

In another article, written for the *Canadian Forum* in 1934, he was blunter still: 'if in order to protect herself from being dragged into overseas wars . . . Canada were to embrace a policy of political isolation and economic rapprochement with the United States, she would become dependent on the United States for her only secure market. . . . This combination of economic and political dependence might well be too much for her nascent nationality, and she would in fact if not in name become part of the United States.'[55] This sounded as though Reid was prepared to risk absorption if only Canada's neutrality could be preserved.

Equally offensive to his masters was Reid's attitude to the Ethiopian crisis that tore apart the League of Nations in the fall of 1935. While still sentimentally in favour of strengthening the Covenant of the League, Reid was no admirer of sanctions as a policy. Therefore his position on the Italo-Ethiopian war, formulated just before the Italian invasion, was one that could not have appealed to supporters of the League such as Dafoe. To Reid, the case was clear: unless the League were to set up a commission to study Italy's problems and to find a peaceful solution to them, then Canada had to oppose sanctions against Italy, 'for sanctions under such circumstances would not be the force of equitable authority but would simply be the old-fashioned private war used by the "haves" to assert their power against the "have-nots".' On the other hand, if such a commission were formed and Italy nevertheless attacked, Canada should not participate in military sanctions but only in economic ones. On the grounds of geographical remoteness and absence of interests in the area, Canada had to be excused from any military role. 'Nations today', he said, 'under any system of collective security can only be expected to pay premiums which are roughly proportionate to their risks.'[56]

Even that was a compromise to Reid, one he must have felt he could propose in the near-certainty that the League would do nothing to examine Italian problems. His base position, therefore, remained as it had been all through the decade of the Depression. Britain was committed to participate in virtually every war that France might wage against Germany, and Canada as a part of the Empire was probably doomed to be dragged along by the British. To avoid this, all Commonwealth countries, all the states of the Americas, and the uncommitted blocs in Europe, had to adopt a hard and fast policy of neutrality and say that under no circumstances short of direct attack on their territory would they intervene. This sweeping view was considered, however, and Reid amended it in a letter to Lord Lothian in 1937: 'I am not prepared to prescribe for any country but my own and for Canada I prescribe a policy of not sending armed forces overseas under any circumstances.'[57] In 1937 other mandarins were saying much the same thing.

If Reid's views offended his employers, they found favour in at least one quarter. Mackenzie King liked them. Reid had denounced the Liberal leader in the past—'the bankruptcy of democracy in Canada is nowhere better exemplified than in the behaviour of the Liberal leaders during the past four years,' he wrote in 1935[58]—but one article he wrote on King's foreign policy in 1937 greatly appealed to the Prime Minister. For this study he ploughed through King's tortuous prose to unearth the principles that, Reid claimed, underlay Canadian foreign policy. The result, as King noted in his diary, was that this 'excellent' article had 'cleared my mind of many points',[59] and the Prime Minister cited Reid in Parliament to counter critics who argued that Canada had no policy.[60] In effect, Reid's analysis made sense of Canadian policy and, because of that, may have become Canadian policy.

Mackenzie King's approval was important because Reid, aware of his low standing with the CIIA National Executive, had become interested in joining the Department of External Affairs. Early in 1936 Dr Skelton had broached the possibility of an appointment and in November of that year the two men discussed this in Ottawa. Reid wrote his wife that Skelton, who was as neutralist in attitude as Reid himself, 'was very cordial but had not thought out the details of my appointment, if I should be appointed. There was no reason why he should have until I told him I was willing to consider a position.'[61] There was to be no quick decision. The Prime Minister's reluctance to expand his department, and Skelton's disinclination to press his chief, combined to drag matters out for two full years, during one of which Reid taught at Dalhousie University.[62] At last, on 27 December, 1938, Escott Reid was appointed Second Secretary in the Department of External Affairs and posted to Washington. His salary was $3,900, his allowances $2,750.[63]

III

For the next two years Reid served in Washington as second secretary in the Canadian Legation. For most of that time, as he later wrote in a memo justifying his case for promotion, 'I was, de facto though not de jure, the senior political officer under the Minister and when there was no Minister or when the Minister was not well enough to discharge his duties, that is to say for two-thirds of the time I was in Washington, I was the senior political officer.'[64] That was true enough, and Reid carried the work of the Legation after the outbreak of war when Loring Christie, the minister, was very ill for most of the year-and-a-half of life that remained to him. The combination of Christie and Reid, both strongly isolationist and neutralist before September 1939, worried some observers. J.W. Dafoe, a man Reid admired but with whom he had clashed repeatedly at the CIIA, fretted over the Washington duo, 'because their private views are closely akin to one another, and they both held attitudes in the period preceding the war which were exasperating to me.'[65]

Even the RCMP was concerned about Reid, although for different reasons. In the summer of 1940 the Commissioner of the force told Skelton that Reid had received an advertisement for Soviet books. Skelton was properly scornful, replying that the receipt of a book list 'could hardly be considered to indicate an intention to buy, much less an indication of sympathy with the doctrines' of Communism; the Under-Secretary could not forbear from adding that several of the books seemed essential for anyone desiring to understand European trends.[66] In fact the RCMP may have been closer to the mark in assessing Reid's sympathies than it realized. As Reid later acknowledged, by the late 1930s 'I had come to believe . . . that Moscow might well be the Mecca of the disenchanted and disinherited for the whole world. I was unhappy about some of the developments in the Soviet Union. I hated what I saw happening in Nazi Germany. I feared that perhaps the western world might have to choose between communism and fascism. I knew that in that event I would choose communism. . . . My spirits therefore rose when Hitler forced the Soviet Union to join the anti-Hitler coalition. . . . I thought that now the war would become a people's war.'[67] Only a few years later Reid's disillusionment with Moscow would be total.

Reid's posting to Washington brought about a new development in his thinking, having to do with American policy towards Canada, though this was not recorded until after his return to External Affairs in Ottawa in the spring of 1941. Reid argued that the United States was following a course that he labelled 'Domination, Coöperation, Absorption'. He had no hesitation in putting the blame for this situation squarely where it belonged: 'We are being treated as children because we have refused to behave as adults. . . . On matters of high policy in the realm of foreign affairs Canada does not make decisions; it has decisions forced on it.'[68] Vincent Massey, anglophilic as ever, saw the new Reid in

London in May 1943 and noted that 'I was interested to see how alive he had become to the danger of American high pressure methods in Canada in connection with the war effort and the implications of this as regards our post-war relations. . . . This is a danger which External Affairs took a long time to discover, being preoccupied as they were with flogging the dead horse of "Downing Street domination".'[69]

Although he had correctly identified the problem, Reid did not immediately see how Canada could handle pressures that had developed because of the need for American troops in northern Canada, the arrogance of the U.S. that went hand in hand with its renewed sense of manifest destiny, and Canadian dissatisfaction with the exclusive nature of the Combined Boards. There were a number of minor alterations that could be made in Canadian tactics, and in representation at the Legation, but Reid's major points all hinged on the necessity of Canada's working toward the creation of an effective international order. In 1942 he called for 'the construction of an effective collective system' to replace the defunct League of Nations as 'the main goal of our policy'.[70] The next year, when he pointed out that American influence on Canada was certain to remain strong in the coming peace, he noted that we 'have not won from London complete freedom to make our own decisions on every issue—including that of peace and war—in order to become a colony of Washington. It would thus appear probable that effective military cooperation between Canada and the United States is possible only within the framework of an effective world order of which both Canada and the United States are loyal members.'[71]

Thus in a curious way Reid had come almost full circle since his neutralist and isolationist period in the 1930s. The war had confirmed his belief that only a strong international organization could safeguard peace—in 1944, characteristically, he tried his hand at drafting a charter for just such a body[72]—and that, equally important for Canada, only such an organization could preserve Canada's independence in the face of a powerful and aggressive United States. Because Britain was weak, Canada's problem was now the United States.

At the Chicago Conference on postwar civil aviation Reid had a chance to work closely with the British and Americans in an important field. As the great powers jockeyed for post-war routes and advantage, civil aviation was a major issue. Reid saw his role—Canada's role—as that of 'honest broker'. The United States and Great Britain were at loggerheads, each pressing schemes to secure their own postwar interests. Canada had been in the middle, touting its own plan, which was a compromise between the positions of the two great powers. In other words, just as Rasminsky had given Canada a much larger role than usual through his expertise in international monetary questions, so too did Reid carve out a place for Canada as 'one of the three great powers at the Conference'. In a sense, he said, outlining a policy and a tactic that he would favour in the postwar years,

> our greatness was thrust upon us. It was thrust upon us in the main because we were the only delegation which came to the Conference with a carefully worked-out comprehensive draft convention which could provide a basis of discussion. . . . The decision of the Conference to take our convention . . . as the basis of discussion was not therefore unnatural. Once it had been adopted as the basis of discussion and once it was generally realized that the main struggle at the Conference was between the United States and the United Kingdom with Canada in between, our role as mediator became obvious.[73]

There was no doubt that Reid himself played an important part in keeping the Canadian delegation to the fore, his fertile mind and quick skills as a draftsman winning him plaudits.[74] As he told Hume Wrong, the Associate Under-Secretary in Ottawa, 'There are, I think, a very large number of important lessons which we can learn from the Chicago Conference for use in succeeding international conferences, especially the strength of Canada's position . . . if before the conference meets Canada publishes a detailed, carefully worked-out draft convention and is in a position at the conference constantly and quickly to revise the draft convention to make it more generally acceptable.'[75] This was Reid at his best, carving out a position far beyond his country's rightful station by dint of verbal and written skills and clever negotiations.

Reid also performed well as an adviser to the Canadian delegation at the 1945 United Nations Conference on International Organization at San Francisco,[76] and particularly in the subsequent meetings that put flesh and organizational structures on the bones of the new United Nations. His perceptions of Canada's potential as a leader of the middle powers, which he had first formed in Chicago, were confirmed at the UN Preparatory Commission meetings. Canada had sent to this international conference a competent and hard-working delegation, and as a result it became almost automatically one of the Big Five of the conference.[77] For all those reasons he had set out during the war for Canada to support a world organization, Reid was a true believer in the worth of the United Nations. In a draft speech he prepared for the Prime Minister in April 1946, this declaration of faith appeared (though it was not finally included): 'Canada intends to use the United Nations as the principal instrument of its foreign policy.'[78]

Nonetheless, true believer in international government though he was, Reid quickly became disillusioned by the actions of the Russian members. His anger at the Soviet Union showed clearly in a paper he prepared describing the UN's first General Assembly in February 1946. 'The tactics of the Soviet delegations', he wrote, 'were to use the proceedings for purposes of propaganda,' adding that they had made it 'apparent that talk of turning the United Nations into an agency of international government, by the delegation to it of a portion of the sovereignty of the members, is in present conditions wholly unrealistic.'[79] His disillusionment was further revealed in a conversation with Grant Dexter, the *Winnipeg Free Press* reporter, in March 1946:

> When [Reid] left Ottawa in 1941 or 1942 [sic], he was a tremendous Russian man. He wanted world government . . .
>
> Escott has learned a great deal. . . . He is cured on Russia, beyond all danger of a relapse. Indeed, I never heard more envenomed comment on Uncle Joe and Co. than from Escott.
>
> To begin with, Escott favours the government's course on spies [i.e., the setting up of a Royal Commission to investigate the situation revealed by Igor Gouzenko's defection and the draconian measures employed by the RCMP]. He is prepared to trust the powers that be. He drew this analogy: We are now up against an ideological conflict without parallel since Elizabethan times. The communists today are the Papists of the last half of the seventeenth century. . . . You have citizens who give an allegiance elsewhere and your normal system of justice and individual rights breaks down.

The spies were one thing; but the real causes of Reid's growing mistrust of the Russians were Soviet actions in the UN and in Eastern Europe:

> He felt quite sure that Russia would not quit UNO. On the contrary, his judgment is that Russia will stay in and hinder the work in every possible way. It would be much better if Russia would get out since we could then go ahead in the noncommunist world (including satellites) and do a better job in raising standards of living, promoting trade and the like, than Russia could do in her neck of the woods. This would be extremely helpful to reversing the play of forces. Russia would have to pass over to the defensive.[80]

The UN man, the believer in the Utopian world of international organization in which Canada could find safety and prosperity, had begun to be replaced by the anti-Soviet hard-liner. The Russians had messed up the United Nations. But he did not abandon it. A paper he drafted in February 1946 on board ship bringing him back to Canada from the first General Assembly in London made clear that Reid preserved his long-term commitment to world government. There was a schism between the West and the USSR, however, and the two worlds were suspicious and fearful of each other. The West must be clear about the moral nature of that split—Christian individualism versus the totalitarian heresy—and wage a war for men's minds. 'In order to be successful,' he said, 'the faith of the Western world must show itself in good works'—a commitment to social justice, decolonization, and a genuine world government. That meant a reconciliation of East and West that would enable the General Assembly to become a true world legislature and the International Court of Justice a true judicial body. It also meant reducing and limiting armaments: only in this way would the West survive and atomic war be averted.[81] Reid sounded as naive as a World Federalist.

He also sounded much like Lester Pearson, whose utopianism, while less fervid and centred more on the North Atlantic area, was no less strong. Significantly, Pearson, who was now in charge of the Department of External Affairs, chose Reid to be his right hand for the next half-dozen years.* Both Reid and Pearson

---

* Reid later noted that '. . . I'm not the kind of person who is interested in jobs which are mostly reporting and representation. If I stay in External Affairs I want to be in a place where I have a good chance to influence the thinking of the government on the bigger issues of foreign policy.' (Reid Papers, Ste Cécile de Masham, N.A. Robertson file, Reid to Robertson, 8 Jan., 1959.)

wanted to participate in the creation of a new world order; they viewed involvement in the world as a good thing in itself, and rejected former policies that stood for no commitments. The new policy was activist utopianism.

By the beginning of 1947 the Soviet Union had become a major military and political threat to the West. Reid wrote in a 'Political Appreciation of the Possibility of the Soviet Union Precipitating War Against the United States' that he did not anticipate any immediate act of aggression. In fact, 'On the assumption that the Soviet Union is out to secure domination of the world, it is clear that the Soviet Union's ambition would be to secure that domination without recourse to a first-class war. The Soviet Union does not want to inherit a desert but a going concern.' Thus, to Reid, the USSR sought dominance by a gradual extension of power, 'an extension of political power over adjoining territory, an extension of economic power, an extension of power over the minds of men . . .'[82]

How to resist this? By the summer of 1947 Reid had found the answer. The Western nations must organize for collective self-defence against the threat of the USSR. He floated this idea in August at the Couchiching Conference of the Canadian Institute of Public Affairs, in a speech devoted to the necessity of making the UN more effective within the limitations imposed by the Charter. In the 1930s he had wanted to see the League Covenant reformed before Canada could pledge its support for sanctions; now, in the 1940s, he was calling for changes in the UN to increase its effectiveness in the face of Soviet obstruction.[83] The nub of his argument was that 'the states of the Western world are not debarred by a Soviet veto or by Soviet membership in the United Nations from the creation of international federal institutions to deal with international economic and social questions if they decide that such institutions are required.' 'Nor', he insisted, 'are they debarred by the Charter of the United Nations or by Soviet membership in the United Nations from creating new international political institutions to maintain peace, if the time should come when it was generally agreed by them that this was necessary. Nothing in the Charter precludes that existence of regional political arrangements,' he went on—giving the first public utterance anywhere to the idea that led to the creation of the North Atlantic Treaty Organization—'and these regional agencies are entitled to take measures of collective self-defence against armed attack.'[84]

Though Reid had no doubts about the Soviet threat and about

the West's need to organize in order to meet it, he remained remarkably cool in his appraisal of the United States and its policies. In a long paper in August 1947 that was circulated to senior officers of his Department at home and abroad, Reid set out his concerns. To him, 'both the Soviet Union and the United States are expanding powers.' Both wanted to expand their defence areas because each believed the other 'constitutes a menace to its way of life. It constitutes a menace because its way of life is so different from the way of life of the other. . . . Each side desires to expand its defence area because each fears the threat to its security which results from the other's expansionist moves.' In other words, either side could begin a war. The Americans might initiate a conflict if they felt the balance of power was tipping against them or, alternatively, they might push the USSR too hard in an emotional burst of anti-Communism. In this atmosphere there was the ever-present danger that the Soviet 'realists' might move to war if they believed the balance of power favoured them, or if they concluded that their chances of achieving their ends without war were not good.[85] Thus in Reid's eyes the United States was also a potential threat to peace. The balance of power was the key. If it tipped too far to either side, war was a possibility.

During the recent war, conscious of the American influence on Canada, Reid had posited a new international organization as one way of putting the bilateral Canadian-American relationship into a new multilateral context. Now, with the USSR negating the usefulness of the UN, yet another organization had to be created to incorporate that unbalanced bilateral relationship within a larger structure.[86] In Reid's view this was essential to protect the interests of Canada, a small North American state overshadowed by the giant with which it shared the continent,[87] but he also believed it was necessary because Soviet aggressiveness demanded a new organization to protect the interests of the democracies and Christian civilization. The rationale was brilliant and persuasive, the concept clear. Reid persuaded his colleagues in External Affairs of the value of his idea, and they persuaded St Laurent, Secretary of State for External Affairs, and Mackenzie King. Canada's two-year crusade for a new collective-security organization then shifted to Washington and London and, eventually, to Paris, Rome, Brussels, and the other Western European capitals. Finally, despite untold difficulties, it would triumph.[88]

In his own way Escott Reid had scarcely changed since the 1930s. The world still needed effective international organization;

security could be guaranteed only by an efficient joint defence system; and Canada could remain independent only if its relations with the United States were subsumed in some broader multilateral arrangement. The North Atlantic Treaty Organization of 1949 was a logical outgrowth of his concerns over two decades.

Since Reid had played a major role in its creation, why was he not rewarded by a grateful government? Why did he never achieve his ambition of becoming Under-Secretary of State for External Affairs? That he was intelligent none could doubt. His Oxford First confirmed this, galling those of his colleagues who had received seconds. But his brilliance sometimes seemed too facile. The memoranda and lengthy papers that poured constantly from his pen contained a jumble of good and bad ideas. 'Reid is flooding us with papers and telegrams,' Hume Wrong complained in 1945.[89] Reid was not unaware of the irritation he caused with his excessive flow of missives. 'You always accuse me of swamping the Department with reports,' he once said to Pearson. 'Usually the charge is greatly exaggerated.'[90] It wasn't. Exasperation was also caused by the content of the reports. Reid's moralism seemed so superior to that of lesser men,* his emphasis on a religious morality (in a Department full of agnostics) insufferable. Who else but Reid could have written that paper of February 1946 about 'good works'? The simplism and idealism of his beliefs did not always sit well with a Department of External Affairs whose style was usually one of amused skepticism. Norman Robertson, not Escott Reid, had the cast of mind that was preferred.

Reid's personal quirks also exasperated his colleagues. He was openly ambitious, jealous of his place, and quick to take offence or stand on his dignity. An officer of the American Embassy in Ottawa reported in 1945 that John Read, the Department's legal specialist, and Arnold Heeney had been joking about the situation in London where Vincent Massey, the High Commissioner, and Escott Reid, heading the delegation to the Executive Committee of the Preparatory Commission of the UN, 'seem so jealous of each other that they communicate . . . via the Department of External Affairs.'[91] An exaggeration, of course, but too many of the

---

* James Eayrs looked at one essay of Reid's about the 'Conscience of the Diplomat: A Personal Testament' (in Queen's Quarterly, LXXIV (1967) and jeered: ' "What are the essential qualities which a diplomat must possess?" [Reid asked.] And he answers as Nicolson answered: "The first quality is honesty." That remark is beyond comment as it is beyond belief.' (Diplomacy and its Discontents, Toronto, 1971, 71.)

Department's officers would have agreed. Indeed, they had all fought with Reid at one time; the only saving grace in such struggles was that Reid held no grudges. He was unloved. That his career advanced as far as it did could only have been because of merit, one officer remembered. Another officer, junior to Reid, remembered him as 'the worst Son of a Bitch I ever worked for', but added quickly that Reid had helped him get accelerated promotion.

Reid's enthusiasm often wore out those around him, and he was not always able to discern easily the worth of the issues for which he fought. A struggle to achieve the North Atlantic Treaty, to some observers, sometimes seemed on a par with a perfectionist crusade for simplified English in international documents.[92] Sometimes this lack of judgement worried those around him. Arnold Heeney once wrote of Reid's 'natural impulses and his natural dispositions to carry the torch high in every direction simultaneously.'[93] Lester Pearson also saw this. In 1947 he wrote that 'Escott is as busy and active and useful as ever, but is emotionally unstable, and I sometimes get worried about him. He came back from the Assembly, as you know, in very bad shape—almost a nervous wreck—and he is showing signs the last two or three weeks of mental fatigue. This always means for him a certain irrationality of conduct, and an intolerance of viewpoint. He has become quite obsessed lately over the export of arms, having exalted it into a crusade against evil.' Anyone who could be carried away by such an inconsequential subject (for so it was seen at the time) could not be taken seriously. Still, Pearson had recommended Reid for promotion to Assistant Under-Secretary and would make him Deputy Under-Secretary of State for External Affairs, the number two position in the Department.[94]

'Mad is he?' George II was supposed to have said of General James Wolfe. 'Then I hope he will bite some others of my generals.' Pearson might have said that of Escott Reid. Unstable or not, on a crusade or not, Reid produced more good ideas (and some bad ones too) than anyone else in his Department. Unfortunately not everyone trusted his ability to separate the wheat from the chaff, and Reid's influence, while strong, was never as great as he might have wished. Still and all, a man who provided the impetus and rationale for NATO, and who was in a major way responsible for the revolution in Canadian foreign policy that it represented, need never hang his head.[95]

9

THE END OF THE
MANDARIN ERA

By the mid-1950s the heyday of the mandarins was nearing its end. Death had already removed some of the most powerful players from the stage. Skelton and Christie died in 1941, early casualties of the pressures of war. Clifford Clark died at the end of 1952 while on a speech-making trip to Chicago. Alex Skelton drowned while sailing off the coast of Nigeria in 1950, a death that many believed to be a suicide. Hume Wrong died in hospital in late 1954 before he could take up the reins as Under-Secretary of State for External Affairs. Still others retired or left the public service. Graham Towers, one of the founders of the mandarinate and a power in the land for twenty years, retired in 1954. Donald Gordon, the hard-driving, driven man who had made the Wartime Prices and Trade Board the great success it was, had left the relatively tame precincts of the Bank of Canada for the presidency of the Canadian National Railways based in Montreal and, although a Crown corporation, a world away from the public service and Ottawa. John Deutsch returned to academe as a professor of economics at the University of British Columbia, while W.A. Mackintosh was Principal of Queen's. Two members of the mandarinate had gone political. Pearson entered the Cabinet in 1948 as Secretary of State for External Affairs and J.W. Pickersgill in 1953 as Secretary of State and then, a year later, as Minister of Citizenship and Immigration—fateful moves that greatly increased Opposition mistrust of the senior bureaucracy's links with the government party. So few of the old group were left that there was a certain poignancy in the remark that Donald Gordon made to Watson Sellar, the Auditor-General, at a reception in Ottawa at the beginning of 1956: 'He had thought he knew most of the people who would attend. Instead he knew very few—much to the point, as official Ottawa has changed to a remarkable degree in the past five years.'[1] So it had.

A few mandarins, however, remained in harness. Arnold Heeney was the Ambassador in Washington, Dana Wilgress was Permanent Representative to the NATO Council, and Norman Robertson was High Commissioner in the United Kingdom. Escott Reid was High Commissioner in New Delhi. Louis Rasminsky, a bit disillusioned at being passed over for Graham Tower's post as Governor of the Bank of Canada—allegedly on the grounds of objections to his religion from the chartered bankers with whom the Bank had to work closely—was still the number-two man at the Bank (though he would assume the governorship in 1960), while his old University of Toronto friend, A.F.W. Plumptre, was Assistant Deputy Minister of Finance. Mitchell Sharp was Deputy Minister of Trade and Commerce. At the top of the pole was the Clerk of the Privy Council, Robert Bryce, now easily the most influential member of the public service, the closest adviser to Prime Minister Louis St Laurent.

Although they had tried to bring along new men, the mandarins' strength was depleted by the passage of years; it was also weakened by other alterations in the structure of the government. By the mid-1950s the civil service was very large, substantially larger than at the peak of the war. In 1945, for example, the total number of federal civil servants was 115,908; in 1950 there were 127,196; and in 1955 there were 181,582. External Affairs had doubled in size, as had National Defence and Agriculture. National Health and Welfare was three times larger, and the RCMP, reflecting the nation's sense of insecurity, had increased from 499 in 1945 to 6,236 in 1955.[2] The public service was bloated. Although they still existed, the intimacy and affection that had bound the senior officials together and given them an extraordinary collective influence were no longer so strong in a vast bureaucracy that precluded arrangement-making over lunch in the Château Laurier cafeteria—even had that room still existed in its old wartime form. Most significantly, the era of the experts was beginning, while that of the generalists was coming to a close. The men with computers and flow-charts were just around the corner, as were new organizations with sweeping and ill-defined mandates. More to the point, the policy consensus among the officials in Finance, External Affairs, Trade and Commerce, and the Bank of Canada that had been such a striking feature of the Ottawa scene through the 1940s was beginning to break down.[3] The problems that had accompanied the Depression, the war, and the 'cold peace', were not too vast or too complex to be handled by the mandarins' almost incredible unanimity. There was agreement on the need for an increased role for the federal government in social welfare and in the management of the economy; on the need for an international policy that saw Canada reject the negativism that so often had characterized the long-ago days of 'Parliament will decide'; on the need for a policy of freer trade, of aid to overseas markets, of close economic links with the United States, all designed to ensure that Canadians enjoyed the highest possible standard of living.

By the early and mid-1950s, however, events had begun to alter these established policies. Ottawa had established its role as the dominant player on the federal-provincial stage and, although the provinces were beginning to stir restlessly, there seemed few new worlds to conquer. The economy had been running well, but inflation was beginning to be a concern and unemployment, except for a few good years, remained substantial. Structural weaknesses had begun to show. Foreign policy was in good hands—Mike Pearson's hands—but relations with the United States in the Dulles years, and with Britain, trying desperately to recapture its place as a great power, were difficult. Most important, perhaps, Canada's trade increasingly flowed in a north-south direction, and while the nation was prosperous, it was disquieting to be so dependent on the American market. The United States also supplied most of Canada's investment capital and had a determining influence on defence policy as well. By the sixth or seventh year of the St Laurent decade, although none of the mandarins could have been called economic nationalists, one or two were becoming concerned about this great reliance on Washington.

The problems were different now, and seemingly harder to resolve. There was one positive note, however. The mandarins did not have to worry about the uncertanties that would have been caused by an unstable political environment in Canada. The Liberals had been in power for so long that they had become 'the government party'. The CCF was a splinter, Social Credit was a tiny Alberta fringe group, and the Progressive Conservatives seemed a weak, dispirited rump, saddled with George Drew's Bay Street image and Anglo style. There were problems, yes, but nothing that time could not resolve. For men like R.B. Bryce, the Clerk of the Privy Council, whose influence on the Prime Minister was almost as great as that of Skelton or Clark in their prime, time did not seem to be in short supply.

I

Robert Bryce was born in Toronto on February 27, 1910, the son of a very tough man. His father and namesake was a mining engineer, a specialist in the hunt for, and development of, mining properties who had gone to work before completing his university degree—drilling Pennsylvania Railroad tunnels under the Hudson River and mining in Mexico and Cobalt, Ont. Bryce Sr was able to afford a good life for his family, but he became wealthy after the Macassa Mines property at Kirkland Lake proved out as a good gold-bearing site for a time. The Bryces lived in a large Rosedale mansion during the 1930s and after, but there was sometimes little cash in hand because the father gambled on ore bodies; the family fortunes rose and fell with the success—or lack of it—of Bryce's enterprises.

The father was a driver who pressed his eldest son to perform well in school, and he was not disappointed. After attending the University of Toronto Schools, Bryce was sent to the University of Toronto to study engineering, at his father's insistence. He graduated in 1932 at the height of the Depression. What then? The father wanted his son to study business, but young Bryce, whose interests had been turned to the left by a Utopian socialist mother and a reaction against his father's entrepreneurial capitalism, persuaded his father that he should study economics at Cambridge. Bryce knew people who had gone there—notably A.F.W. Plumptre, who had taught Bryce's sister at the University of Toronto—and although an engineering graduate, he had broad interests that had led him into debating and current events and to acquaintanceships with bright young men like Lorie Tarshis, who was also destined for Cambridge economics.

The one problem was that Bryce had taken no economics courses at the University of Toronto. Fortunately that did not trouble Cambridge, which was prepared to admit him with senior standing on the basis of his high grades and good recommendations; but it troubled Bryce, who spent the summer of 1932 at a family cottage on Go Home Bay, immersing himself in the classics of economics and in Keynes to prepare himself for Keynes's seminar, his goal. Bryce recalled that most of the other members of that seminar had had their views contaminated by studying Keynes's early works; unlike Bryce, they could not readily adapt to the new Keynes of the General Theory. Bryce, unsteeped in the great man's earlier doctrines and with the god-given gift of being a fast study, which the discipline of engineering had honed, began to immerse himself in Keynesian economics. He became a member of the Political Economy Club and a regular attendant at its sessions, an admirer of Keynes's analytical skills and of his understanding of the way institutions truly operated. The two years at Cambridge flew by, and by late 1934 Bryce was working as a doctoral student, writing 'The Fluctuations in Real Investment in the U.S.A. Since the Great War and Their Relationships to Other Economic Changes', an attempt to apply Keynes's monetary theories of employment and interest to the American experience. But the more he had to explain Keynes to others, the farther Bryce got from his own research. In the spring of 1935, for example, he went several times to the London School of Economics ostensibly to sit in on Friedrich Von Hayek's class on monetary and cycle theories but really to preach Keynes's General Theory to the unconverted. A paper Bryce prepared for this class, in fact, was the first exposition of the Theory. When Keynes read it he pronounced it 'excellently done' and 'so comparatively complete . . . a theory which is unfamiliar anyhow does not become easier through compression. All the same you have got into it the main elements in my theory.'[4]

As Keynes introduced Bryce to revolutionary theories of economics, Cambridge itself exposed him to revolutionary political ideas. The son of a capitalist, Bryce was ideally suited to be swept up in the leftist fervour of the university in the mid-1930s. At the same time, fascism was on the march, and to Bryce's great credit he found his friends among those who were trying to resist what then seemed to be the inevitable triumph of the right. He joined socialist clubs and spoke for Labour candidates; he participated in demonstrations, some of which became violent; and he became close to a number of men, including his fellow Canadian Herbert Norman; through him he met the poet John Cornford, a Communist destined to be killed fighting against Franco.[5]

Bryce's Cambridge connections on the left arouse a natural interest today, especially given the revelations of Soviet spy recruiting at the university at that time. One scurrilous Toronto newspaper even reported in 1981 that Bryce, Lester Pearson, Herbert

Norman, and Kim Philby, the Soviet spy who rose to high places in British intelligence, were photographed together at the university. Bryce replied that he did not know Pearson while he was at Cambridge (Pearson, of course, went to Oxford in the twenties), and that he never met Philby—a reply, while correct, that failed to satisfy the *Toronto Sun* and the RCMP sources that feed it. The same newspaper also claimed that O.D. Skelton had been recruited by the Comintern in 1923, another ridiculous charge that says little for the *Sun*'s credibility or the RCMP's investigative powers.[6]

Bryce went to Harvard in 1935 on a Commonwealth Fund Fellowship won on Keynes's recommendation that he had a strong personality and a practical bent, but was perhaps out of his depth in advanced branches of economics![7] Even so, he arrived in Boston, as John Kenneth Galbraith later noted, with 'a special license to explain what Keynes meant in his more obscure passages.'[8] Bryce himself put it this way when he tried to justify to his Cambridge supervisors why his dissertation work was slow:

> I expected at Harvard to round off the theoretical portion of my work rather quickly and to have the necessary historical material available for the applied work. I found Harvard highly critical of the theoretical views I held and I spent a good deal of my time in learning what I could of their methods of analysis. It was at this time that Mr. Keynes's General Theory of Employment, Interest and Money appeared and it evoked a great deal of interest. Being one of the few in Harvard—indeed in the U.S.A.—who had studied these ideas at Cambridge, my time was very much taken up in discussion of them. In view of their importance and the reception accorded them, I considered this time well spent from a broad point of view, while the experience gained was of considerable value in formulating my own ideas.[9]

Of value, yes, but Bryce's own work proceeded not at all, so caught up was he in his discussions. 'Furthermore,' as he later wrote to Cambridge with a somewhat tart tone, 'I found, somewhat unexpectedly, there was a good deal of economics, both theoretical and practical, which I had to learn at Harvard to supplement the rather specialized, though excellent training one receives at Cambridge.'[10] At Harvard Bryce studied under Schumpeter, Leontief, Haberler, and Harris, among others.

He also continued his friendship with Herbert Norman, who was now at Harvard, and through Norman became acquainted with the Japanese Marxist economist, Shigeto Tsuru. Probably also through Norman, and his acquaintance with Dr Paul Sweezy, an American Marxist, Bryce was asked to deliver a paper to a Marxist study group on the American New Deal's Agricultural Adjustment Act 'as seen in the light of Lenin's analysis of American agriculture in the 19th century.' That provoked an eventual RCMP investigation of his academic past in the 1950s, Bryce said, although when the spy-hunters read through the paper they got only a few pages into it before deciding that 'it wasn't very interesting'.[11] Bryce also suffered from the public comments of American Congressional committees, but the RCMP investigations produced nothing substantive against him.[12] Herbert Norman would not be so lucky.

By 1937 Bryce was twenty-seven and married to a social worker he had met in Cambridge, Mass. Harvard offered him a position but he was anxious to return to Canada and, in any case, his Commonwealth Fund Fellowship obliged him to leave the United States. He applied to Clifford Clark for a job with the Department of Finance; at the same time he approached the Sun Life Assurance Company in Montreal. Clark was slow in reading the papers Bryce sent him, so the anxious applicant accepted the insurance company's offer, two hours before Clark telephoned with his own.[13] Thus it was the business world of Montreal for a year,[14] working on the Sun's investments in the United States. Bryce said of this position that it 'involved following the American economic situation from day to day.' He took the post, he told Cambridge University, because he believed the experience could only benefit him in his dissertation research. Despite extension after extension from a compliant Faculty of Economics, however, Bryce's thesis (like Clark's) would never be finished.[15]

In the middle of 1938 Clark approached Bryce again and this time Bryce willingly joined the Department of Finance, arriving in Ottawa the weekend of the Munich crisis to be assigned, as his first chore, the task of looking up details on war-risk insurance for shipping.[16] The pressure, once begun, never let up, and Clark soon discovered that he had a gem in Bryce. Peering out from behind his thick-lensed spectacles, Bryce brought enormous intelligence and energy to his work, and his duties encompassed almost every aspect of government finance. He managed to insert some

Keynes into the Dominion budget of 1939; he wrote papers on the problems of the Canadian exchange rate; he gave a paper to the Canadian Political Science Association that applied both Keynes and his Harvard training to the problem of Canada's international economic vulnerability; and he participated actively in the manifold activities and conferences of the Canadian Institute of International Affairs.[17] These activities were more than enough to justify a Montreal friend's comment that 'Just to read in your letter how hard you have been working very nearly gave me a nervous breakdown!'[18]

The war ensured that the pace never altered. Bryce prepared some of the original studies on the proportion of the National Income that Canada could devote to the war,[19] and he became secretary of the Economic Advisory Committee when it was set up in September 1939, and the draftsman of its minutes and many of its reports. He served on committee after committee, sometimes in his own right, sometimes as Clark's deputy—along with Mitchell Sharp, another of the wartime recruits to the Department. Although he was still relatively junior, his voice was listened to. In 1944, for example, he and Sharp worked closely with J.G. Gardiner, the Minister of Agriculture and the *bête noire* of the mandarins, on the price-support bill, and Gardiner treated them well. On the Mutual Aid Board, a Cabinet committee, Bryce as the chief expert on the subject was heard with respect, primarily as Clark's man but also for his own obvious abilities. If there was a problem, Clark could be relied upon to back up his men, the ideal relationship between superior and subordinate. Equally important, the Finance Department still had short lines of authority—there was no one on the organization chart between Bryce and the Deputy—and he had access to Clark whenever necessary. In a true sense Bryce became Clark's work-horse, the man to tackle any difficult job. He was also becoming a negotiator as well and participated with Keynes in discussions on Canadian aid to Britain when the great economist came to Ottawa to persuade the government, successfully, to give more assistance.

The war made Bryce's reputation. If a question arose, he could tackle it and produce a well-written thirty-page memorandum on the subject overnight. His capacity to assimilate data was enormous, his fund of ideas impressive. Professor Vincent Bladen remembered sitting with Bryce on a committee where Bryce brainstormed, throwing out ideas and hoping and expecting to see them challenged. This wasn't how the mandarins usually worked; most simply reached into their file folder for a solution, presenting it as the end of the discussion. That was not Bryce's way.[20]

Peace changed the pressure very little. Bryce played an important part in working out the loan to Britain in 1946, and in repeated attempts over the next few years to keep Canadian-British trade flowing despite London's perilous economic condition. He helped to deal with the Canadian dollar shortage of 1947-8, bringing his academic studies to bear once more on current events and demonstrating his expanding talents by working on Finance Minister Douglas Abbott's speech announcing the dollar conservation measures of November 19, 1947.[21] Finally, as Canada began to get caught up in the Cold War he threw out ideas galore on ways to strengthen NATO's economic underpinnings—and to facilitate Canadian exports.[22]

In 1947 Bryce was promoted to Assistant Deputy Minister of Finance and made secretary of the Treasury Board. This was a crucial post because the Board was a Cabinet Committee that acted as the executive body responsible for internal administration and the surveillance of expenditures. During the Depression, Treasury Board had viewed its functions in a negative way, taking every opportunity to reduce expenditures; during the war it had been called upon to manage expanding services, but again its control was exercised in an essentially negative fashion. The war changed Ottawa's role in the economy, and the Board could no longer be pinch-penny. 'What the Treasury Board needed', one history of the organization noted, 'was a strong Secretary with an appreciation of the priorities in expenditure which could affect employment, income, prices, interest rates and other fiscal matters.'[23] The post might have been made for Bryce, who tried to interpret his mandate creatively, assisting in the general management of government. 'He had experience in the policy divisions of the Department of Finance, was a trained economist and engineer and wanted the Board to be a positive agency. . . . The result was that the Treasury Board became more deeply involved in departmental activities and responsibilities.' In fact, as the Treasury Board historians note, 'The Secretary was in effect downgrading the responsibility of the Deputy Ministers of other Departments. . . .'[24] The role of busybody, prying into everyone's affairs, was a delicate one, but Bryce carried it out with great success. Significantly, two years later when Arnold Heeney was about to leave his post as Clerk of the Privy Council, Bryce was the initial choice as his successor to the pre-eminent position in the public service, and his selection was widely acceptable to all—except Clifford Clark, who was unhappy at the prospect of losing his right-hand man. That was a high tribute, particularly as Bryce was only thirty-nine and virtually the cadet of the mandarinate. As it turned out, however, other factors impinged on choosing Bryce, and Norman Robertson was brought from London to take the job.[25]

By 1950 Bryce had as detailed a knowledge of the federal bureaucracy as anyone in Ottawa. The Treasury Board post virtually required that, and Bryce took advantage of every opportunity to learn more. For example, as a man who was temperamentally a hawk on defence questions, and as defence at the beginning of the 1950s absorbed so great a percentage of the budget, Bryce took a detailed interest in the Department of National Defence, probing everywhere. He even had himself put on the rank-structure committee, which was far removed from budgetary matters, and came to know officers across all three services.[26]

Bryce's career was not a succession of triumphs, however. In December 1952, when Clifford Clark died, Bryce might have expected to become his successor. But the Minister of Finance, Douglas Abbott, chose instead Kenneth Taylor, a one-time academic who had worked with the Wartime Prices and Trade Board during and after the war. Taylor was politically astute and an able and decent man, but he totally lacked Bryce's energy, ability, and flair. Abbott later claimed that his selection had been based on Taylor's seniority,[27] despite the fact that Bryce had more Department service than Taylor. Later Abbott said he had not wanted Bryce because his prose was too convoluted![28] Bryce's eventual reward came a year later when Pickersgill left the Privy Council Office to enter the Cabinet. No one, Bryce remembered, asked him if he wanted to become Clerk of the Privy Council. Pickersgill simply assumed that he would. So he did, and 'it was the best job I ever had.'[29] When the appointment was announced in September 1953, the Auditor-General noted in his diary that 'Bryce had been appointed. . . . A good man, but he finds it hard to say "no" and is an empire builder so far as staff are concerned,'[30] a ref-

erence to Bryce's expansion of the Treasury Board staff. Whether
those criticisms were apt is hard to determine, though if Bryce
was a man who found it hard to say no, he was the first Secretary
of Treasury Board of whom that could be said.

II

As we have seen, by the mid-1950s there was beginning to be substantial and widespread unease about the influence of the civil service on government decisions and on the apparently close links between the Liberal Party and the senior bureaucracy. This was not a
new development, of course. In 1942 the Leader of the Opposition, R.B. Hanson, lashed out at the 'masterminds who behind the
scenes are formulating our war-time financial policies. . . . These
men have responsibilities, they have great power; but they are not
answerable to anybody.'[31] George Drew, the Ontario Conservative premier, took a similar view, stating darkly that overworked
ministers had delegated power 'to a hidden form of government in
the form of officials.' Worse yet, those officials were in his mind
'extremely dangerous men', pursuing centralization, and perhaps
intending to set up 'an effective dictatorship behind the mask of
Responsible Government'.[32] That was one avenue of the attack;
another was by criticizing the way appointments were made, and
occasionally those who received them. When, late in the war, a
new Deputy Minister of Trade and Commerce was named, a senior civil servant (not a mandarin) and a businessman with Ottawa
connections commiserated together, 'His opinion of the man is
low,' Watson Sellar noted in his diary of his conversation with
Fraser Bruce of the Aluminium Company of Canada. 'He says it is
a sample of the "men with the money bags"—Clark and Towers
in dictating appointments. When I told him the salary was $12,000
he hit the roof.'[33] A third line was that the bureaucracy was too
autocratic for the nation's good. 'I do not find bureaucrats as persons terrifying at all,' the Canadian historian and civil libertarian,
A.R.M. Lower, wrote to his former teaching colleague, J.W.
Pickersgill, 'and many of them are the nicest possible people.
Have we not, for example, been sending our best students into the
bureaucracy for years past? (It might have been safer for liberty if
we had been sending our poorest!)'[34] Yet another approach was
that the civil service was spendthrift. The Auditor General, particularly concerned with this in 1952 when expenditures were being

processed with great speed, complained in his diary that 'Financial people, and the Government generally, are uninterested in the amounts paid out. The Big Idea seems to be to reduce the surplus to an amount which will "save face" of those who forecast a smaller surplus.'[35] 'The truth is,' George V. Ferguson of the *Montreal Star* wrote to a diplomat friend, 'that the Liberals are not running the Govt. The civil service is.'[36]

That was what troubled many serious observers who feared that the civil service had turned into the directing agency of the government. J.E. Hodgetts wrote in 1955:

> At the national level, the Liberals have now held office for two decades. Over that period the civil service has not only quadrupled but has vastly improved in the quality of its personnel. Is there a connection between the Liberals' longevity and the growth of the bureaucracy? Might it not be that the monopoly of one party is broken only when it makes enough serious mistakes to become thoroughly discredited? And could it also be said that the emergence of an efficient bureaucracy makes it increasingly unlikely that such mistakes will now occur?

There was some truth in this criticism of the bureaucracy that the mandarins had helped to create, although it implied that they were both more influential and efficient than they truly were. They provided the skills the government needed—Bryce's mastery of Keynesian techniques is but one example—and they gave the Liberal government many of its policy ideas. This too worried Hodgetts:

> A generation of Liberal politicians and a generation of presumably neutral senior permanent officials have worked hand-in-hand to create what is now advertised as the Liberal programme. One imputes no blame to these senior officials if one argues that they are now as fully committed to the Programme as their political chiefs. Suppose, then, a change in the party in power? Could we expect impartial service from the permanent servants . . .? . . . Will the long-term involvement of senior permanent officials create a situation where their objective consideration of alternatives may be impaired? . . . The line between politics and administration is difficult to maintain under normal party circumstances, but it

is likely to disappear altogether when one party holds office for a long period.[37]

There were other wrinkles. Looking at the formulation of the Liberal and Conservative party platforms for the 1957 election, John Meisel concluded that the government's platform had emerged from within the ministry, not from the party, and had therefore been produced by the public service. 'This, it has been alleged, made the Liberal point of view highly centralist and relatively insensitive to regional needs and demands as expressed particularly in the Prairies and the Maritimes.'[38] As Reginald Whitaker noted in *The Government Party* (1977), 'the Liberal Party had indeed become the Government party to the extent that the question of whether, for example, the bureaucrats were Liberals or whether, conversely, the Liberals had themselves become bureaucrats, is rather problematic.'[39] Sandra Gwyn later put it much the same way: 'It isn't that the bureaucrats are all Grits. . . . It's that the Grits are all bureaucrats.'[40]

On the other hand, there was nothing new or startling in the participation of civil servants in policy making, J.W. Pickersgill argued correctly. An official who was merely an administrator was unlikely to be a good administrator, for unless he understood the policy he was running he could not do his job well; if he did understand it, then he would see the faults in it; if he reported those to his minister, then he would be seeking to change or make policy.[41] And Mitchell Sharp, rejecting the idea of a bureaucracy that had to wait on the politicians to initiate the policy process, pointed to the occasions when 'civil servants by fruitful initiatives led the Government to adopt lines of policy which would never have occurred to them otherwise. . . .'[42]

What did seem clear was that the lines had blurred between Minister and adviser. When Pearson moved into the Cabinet in 1948, Mackenzie King inexplicably remarked to the country that the civil service should be regarded as 'the stepping-stone to the Ministry', an amazing *faux pas* that Eugene Forsey properly described at the time as 'the most extraordinary statement of his career', one asserting 'a constitutional principle as novel as it is subversive of parliamentary government.'[43] The elevation of Pearson had been bad enough; Jack Pickersgill's was worse in the eyes of the Opposition. He had been a very political servant under King and St Laurent, he was considered by some to have besmirched the impartiality of the senior position in the public service as Clerk of the Privy Council, and by entering the Cabinet in 1953 had appeared to prove the complaints against him. This event fuelled the Tories' suspicions that the civil service was partisan.

Thus when John Diefenbaker unexpectedly led the Progressive Conservative party to victory in the 1957 election, the incoming government was filled with mistrust of its senior bureaucratic advisers, and the mandarins for their part were nervous about the change and the challenge that awaited them. The most suspicious Tory of all was Diefenbaker, who wrote in his memoirs: 'When a government has been in power as long as the Liberals, it was natural that many public officials absorbed the political faith of the government, which in their opinion seemed destined to endure forever. Following the election in 1957 one or two high-ranking public servants suggested that my government would be at best short-lived.'[45] Who those doubters were remains unknown. Diefenbaker also noted that 'Pearson and Pickersgill, having been civil servants themselves, knew all the higher echelon public servants', thus implying that the Liberals used these connections to secure information harmful to the new government. The Conservative leader then added that 'Perhaps there were a number of high-ranking public servants who should have been dismissed without delay when we took office. . . .' Nonetheless he was reluctant to do this 'on the sole ground that they had served another administration. I thought that course most unjust. . . .' But 'had I been returned to office in 1965, there would have been some major changes made. It became obvious as soon as we were out of office in 1963 that there were quite a number of senior people in the public service, about whom I had not known, who had simply been underground, quietly working against my government and waiting for the Liberals to return to power.'[46] Again, no names were mentioned.

Other Conservatives were blunter. A British Columbia backbencher, A.D. McPhillips, told a constituency meeting in 1957 that 'All the top Civil Servants and the Deputy Ministers are Grits.'[47] Gordon Churchill, the Minister of Trade and Commerce in the new government, later said that 'One of the strange things . . . was that Mitchell Sharp phoned me and said that the department offices . . . would not be available for ten days because they were re-decorating. Actually they were getting rid of the files.'

Churchill added that he and his personal staff met 'the coldest reception I had ever received' at Trade and Commerce, and one of his own appointees after the 1958 election told him 'quite frankly, "When you first came down here you were hated by everybody in the department, right down to the most junior office boy." '[48] This was told to him by James Roberts, a wartime Brigadier, a businessman and an active Conservative, who recounted his own welcome to the Department as an Associate Deputy Minister:

> I next met the deputy minister . . . a long-serving career trade commissioner. He stated bluntly that he had not asked for me as a member of the department and that it would be a long time before I could be of any use to the department. I would be given an office and would participate in all departmental meetings but it would be my own responsibility to inform myself of the working of the ministry. . . . His words were blunt and to the point and I had no quarrel with them, but it was abundantly clear that he did not intend to take me into his confidence.

Roberts added that over the year they served together 'our personal relationship remained cool and distant and I was not asked to join in many meetings . . . with other senior officials.'[49]

After the 1958 election the Toronto *Globe and Mail* also weighed in with a call for a wholesale house-cleaning. In its first few months in power in 1957, the government had had to postpone decisions, for it 'had to be certain that they were getting sound advice from sound advisers'. But the *Globe* cautioned that now the government had the right and duty to dismantle the bureaucratic 'establishment', to assess the outlook, attitude, and state of mind of the senior civil servants. It was not their competence that was in question, the *Globe* argued, but whether they were a help or a hindrance. The Liberals had hired them, and as a result the civil servants might not be the ones a Conservative government wanted to do the job.[50] A few days later the paper's Ottawa columnist noted that changes at the top of the civil service would be a good thing and could be managed without hurting either the nation or individuals. There were, Robert Duffy admitted, some possibilities of a temporary sacrifice of accumulated administrative experience, but this could be outweighed by the gain in freshness of approach and, most important, in a reassertion of the supremacy of elected authority.[51] This mindless advice, if taken, could have destroyed the public service; it could have been justified only had there been outright opposition to the Diefenbaker government from the mandarinate.* No one—not even James Roberts—suggests that there was.

A better perspective is given by Gowan Guest, a prime ministerial aide, who remembered getting 'a couple of calls a day from [Ministers'] executive assistants . . . practically all of them saying they had problems, that they were not getting cooperation, or they were having difficulty communicating or that these people were giving them stupid reasons [for objecting to proposals].' Guest went on:

> They were in a position where they knew what was the best thing to do. It could be in connection with anything—the Seaway, anything. They had the position papers and the study and so on, and sometimes they'd be indifferent, and they'd let you fan the air and try to figure it out. . . .
>
> I think the fault was, on the part of the senior civil service, that they never got on the team. On the other side, on the part of the government, the fault was that they never really invited them to be part of the team.[52]

That was probably a fair assessment.

So too was that of Charles Ritchie, a senior officer in the Department of External Affairs who visited Ottawa from his post at the UN in the middle of 1959 to find 'suspicion of Ministers, and particularly of the Prime Minister, that the higher civil servants

---

* Arnold Heeney, the Chairman of the Civil Service Commission at the time of the change in government, told the Empire Club in Toronto that the transition was 'accomplished with extraordinarily little administrative disturbance and surprisingly little fuss', that 'working relations between the principal civil servants and the Ministers . . . are, I believe, firmly established on the basis of mutual confidence, respect and understanding.' (*Empire Club Addresses 1957-8* (Toronto, 1959), 176-7.) On the other hand, when Sharp and Claude Isbister, another senior official, left Trade and Commerce in 1958, Heeney urged J.H. Warren to apply for the post of Assistant Deputy Minister. (Warren interview, 15 May, 1979.) This appears to have been an attempt to have a junior mandarin in place to ensure that matters did not get too far out of hand, although Warren's merits were very great and there was much to be said in favour of filling senior posts by selection and opening the process to candidates outside the department concerned.

Howard Green, however, told the House of Commons that the government had received 'splendid cooperation' from the bureaucracy. (*Debates*, 18 Dec. 1957, 2515. See also Green in *ibid.*, 15 Nov.1957, 1211.)

may be disloyal to the government, or even plotting with the Liberals against them. In a way,' Ritchie observed in his diary,

> this suspicion is comprehensible. In the long years in Opposition the Conservative Members of Parliament, particularly the Western Members of Parliament, have been living a somewhat isolated life in their rented houses and apartments in Ottawa. They have seen the cozy, intimate relationship between Liberal Ministers and civil servants, mostly living cheek-by-jowl in Rockcliffe, their children attending the same schools, their wives in and out of each others' houses, intimate old friendships between senior civil servants and Ministers, and so they have come to believe in a sort of conspiracy against the government. It is true, I imagine, that most of the influential civil servants in Ottawa have Liberal sympathies, certainly very few are Conservatives, but I think they are much too loyal to the tradition of an impartial civil service to work against the government. Unfortunately, this intense suspicion of their motives and behaviour may create the very animosity that it fears.[53]

At the very least, then, even if Diefenbaker's and Churchill's complaints are disregarded, there was certainly a period of difficulty and discomfort that accompanied the Conservative takeover. Perhaps this was inevitable after twenty-two years of Liberal government,[54] and possibly the Conservatives might have been expected to treat the mandarins harshly. In fact, the myth to the contrary, the treatment was markedly gentle, Sharp being the sole mandarin deputy minister to resign well ahead of his retirement age[55] (although some senior officials—George McIvor of the Wheat Board, W.J. Bennett of Atomic Energy of Canada, and Davidson Dunton of the CBC—also left).[56] The Tory mistrust of the mandarins was as strong as ever, however. This was a worrisome problem for a prime minister without leadership experience; a critical one for a new government that needed all the help it could get to learn how to pick up, hold, and manage the reins; and a crucial one for a civil service that needed the opportunity to demonstrate that it served the nation and the administration elected to run it, not the old Liberal régime. In this difficult time the task of reconciling government and bureaucracy fell to Robert Bryce.

A more thankless task could hardly be conceived. In the begin-

ning Diefenbaker was suspicious of Bryce. Had he not worked for
the Grits since 1938? Had he not been *the* closest adviser to St
Laurent since 1953? On the other hand, Bryce's father had been a
Tory, a redeeming factor with the Prime Minister and something
he never forgot.[57] More to the point, Bryce instantly began to
provide the Chief and his government with straightforward and
correct advice, and assistance of every kind, carefully choosing his
words when he disagreed with a proposed course to suggest the
probable consequences tactfully but frankly. In addition he made
it his job to learn to understand the Prime Minister, talking with
his executive assistants at length, searching for the directions the
government wanted to follow.[58] As always, too, Bryce brought
the same enormous drive to serving John Diefenbaker that he had
formerly shown under Clifford Clark, Louis St Laurent, and his
other masters. When the Prime Minister asked for a paper, he received a well-worked out memorandum—and on time. Bryce
produced the goods, and within two or three months Diefenbaker
began to trust him, to become dependent on him, and to be very
frank with him. A few months before his death, Diefenbaker described his Clerk of the Privy Council as a wonderful man, loyal,
intelligent, hardworking. 'I could not have carried on without
him,' he said.[59]

But Bryce was almost the only mandarin Diefenbaker trusted.
No other official (except an Assistant Secretary) was allowed in
the Cabinet room. 'There were enough leaks without officials,'
Diefenbaker said.[60] All the senior officials were Grits, all 'Pearson-
alities', too close to the party leader who had been elected by the
Liberal convention early in 1958.[61] The Prime Minister considered
External Affairs in particular to be a haven for his enemies. This
mistrust was not relieved when Norman Robertson was brought
back from the Washington Embassy in the fall of 1958 to be
Under-Secretary again, though the appointment was made with
Diefenbaker's concurrence. It was not that Robertson, a careful
and cautious man who hid the way he voted even from his friends
and family, put a foot wrong; it was simply that the Prime Minister thought that he might. And there was always the fear that
Robertson and other mandarins were making unfavourable comparisons between him and his Liberal predecessors. Robertson
rarely saw the Prime Minister, even though his office was very
close to Diefenbaker's on the second floor of the East Block. Diefenbaker was thus deprived of the advice of a wise counsellor,

something he should have treasured. External Affairs therefore lost its direct influence on the Prime Minister. This put a very heavy burden on Basil Robinson, a young foreign-service officer who served as the liaison between External Affairs and the Prime Minister's Office and had the duty of staying loyal both to the Prime Minister and to his Department. Diefenbaker's mistrust of External also put a load on the Clerk of the Privy Council. Bryce, a friend of Robertson's, was forced into an intermediary role, conveying as much of Robertson's advice as he could to the Prime Minister.[62] Policy differences made this particularly difficult at the time of the debate within the government over nuclear weapons. Bryce (and National Defence) wanted them; External Affairs did not; and Bryce had to convey information to a wavering Prime Minister without misrepresenting Robertson's views, no matter how much he disagreed with them.[63]

It was not only here that Bryce was intermediary. He played that same role—Basil Robinson called him 'the universal joint'[64]— for virtually all the mandarins. He was the man in the middle, reassuring the Prime Minister and his Cabinet that the public service was there to assist any and all governments, and reassuring the mandarins that the Prime Minister was a man who, despite his instinctive mistrust of them, wanted to serve the country as best he could. Unfortunately Diefenbaker's memoirs imply that Bryce was unable to carry out this mission. To the end of his days the Chief remained convinced that he had been done in by 'them', an omnibus group that included many senior officials—as well as by numerous Conservatives. However, some ministers—George Hees, Alvin Hamilton, R.A. Bell, George Nowlan—got on well with their deputies;[65] but because they seem not to have conveyed this to Diefenbaker and their colleagues, Tory suspicions stayed alive and grew stronger as former public servants began to enlist under Pearson's banner. Mitchell Sharp; C.M. Drury, a former deputy minister of National Defence; Guy Favreau, a senior Justice Department official; Maurice Lamontagne, an economics adviser to the Privy Council Office—the list of retired civil servants who ran for office in the elections of 1962 and 1963 went on and on, confirming the Tories' darkest misgivings.

Despite his best efforts, and the trust in which he was held by the Prime Minister and his fellow mandarins, Bryce failed as the middleman. No one could have succeeded, given the character of the Prime Minister and several of his ministers. But the downfall of the government, its collapse in confusion in early 1963, had nothing to do with the mandarins and their advice or their alleged leanings toward the Liberals. It was John Diefenbaker's failure. His doubts and fears, his indecisiveness,[66] his very style ultimately led to its collapse. 'They' had opposed him and 'they' apparently included some of the mandarinate; but the civil servants, especially Bryce, are largely blameless for the end result. Some of his friends used to complain that the Clerk of the Privy Council actually seemed to like Diefenbaker. This, in fact, was true. As Bryce said later, when Diefenbaker trusted someone, 'he was a good man to work for. He treated his official and personal staff considerately and in a friendly way.'[67] Certainly Bryce was loyal to the Chief, and it was largely owing to him that the government functioned as well as it did. Bryce kept the public service working as efficiently and smoothly as possible.

Few emerge from the Diefenbaker period with their credit enhanced. The Prime Minister's viciousness was matched by that of his critics, and the coincident hard times that came with the Tory election victories of 1957 and 1958 made futile many initiatives that might otherwise have succeeded. But all agree—Diefenbaker, the mandarins, the ministers—that Bob Bryce played his role superbly. It is an irony that in his three volumes of memoirs Diefenbaker referred to Bryce only twice in passing. But anonymity is and should be a tradition in the public service,[68] and given the tenor of Diefenbaker's apologia, his neglect of Bryce might be the highest tribute of all.

III

The Liberal Party, led by Lester Pearson and including among its senior figures Jack Pickersgill and Mitchell Sharp, came to power in the election of 1963, accompanied by almost audible sighs of relief from the surviving mandarins, who rejoiced in the prospect of an end to the turmoil and uncertainty of the Diefenbaker interregnum. Canada could now return to safe, certain, careful progress under Pearson, himself a former mandarin. But this was not to be. The chaos of the Diefenbaker years was succeeded by a different chaos in the mid-1960s. The Liberals staggered and lurched from the 'sixty days of decision' and the unpopular Gordon budget, which in action turned out to be a disastrous parody of election promises, to recurrent scandals that wracked the government and played into the hands of the Leader of the Opposition. Governability as a Canadian trait, and competence as a characteristic of Canadian government, seemed to have disappeared. And with these successive crises the heyday of the mandarins appeared to have come to an end. In retrospect, however, the break in the power of senior civil servants had occurred years before, in 1957 with the accession of Diefenbaker.

What did the mandarins accomplish from 1935 through to the defeat of the St Laurent government? They played a crucial role in centralizing power in Ottawa. They created a Canadian foreign policy that was by their lights nationalist and at the same time internationalist. They provided the ideas and the intellectual rationale for the establishment of the Canadian welfare state. And they developed close links with two governments—those of Mackenzie King and Louis St Laurent—though to those outside the Liberal Party this alliance seemed to violate the proper relationship of a civil service to the government it served.

The Ottawa Men were centralists first and foremost. The Depression had demonstrated that Canada could work satisfactorily only if the central government had the power to create and implement national programs, to equalize services across the land, and to establish and maintain a national minimum standard of social services that would be the same in Summerside, Toronto, or Kamloops. Power had to be concentrated in the hands of the only government that could achieve these ends—and at the disposal of the only civil servants in the nation with the vision and skills to make Canada the kind of country it could and should be. In this construct the provinces were in the hands of backward satraps, in charge of venal politicians and file clerks, their outlook limited by narrow geographical boundaries.

There was some truth in that harsh judgement. Parochialism was the norm as each province resisted efforts to co-ordinate policies and fought bitterly against common solutions that might diminish their constitutional powers. As early as 1933, for example, at the very nadir of the Depression, Ontario and Quebec had flatly refused to co-ordinate unemployment policies with the other provinces and Ottawa. In the circumstances, federal politicians were leery of any steps that might upset the delicate relationships with the nine provinces. It took extraordinary efforts on the part of Graham Towers and Clifford Clark to persuade the King government to assist the near-bankrupt Prairie Provinces and to launch that grand inquest into dominion-provincial relations, the

Rowell-Sirois Commission. Such caution became unnecessary once the war began: the constitution granted Ottawa vast emergency powers, and the war also seemed to make the politicians more willing to accept the centralist advice of their officials. The results were an intrusion of the federal government into areas that hitherto had seemed safely provincial, and a huge increase in federal powers. The provinces resisted, on occasion, sometimes fiercely.[69] But during the war and postwar years the balance of power in Canada shifted decisively in Ottawa's direction. To the mandarins, to the Liberals, the rising prosperity of the nation proved the worth of massive federal power.

There was one major problem here: Quebec was resistant. It was ordinarily treated by Ottawa as a province like the others, but this was never so. French Canadians enjoyed economic benefits as much as Albertans or Ontarians, but they still had special concerns—for their language, culture, and religion—that the rest of the country could not share. King and St Laurent were aware of this—as politicians leading a party heavily dependent on the votes of Quebec, they had to be—but their political interests did not seem to affect the general drift of policy. And the mandarins, English Canadians to a man, somehow forgot about Quebec. It was not that they were assimilationists or anti-French; they weren't. It was simply that it was neater on the charts and plans if Quebec received the same treatment as the rest of the country. This curious blindness to the fundamental reality of Canadian life was to cost the country dearly.

Other regions also came to be exceedingly unhappy with the treatment they received from a nationalist and centralist Ottawa. Consultation was sporadic, consideration was minimal, and resentment increased by leaps and bounds. But the provincial public services were growing. By the early 1960s Quebec and Ontario were beginning to deploy mandarins of their own, men and women every bit as bright and tough as the federal representatives they dealt with at meetings and conferences. British Columbia and Alberta followed. And Saskatchewan, under a CCF government since 1944, had a small but very able and dedicated bureaucracy that had been attracted to the province by the idealism of Premier Tommy Douglas. The balance of intellectual power began to approach equilibrium; a change in the balance of real power was inevitable.

But the balance of power in the world was also changing. In the

1930s, when Canada attempted to move toward autonomy within the Empire, the tactic was revealed to be hollow by the virtually automatic Canadian declaration of war in September 1939, just one week after that of Britain. Canada had played almost no part in the decision-making of the late 1930s and indeed, had deliberately turned its back on the world for the sake of domestic political tranquillity. But the events of the war altered this balance too. Ottawa—represented by supremely able men—began to state the Canadian case in the councils of the Great Powers, and in the space of three or four years Canada put aside the trappings of a colony. The mandarins were all nationalists, all concerned to see their country achieve independence, unity, and a proper place in the world. Internationalists as well, they were certain that Canada had a genuine role to play. The war had irrefutably demonstrated that Canada could produce the necessary goods and raise large, effective fighting forces. War conditions had also shown that Canada could discern and protect its national interests through skilful diplomacy and a willingness to deploy forcefully such power as it possessed. The peace that followed the war emboldened the mandarins to believe that Canada's goals could continue to be pursued. They had already achieved Canada's independence within the Commonwealth and had dealt effectively with the United States throughout the war.

But after Moscow revealed itself to be a threat, the Cold War became even trickier to manage than the hot war had been. The Communist danger demanded the establishment of a western alliance in which the United States inevitably took the leading role. The United Nations itself became an arena of the Cold War, one in which the Western case had to be maintained and in which independent initiatives were rare. And the economic position was so difficult that Canada always had to consider the need for earning American dollars required to pay for imports from the south. Canada's independence, so recently won from Britain, seemed to be eroding as the United States became aggressive and expansionistic. The Canadians had seen the UN as a makeweight that would offset the continental power of the United States. But then the North Atlantic Treaty was created—partly through Canadian initiative—to contain the USSR and USA, and even the Commonwealth would again be summoned forth in an attempt to seek succour from the American embrace. Nothing worked. Canadian independence, Canadian nationalism, as envisaged by the mandarins during the 1930s, the war, and the early postwar years had disappeared.

There was greater success in the area of social welfare. Back in the 1930s the Ottawa Men had looked on appalled as Canada collapsed, factories and mines shut down, soup kitchens and bread lines multiplied. The war rescued and rejuvenated the country, creating jobs and, even with wartime restrictions, raising the standard of living substantially. The mandarins feared that with peace the machine would break down, plunging the nation into another Depression. After the Great War there had been general strikes, riots, and disillusion. How much worse could it be this time? The solution, in good Keynesian fashion, was to have the state intervene. The government would put money into the hands of those who needed it and would spend it, simultaneously helping the common people and assisting the maintenance of a high level of employment. The archetypal legislation was the Family Allowances Act, passed in 1944. Monthly cheques to each mother in the land would give hefty support to community buying power, keeping up the demand for consumer goods and maintaining jobs. That was good economic sense, and if Ottawa lacked the revenues to meet its commitments to the baby bonus and other social legislation, it could always borrow to pay the bills. Deficit financing could be a built-in stabilizer for the whole economy, while the social legislation it helped to support could better the lot of the people and help the entire economy. The White Paper of 1945 also committed the government to maintaining a high level of employment. It was a brilliant conception, one with political benefits for the Liberal Party that had presided over the humanization of capitalism—and one that had served the interests of the bureaucracy by strengthening the powers of the central government.[70]

The Liberals, in fact, greatly benefited from the ideas and talents of the mandarins. Compare the Mackenzie King government of the 1920s to that of the war and postwar years. The first was cautious and careful, a small government devoted to *laissez-faire*. The second, while often still cautious and careful (in the manner of the Prime Minister), was the creator of a wartime government that was interventionist, centralist, forceful in social measures and on the world stage. What had changed? The times and the advisers. King himself might have changed as well, reacting to the events of the 1940s; but as so many of the new policies were sold only with difficulty to the Prime Minister, one can be forgiven for doubting this. Still, there is no argument that King and his successor reaped enormous rewards from the policies the Ottawa Men pressed on sometimes unwilling politicians.

Much more sympathetic to the mandarins' goals were some key politicians. Such ministers as Brooke Claxton and Paul Martin in the Department of National Health and Welfare knew the Ottawa Men well and shared many of their attitudes. Others, like C.D. Howe, were willing to take good ideas and run with them. Still others, like Pearson and Pickersgill, were mandarins transformed into Liberal politicians, and certainly they knew the worth of the ideas advanced by their friends and former colleagues. The officials worked with their ministers, developing the policies and programs that the Liberal Party used to win election after election, and helping the politicians defend themselves and the programs when under attack. They were aware of politics; they had to be. They deserved criticism only if they placed the party interest ahead of the public interest.[71] The relationship between bureaucrat and politician is not an easy one, but in the Liberal hegemony it was a relationship marked by mutual regard and trust, and one that on balance served the nation well.

The Opposition can be forgiven for not seeing matters that way. To them the mandarins had been in bed with the Grits for so long that the two had become almost coupled, in their minds, in a marriage of state and party—a perception that was heightened by the entry into politics of Pearson, Pickersgill, and Sharp. What the Conservatives disregarded was that the mandarins felt deeply that it was the duty of the bureaucracy to serve the government of the day to the best of its ability, to provide ideas, advice, and the competent administration of policies that the government passed into law. Such advice and service were awaiting the Conservatives in June 1957, had they wanted them and been able to use them. Some ministers of the Diefenbaker administration did, and the mandarins served them well; others, including the Prime Minister, were suspicious, and failed to make use of the abilities and ideas at their disposal. However understandable these suspicions may have been, they were unjustified: there is no reason to doubt that the Ottawa Men were willing, even anxious, to demonstrate their competence and impartiality to the incoming administration. To the Tory government's credit, there were no purges (like those of the NDP in Saskatchewan, British Columbia, and Manitoba when it toppled entrenched governments),[72] nor should there have been. Whether such a judgement could now be made—after almost a decade and a half of Trudeau government, and the politicization of the bureaucracy from the office of the Clerk of the Privy Council downward—is much less certain.[73]

If it was the mandarins' fate to be misunderstood and mistrusted by the Diefenbaker government of 1957, that was a consequence of their long administrative life. The Ottawa Men retained their influence for an extraordinarily long period, primarily because the generation that Skelton, Clark, and Towers had recruited was so young when it came to Ottawa. Norman Robertson, for example, remained a civil servant from 1929 until his retirement at the end of 1965; and for the next three years he played an important advisory role to External Affairs. Robert Bryce's career extended from the end of the Depression into the 1980s, if one considers appointments and advisory roles. Long service was the norm, and this provided a continuity of policy that was rare in democratic states. More to the point, because the mandarins reached their positions of influence while still young, in the forties and fifties the influence of the Robertsons, Bryces, Reids, and Rasminskys seemed to be never-ending.

Long service gave the Ottawa Men enormous clout and allowed them to develop all the skills of bureaucratic negotiation.[74] As Mitchell Sharp noted: 'In many cases, they have a greater influence upon the course of events than have Ministers, particularly the weaker and less competent Ministers.' That was certainly so of the King and St Laurent years. But, as Sharp says, the real questions were whether the mandarins exerted too much influence and whether they turned their ministers into puppets. He admits that these questions are difficult to answer. To Sharp, it was enough that a minister such as C.D. Howe was never manipulated and yet retained a close working relationship with his officials. He adds:

> When I was a civil servant, I think it is fair to say that individual Ministers and the Cabinet as a whole depended more upon the advice of senior civil servants than they do today and they did so deliberately. When a difficult problem arose, the customary response was to refer it for study and report to a committee of senior public servants. There was also a period during the war and in the immediate post-war years when influential public servants . . . were active promoters of new ideas and approaches that they persuaded their Ministers and the Cabinet to adopt.

Today, Sharp agrees, it is different. Contentious questions now are referred to ministerial not officials' committees—perhaps in an attempt to counter bureaucratic influence and to keep the ministers atop the policy process. 'Innovative ideas still emerge from the civil service, but the process of decision-making at the Cabinet level is so complex nowadays that individual contributions are quickly submerged in a deluge of documentation.'[75] The net result, as Robert Bryce has recently noted, is that today the 'Ottawa game is much more competitive, much more criticized, more highly paid, and somewhat less fun.'[76]

Changes in Cabinet procedures are not the only reasons for the decline in the innovative powers of the bureaucracy. The public service today is so much larger than it was in 1936, 1946, or 1956 that comparisons are almost futile.[77] Intelligent generalists, such as the Ottawa Men, came to be replaced by hordes of 'experts'. For example, in the late 1950s there were still only a handful of economists in Ottawa; but by 1975, Bryce reported, there were 2,374 civil servants classified as economists.[78] The babble of competing advice on ways to deal with insoluble questions must have been overwhelming. Similarly there are now advisory boards, commissions, study groups, and the like to offer politicians alternate sources of advice on a host of questions. The Prime Minister's Office and the Privy Council Office have been vastly expanded and made co-ordinating bodies—central agencies, in the current jargon—with the capacity to provide supplementary or competing advice to the Prime Minister and Cabinet.[79] Also, the whole question of civil-service unionization greatly altered the way the mandarins could employ their staffs. The government and the senior officials have become a 'them' against which the lower ranks rail and occasionally strike. And even in departments like External Affairs—once, but no longer, the élite of the public service—conditions of employment abroad and prospects of promotion became so much a source of grievance that a Royal Commission had to be established to study them. The report's very modern suggestion that spouses receive stipends was an idea that would have been incomprehensible to the mandarins' wives.[80] They may have been unhappy occasionally, and frustrated by the cocktail circuit to which they were condemned in Ottawa and abroad, but in the convention of the time, almost all of them seemed willing to endure anything for the sake of their husbands' careers.

The huge bureaucracy that is the civil service of today is formal and rigid. Decisions are slow and grudging, initiative is blocked, procedures are everything. Formality and rigidity were not entirely absent in the past, but they did not constrain the mandarins of the thirties and forties. One student of bureaucracy has observed that if the public service 'is to operate successfully, it must attain a high degree of reliability of behaviour, an unusual degree of conformity with prescribed patterns of action.' Discipline is as necessary in any senior civil service as in the army.[81] The mandarins were both disciplined and reliable (although Norman Robertson could bury contentious files in the hope that problems they contained would go away, and Escott Reid was occasionally erratic), but they can hardly be described as conformists, except in matters of style. And perhaps of thought. If they had been on the Left in their youth, like Robertson and Bryce, or if they had been Round Tablers, like Wrong, or almost apolitical, like Pearson—once they adjusted to the Ottawa scene they became men of political moderation. They were interested in ideas, tolerant of those who differed. But as good tacticians they were wisely unwilling to go too far out in front of their Cabinet ministers, and almost none ever did. While the minister's responsibility was to formulate policy and the deputy's to implement it, sensible ministers most often acquired ideas wherever they found them—usually from their mandarins.[82] (Foolish ministers, arriving at their departments with simplistic notions about the ease of securing change, were quickly brought down to earth by ramifications of which they had been entirely innocent.) During the war, their period of greatest influence, the mandarins served under the ablest ministers in Canadian history, men who were willing to accommodate themselves to changing conditions by accepting the new ideas that a united group of civil servants presented to them. Often, because of ministerial exhaustion, these ideas were virtually assured of implementation.[83]

There is one final point worth noting. At the beginning of the period under study here, Canadian public servants dealt almost entirely with events from an Ottawa context. The capital was the centre of their existence. Once the Second World War began, however, the mandarins quickly learned to deal with events in an international context. This thrust applied not only to officers of External Affairs but to those in Finance, Trade and Commerce, the Bank, and the PMO and PCO. The mandarins travelled extensively to meetings and conferences, they negotiated treaties and pacts, they accompanied their ministers abroad. Perhaps to their surprise they discovered that they were not only Ottawa men but mid-Atlantic men; and further that they shared their training, attitudes, and ideas not only with contemporaries in Britain and the United States certainly, but with those in Western Europe.[84] Also surprising—Canadians are a modest people—the mandarins discovered that they were every bit as able as those non-Canadians with whom they dealt. After the war—when the Americans considered Canada to be a sideshow, a country not deserving too much attention—relations with the U.S. became so important that only the best minds were assigned to American negotiations. Rasminsky, Heeney, Bryce, Towers and the rest took a back seat to no one, and in the negotiations they conducted with the United States they usually proved stronger in argument than their friends across the table (an expertise that allowed them to win battles, but no wars). That built-in advantage, however, was not great enough in the complex world of the Cold War years to preserve the kind of independent Canadian nationalism that the mandarins they could shape.

The historian Arthur Lower has said that our civil service 'is full of excellent and upright men, but it is primarily a Civil Service and as such it has its own characteristics that nothing is going to change much.' Lesser bureaucrats, he went on, were interested in salaries, holidays, and promotions, and some of them in their work. 'Civil Servants of the higher ranks are interested in what they are doing, and many of them, perhaps most, in power.'[85] Lower had been a close friend of Jack Pickersgill's, and perhaps that observation was based on an assessment of his Wesley College office-mate; perhaps it was even correct as a generalization. It would be impossible to deny that the mandarins had power—or at least a share of it. They did, after all, see many of their ideas implemented. They could speed the careers of the bright young graduates they spotted in the universities and brought to Ottawa: that also is power. They could assist the politicians they served and, if they were crossed, they could frustrate others: that too is power. Finally, beyond Canada's boundaries they helped to shape the world we live in.

But all this was only power of a sort. The Ottawa Men lacked the ultimate power that comes from the ballot box: the power to move men. All the mandarins had, essentially, was influence on politicians. Pickersgill, Pearson, and Sharp no doubt realized this when they abandoned the secure world of the mandarins for the less certain one of politics. From 1935 to 1957 the influence of the mandarins had been paramount. It helped to alter the way Canadians lived, acted, and thought about themselves; it played a large part in transforming the country. Since their day, however, Canada and the world have changed so much that it is unlikely that a group of civil servants could ever again have such an influence on the country.

NOTES

1. THE MANDARINS

1. H. Heclo and A. Wildavsky, *The Private Government of Public Money* (London, 1974), 76.
2. J.W. Pickersgill Papers (Ottawa), Heeney file, Heeney to Pickersgill, 3 Nov., 1952.
3. Peter C. Newman, *The Canadian Establishment* (Toronto, 1975), 321, note. Other accounts of the bureaucracy's socio-economic background are: Colin Campbell and George Szablowski, *The Super-Bureaucrats* (Toronto, 1979), 105ff.; Dennis Olsen, *The State Elite* (Toronto, 1980); John Porter, *The Vertical Mosaic* (Toronto, 1965), 417ff.; and Robert Presthus, *Elite Accommodation in Canadian Politics* (Toronto, 1973). Even when women could be recruited into the Department of External Affairs, few were. Of 570 foreign service officers serving between 1945 and 1965, only 5.8 per cent were female and in 1965 only 3.24 per cent of serving officers were women. See John English, 'The Professional Diplomat in Canada', (a paper presented to a Conference on Professionalization, University of Western Ontario, March 1981), 14.
4. Public Archives of Canada [PAC], Department of Finance Records, vol. 2694, file 100-7, Memo, 8 Jan., 1940.
5. Porter, 441.
6. PAC, W.L.M. King Papers, Diary, 22-3 April, 1937.
7. Interview, 22 June, 1978.
8. Joseph Schull, *The Great Scot* (Montreal, 1979), 25.
9. University of Oxford, *Supplement to the Historical Register of 1900 . . . 1901-30* (Oxford, 1934). Pickersgill is omitted from this listing.
10. J.L. Granatstein, *A Man of Influence: Norman A. Robertson and Canadian Statecraft, 1929-68* (Ottawa, 1981), 25.
11. King Papers, list of personnel on EAC, f.C260230.
12. *Ibid.*
13. *Ibid.*
14. PAC, Privy Council Office Records, PARC Box 287421, file C-11, memo, 're Commission on the Civil Service', 10 Dec., 1945.
15. Walter Gordon, *A Political Memoir* (Toronto, 1977), 45.
16. See Department of Finance Records, vol. 3599, file A-06 for the proceedings of the Commission.
17. Mrs A.D.P. Heeney Papers (Ottawa), Heeney to Mrs Heeney, 18 Aug., 1946.
18. Based on advertisements in the Ottawa *Citizen*. On Rockcliffe, see Bill Ste-

phenson, 'The Haughtiest Suburb of them all,' *Maclean's*, 15 Sept., 1954, 29ff.; Shirley Woods, Jr., *Ottawa the Capital of Canada* (Toronto, 1980), 251-3.

19. Mrs Heeney interview, 20 Nov., 1978.

20. James Eayrs, *Diplomacy and Its Discontents* (Toronto, 1971), 34.

21. Kildare Dobbs, *Reading the Time* (Toronto, 1968), 161.

22. H.I. Macdonald interview, 9 Feb., 1978.

23. See R. Faris, *The Passionate Educators* (Toronto, 1975), 15.

24. Wilfrid Eggleston, *While I Still Remember* (Toronto, 1968), 273-4.

25. Brian Heeney interview, 21 Mar., 1978. Graham Fraser interview, 26 Jan., 1978.

26. Queen's University Archives, J.A. Stevenson Papers, docs. on vol. 1, folders 4, 22.

27. Dana Wilgress, *Memoirs* (Toronto, 1967), 101.

28. Kenneth Clark Papers (Toronto), Clark to Gagnon, 13 Nov., 18 Dec., 1937.

29. *Ibid.*, 'John Gilmour Estate Fishing & Hunting Property,' mimeo, n.d.

30. *Ibid.*, Clark to Mackintosh, 5 Aug., 1939.

31. *Ibid.*

32. *Ibid.*, Clark to Mackintosh, 14 Aug., 1939; Clark to Stewart, 23 Aug., 1939.

33. *Ibid.*, Clark to J.F. Davey, 14 Feb., 1940.

34. Lists on *ibid.*

35. PAC, N.A. Robertson Papers, G.F. MacLaren to members, 20 June, 1940.

36. *Ibid.*

37. Queen's University, W.A. Mackintosh Papers, D.G. Marble to members, 5 March, 1942.

38. Schull, 72, 100.

39. Clark Papers, 'Report of a Biological Survey . . .,' n.d.

40. *Ibid.*, List of Ordinary Members 1952.

41. 432ff.

42. 'The Establishment that Governs Us,' *Saturday Night* (May, 1968), 23-4. See also Peter Newman, 'The Ottawa Establishment,' *Maclean's* 22 Aug., 1964, 7ff. and *ibid.*, 4 June, 1960, 2.

2. THE EARLY CIVIL SERVICE

1. Cited in R.M. Dawson, *The Civil Service of Canada* (London, 1929), 233.

2. J.E. Hodgetts, *Pioneer Public Service* (Toronto, 1955), 35.

3. *Ibid.*, 36.

4. J.M. DesRoches, 'The Evolution of the Organization of Federal Government in Canada', *Canadian Public Administration*, V (December, 1962), 411, 413.

5. *The Red Tapeworm* (London, 1955), 15-16.

6. Dawson, 94.

7. *Ibid.*, 76.

8. James Manion, *A Canadian Errant* (Toronto, 1960), 57ff.

9. *Ibid.*, 55.

10. Hodgetts, 57.

11. J.E. Hodgetts, *The Canadian Public Service* (Toronto, 1973), 34-35.

12. Public Record Office (PRO), Dominions Office Records, Do35/68/D6765, extract from letter, Hadow to Whiskard, 30 April, 1929.

13. O.M. Hill, *Canada's Salesmen to the World* (Montreal, 1977), 512.

14. Cited in H.G. Villard and W.W. Willoughby, *The Canadian Budgetary System* (New York, 1918), 268.

15. Cited in Dawson, 29.

16. *Ibid.*, 30. Cf. D.J. Hall, *Clifford Sifton*, Vol. I: *The Young Napoleon 1861-1900* (Vancouver, 1981), 124-6.

17. R.M. Dawson, 'The Canadian Civil Service', *Canadian Journal of Economics and Political Science*, II (1936), 290.

18. *Ibid.*, 291.

19. W.L. Grant, 'The Civil Service of Canada', *University of Toronto Quarterly*, III (July, 1934), 431.

20. Cited in W.L. Grant, 'Civil Service Reform', *Manitoba Free Press*, 16 Dec., 1930.

21. See Sonja Sinclair, *Cordial but not Cosy* (Toronto, 1979), 43 and chap. II; R.D. MacLean, 'An Examination of the Role of the Comptroller of the Treasury', *Canadian Public Administration*, VII (March, 1964), 44ff.; A.S. Sterns, *History of the Department of Finance* (mimeo, Ottawa, 1965), 30.

22. See J. Swettenham and D. Kealy, *Serving the State* (Ottawa, 1970), Appendix A for 'The Story of the Professional Institute [of the Civil Service of Canada], 1920-1945'. Cf., 'The Large and Generous View: The Debate on Labour Affiliation in the Canadian Civil Service, 1918-28', *Labour*, II (1977), pp 121-2 for a revealing look at the professionals' attitudes.

23. See M. Pope, ed., *Public Servant: The Memoirs of Sir Joseph Pope* (Toronto, 1960), passim.

24. See Taylor Cole, *The Canadian Bureaucracy* (Durham, 1949), 10-11.

25. C.A. Magrath, 'The Civil Service', *University Magazine* (1913), 252.

26. H. Borden, ed., *Robert Laird Borden: His Memoirs* (Toronto, 1938), II, 803-4.

27. Dawson, *Civil Service of Canada*, 95.

28. Hill, 230-1.

29. Cited in S.E.D. Shortt, *The Search for an Ideal* (Toronto, 1976), 101.

30. Dawson, *Civil Service of Canada*, 96.

31. Grant, *University of Toronto Quarterly*, 436-7.

32. Cited in Cole, 40-1.

33. Grant, *University of Toronto Quarterly*, 436-7.

3. THE FOUNDERS

1. Queen's University Archives, Mss. Collection 203, vol. 5B, University Register, f. 518 and *ibid.*, W.A. Mackintosh Papers, vol. 9, file 220, J.F. Macdonald to Mackintosh, 18 March, 1941.

2. S.E.D. Shortt, *The Search for an Ideal* (Toronto, 1976), 95.

3. K.P. Kirkwood, 'The Department of External Affairs: A History', (mimeo, Ottawa, 1958), IV, 959ff.

4. G.N. Hillmer, 'The Anglo-Canadian Neurosis: The Case of O.D. Skelton', in P. Lyon, ed., *Britain and Canada* (London, 1976), 63.

5. Skelton's obituary in *The Times*, 30 Jan., 1941.

6. Queen's University Archives, Adam Shortt Papers, Skelton to Shortt, 22 Feb., 1902.

7. *Ibid.*

8. *Ibid.*, 1 March, 1902.

9. PAC, W.L. Grant Papers, vol. 9, Skelton to Grant, 12 Feb., 1904.

10. *Ibid.*, 29 Jan., 1904.

11. See W. Gordon, 'The Late Mrs. O.D. Skelton', *Queen's Review* (November, 1956), 210ff.

12. Shortt Papers, Skelton to Shortt, 29 June, 1905.

13. *Ibid.*, 9 Jan., 1906.

14. *Queen's University Journal*, 2 Nov., 1908, 39ff.

15. Shortt Papers, Skelton to Shortt, 25 March, 1906. I have throughout this section benefited greatly from reading Barry Ferguson's draft York University thesis on Queen's University's Political and Economic Science Department.

16. Shortt Papers, Skelton to Shortt, 24 Sept., 1907.

17. *Ibid.*, 12 Aug., 1908; W.A. Mackintosh, 'Adam Shortt', *Canadian Journal of Economics and Political Science*, IV (May, 1938), 172.

18. Shortt Papers, Skelton to Shortt, 31 Aug., 1908.

19. *Queen's University Journal*, 2 Nov., 1908, 39ff.

20. Shortt Papers, Skelton to Shortt, 14 Jan., 1909.

21. See e.g., D.M.L. Farr's introduction to Skelton's *Life and Letters of Sir Wilfrid Laurier* (Toronto, 1965), I, p.xi and Carl Berger, *The Writing of Canadian History* (Toronto, 1976), 48. Some people—Prof. H.S. Ferns, for one—claim to have seen Lenin's letter to Skelton. If it existed, the letter does not seem to have survived.

22. PAC, W.L.M. King Papers, Skelton to King, 9 Aug., 1911, f.16959.

23. Docs. on *ibid.*, ff.16961ff.

24. *Ibid.*, Skelton to King, 24 Sept., 1911, ff.16965ff.

25. *Queen's University Journal*, 1 Dec., 1911, 1.

26. Queen's University Archives, D.M. Gordon Papers, box 2, file 9, Memo on Economic Research . . ., 15 Oct., 1918. I am indebted to Mr Barry Ferguson for this reference.

27. K.W. Taylor, 'Economic Scholarship in Canada', *Canadian Journal of Economics and Political Science*, XXVI (February, 1960), 7-8.

28. Queen's University Archives, Board of Trustees Minutes, 30 Apr., 1913, 7 May, 1924.

29. 'Electoral Reform', *Queen's Quarterly*, XXI (Winter, 1913-4), 515.

30. Grant Papers, vol. 9, Skelton to Grant, 13 Aug., 1917. See Skelton's piece on conscription in *Queen's Quarterly*, XXV (1917), 219ff.

31. PAC, W.C. Good Papers, Skelton to Good, 9 Jan., 1918, f.2677.

32. Grant Papers, Skelton to Grant, 19 March, 1917.

33. PAC, O.D. Skelton Papers, vol. 1, contain some drafts of the book and a few comments from authorities to whom Skelton sent chapters. See also Berger, 49-50.

34. W.A. Mackintosh, 'O.D. Skelton', *Canadian Journal of Economics and Political Science*, VII (May, 1941), 272.

35. Mrs W.A. Mackintosh interview, 6 Sept., 1978.

36. Queen's University Archives, D.A. Skelton Papers, vol. 1, Skelton to son, 25 Aug., 1922; PAC, Sir Robert Borden Papers, Skelton to Borden, 13 Aug., 1927, f.158567.

37. W.A. Mackintosh, 'O.D. Skelton', in R.L. McDougall, ed., *Canada's Past and Present* (Toronto, 1965), 68-9.

38. Berger, 52.

39. Cited in R.M. Dawson, *William Lyon Mackenzie King*, vol. I: *1874-1923* (Toronto, 1958), 454.

40. Cited in Hillmer, 74.

41. Kirkwood, IV, 966.

42. Ramsay Cook, 'J.W. Dafoe at the Imperial Conference, 1923', *Canadian Historical Review*, XLI (March, 1960), 23.

43. Robert Bothwell, 'Loring Christie and the Failure of Bureaucratic Imperialism', Ph.D. thesis, Harvard University, 1972, 323ff.

44. Philip G. Wigley, *Canada and the Transition to Commonwealth* (Cambridge, 1977), 186-7.

45. Cook, 36-7.

46. Dawson, I, 471. See Skelton's 'The Imperial Conference of 1923', *Journal of the Canadian Bankers' Association*, XXXI (1923-4), 153ff.

47. Kirkwood, IV, 966ff.; Queen's University Archives, Lorne Pierce Papers, Skelton to Pierce, 4 April, 1925.

48. Kirkwood, IV, 1311; H.B. Neatby, *William Lyon Mackenzie King*, Vol. II: *1923-32* (Toronto, 1963), 195.

49. Massey College, Vincent Massey Papers, Box B-12, original estimates file, Skelton to Massey, 8 Feb., 1927. Ten years later in London, Massey complained that Skelton's parsimony was such that he had had only two telephone conversations with Ottawa in three years. *Ibid.*, Diary, 16 Sept., 1938.

50. *Ibid.*, Box B-12, estimates file, Skelton to Massey, 25 Feb., 1927. For detail on Massey's expenses, see W.D. Herridge Papers (Toronto), file G4. See also Claude Bissell, *The Young Vincent Massey* (Toronto, 1981), 122ff. and Hugh Keenleyside, *Memoirs of Hugh Keenleyside*, vol. I: *Hammer the Golden Day* (Toronto, 1981), 247-8.

51. Massey Papers, unboxed material, Skelton to Massey, 21, 23 May, 1927.

52. Vincent Massey, *What's Past is Prologue* (Toronto, 1963), 139.

53. Based on Wrong's letters in Mrs C.H.A. Armstrong Papers (Toronto).

54. Massey Diary, 20 May, 1929. The British agreed. See, e.g., Dominions Office Records, DO35/68/D7665, Hadow to Batterbee, 10 June, 1929.

55. See, e.g., PAC, Georges Vanier Papers, vol. 7, 1929 External Affairs file, extract of letter, Skelton to Dandurand, 20 Aug., 1929.

56. PAC, External Affairs Records [EAR], vol. 787, file 408, flyer, 20 June, 1927. See also Gilles Lalande, *The Department of External Affairs and Biculturalism* (Ottawa, 1969), 34-5, and Keenleyside's account of the examinations, 212-13.

57. Cited in Lalande, 36. See also Skelton's testimony in House of Commons Standing Committee on Industrial and International Relations, 25 March, 1930, 10-11.

58. Kirkwood, IV, 973-4.

59. EAR, vol. 787, file 408, 'List of Names . . .', 24 Sept., 1931.

60. *Ibid.*, Memo for Prime Minister, 18 June, 1928.

61. King Papers, Memo to Prime Minister, 5 July, 1929, ff.C51416ff.

62. EAR, vol. 787, file 408, 'Staff, Canada and Abroad', 8 Aug., 1930.

63. See Mrs Armstrong Papers, *passim.*, and K. Kirkwood, *The Diplomat at Table* (Metuchen, N.J.), 1-2, on Kirkwood's arrival at the Washington Legation.

64. W.A. Riddell, *World Security by Conference* (Toronto, 1947), 75ff.

65. University of British Columbia Archives, N.A. MacKenzie Papers, folder 5/4, Skelton to MacKenzie, 23 July, 1929.

66. King Papers, Skelton to King, 8 Feb., 1930, ff.155121-2.

67. Norman Hillmer, 'O.D. Skelton, the scholar who set a future pattern', *International Perspectives* (September-October, 1973), 48-9.

68. Queen's University Archives, Grant Dexter Papers, Memo, 16 Sept., 1941,; L.B. Pearson, *Mike: The Memoirs of the Rt. Hon. Lester B. Pearson* (Toronto, 1972), I, 75-6. Cf., the extraordinary argument in R.F. Holland, *Britain and the Commonwealth Alliance 1918-39* (London, 1981), 185.

69. EAR, vol. 793, file 454(3), Skelton to Herridge, 2 Feb., 1943. See also R.M. Dawson, 'The Canadian Civil Service', *Canadian Journal of Economics and Political Science*, II (1936), 299-300.

70. W.A. Mackintosh, 'William Clifford Clark', *Queen's Quarterly*, LX (Spring, 1953) 2; Corolyn Cox, ' "Cliff" Clark has an old carpet', *Saturday Night*, 1 May, 1943, 20; K.S. Clark Papers (Toronto), Clark's pencilled biographical notes, n.d.

71. *Calendar of Queen's College and University . . . 1907-8*, 173.

72. *Ibid.*, 181ff.; *1908-10*, 154, 164; *Queen's University Journal,* 4 May, 1910, 440-1; Clark Papers, biographical notes.

73. Mackintosh, 'Clark', 2.

74. Austin Cross, 'Watchdog of our Treasury', *Canadian Business* (March, 1942), 20-1.

75. Clark Papers, Biographical notes; Margaret Clark Johnston Papers (Niagara Falls, Ont.), Harvard correspondence, *passim.*

76. Queen's Board of Trustees Minutes, 28 April, 1915, 3 Feb., 1920, etc.

77. R.B. Bryce, 'William Clifford Clark', *Canadian Journal of Economics and Political Science*, XIX (1953), 414.

78. *Bulletin of the Departments of History and Political and Economic Science in Queen's University . . .*, No. 20 (1916).

79. W.C. Clark, 'Inflation and Prices', *Journal of the Canadian Bankers' Association*, No. 25 (1917-18), 133; Clark, 'Should Maximum Prices Be Fixed?', *Bulletin . . .* (1918).

80. James Struthers, 'No Fault of their Own: Unemployment and the Canadian Welfare State, 1914-41', Ph.D. thesis, University of Toronto, 1979, 74; Clark Papers, biographical notes.

81. *Ibid.*; Bryce, 414.

82. Cross, 21-2.

83. Mackintosh, 'Clark', 6; Clark Papers, N. Roberts to W.C. Clark, 22 Dec., 1926.

84. Mrs Mackintosh interview; David Mansur interview, 30 Oct., 1978; K.S. Clark interview, 4 March, 1981.

85. Queen's Board of Trustees Minutes, 6 May, 1931; Clark Papers, M.A. Fyfe to Clark, 27 July, 1931.

86. Bryce, 414; King Diary, 2 Aug., 1934, indicates that Skelton had recommended Clark to Robb, King's Minister of Finance in the late 1920s. Skelton also tried to have Clark appointed to the civil service in 1931. Documents on Clark Papers.

87. Derek Chisolm, 'Canadian Monetary Policy, 1930-4: Was the Bank of Canada Necessary?', (mimeo, unpaginated).

88. For Clark on gold, see 'The Flight from the Gold Standard', Queen's Quarterly, XXXVIII (Winter, 1931-2), 751ff.; for his views on the general world economic situation, see 'What's Wrong with us?', in the Institute Bulletin, copy in PAC, Department of Finance Records, vol. 3993, Clark publications file. See also I.M. Drummond, The Floating Pound and the Sterling Area, 1931-39 (Cambridge, 1981), 65.

89. Derek Chisolm, 'Precursors of the Monetary Approach to External Equilibrium and the Origins of Canadian Central Banking 1932-4', Research Report 7926, University of Western Ontario Economics Dept., August, 1979, 13-15. Clark's memo is in Finance Records, vol. 4666 and in PAC, R.J. Manion Papers, vol. 78, file 32. See also H.B. Neatby, William Lyon Mackenzie King, Vol. III: 1932-9 (Toronto, 1976), 33-4.

90. EAR, vol. 811, file 621, Clark to Skelton, 12 May, 1932.

91. Bennett Papers, Mf. M-1176, ff.112697ff.; Chisolm, 'Precursors', table, 15-15a; Clark Papers, W.W. Swanson to Clark, 17 Sept., 1932 and H. Michell to Clark, 16 Jul 32.

92. R.S. Sayers, The Bank of England 1891-1944 (London, 1976), II, 448, 513 and III, 273-5.

93. J.R.H. Wilbur, 'H.H. Stevens and the Reconstruction Party', Canadian Historical Review, XLV (March, 1964), 5.

94. Mrs Johnston Papers, Whitton radio broadcast transcript, 25 Oct., 1959.

95. Bennett Papers, Mf. M-1045, Clark to Bennett, 15 Oct., 1932, ff.203512ff., and P.C. 2361, 24 Oct., 1932; Clark Papers, Dr Stevens to Clark, 4 Oct., 1932.

96. Mansur interview. There is nothing in Public Archives of Nova Scotia, E.N. Rhodes Papers, to suggest that the Minister was consulted.

97. Chisolm, 'Canadian Monetary Policy'; Grattan O'Leary, Toronto Star Weekly, 9 May, 1942.

98. Chisolm, 'Canadian Monetary Policy'; Globe and Mail, 29 Dec., 1952.

99. Chisolm, 'Canadian Monetary Policy'. On Clark's more routine tasks, see his 'Financial Administration of the Government of Canada', Canadian Journal of Economics and Political Science, IV (August, 1938), 391ff.

100. Irving Brecher, Monetary and Fiscal Thought and Policy in Canada 1919-1939 (Toronto, 1956), 40.

101. Good Papers, vol. 5, Clark to Good, 16 June, 1923, ff.4091-2; Linda Grayson, 'The Formation of the Bank of Canada', Ph.D. thesis, University of Toronto, 1974, 53.

102. Brecher, 102.

103. Grayson, 92. At a Canadian Political Science Association meeting in May 1933 all the academics present were said to favour a central bank. PAC, Alex Johnston Papers, Mf. M-64, Diary, 23 May, 1933.

104. A.F.W. Plumptre, *Central Banking in the British Dominions* (Toronto, 1947), 192ff.; Grayson, 130; G.S. Watts, 'The origins and background of central banking in Canada', *Bank of Canada Review* (May, 1972), 15ff.

105. Floyd Chalmers Papers (Toronto), Chalmers to Col. Maclean, 27 Jan., 1933.

106. Bryce, 416-7

107. Grayson, 135. For Clark on Macmillan, see Clark Papers, Clark to J.B. Rosenwald, 14 Dec., 1931.

108. Watt, 22ff. For a digest of the testimony, see A.F.W. Plumptre, 'The Evidence Presented to the "Canadian Macmillan Commission" ', *Canadian Journal of Economics and Political Science*, II (February, 1936), 54ff. and Grayson, 143ff. See also documents on Rhodes Papers, vol. 1122, file 3.

109. Plumptre, *Central Banking*, 145, 188. The Liberals focused their criticism on this aspect. Neatby, III, 52ff.

110. Plumptre, 'Evidence', 65. See also Merrill Denison, *Canada's First Bank* (Toronto, 1967), 385. On the Royal Bank's different views, see Drummond, 60-1.

111. Grayson, 144. See also Clark's address on the need for a central bank in *Financial Post*, 15 Sept., 1934.

112. Clark to Bennett, 27 March, 1934, cited in Grayson, 240.

113. Bennett Papers, Mf. M-963, Clark to Bennett, 27 June, 1934, ff.63597-8.

114. Grayson, 283-4; *Proceedings of the Canadian Political Science Association 1934*, 276; J.R. Beattie interview, 10 June, 1979; Clark Papers, Towers to Clark, 27 Oct., 4 Nov., 1932.

115. Mackintosh, 'Clark', 8.

116. Clipping of 7 Sept., 1934 in Dexter Papers, vol. 24, file 332.

117. D.C. Abbott interview, 11 Jan., 1979.

118. R.T.L., 'Mr. Towers', *Macleans*, 15 Oct., 1934. Other articles on Towers' background: 'Men of Action', *The Montrealer* (April, 1951); *Montreal Standard*, 19 March, 1938; *Saturday Night*, 15 April, 1944.

119. *Toronto Mail*, 8 Sept., 1934.

120. Bennett Papers, Mf. M-962, ff.63188ff.

121. *Toronto Mail*, 8 Sept., 1934.

122. King Diary, 8 Jan., 1937. Mrs Mackintosh interviews; Mrs N.A. Robertson interview, 22 June, 1979.

123. *Financial Times*, 4 Dec., 1934, cited in Grayson, 283-4. For Sir Thomas White's glowing praise, see Rhodes Papers, vol. 1150, file 4, White to Rhodes, 7 Sept., 1934.

124. J.R. Beattie interview, 10 June, 1979; Louis Rasminsky interview, 4 May, 1979; Mrs Walter Gordon interview, 1 Aug., 1978.

125. J.D. Gibson interview, 13 Sept. 1978; Mansur interview; G.S. Watts interview, 22 Jan., 1979; Rasminsky interview.

126. Joseph Schull, *The Great Scot: A Biography of Donald Gordon* (Montreal, 1979), 25.

127. Plumptre, 145ff.; G.S. Watts, 'The first phase of the Bank of Canada's operations; 1935-39', *Bank of Canada Review* (November, 1972), 8; King Diary, 28 March, 1938.

128. Watts interview.

129. Department of External Affairs, *Statements & Speeches* 54/45, Towers' address to Canadian Club, Montreal, 18 Oct., 1954.

130. Watts, 'Legislative Birth', 23-4.

131. *Statements & Speeches* 54/45.

132. *Report of the Royal Commission on Dominion-Provincial Relations* (Ottawa, 1954), Book I, 237.

133. *Ibid.*, 168-9.

134. Bank of Canada Archives, Graham Towers Papers, Memo #8, 16 May, 1935.

135. *Ibid.*, Memo #10, 5 June, 1935.

136. *Ibid.*, Bank of Canada Records, file Loan Councils . . . PF-1, Memo, n.d.

137. *Ibid.*, Towers to Dunning, 18 Dec., 1935.

138. Neatby, III, 152, 157.

139. *Ibid.*, 157ff.; E.J. Hanson, 'Public Finance in Alberta Since 1935', *Canadian Journal of Economics and Political Science*, XVIII (August, 1952), 322ff; J.R. Mallory, *Social Credit and the Federal Power in Canada* (Toronto, 1954), Chap. VI.

140. Towers Papers, Memo #14, 18 April, 1936.

141. Neatby, III, 161.

142. W.L. Morton, *Manitoba: A History* (Toronto, 1957), 429.

143. Towers Papers, Memo #48, 9-14 Dec., 1936.

144. John Kendle, *John Bracken: A Political Biography* (Toronto, 1979), 148.

145. King Diary, 16 Dec., 1936.

146. Towers Papers, Memo #51, 5 Jan., 1937.

147. Bank of Canada Records, Royal Commission on Dominion-Provincial Relations files, Memoranda file, 'The Bank of Canada and the West', 19 Jan., 1937.

148. King Diary, 21 Jan., 1937.

149. Department of Finance Records, vol. 3986, file P-1-370, 'Report on the Financial Position of Manitoba, 11 Feb., 1937'. See Kendle, 152ff. and Bank of Canada Records, Provincial financing—Manitoba file, Towers to Bracken, 12 Feb., 1937.

150. *Ibid.*, Towers to Dunning, 12 Feb., 1937.

151. King Diary, 16 Feb., 1937. Kendle, 154, had the date of this Cabinet as 15 Feb., 1937.

4. THE ISOLATIONIST NATIONALISTS

1. See E.J. Tarr, 'Canada in World Affairs', *International Affairs*, XVI (Sept., 1937), 676ff. for a good appraisal of Canadian opinion.

2. See P.E. Corbett, 'Isolation for Canada?', *University of Toronto Quarterly*, VI (October 1936), 120ff.; C.P. Stacey, *Canada and the Age of Conflict*, Vol. II (Toronto, 1981), 231ff.

3. PAC, John Read Papers, vol. 10, interview transcript, 7.

4. Keenleyside interview, 4 May, 1978; letter, Escott Reid to author, 23 Aug., 1981.

5. Library of Congress, Frankfurter Papers, Diary, 29 Oct., 1911.

6. Max Freedman, ed., *Roosevelt and Frankfurter: Their Correspondence, 1928-45* (Boston, 1967), 308. Walter Lippmann was also close the the House of Truth group.

7. Robert Bothwell, 'Loring Christie and the Failure of Bureaucratic Imperialism', Ph.D. thesis, Harvard University, 1972, 320.

8. See, e.g., PAC, Loring Christie Papers, 'Memorandum on Derby Recruiting Scheme', and attached notes, 5 June, 1917, ff.1241ff.

9. Toronto Public Library, Main Johnson Papers, Diary, 27 Dec., 1917.

10. Frankfurter Papers, box 43, folder 763, Christie to Frankfurter, 13 May, 1921.

11. *Ibid.*, 13 Feb., 1921.

12. Mrs C.H.A. Armstrong Papers (Toronto), Christie to wife, 26 June, 1925.

13. *Ibid.*, 2 June, 1925.

14. Bothwell, 323ff.

15. Cited in A.I. Inglis, 'Loring C. Christie and the Imperial Idea, 1919-26', Canadian Historical Association paper 1970, 3; published in *Journal of Canadian Studies*, VII (May, 1972), 19ff.

16. Queen's University, Grant Dexter Papers, Memo, Nov., 1939.

17. See, e.g., Inglis, 2.

18. See P.G. Wigley, *Canada and the Transition to Commonwealth* (Cambridge, 1977), esp. 129ff.

19. Robert Bothwell, 'Loring Christie and the Failure of Foreign Policy, 1919-20', American Historical Association paper 1971, 8.

20. *Ibid.*, 9.

21. *Ibid.*, 13.

22. Mrs Armstrong Papers, Jane Christie to Jack Armstrong, 13 Nov., 1923.

23. *Ibid.*, Christie to wife, 18 June, 1925.

24. Christie Papers, Christie to Kerr, 8 Nov., 1925, f.23694.

25. See Wigley, 246-7.

26. As late as 1927, however, Christie had agreed to act as a member of a provisional Round Table Committee in Canada. Bodleian Library, MSS. Eng. Hist. c819, f186-7, A.J. Glazebrook to Dove, 10 May, 1927, Cf. C.P. Stacey, 'Nationality: The Experience of Canada', *Canadian Historical Assn. Report 1967*, 15, n.5.

27. Frankfurter Papers, box 43, file 758, Christie to Frankfurter, 10 Sept., 1914.

28. Mrs Armstrong Papers, Christie to wife, 13 Feb., and 27 Aug., 1925.

29. *Ibid.*, Jane Christie to C.H.A. Armstrong, 8 May, 1928.

30. Sir Robert Borden Diary (Toronto), 3, 4 Jan., 1930.

31. PAC, J.W. Dafoe Papers, Christie to Dafoe, 22 Oct., 1935.

32. See Dafoe's obituary comment on Christie, *Winnipeg Free Press*, 9 April, 1941.

33. K.P. Kirkwood, 'The Department of External Affairs: A History' (mimeo, Ottawa, 1958), IV, 1021ff.

34. Dafoe Papers, Christie to Dafoe, 22 Oct., 1935. John Read (Read Papers, In-

terview transcript, 5-6) suggested that Christie's nose was somewhat out of joint at returning to a Department he had largely founded only to serve under Skelton, Read and Laurent Beaudry, all of whom by 1935 were senior to him.

35. Christie Papers, 'Notes on Canada and "Collective Security" ', 24-26 May, 1935, ff.24161ff.

36. Escott Reid Papers (Ste Cécile de Masham), Christie file, Reid to Christie, 10 Oct., 1935. On Stuart's views, see G.N. Hillmer, 'Defence and Ideology: The Anglo-Canadian Military "Alliance" in the 1930s', International Journal, XXXIII (Summer, 1978), 600-1.

37. PAC, Escott Reid Papers, vol. 13, Reid to J.M. Macdonnell, 30 Aug., 1934, indicates that this was precisely the view of Reid, F.R. Scott and others.

38. Christie Papers, Christie to Lothian, 30 May, 1935, ff.11555ff.

39. Reid Papers (Ste Cécile), Skelton file, Skelton to Reid, 20 May, 1935.

40. See Documents on Canadian External Relations [DCER], Vol. V: 1931-35 (Ottawa, 1973), 379-80; PAC, W.L.M. King Papers, Diary, 25 Oct., 1935.

41. PAC, Newton Rowell Papers, Skelton to Rowell, 2 Oct., 1935, ff.6114ff.; DCER V, 391.

42. Reid Papers (Ste Cécile), Christie file, Reid to Christie, 10 Oct., 1935.

43. Ibid., Christie to Reid, 25 Oct., 1935. On the League of Nations Society, see D.M. Page, 'The Institute's "Popular Arm": the League of Nations Society in Canada', International Journal, XXXII (Winter 1977-8), 28ff.

44. Christie Papers, 'Notes on the European Crisis', 5 Oct., 1935, ff.24126ff.

45. Reid Papers (Ste Cécile), Christie file, Christie to Reid, 30 Oct., 1936.

46. Ibid., Skelton file, Skelton's notes on F.R. Scott, 'Canada and the Commonwealth', a paper for British Commonwealth Relations Conference, 1938, Dec., 1937.

47. The best account is R. Bothwell and J. English, ' "Dirty Work at the Crossroads" . . .', Canadian Historical Assn. Report 1972, 263ff. See also DCER V, 396ff.

48. Rowell Papers, Skelton to Rowell, 21 Oct., 1935, ff.6133-4. See also King Diary, 29 Nov., 1935 and 30 Jan., 1936.

49. Frankfurter Papers, vol. 43, file 769, Christie to Frankfurter, 30 Jan., 1937. See also Yale University Archives, Walter Lippmann Papers, box 61, Christie to Lippmann, 4 Oct., 1937.

50. PAC, Norman Robertson Papers, Skelton to Robertson, 27 Sept., 1938.

51. Dafoe papers, Dexter to Dafoe, 23 April, 1937.

52. Christie Papers, 'Note on the Canadian Position . . .,' 8 Sept., 1938, ff.24114ff.

53. See Pearson's 'Reflections on Inter-War Foreign Policy', Journal of Canadian Studies, VII (May, 1972), 39.

54. Cited in J.A. Munro, 'Loring Christie and Canadian External Relations, 1935-39,' Canadian Historical Association paper, 1970, 12, 13.

55. PAC, L.B. Pearson Papers, Diary, 13 Sept., 1939; Queen's University, Norman Lambert Diary, 10 Nov., 1938; Frankfurter Papers, box 43, file 769, Christie to Frankfurter, 11 Nov., 1938.

56. See Christie's letter to King in King Papers, 19 Sept., 1939, ff.224884 and King Diary, 14 Sept., 1939. On the appointment, see EAR, vol. 1963, file 853, and especially Skelton's comment: 'I cannot see any possible ground for objecting

to the appointment of a North American to a North American post.' *Ibid.*, Skelton to E.J. Tarr, 4 Oct., 1939.

57. Pearson Diary, 13 Sept., 1939.

58. *Ibid.*, vol. 3, Wrong to Pearson, 27 June, 1939 and reply 29 June, 1939. Christie's memo was 'The Propagation of Allied Political Aims in the Event of a General European War', copy in *ibid.*, vol. 6.

59. J.R. Beal, *The Pearson Phenomenon* (Toronto, 1964), 30.

60. Pearson's application form for External Affairs on PAC, Civil Service Commission Records, Historical Personnel files, vol. 536, Pearson file.

61. Peter Stursberg, *Lester Pearson and the Dream of Unity* (Toronto, 1978), 19ff.

62. University of Toronto Archives, Board of Governors Minutes, 10 June, 1926.

63. *Ibid.*, 8 June, 1927.

64. W.D. Meikle, 'And Gladly Teach: G.M. Wrong and the Department of History at the University of Toronto', Ph.D. thesis, Michigan State University, 1977, 175.

65. Historical Personnel files, vol. 536, Pearson file, letters, 10, 19 May, 1928.

66. *Ibid.*, History sheet.

67. PRO, Admiralty Records, ADM 116/2717, Extract of letter from Hadow, n.d. covering letter, 3 Jan., 1930. I am indebted to Norman Hillmer for this reference.

68. United States National Archives, Department of State Records, 893.01 Manchuria/720, Boal to Secretary of State, 15 Dec., 1932. Cited in D.C. Story, 'Canada's Covenant: The Bennett Government, the League of Nations and Collective Security, 1930-35', Ph.D. thesis, University of Toronto, 1976, 230-31.

69. University of British Columbia Archives, N.A. MacKenzie Papers, folder 4/4, Main correspondence 1928, Pearson to MacKenzie, 'Tuesday' [Oct., 1928].

70. Pearson Diary, 19 Jan., 1930 [?].

71. *Ibid.*, 21 Jan., 1930.

72. Beal, 55. See also Pearson's mock-diplomatic notes challenging the U.S. legation to a baseball game with External Affairs. Pearson Papers, vol. 19. Also the account in James Manion, *A Canadian Errant* (Toronto, 1960), 77.

73. G.F. Henderson, *Federal Royal Commissions in Canada, 1867-1966* (Toronto, 1967), 120-21.

74. Stursberg, 25.

75. PAC, R.B. Bennett Papers, Mf.M-1048, f.277607.

76. Historical Personnel Records, vol. 536, Pearson file, History sheet; L.B. Pearson, *Mike: The Memoirs of the Rt. Hon. L.B. Pearson*, vol. I: *1897-1948* (Toronto, 1972), 77-78.

77. MacKenzie Papers, folder 12/6, Main Correspondence ja4ÎfiË, Pearson to MacKenzie, 14 June, 1935.

78. Massey College, Vincent Massey Papers, Box B-57, Personal—Pearson file, Pearson to Massey, 16 Sept., 1935.

79. *Ibid.*, unboxed Pearson file, Skelton to Massey, 18 Feb., 1937. Pearson Diary, 1 Jan., 1936, indicates his salary and allowances totalled $8000.

80. Dexter Papers, Dexter to Ferguson, 12 Nov., 1937.

81. Pearson Papers, vol. 8, Plaunt to Pearson, 7 Jan., 1937.

82. Pearson was not entirely happy with conditions in his Department. See above, p. 000. and Mrs Armstrong Papers, H. Wrong to Marga Wrong, 6 June, 1929 [?] and York University Archives, W.R. Riddell Papers, Diary, 11 April, 1932.

83. University of British Columbia Archives, Plaunt Papers, folder 8-4, Pearson to Plaunt, n.d.

84. Massey Papers, unboxed Pearson file, Massey to Skelton, 15 Dec., 1936.

85. *Ibid.*, Massey to Skelton, 19 Jan., 1937.

86. *Ibid.*, Skelton to Massey, 18 Feb., 1937.

87. Pearson Papers, vol. 8, Murray to Pearson, 1 March, 1937.

88. *Ibid.*, Plaunt to Pearson, 19 July, 1937; Plaunt Papers, box 4-8, Pearson to Plaunt, 28 July, 1937, tel.

89. King Diary, 21 Oct., 1937.

90. Massey Papers, unboxed Pearson file, Massey to King, 11 Nov., 1937.

91. Pearson Papers, vol. 8, Murray to Pearson, 27 Nov., 1937.

92. *Ibid.*, Pearson to Skelton, 16 Dec., 1937.

93. Historical Personnel Records, vol. 536, Pearson file, Skelton to King, 26 Jan., 1938.

94. *Ibid.*, tel., 28 Feb., 1938.

95. *Ibid.*, 3 March, 1938.

96. Pearson Papers, vol. 8, Murray to Pearson, 3 April, 1938; King Papers, King to Massey, 20 Dec., 1938, ff.217574-5.

97. Pearson Papers, vol. 2, Skelton to Pearson, 6 Nov., 1935.

98. *Ibid.*, reply, 22 Nov., 1935; *Mike*, I, 108-9.

99. EAR, vol. 2, file 4, extract, n.d. [late 1935?]. For Pearson on collective security, see T [Pearson], 'Canada and the Far East', *Foreign Affairs*, XIII (1934-5), 388ff.

100. Pearson Papers, vol. 1, Pearson to Crerar, 14 May, 1936.

101. King Papers, Pearson to Skelton, 19 Feb., 1937, f.206227.

102. *Mike*, I, 122.

103. *Ibid.*, 123-4.

104. Vincent Massey, *What's Past is Prologue* (Toronto, 1963), 262ff.; DCER VI, 1100-03; King Papers, Memo, 27 Jan., 1939, ff.118579ff.; J.L. Granatstein and R. Bothwell, 'A Self Evident National Duty . . .', *Journal of Imperial and Commonwealth History*, III (January, 1975), 221ff.

105. Dexter Papers, box 8, file 4, Diary, 20 Sept., 1938. See *ibid.*, Dexter to Ferguson, 6, 20 Sept., 1938, which indicate how Pearson kept Dexter informed of U.K. policy during the crisis.

106. Pearson Papers, vol. 2, Pearson to Skelton, 16 Sept., 1938.

107. PRO, Prime Minister's Office Records, PREM 1/242, Record of Meetings of High Commissioners, 29 Sept., 1938.

108. Pearson Papers, vol. 2, Pearson to Skelton, 4 Nov., 1938.

109. See King Diary, 12, 13 Sept., 1938.

110. EAR, vol. 767, file 319, Pearson to Skelton, 17 March, 1939; DCER VI, 1137ff.

111. EAR, vol. 767, file 319, Pearson to Skelton, 24 March, 1939; DCER VI, 1155ff.

112. Dexter Papers, Memo, 30 June, 1939. Cf. DCER VI, 1080-1. Massey on the

other hand told King that 'I don't believe that any government could remain in power in this country and say less [than Chamberlain in guaranteeing Poland and Romania]. All classes, all parties and all ages are now united. . . . ,' Massey, 276.

5. THE ROAD TO FUNCTIONALISM

1. PAC, N.A. Robertson Papers, vol. 2, Personal and Family file, Robertson to his parents, 30 Jan. 1941. This account of Robertson's career is based on my *A Man of Influence: Norman A. Robertson and Canadian Statecraft, 1929-68* (Ottawa, 1981).

2. See PAC, W.L.M. King Papers, Memo, 6 Jan., 1939, f. C107533; *Foreign Relations of the United States [FRUS] 1938* (Washington, 1955), II, 298ff.

3. Queen's University, Norman Rogers Papers, Notes of Conversations, 29 April, 1940, 40ff.

4. PAC, Department of Finance Records, vol. 2691, file France 1939-40, Towers to Ralston, 17 May, 1940; *DCER* VIII, 485ff., 515-6.

5. PRO, Foreign Office Records, documents on F.O. 371/25224 and F.O. 800/312, Halifax Papers, Memo, 27 Aug., 1940.

6. Dupuy's mission, agreed to reluctantly by Ottawa, had been manoeuvered by Vincent Massey. See Massey College, Massey Papers, Diary, 11 Nov., 20, 31 Dec., 1940, 3 Jan., 1941, etc. See *DCER* VIII, 631ff.

7. Foreign Office Records, F.O. 371/28234, Churchill to Foreign Secretary, 29 Dec., 1940.

8. *Ibid.,* F.O. 371/28235, D. Morton to Churchill, 2 June, 1941 and 6 Oct., 1941, Cadogan to Ismay, 17 Oct., 1941.

9. Harvard University, Pierrepont Moffat Papers, Memo, 9 May, 1942; Royal Archives, Windsor Castle, Geo. V CC53/862, King to Athlone, 20 May, 1941. See Dupuy's account, 'Mission à Vichy: Novembre 1940', *International Journal,* XXII (Summer, 1967), 395ff.

10. PRO, Cabinet Records, Cab. 66/12, W.P. (40) 389, 27 Sept., 1940; PRO, Dominions Office Records, D.O. 35/1004 minutes on file; Foreign Office Records, F.O. 371/24335, tel. Butler to F.O., 26 Oct., 1940; *DCER* VIII, 723ff.

11. King Diary, 5 July, 1940. On Quebec attitudes, see J.F. Hilliker, 'The Canadian Government and the Free French', a paper presented to Canadian Committee on History of Second World War Conference, October, 1977, and P.M. Couture, 'The Vichy-Free French Propaganda War in Quebec, 1940 to 1942', *Historical Papers 1978,* 200ff. This chapter has benefited greatly from Dr Couture's 1981 Ph.D. dissertation (York Univ.) on Canada and France 1940-42.

12. Dominion Office Records, D.O. 35/1004, tel., Newfoundland to D.O., 20 May, 1941.

13. *Ibid.,* Minutes, 19, 23 June, 1941.

14. Moffat Papers, Memo, 17 May, 1941; *DCER* VIII, 806.

15. King Papers, Memo, 15 May, 1941, f. C283110.

16. Moffat Papers, Memo, 28 May, 1941; *DCER* VIII, 809.

17. Department of External Affairs [DEA], file 1497-40, Memo for Prime Minister, 8 July, 1941; *DCER* VIII, 827-8.

18. King Papers, Hankinson to Robertson, 9 July, 1941, f. C284583, and Memo,

15 July, 1941, f. C284582; *DCER* VIII, 829-30.

19. PAC, Privy Council Office Records, Cabinet War Committee Minutes, 6 Aug., 1941 and Documents, Wood to Robertson, 4 Aug., 1941. On opinion on St Pierre, see W.A. Christian, Jr., *Divided Island* (Cambridge, 1969), esp. chap. V-VIII.

20. Cabinet War Committee Minutes, 29 Oct., 1941 and Documents, MacDonald to Robertson, 21 Oct., 1941.

21. Moffat Papers, Memo, 3 Nov., 1941; *FRUS 1941*, II, 540.

22. Moffat Papers, Memo, 13, 14 Nov., 1941.

23. Cabinet War Committee Minutes, 26 Nov., 1941; *FRUS 1941*, II, 544.

24. King Diary, 1 Dec., 1941; Cabinet War Committee Minutes, 1 Dec., 1941; *DCER* VIII, 854-6.

25. Cabinet War Committee Minutes, 2 Dec., 1941.

26. King Diary, 2 Dec., 1941.

27. Cabinet War Committee Minutes, 3 Dec., 1941; *FRUS 1941*, II, 542-3.

28. King Papers, Memo, 3 Dec., 1941, ff. C284624, copy on EAR, vol. 779, file 375; *DCER*, VIII, 856-9.

29. *FRUS 1941*, II, 544-5.

30. Moffat Papers, Memo, 15 Dec., 1941; King Papers, Memo, 15 Dec., 1941, ff. C284647-9.

31. Cabinet War Committee Minutes, 16 Dec., 1941.

32. *FRUS 1941*, II, 546, 549-51. Wrong reported that the U.S. 'seemed to feel that they want to have as little to do with [de Gaulle] as possible.' King Papers, Memo, 16 Dec., 1941, ff. C284663-4.

33. King Papers, Memo, 16 Dec., 1941, ff. C284652-3; Moffat Papers, Memo, 16 Dec., 1941; *FRUS 1941*, II, 547.

34. Cabinet War Committee Minutes, 16 Dec., 1941. Memo, 29 May, 1943, indicates that the Minister stayed in Canada until June 1943 when he received a posting to Algiers.

35. *Ibid.*, 19 Dec., 1941.

36. Moffat Papers, Memo, 19 Dec., 1941. Stone was considered by the British 'a great comforter and support' for the Free French, one who 'lent sympathetic ear to their anti-American outpourings.' Foreign Office Records, F.O. 371/36603, Maitland to Greenway, 8 Sept., 1943.

37. Moffat Papers, Memo, 22 Dec., 1941.

38. Muselier apparently was embarrassed at having to break his pledge to the U.S. and Canada, but as he explained to Adm. L.W. Murray in Newfoundland, he had been given direct orders by de Gaulle. PAC, Murray Papers, vol. 4, Recollections, 46.

39. King Diary, 25 Dec., 1942.

40. N.H. Hooker, ed., *The Moffat Papers* (Cambridge, 1956), 363-4. Some evidence, as yet unpublished, indicates that the Canadians were aware of Muselier's plan. The story is expected in the forthcoming history of External Affairs by Donald Page.

41. Hooker, 366.

42. *FRUS 1941*, II, 551. Cordell Hull, *The Memoirs of Cordell Hull* (New York, 1948), II, 1130.

43. Hooker, 367; EAR, vol. 778, file 375, Memo, 26 Dec., 1941.

44. DEA, Pickersgill interview.

45. King Diary, 25 Dec., 1941.

46. D.G. Anglin, *The St. Pierre and Miquelon Affaire* (Toronto, 1966), 105. The message was not sent, but as it was shown to Moffat its purpose was achieved.

47. Hull, II, 1131ff.; Library of Congress, Cordell Hull Papers, Box 58, Memos, on file 215.

48. Moffat Papers, Memo, 31 Dec., 1941.

49. Anglin, 125.

50. The British had difficulty in persuading the U.S. that they had not put up Muselier to act. Muselier, who had long intrigued against de Gaulle, resigned his post in 1942. See François Kersaudy, *Churchill and de Gaulle* (London, 1981), Chap. VII. Kersaudy cannot be relied on in his account of the St Pierre affair.

51. Moffat Papers, 372-3.

52. e.g., Foreign Office Records, F.O. 371/28436, tel., D.O. to High Commissioner, 19 May, 1941.

53. Dominions Office Records, D.O. 114/113, 135-6.

54. Moffat Papers, Memo, 17 May, 1941.

55. *Ibid.*, 28 May, 1941.

56. Dominions Office Records, D.O. 114/113, 137.

57. *Ibid.*, 138 and Cabinet Records, Cab. 65/20, W.M. (41), War Cabinet Conclusions, 1 Dec., 1941.

58. *DCER* VIII, 605-6.

59. *Ibid.*, 617-8.

60. Hilliker, 'Free French', 6-7.

61. Moffat Papers, Memo, 9 Feb., 1942.

62. See the Miribel report on Quebec opinion, copy on Dominions Office Records, D.O. 35/1003, att. to MacDonald to Attlee, 13 Mar., 1942.

63. Cabinet War Committee Minutes, 22 April, 1942; United States National Archives, State Department Records, Hickerson Papers, Memo, 25 April, 1942; Hull Papers, box 59, file 215, Memos, 25 April, 1942 and ff. There was similar advice from Dupuy who returned to Canada in May, 1942. See Massey Papers, Diary, 2 May, 1942.

64. Cabinet War Committee Minutes, 8 May, 1942.

65. Hickerson Papers, Memo, 25 April, 1942.

66. House of Commons *Debates,* 19 May, 1942, quoted on Foreign Office Records, F.O. 371/31957, tel. S.S.E.A. to S.S.D.A., 19 May, 1942. This upset the Foreign Office. See minutes on *ibid.*

67. Cabinet War Committee Minutes, 8, 22 May, 1942; Hull Papers, box 57, file 196, Memo, 22 May, 1942; Moffat Papers, Memo, 28 May and 15 June, 1942.

68. DEA, Glazebrook interview, 12 Jan. 1977.

69. Moffat Papers, Memo, 8 Nov., 1942.

70. DEA, Pickersgill interview, 3 Dec., 1977.

71. See Dominions Office Records, D.O. 114/113, 140.

72. DEA, Pickersgill interview.

73. Moffat Papers, Memo, 8 Nov., 1942.

74. King Diary, 9 Nov., 1942; Hull Papers, box 57, file 196, Memo, 9 Nov., 1942.

75. King Diary, 9 Nov., 1942.

76. Cabinet War Committee Minutes, 9 Nov., 1942.

77. King Diary, 9 Nov., 1942; DEA, file 1-AS, Memo for Prime Minister, 11 Nov., 1942; Moffat Papers, Memo, 23 Nov., 1942. DEA, file 4587-B-40, Memo, 29 May, 1943, indicates that the Minister stayed in Canada until June 1943 when he received a posting to Algiers.

78. Hilliker, 'Free French', 13; DEA, file 1-AS, Memo for Prime Minister, 23 Aug., 1943.

79. Letter, Mrs N.A. Robertson to author, 26 Oct., 1979.

80. '. . . a rather unattractive structure, with a Mansard roof, and a tower. It came to my wife . . . and there four of my five children were born.' George M. Wrong, *Chronicle of a Family* (privately printed; in the possession of Mrs C.H.A. Armstrong, Toronto),

81. Mrs C.H.A. Armstrong Papers (Toronto), Draft Family History, chap. I, 5; Mrs Armstrong interview, 27 Jan., 1978; Vincent Massey, *What's Past is Prologue: The Memoirs of Vincent Massey* (Toronto, 1963), 21–2; Claude Bissell, *The Young Vincent Massey* (Toronto, 1981), 36ff. Mrs Armstrong is Hume Wrong's sister.

82. Interview, 27 Jan., 1978.

83. See, on the University at this period, A.F. Bowker, 'Truly Useful Men: Maurice Hutton, George Wrong, James Mavor and the University of Toronto, 1880-1927', Ph.D. thesis, University of Toronto, 1975.

84. Balliol College Records, Oxford, Hume Wrong file, Hutton to Bailey, 29 Mar., 1914.

85. *Ibid.*, 5 Aug., 1914.

86. Mrs Armstrong Papers, Wrong to Murray Wrong, 3, 21 Sept., 2 Nov., 1916; to Marga Wrong, 22 July 1916. Much information on Wrong's war service is to be found in the Gerald Blake Papers, now in the possession of Mrs James Bacque, Toronto.

87. Mrs June Wrong Rogers Papers (Ottawa), fragment, Nov., 15. (Mrs Rogers is Hume Wrong's daughter.)

88. Mrs Armstrong Papers, Wrong to Murray Wrong, 24 Feb., 1918.

89. *Ibid.*, 23 March, 1917.

90. *Ibid.*, 27 May, 1918, 30 March, 1918.

91. Balliol College Records, Wrong file, Wrong to Pickard-Cambridge, 24 Dec., 1918; University of Oxford, *Supplement to the Historical Register of 1900 . . . 1901-30* (Oxford, 1934).

92. Mrs Armstrong Papers, Wrong to G.M. Wrong, 31 Jan., 1920.

93. *Ibid.*, 15 March, 1919.

94. *Ibid.*, 23, 31 Jan., 1920.

95. See W.D. Meikle, 'And Gladly Teach: G.M. Wrong and the Department of History at the University of Toronto', Ph.D. thesis, Michigan State University, 1977, 120-21, 170n.

96. University of Toronto Archives, Board of Governors Minutes, 13 Nov., 1924; 26 March, 1925.

97. Mrs Armstrong Papers, Wrong to Murray Wrong, 9 Feb., 4 June, 7 July, 1917, 27 Nov., 1922.

98. Hon. Paul Martin interview, 16 June, 1978.

99. PAC, Hume Wrong Papers, vol. 1, file 1, Wrong to McGhee, 30 April, 1923;

ibid., Wrong memo, 24 May, 1922. See esp. John Kendle, *The Round Table Movement and Imperial Union* (Toronto, 1975), 278.

100. Mrs Armstrong Papers, Wrong to Murray Wrong, 15 July, 1924.

101. *Ibid.,* Wrong to G.M. Wrong, 12 May, 1926.

102. *Ibid.,* 20 June, 1926.

103. *Ibid.,* 19 July, 1926. The Round Tablers, however, would have been delighted to keep Wrong at work in Toronto. See Bodleian Library, Oxford University, Mss. Eng. Hist., c819, f.179, A.J. Glazebrook to Dove, 14 April, 1927.

104. Massey College, Vincent Massey Diaries, 1 Feb., 1927 and *passim.*

105. PAC, Civil Service Commission Records, Historical Personnel files, v.358, Wrong file, History sheet. That salary did not always meet expenses. In 1933, Wrong said that 'I hope to keep to $9000 expenses this year.' Mrs Armstrong Papers, Wrong to Marga Wrong, 23 Nov., 1933.

106. *Ibid.,* 3 Oct., 25 Nov., 28, 29 March, 1929.

107. Massey Diary, addenda to 12 April, 1928 entry. Massey's *Memoirs* say nothing of this—and nothing of substance on his period in Washington; Bissell is marginally better on Washington, but inaccurate in saying Wrong-Massey relations were satisfactory for 'several years'. Bissell, 125-7.

108. Mrs Armstrong Papers, Wrong to parents, 12, 15, 27 April, 1927.

109. *Ibid.,* Wrong to mother, 17 July, 1927.

110. *Ibid.,* Wrong to Marga Wrong, n.d. [1927].

111. *Ibid.,* 16 Dec., 1928, 20 Jan., 1929. Marga Wrong was secretary of the International Committee of Christian Literature for Africa from 1926. She died in Uganda in 1948.

112. *Ibid.,* 31 Jan., 2 April, 1933.

113. *Ibid.,* 18 June, 1933.

114. *Ibid.,* e.g., 18 June, 1933, 24 Nov., 1935.

115. *Ibid.,* dates as noted.

116. Mrs Rogers Papers, Wrong to J.W. Dafoe, 7 May, 1930.

117. See, e.g. Wrong Papers, vol. 3, file 14, Minute Sheet, 8 May, 1934; vol. 1, file 2, 'What has the good neighbour policy accomplished . . . ,' 6 July, 1935.

118. Mrs Armstrong Papers, Wrong to Marga Wrong, 20 Jan., 1929; Prof. Dennis Wrong interview, 15 June, 1978; PAC, R.B. Bennett Papers, Wrong dispatch, 13 July, 1935, f.183238.

119. e.g., see PAC, L.B. Pearson Papers, N1, vol. 3, Wrong to Pearson, 15 July, 1936, and 17 Oct., 1937.

120. Mrs Armstrong Papers, Wrong to Marga Wrong, 25 June, 1934; and *passim.*

121. e.g., *ibid.,* 29 March, 1929.

122. H.L. Keenleyside interview, 4 May, 1978.

123. Mrs Armstrong Papers, Wrong to Marga Wrong, 29 Sept., 1936.

124. e.g., *ibid.,* 13 Aug., 1938; King Diary, 14 March, 1938.

125. George Glazebrook Papers (Toronto), Glazebrook to J.W. Holmes, n.d. [1968].

126. Mrs Armstrong Papers, Wrong to Marga Wrong, 5 Jan., 25 Sept., 1938. Still, as he wrote Pearson, 'it does seem a poor time to leave, just when the inter-

national situation may break at any moment.' Pearson Papers, N1, vol. 3, 6 April, 1938.

127. *Ibid.*, 7 Nov., 1937.

128. Wrong Papers, vol. 3, file 14, Wrong to Skelton, 18 Dec., 1935, unsent.

129. Mrs Armstrong Papers, Wrong to Marga Wrong, 17 Sept., 1938.

130. *DCER*, VI, 1104ff. See Pearson Papers, N1, vol. 3, Wrong to Pearson, 31 Dec., 1938; Miller, 813-14.

131. Wrong Papers, vol. 3, file 17, Skelton to Wrong, 2 March, 1939.

132. *DCER* VI, 1247, Memo by Skelton, 25 Aug., 1939.

133. Escott Reid interview, 14 Oct., 1978.

134. Pearson Papers, N1, vol. 3, Wrong to Pearson, 11 Sept., 1939.

135. e.g., Massey Diary, 10, 14 Oct., 1939.

136. Pearson Papers, N8, Diary, 17-20 Oct., 1939, 10 Nov., 1939; Civil Service Commission Records, Historical Personnel files, vol. 536, Pearson file, Pearson to McCloskey, 14 Feb., 1940.

137. King Papers, Memo for Prime Minister, 12 Sept., 1940, ff. C163164-5.

138. 'No. No', was King's comment. *Ibid.*, Memo, Skelton to King, 19 Aug., 1940, f. C220893.

139. *Ibid.*, Memo for Prime Minister, 12 Sept., 1940, f. C163165.

140. Mrs Armstrong Papers, Wrong to Marga Wrong, 2 Jan., 1941.

141. Documents on Civil Service Commission Records, Historical Personnel files, vol. 358-9, Wrong file. See also EAR, vol. 1890, file 40-K and vol. 2122, file AR 1184/1.

142. Mrs Armstrong Papers, Wrong to Marga Wrong, 2 Feb., 1941.

143. See Granatstein, 101ff.

144. *Ibid.*, 183ff.

145. Pearson Papers, N1, vol. 1, Crerar to Pearson, 7 Feb., 1941; Moffat Papers, Memo, 13 Feb., 1941. Copy in Hickerson Papers.

146. See King Diary, 19-20 Feb., 1941; King Papers, Memos, 22 Feb., 1941, ff. C162791ff; Moffat Papers, Memo, 24 Feb., 1941; Pearson Papers, N8, Diary, 24 Feb., 1941.

147. Mrs Armstrong Papers, Wrong to Marga Wrong, 27 April, 8 June, 1941.

148. See J.L. Granatstein, *Canada's War: The Politics of the Mackenzie King Government, 1939-45* (Toronto, 1975), 147-48; documents on DEA, file 2341-40C.

149. C.P. Stacey, *Arms, Men and Governments: The War Policies of Canada* (Ottawa, 1970), 370ff.

150. Wrong Papers, vol. 8, file 43, Memo, 14 Dec., 1941.

151. Cabinet War Committee Minutes, 29 Dec., 1941.

152. DEA, file 3265-A-40C, Memo for Prime Minister, 17 Jan., 1942.

153. *Ibid.*, Wrong to Robertson, 20 Jan., 1942.

154. *Ibid.*

155. See A.J. Miller, 'The Functional Principle in Canada's External Relations', *International Journal*, XXV (Spring, 1980), 316-17 for a brief discussion of works by Woolf and Mitrany on functionalism. Miller, 318, presents evidence that Wrong had read Mitrany by November 1943, at least.

156. See, e.g., the apparent lack of follow-up to the discussion in Cabinet War Committee Minutes, 12 Feb., 1942.

157. DEA, file 3265-A-40C, Wrong to Pearson, 3 Feb., 1942. On Wrong's constant concern that efficiency not be jeopardized by Canada, see Wrong Papers, vol. 4, file 20, 'Canada, the United Nations, and the Combined Boards', 8 Aug., 1942.

158. DEA, file 3265-A-40C, Tel., SSEA to Canadian Minister, Washington, 2

159. Quoted from a now lost Wrong diary of September 1942 in George Glazebrook, 'Humphrey Hume Wrong, A Biographical Sketch', unpub. MSS. I am grateful to Professor Glazebrook for allowing me to see and use his MSS.

160. PRO, Treasury Records, T188/252, Memo, 30 July, 1942. See also generally, Dominions Office Records, DO 114/112 and DEA, file 3265-A-40C, Wrong to Pearson, 22 Sept., 1942.

161. DEA, file 2295-G-40, Memo for Prime Minister, 3 Feb., 1943.

162. Wrong Papers, vol. 4, file 24, Memo for Under-Secretary, 19 March, 1943.

163. See Robert Bothwell and J.L. Granatstein, 'Canada and the Wartime Negotiations over Civil Aviation: The Functional Principle in Operation', *International History Review*, II (Oct., 1980), 585ff.

164. House of Commons *Debates*, 9 July, 1943, 4558.

165. *Ibid.*, vol. 4, file 24, Memo for Under-Secretary, 19 March, 1943.

166. *Times Literary Supplement*, 21 Dec., 1979, 148.

6. NEW MEN, NEW IDEAS

1 V.W. Bladen, *Bladen on Bladen* (Toronto, 1978), 44.

2. Confidential interview.

3. University of Toronto Archives, Department of Political Economy Records, vol. 7, 1929 file, Rasminsky to Innis, 26 Jan., 1929. I am indebted to Prof. Brian McKillop for this reference.

4. University of British Columbia Archives, Norman MacKenzie Papers, file 6/4 Main Correspondence, Rasminsky to MacKenzie, 21 April, 1930.

5. *Ibid.*

6. Rasminsky interview, 30 Nov., 1978; Bank of Canada Archives, L. Rasminsky Papers, Appt. to League file, Sec.-Gen. to Rasminsky, 1 Aug., 1930. The appointment had been announced earlier. See Toronto *Telegram* 10 March, 1930, 1 in *ibid.*

7. Mrs N.A. Robertson interview, 30 Nov., 1978. By 1938, Rasminsky's salary had risen to 20,900 Swiss francs. Rasminsky Papers, Salary file, Avenol to Rasminsky, 7 Jan., 1938.

8. See Rasminsky Papers, file LR76-6, Memorandum, n.d. [1941] and attached correspondence; Nutrition Trip 1936 file and especially editorials (Sept., 1937) in *New York Times, Times* of London, etc.; League Drafts file; and Depressions Report file.

9. Rasminsky interview, 30 Nov., 1978; Bank of Canada Archives, Bank of Canada Records, Deputy Governor's clipping file 1B-292; A.F. Cross, 'Oligarchs at Ottawa', *Public Affairs* (Autumn, 1951), 23; Rasminsky Papers, Bolivia Mission file, Rasminsky to Loveday, 30 Dec., 1939 and Report on Bolivian Mission, n.d.

10. *Ibid., file LR*76-1, tel., Rasminsky to Acting Secretary-General, 24 June, 1943. Departure from League 1943 file, Lester to Rasminsky, 3 July, 1943.

11. *Ibid.*, file LR76-2, file 76-10, etc.

12. *Ibid.*, Misc. Correspondence 1930-5, W.C. Clark to Rasminsky, 5 Nov., 1933; Public Archives of Canada, W.L. Grant Papers, vol. 9 Skelton to Grant, 3 Feb., 1934. In July 1934, however, Rasminsky applied for a post as Assistant Deputy Governor of the Bank of Canada and failed to get the job. Rasminsky Papers, W.C. Clark Correspondence 1930-5 file, Rasminsky to Clark, 11 July, 1934.

13. See Rasminsky's account of the work of the FECB in 'Foreign Exchange Control in Canada; Purposes and Methods', in J.F. Parkinson, ed., *Canadian War Economics* (Toronto, 1941). As an employee of the Bank, Rasminsky was not quite a civil servant although I have treated him as such throughout. Dr W.A. Mackintosh at one point described him as being in 'an institution on the fringe of the Government'. PAC, CIIA Records, vol. 3, Mackintosh to Edgar Tarr, 13 June, 1943. See also Rasminsky Papers, Loveday Correspondence 1939-40 file, Rasminsky to Loveday, 22 Feb., 1940.

14. DEA, file 6000-D-40c, tel., 22 May, 1942. This message and many others cited in this paper are printed in *DCER,* IX, 612ff. On Keynes's ideas on this subject, see the brief account by Sir Roy Harrod, 'Problems Perceived in the International Financial System', in A.L.K. Acheson, *et al., Bretton Woods Revisited* (Toronto, 1972), 6ff. See also Thomas Balogh, 'Keynes and the IMF', *Times Literary Supplement,* 10 Oct., 1975, 1211. The two basic books on the wartime international financial discussions are R.N. Gardner, *Sterling-Dollar Diplomacy* (New York, 1969) and Armand Van Dormael, *Bretton Woods: Birth of a Monetary System* (London, 1978).

15. 27 Sept., 1980, 111-12.

16. See Rasminsky's clear account of interwar international monetary problems in his 'Plans for Post-War Currency Stabilization', *Canadian Banker,* LI (1944), 31ff.

17. *Ibid.,* 40.

18. See e.g., the reactions of Clark, Towers and Wilgress on DEA, file 6000-D-40c, 26, 27, 28 May, 1942.

19. Rasminsky Papers, file LR76-6, Memo, n.d.

20. J.K. Galbraith, 'How Keynes Came to America', in Milo Keynes, ed., *Essays on John Maynard Keynes* (Cambridge, 1975), 137.

21. 'Basic Issues in Postwar International Economic Relations', XXXII (1942), esp. 176ff.

22. DEA, file 6000-D-40c, Memo to Wrong, 1 Sept., 1942.

23. *Ibid.* and *ibid.,* Wrong to Prime Minister, 3 Sept., 1942.

24. *Ibid.,* memo, 6 Oct., 1942. See also Mackintosh's discussion memo of talks with U.S. officials on 21 Sept., 1942. *Ibid.,* memo, 2 Oct., 1942.

25. L. Rasminsky, 'Canadian Views', in *Bretton Woods Revisited,* 34.

26. PAC, Hume Wrong Papers, vol. 4, file 23, Diary of London Trip, 29 Oct., 1942.

27. DEA, file 6000-D-40c, Rasminsky to Towers, 4 Nov., 1942.

28. Rasminsky Papers, file LR76-103-19, 'Report of the Canadian Representatives at the "Post-War Economic Talks" . . .'

29. W.C. Clark, 'Postwar International Monetary Stabilization', *New York University Institute on Postwar Reconstruction,* series 11, no. 11, 15 Dec., 1943, 216. Keynes's plan, Rasminsky said later, was 'in fact not much more than a set of books, but one which has the great merit of revealing at a glance the state of unbalance in the international accounts of the member countries. . . .' Rasminsky Papers, file PWCP-General, 'Notes for Meeting on International Currency Plans, Chicago, Aug. 26, 1943', 2.

30. DEA, file 6000-D-40c, Rasminsky to Towers, 4 Nov., 1942.

31. *Ibid.*

32. Rasminsky Papers, file PWCP Anglo/Canadian, 'Report on Visit to London, October-November 1942'.

33. PAC, Department of Finance Records, vol. 3593, file L-10D, Memo, 29 Oct., 1942. According to Walter Lippmann, Keynes was thinking in terms of a $30 billion commitment. See Ronald Steel, *Walter Lippmann and the American Century* (Boston, 1980), 396.

34. Rasminsky interview, 4 May, 1979.

35. Rasminsky Papers, file LR 76-103-19, 'Report of the Canadian Representatives at the "Post-War Economic Talks" . . .,' 23 Oct., 9 Nov., 1942; Rasminsky interview, 4 May, 1979.

36. DEA, file 6000-D-40c, Rasminsky to Towers, 4 Nov., 1942; *ibid.,* Wrong to Pearson, 11 Dec., 1942.

37. *Ibid.,* Plumptre to Clark, 16 Jan., 1943. A copy of White's final draft is in *ibid.,* attached to Memo to Under-Secretary, 3 Mar., 1943. See on White, David Rees, *Harry Dexter White: A Study in Paradox* (New York, 1973), esp. Chap. XIV. See also Gabriel Kolko, *The Politics of War* (New York, 1968), 255ff. and A.F.W. Plumptre, *Three Decades of Decision* (Toronto, 1977), 36ff.

38. e.g., DEA, file 6000-D-40c, Rasminsky to Wrong, 24 Dec., 1942 and attached memo of 21 Dec., 1942.

39. Rasminsky Papers, file LR76-104-41, Memo to Governor, 22 Dec., 1942. Much later, Rasminsky told Towers that 'if one uses international conferences for their propaganda value they are more likely than not to be a boomerang.' *Ibid.,* file LR76-74, 8 Feb., 1944. See also, *ibid.,* Council on Foreign Relations file, 'Meeting of Council . . . ,' 24 Jan., 1942 for similar thoughts.

40. Department of Finance Records, vol. 3447, International Clearing Union file, Plumptre to Clark, 16 Jan., 1943.

41. *Ibid.,* Memo for Clark, 25 Jan., 1943.

42. DEA, file 6000-D-40c, Wrong to USSEA, 8 Feb., 1943.

43. *Ibid.,* Deutsch memo to USSEA, 3 March, 1943.

44. Queen's University, John Deutsch Papers, file 1228, Sub-Committee minutes, 11 March, 1943.

45. Department of Finance Records, vol. 3447, ICU file, Rasminsky to Mackintosh, 24 March, 1943.

46. Rasminsky Papers, file PWCP-Can, Rasminsky to Mackintosh, 24 March, 1943 and enclosure. See also Rasminsky's article in *Canadian Banker,* 42ff.

47. Department of Finance Records, vol. 3447, ICU file, Rasminsky to Mackintosh, 24 March, 1943; DEA, file 6000-D-40c, Ilsley to Morgenthau, 8 April, 1943; Princeton University Library, Harry Dexter White Papers, 'Canadian

Questions on the Fund', n.d. The minutes of the discussions are in Department of Finance Records, vol. 3447, ICU file, dated 21-26 April, 1943.

48. PAC, Laurent Beaudry Papers, vol. 4, Press Conference, 8 April, 1943.

49. Floyd Chalmers Papers (Toronto), Conversations 1943 file, Memo, 26 April, 1943.

50. Rasminsky Papers, file PWCP-Canada, 'International Financial Arrangements Post-War', 30 April, 1943.

51. Department of Finance Records, vol. 3981, file M-1-7-1, Keynes to Wrong, 19 May, 1943.

52. Ibid., vol. 3579, file M-01, Memo for Minister, 2 June, 1943; copy on DEA, file 6000-D-40c; see also R.N. Gardner, 'The Political Setting', in Bretton Woods Revisited, 23-4.

53. DEA file 6000-D-40c, Memo for Prime Minister, 29 May, 1943.

54. Ibid., Rasminsky to Robertson, 29 May, 1943.

55. Rasminsky Papers, file PWCP-General, 'Summary of Tentative Draft Proposals . . .,' n.d.

56. Ibid., file PWCP-UK, Rasminsky to Keynes, 3 June, 1943. See Department of Finance Records, vol. 3555, file DO3b, Mackintosh to Keynes, 3 June, 1943.

57. PAC, Privy Council Office Records, Cabinet War Committee Minutes, 2 June, 1943.

58. PAC, W.L.M. King Papers, Memo, 11 June, 1943, f.C212601. See Department of Finance Records, vol. 3593, file L-11-F, Memo, 22 June, 1943.

59. EAR. vol. 2110, file AR 405/9/2, tel., Mackintosh to Robertson, 14 June, 1943; DEA, file 6000-D-40c, Deutsch to Mackintosh, 23 June, 1942. The plan was eventually tabled in Parliament and circulated widely by the Wartime Information Board. It was soon the subject of study by the U.S. Embassy in Ottawa. See U.S. Treasury Department, Records, Acc. 67-A-245, Box 41, Canada Bretton Woods file, J.W. Tuthill's 'Canadian Views on International Monetary Stabilization', 30 June, 1943. See also White Papers, Memo, Hannay to White, 2 Aug., 1943 for comments on Tuthill's paper.

60. Van Dormael, 88.

61. Rasminsky interview, 4 May, 1979.

62. Rasminsky Papers, PWCP-Anglo-U.S. file, Keynes to Rasminsky, 18 Sept., 1943. For notes on the Anglo-U.S. discussions, as given to Commonwealth representatives in Washington, see DEA, file 6000-40c, 22, 30 Sept., 1943 and Rasminsky Papers, PWCP Anglo-U.S. file, 'Notes on Washington Conversations, September 28-9', 1943.

63. This is printed, along with the texts of all the major documents leading to the establishment of the IMF, in J.K. Horsefield, The International Monetary Fund 1945-65 (Washington, 1969), III, 128ff.

64. The Bretton Woods records are printed by the U.S. Department of State as Proceedings and Documents of the United Nations Monetary and Financial Conference . . . (Washington, 1948). There also exist mimeographed 'Informal Minutes, Commission I, United Nations Monetary and Financial Conference . . .' (1951), a copy of which is in Mr Rasminsky's possession.

65. Mrs A.F.W. Plumptre Papers (Ottawa), Plumptre to Mrs Plumptre, 18 July 1944. The allocation of Canadians to committees is in DEA, file 6000-F-40, encl.

with Deutsch to Robertson, 5 July, 44.

66. 'International Credit and Currency Plans', XXII (July, 1944), 589ff. See also J.W. Holmes' account in *The Shaping of Peace: Canada and the Search for World Order 1943-57* (Toronto, 1979), I, 52ff.

67. Rasminsky Papers, PWCP-BW Comm I file, 'Report of Commission I', 29 July, 1944.

68. The instructions given the Canadian delegation are on DEA, file 6000-F-40, attached to Deutsch to Robertson, 5 July, 1944. See *ibid.*, Memo, 10 July, 1944; and Department of Finance Records, vol. 3347, file 4747-P-13, Memo, 7 July, 1944.

69. *Ottawa Citizen*, 5 Aug., 1944, on PRO, Treasury Records, file T247/64.

70. PRO, Dominions Office Records, DO 35/1216, Report by Snelling, 1 Aug., 1944. See also Department of Finance Records, vol. 3391, file u4747P-13, Clark to Rasminsky, 15, Aug., 1944. Rasminsky himself told a friend that Canada was 'listened to with great attention, not only by the big powers but also by the smaller countries including the Europeans and the Latinos. If we wanted to do it, I am quite sure that we could establish for ourselves a position of natural leader of the smaller countries.' Rasminsky Papers, file PWCP-BW, Rasminsky to T.A. Stone, 7 Aug., 1944.

71. Queen's University Archives, W.A. Mackintosh Papers, box 8, file 19F, Dafoe to Mackintosh, Christmas 1941.

72. F.A. Knox, 'W.A. Mackintosh, 1895-1970', *Proceedings of the Royal Society of Canada*, ser. IV, vol. IX, (1971), 69ff.

73. Queen's University Archives, Board of Trustees Minutes, 3 Feb., 1920.

74. Mackintosh Papers, box 8, file 206, Mackintosh to Taylor, 30 July, 1925.

75. *Ibid.*, Mackintosh to Skelton, 1 June, 1925.

76. Board of Trustees Minutes, 7 May, 1937.

77. See Barry Ferguson and Doug Owram, 'Social Scientists and Public Policy from the 1920s through World War II', *Journal of Canadian Studies*, XV (Winter 1980-1). I am much indebted here to Mr Ferguson's bibliographical work on Mackintosh, done in connection with his York University dissertation on the Queen's Political and Economic Science Department.

78. Cited in Carl Berger, *The Writing of Canadian History* (Toronto, 1976), 92.

79. e.g., *Queen's Quarterly*, XXXIII (1925-6), 115ff.; 'Trade Barriers as an Obstacle to Prosperity', *Annals of the American Academy* . . . (July 1936).

80. Dales's introduction to the Carleton Library edition of *The Economic Background of Dominion-Provincial Relations* (Toronto, 1964), 6.

81. Cited in Ferguson and Owram, 9.

82. Queen's University Archives, Norman Rogers Papers, Box 2, Mackintosh to Rogers, 20 Feb., 1935.

83. James Struthers, 'No Fault of their Own: Unemployment and the Canadian Welfare State, 1914-41', Ph.D. thesis, University of Toronto, 1979, 488ff.

84. King Diary, 25 Jan., 1938. See also Struthers, 539ff. and H.B. Neatby, *William Lyon Mackenzie King* (Toronto, 1976), III, 247-8.

85. Struthers, 555. See Mackintosh's paper for the NEC, 'Public Works as a Recovery Measure', Mackintosh Papers, box 4, file 100. See also D. McGinnis, 'The "Keynesian Revolution" in Canada, 1929-45', in R.D. Francis and H. Gan-

zevoort, eds., *The Dirty Thirties in Prairie Canada* (Vancouver, 1980), 54.

86. Bladen interview, 2 Nov., 1978.

87. Bladen, *Bladen on Bladen*, 70-1.

88. Board of Trustees Minutes, 19 May, 1939.

89. Mrs W.A. Mackintosh interview, 6 Sept., 1978.

90. R.B. Bryce interview, 28 Nov., 1978; EAR, vol. 824, file 705, Memo for Dr Skelton, 1 Sept., 1939.

91. *Ibid.*, Memo for Prime Minister, 9 Sept., 1939.

92. *Ibid.*

93. King Diary, 12 Sept., 1939.

94. *Ibid.* suggests otherwise. But cf. Department of Finance Records, vol. 4660, file 187-EAC-1, Heeney to Ralston, 12 Sept., 1939.

95. The problem of French-Canadian representation was continuous. When DesRosiers became ill in 1943, Clark was told that no substitute could be found, although Bryce, the EAC Secretary, said 'I think it is highly desirable that there should be at least one French-Canadian on the list.' *Ibid.*, Bryce to Clark, 13 Dec., 1943.

96. See J.L. Granatstein, *Canada's War: The Politics of the Mackenzie King Government, 1939-45* (Toronto, 1975), 59ff. See also EAC minutes on Department of Finance Records, vol. 4660, file 187-EAC-3.

97. *Ibid.*, Minutes, 11, 13 Dec., 1939.

98. *Ibid.*, vol. 3989, file U-1-1, Memo on Draft Unemployment Insurance Bill, n.d. [20 Jan., 1940].

99. *Ibid.*, vol. 4660, file 187-EAC-3, Minutes, 1 May, 1940.

100. Rasminsky Papers, file LR 76-130-1, 'Interim Memo . . .,' 19 Feb., 1940; Department of Finance Records, vol. 3551, file B-04a, Robertson to Mackintosh, 17 June, 1940; *ibid.*, vol. 4660, file 187-EAC-4, 'Report of EAC on the formulation of measures . . . ,' 15 Aug., 1940.

101. *Ibid.*, Minutes, 3 Feb., 1941.

102. Privy Council Office Records, PARC Box 287415, Memo, 30 Oct., 1942 [?] and *ibid.*, Memo to Mr Heeney, 21 Oct., 1942.

103. See Granatstein, 254ff.

104. Department of Finance Records, vol. 4660, file 187-EAC-3, Minutes, 10 Nov., 1942; Privy Council Office Records, PARC Box 287415, Memo for Mr Heeney, 10 Nov., 1942; McGill University Archives, F. Cyril James Papers, box 334, James to Mackenzie, 6 July, 1942, which indicated Norman Robertson's early concerns about a lack of liaison between James's Committee and departments.

105. Department of Finance Records, vol. 4660, file 187-EAC-47, Report, 30 Nov., 1942.

106. DEA, file 1843-A-40C, Memo for Prime Minister, 10 Dec., 1942; Department of Finance Records, vol. 4660, file 187-EAC-1, Heeney to Clark, 26 Dec., 1942; *ibid.*, James to Mackintosh, 28 Dec., 1942 and Clark memo, n.d.

107. Queen's University Archives, Norman Lambert Diary, 2, 4 Jan., 1943.

108. Department of Finance Records, vol. 4660, file 187-EAC-3, Minutes, 16 Jan., 1943.

109. Copy in PAC, Ian Mackenzie Papers, vol. 40, file G25(4), 20 Jan., 1943.

110. King Papers, Mackenzie to King, 20 Jan., 1943, ff. 87367ff. Cf. Mackenzie Papers, documents on vol. 40, file G25(4).

111. See Granatstein, 263n.; King Diary, 22 Jan., 1943. The best account of the whole question of health insurance is Robert Bothwell, 'The Heagerty Plan', Canadian Historical Association paper, 1975.

112. Department of Finance Records, vol. 4660, file 187-EAC-3, Minutes, 7 Jan., 1943.

113. See Queen's University Archives, John Deutsch Papers, file 1284, 'Report of Economic Advisory Committee on Constitutional Problems . . .,' 7 June, 1943.

114. See Granatstein, 267ff.

115. See R.M. Burns, *The Acceptable Mean: The Tax Rental Agreements 1941-62* (Toronto, 1980), 38-9.

116. See Department of Finance Records, vol. 4660, file 187-EAC-1, documents for Oct., 1944 and March-April, 1945.

117. Queen's University Archives, Grant Dexter Papers, Memo, 1 March, 1945. On Howe, his Department, and the *White Paper,* see Robert Bothwell and W. Kilbourn, *C.D. Howe* (Toronto, 1979), Chap. XII.

118. *Canadian Economic Policy Since the War* (Ottawa, 1966), 15.

119. *Ibid.,* 15-6.

120. Bank of Canada Archives, Bank Records, Department of Reconstruction, 1944-8, file 3B-176, Memo Mackintosh to Robertson, *et al.,* 27 March, 1945.

121. *Canadian Economic Policy,* 16.

122. House of Commons *Debates,* 12 April, 1945, 808ff.

123. *Employment and Income with Special Reference to the Initial Period of Reconstruction* (Ottawa, 1945), *passim.*

124. *Canadian Economic Policy,* 21.

125. See Mackintosh's disquisition on Keynesianism in *ibid.,* 15. See also R.B. Bryce, 'William Clifford Clark, 1889-1951', *Canadian Journal of Economics and Political Science,* XIX (1953), 419. For an examination of the Australian, British and Canadian White Papers, see D.H. Merry and G.R. Bruns, 'Full Employment', *Economic Record,* XXI (December, 1945), 226, 228. The Australian authors noted that the Canadian paper gave more emphasis to private enterprise than did the other two.

7. ORGANIZATION AND POLITICS

1. PAC, W.L.M. King Diaries, 27 March, 1937.

2. H.B. Neatby, *William Lyon Mackenzie King,* Vol. III: *The Prism of Unity* (Toronto, 1976), 262.

3. *Ibid.,* 262-3.

4. Queen's University Archives, Tweedsmuir Papers, Bickersteth to Tweedsmuir, 4 Jan., 1936 and attached memo, 'The Introduction of Certain Features of the British Cabinet Office into Canada,' Aug., 1927.

5. *Ibid.,* Tweedsmuir to King, 31 Dec., 1935, and attached memo, 'Notes on a Prime Minister's Chef du Cabinet'. See also Churchill College, Cambridge,

Bickersteth Papers, 'Some Observations on the Present Political Situation in Canada', April, 1936.

6. King Diary, 10 Dec., 1937.

7. J.W. Pickersgill, *My Years with Louis St. Laurent* (Toronto, 1975), 8.

8. On the background, see Brian Heeney Papers (Peterborough), Arnold Heeney draft memoirs, 1ff.

9. See PAC, Arnold Heeney Papers, vol. 8, School Days Scrapbook; Brian Heeney interview, 21 March, 1978 and Heeney draft memoirs, chapter III, 7.

10. Arnold Heeney Papers, vol. 8, scrapbook.

11. Brian Heeney Papers, Heeney to mother, 27 June, 1919.

12. *Ibid.,* Heeney to father, 9 Aug., [?].

13. *Ibid.,* Heeney to mother, 21 Nov., 1922.

14. PAC, Bertal Heeney Papers, Hasted [Dowker] to Rev. Heeney, 24 May, 1924.

15. Arnold Heeney Papers, vol. 8, scrapbook.

16. Brian Heeney Papers, Heeney to father, 15 Dec., 1930.

17. Arnold Heeney Papers, vol. 8, Diary, 27 May, 1925.

18. *Ibid.,* 2 March, 1925.

19. *Ibid.,* 3 May, 1925.

20. *Ibid.,* 11 June, 1925.

21. *Ibid.,* 3 Aug., 1925.

22. Rhodes House, Oxford, Wylie Confidential Notebook, Heeney entry.

23. Arnold Heeney Papers, vol. 8, Diary, 19 July and 5 Dec., 1925.

24. Pickersgill in *International Perspectives,* (March–April 1973), 56.

25. Arnold Heeney Papers, vol. 8, Diary, 1 March, 1925.

26. Brian Heeney Papers, Heeney to sister, 11 Oct., 1926.

27. *Ibid.,* Heeney to mother, 16 Oct., 1926.

28. PAC, Brooke Claxton Papers, vol. 5, Claxton to G. Spry, 11 Feb., 1927.

29. Brian Heeney Papers, Heeney to father, 30 Oct., 1927 and Mrs Heeney's note on letter.

30. *Ibid.,* Heeney to father, 26 Feb., 1928.

31. A.D.P. Heeney, *The Things that are Caesar's* (Toronto, 1970), 38.

32. Brian Heeney Papers, Heeney to mother, 11 Sept., 1933. In *The Things* the meeting of the Canon and King is incorrectly dated as 1934.

33. Bertal Heeney Papers, vol. 1, King to Canon Heeney, 22 July, 1934.

34. Brian Heeney Papers, Heeney to father, Thursday [fall 1935]; Arnold Heeney Papers, vol. 1, King to Heeney, 10 Aug., 1935.

35. King Diary, 10 Dec., 1936.

36. Bertal Heeney Papers, vol. 1, King to Heeney, 8 Jan., and 27 Sept., 1937.

37. Arnold Heeney Papers, vol. 1, Heeney to King, 4 Oct., 1937.

38. Brian Heeney Papers, Heeney to father, Monday [Oct., 1937]. A few months earlier, Heeney had been suggested for a place on the CBC board by Alan Plaunt: 'Leisurely, well to do . . . actively Liberal . . . persona grata with the business community, the university authorities and the french-speaking population.' University of British Columbia Archives, Plaunt Papers, box 8-2, Plaunt to E.A. Pickering, 7 April, 1937.

39. Arnold Heeney Papers, vol. 1, King to Heeney, 13 July, 1938.

40. Brian Heeney Papers, Heeney to father, 18 July 1938.

41. Arnold Heeney Papers, vol. 1, Personal Memo, 26 July, 1938.

42. *Ibid.,* Heeney to King, 24 Aug., 1938. See also Brian Heeney Papers, draft memoirs, chap. VII, 9ff, and Heeney to father, 25 July, 1938; King Diary, 27 July, 1938.

43. Arnold Heeney Papers, vol. 1, Father to Heeney, 29 Aug., 1938.

44. *Ibid.,* PC 2238, 8 Sept., 1938; EAR, vol. 796, file 482, Skelton to King, 29 Aug., and 6 Sept., 1938.

45. Brian Heeney Papers, fragment, n.d.

46. King Diary, 5 Oct., 1938.

47. Pickersgill, 9.

48. Brian Heeney Papers, Heeney to father, 28 Oct., 1938.

49. A.D.P. Heeney, 'Cabinet Government in Canada . . . ,' *Canadian Journal of Economics and Political Science,* XII (August 1946), 285. See also Heeney's later article, 'Mackenzie King and Cabinet Secretariat,' *Canadian Public Administration,* X (September, 1967).

50. PAC, Privy Council Office Records, Cabinet War Committee Minutes, Cabinet Sub-Committee on Defence Minutes, 14 Nov., 1938 ff.; King Diary, 14 Nov., 1938.

51. Brian Heeney Papers, Heeney to father, Spring, 1939.

52. *Ibid.,* 19 Jan., 1939.

53. Queen's University Archives, Norman Lambert Papers, Diary, 15 April, 1939 and 30 June, 1939.

54. King Diary, 23 June, 1939.

55. Arnold Heeney Papers, vol. 1, Memo for Prime Minister, 25 July, 1939.

56. Heeney, *Canadian Public Administration,* 369.

57. King Diary, 22 Aug., 1939.

58. See King Papers, PC 2474, 30 Aug., 1979, ff. C155890-1 and PC 4017½, 5 Dec., 1939, ff.C155892ff.

59. Cabinet War Committee Minutes, 28 Sept., 1939 ff. and 8 Dec., 1939 ff.

60. EAR, vol, 822, file 701, 'Note on the War-Time Organization of the Cabinet,' n.d.

61. King Diary, 19 Jan., 1940.

62. Lambert Diaries, 27 Jan., 1940.

63. Brian Heeney Papers, Heeney to mother, 25 Feb., 1940.

64. *Ibid.,* Heeney to parents, 13 March, 1940.

65. King Diary, 22 March, 1940.

66. Arnold Heeney Papers, vol. 1, PC 1121, 25 March, 1940.

67. King Diary, 28 March, 1940.

68. Bertal Heeney Papers, father to Heeney, 27 March, 1940.

69. Cabinet War Committee Minutes, 4 April, 1940 ff.

70. Brian Heeney Papers, Heeney to father, 11 Dec., 1940.

71. Harvard University, Pierrepont Moffat Papers, Memo of Conversation, 12 Feb., 1941.

72. Brian Heeney Papers, Heeney to parents, 20 March, 1941.

73. Heeney, *Canadian Public Administration,* 370.

74. Cabinet War Committee Minutes, 10 Sept., 1941.

75. Conacher interview, 23 May, 1980.
76. Heeney, *Canadian Public Administration,* 370-1.
77. PAC, Department of Finance Records, vol. 4660, file 187-EAC-1, Memo to Dr Clark, 11 July, 1941.
78. Franklin D. Roosevelt Library, Wayne Coy Papers, Box 22, 'Top-Level Coordination in the Government of Canada,' 20 Sept., 1943. I am indebted to my colleague Robert Cuff for this reference.
79. Privy Council Office Records, PARC Box 1002, file P-50 (1941-6), Heeney to Walter Gordon, 5 April, 1946 and attached memo.
80. See, e.g., Heeney's role in eliminating the Advisory Committee on Reconstruction. Documents on DEA, file 1843-A-40C. A number of special boards and bodies reported to Cabinet through Heeney, including the Special Commissioner for Defence Projects in North West Canada, the Canadian Information Service, established at the end of the war, and the Security Panel, the key committee dealing with security problems, created in 1946.
81. King Diary, 3 Feb., 1941.
82. *Ibid.,* 29 Jan., 1941, 3 Feb., 1941.
83. *Ibid.,* 28 Nov., 1944.
84. Heeney, *The Things,* 90.
85. DEA, file 270-40, memo for Prime Minister, 16 June, 1945; Heeney, *CJEPS,* 290ff.
86. DEA, file 270-40, letter King to Ministers, 25 July, 1940; Privy Council Office Records, PARC Box 1002, file P-50 (1941-6), Heeney to W. Gordon, 5 April, 1946 and attached memo.
87. Mrs A.D.P. Heeney Papers, R.G. Robertson to Mrs Heeney, 20 Dec., 1970.
88. Pickersgill, *My Years,* 5. The other source of information on Pickersgill's family is George Ford, ed., *The Making of a Secret Agent: The Pickersgill Letters* (Toronto, 1978).
89. J.W. Pickersgill Papers (Ottawa), Congratulations re Appointment to PCO file, E.N. Hunter to Pickersgill, 24 March, 1952.
90. *Ibid.,* Oxford degree file, Pickersgill to A.H. Smith, 10 April, 1953 and reply 14 April, 1953.
91. Queen's University Archives, A.R.M. Lower Papers, Box 26, file D1, Riddell to Lower, 8 June and 25 July, 1929.
92. *Ibid.,* Assistant Registrar to Pickersgill, 6 Dec., 1935 and Lower memo, 10 Dec., 1935.
93. See Ford, *passim;* A.R.M. Lower interview, 30 Oct., 1978.
94. Lower Papers, Box 26, file D1, undated clipping.
95. Lower interview.
96. PAC, F.H. Underhill Papers, Pickersgill file, Pickersgill to Underhill, 22 April, 1936.
97. X (1931-2).
98. LIV (March, 1939).
99. XV (April, 1935), 253.
100. J.W. Pickersgill interview, 13 Oct., 1978.
101. Lower Papers, Box 26, Pickersgill to Riddell, 4 Feb., 1932; Lower interview.

102. DEA, Pickersgill interview, 4 Dec., 1977.

103. Ford, 23, 25.

104. Pickersgill Papers, Dafoe file, Dafoe to Pickersgill, 3 Sept., 1937; J.H. Stitt, 'That Man Pickersgill', speech copy in Queen's University Archives, Grant Dexter Papers, vol. 22, file 274.

105. DEA, Pickersgill interview; Lower wrote that 'there was no future for him and . . . his position had been the subject of intrigue ever since he came here.' Lower Papers, vol. 1a, Lower to H.A. Innis, 4 Nov., 1937.

106. *Ibid.*, vol. 26, Pickersgill to Lower, 22 April, 1937; EAR, vol. 839, file S-1-AA, List of names, 28 Aug., 1940; Pickersgill interview, 13 Oct., 1978; 'That Man Pickersgill'.

107. Documents on Lower Papers, vol. 26.

108. PAC, Civil Service Commission Records, Historical Personnel files, vol. 351, Skelton file, McCloskey to Skelton, 5, 7 Oct., 1937.

109. Pickersgill interview, 13 Oct., 1978.

110. *Ibid.*

111. *Ibid.*

112. *Ibid.*; King Diary, 2 Aug., 1938.

113. Finance Department Records, vol. 3990, file U-1-10, Clark to Pickersgill, 1 Nov., 1938.

114. e.g., EAR, vol. 817, file 651, Note, Pickersgill to Skelton, 6 Dec., 1938.

115. King Diary, 20 Jan., 1939.

116. *Ibid.*, 11 Aug., 1939.

117. *My Years*, 10.

118. J.W. Pickersgill, 'Bureaucrats and Politicians', *Canadian Public Administration*, vol. XV, (Fall, 1972), 421.

119. DEA, Maurice Pope interview, 2-9 June, 1977; Walter Turnbull interview, 16 Oct., 1978. Cf. *My Years*, 10-11.

120. Underhill Papers, Pickersgill file, Pickersgill to Underhill, 9 Oct., 1939.

121. Turnbull interview.

122. DEA, Pickersgill interview, 3 Dec., 1977; Pickersgill interview, 13 Oct., 1978; King Diary, 13 Sept., 1940.

123. Moffat Papers, Memo of Conversation, 11 Dec., 1941.

124. King Diary, 19 June, 1942.

125. Pickersgill Papers, loose letter, Pickersgill to Ross Macdonald, 8 Sept., 1943.

126. Pickersgill interview, 13 Oct., 1978.

127. e.g., King Diary, 10 Sept., 1942.

128. *Ibid.*, 5 Feb., 1944. Pickersgill later became a good 'leak'. See, e.g., Dexter Papers, Memos, 1 May, 1951 and 14 April, 1952.

129. J.L. Granatstein, *Canada's War: The Politics of the Mackenzie King Government 1939-45* (Toronto, 1975), 281-2.

130. *Ibid.*, 267-8; Pickersgill Papers, Claxton file, *passim.*

131. *Ibid.*, Lower file, Pickersgill to Lower, 11 Dec., 1944.

132. King Diary, 12 Dec., 1944.

133. On Pickersgill's duties, see Privy Council Office Records, PARC box 1002, file P35-3, Heeney memo, 30 June, 1945.

134. *My Years,* 48.

135. King Diary, 27 Aug., 1948; *My Years,* 50.

136. Privy Council Office Records, PARC box 287334, file P-35-3, staff list, 7 May, 1948.

137. PAC, Louis St Laurent Papers, vol. 40, Memo for Acting Prime Minister, 18 Sept., 1948.

138. e.g., Pickersgill Papers, Keenleyside file, Memo for Prime Minister, 18 Oct., 1949 and Keenleyside to Pickersgill, 31 Oct., 1949.

139. PAC, N.A. Robertson Papers, vol. 2, Pickersgill to Robertson, 9 Jan., 1949.

140. *My Years,* 64.

141. *Ibid.,* 87.

142. *My Years,* 92ff.

143. Austin Cross, 'Oligarchs at Ottawa', *Public Affairs* (Autumn, 1951), 21.

144. Queen's University Archives, T.A. Crerar Papers, Box 105, file 7, Crerar to Dexter, 30 May, 1951.

·5. Dexter Papers, Hutchison memo, 23 Jan., 1952.

146. Cited by P. Newman in *Maclean's,* 22 Oct., 1960.

147. Privy Council Office Records, PARC box 287293, file P-35-3, Memo for Mr Beach, 8 June, 1951.

148. *My Years,* 174.

149. See J. and G. Fraser, eds, *Blair Fraser Reports* (Toronto, 1969), 23-4.

150. See Dexter Papers, Memo, Mackie to Dexter, 2 Dec., 1952; Toronto *Globe and Mail,* 1 Dec., 1952.

151. *My Years,* 175-6.

152. See on this incident, *My Years,* 179; Joseph Schull, *The Great Scot* (Montreal, 1979), 161-3; *Globe and Mail,* 1 Dec., 1952; *Winnipeg Free Press,* 11 Dec., 1952.

153. St Laurent Papers, vol. 140, Pickersgill to St Laurent, 28 April, 1953; *My Years,* 178.

154. *Ibid.,* 179; Pickersgill memo to author, n.d.

155. Pickersgill Papers, 1953 Election Campaign file, Pickersgill to Robertson, 22 May, 1953; *My Years,* 181ff.

156. Pickersgill Papers, Regarding Cabinet Post file, Pickersgill to J.T. Hackett, 12 June, 1953.

157. Dexter Papers, Dexter to V. Sifton, 22 May, 1953.

158. Bishop's University Archives, T.W.L. MacDermot Papers, file/71, Ferguson to MacDermot, 17 June, 1953.

159. *Ibid.,* 12 July, 1953.

160. Pickersgill Papers, loose letter, Pickersgill to Macdonnell, 15 Sept., 1953.

8. THE RUSSIANS, THE AMERICANS, AND US

1. Dana Wilgress, *Memoirs* (Toronto, 1967), 13-14.

2. Based on docs on PAC, Department of Trade and Commerce Records, vol. 1426, file A-817, and PAC, Civil Service Commission, Historical Personnel Records, vol. 358, Wilgress file. The article was 'The London Money Market,' XX (April, 1913).

3. Trade and Commerce Records, vol. 1426, file A-817, Grigg to Murray, 7 July, 1915.

4. Wilgress, 22.

5. Trade and Commerce Records, vol. 1426, file A-817, Wilgress to O'Hara, 16 July, 1916.

6. Wilgress, 39.

7. *Ibid.*, 50.

8. *Ibid.*, 59.

9. EAR, vol. 793, file 454, Skelton to Herridge, 2 Feb., 1934.

10. Harvard University, Pierrepont Moffat Papers, Armour to Moffat, 4 Jan., 1937. The British later said the same thing. See PRO, Dominions Office Records, DO 35/1211, Garner to Cockram, 22 Oct., 1946.

11. On the trade negotiations, see J.L. Granatstein, *A Man of Influence: Norman A. Robertson and Canadian Statecraft, 1929-68* (Ottawa, 1981), Chaps. II–III.

12. Queen's University Archives, W.A. Mackintosh Papers, box 8, file 206, Mackintosh to A.B. Purvis, 4 Feb., 1939.

13. See Wilgress's later and very revealing exchange of correspondence in 1952-3 with A.D.P. Heeney. PAC, Heeney Papers, vol. 1.

14. PAC, J.W. Dafoe Papers, Dexter to George Ferguson, 25 April, 1941.

15. U.S. National Archives, State Department Records, Hickerson files, Moffat memo, 1 Oct., 1942.

16. Cf. Wilgress, 122.

17. *Ibid.*, 123. PAC, Watson Sellar Diary, 2 Dec., 1942; Dominions Office Records, DO 35/664, Duff to Machtig, 6 Nov., 1942.

18. In addition to his memoirs, see also Wilgress's article, 'From Siberia to Kuibyshev,' *International Journal,* XXII (Summer, 1967), 364ff.

19. PAC, W.L.M. King Papers, dispatch, 9 Oct., 1945, vol. 340.

20. See Donald Page, 'The Wilgress Despatches from Moscow, 1943-6,' a paper presented to the Canadian Committee on History of Second World War Conference, St-Jean, Qué., 1977, 16.

21. Dominions Office Records, DO 35/1601, minute by N.E. Costar, 30 Dec., 1944; PRO, Foreign Office Records, FO 371/43413, Minute, 19 May, 1944; Page, 18.

22. Minute by J.G. Ward, 8 Dec., 1945, on *ibid.,* FO 371/47861. On British attitudes to the USSR, see P.G. Boyle, 'The British Foreign Office View of Soviet-American Relations, 1945-6', *Diplomatic History* (Summer, 1979), 307ff.

23. Cited in Page, 8.

24. See King Papers, dispatches, 29 Sept., 1945, ff.C237726ff.; 9 Oct., 1945, vol. 340; 15 Oct., 1945, ff.C237731ff.; 29 Oct., 1945, ff.C237739ff.; PAC, Laurent Beaudry Papers, dispatches, 31 May and 14 June, 1946.

25. King Papers, dispatch, 9 Oct., 1945, on vol. 340.

26. Page, 13, dispatch of 3 July, 1943.

27. King Papers, dispatch of 9 Oct., 1945, on vol. 340.

28. Page 13, letter of 20 Jan., 1945.

29. King Papers, dispatch of 29 Oct., 1945, ff.C237739ff.

30. Reid to his wife, 27 April, 1945, cited in Reid's MS. 'The Making of the United Nations: San Francisco, London, 1945-6,' 46.

31. Smith interview, 18 Feb., 1978.

32. See King Papers, Memo, J.E. Read to Prime Minister, 20 June, 1945, ff.C237899ff.

33. *Ibid.*, dispatch of 9 Oct., 1945, vol. 340; and *ibid.*, dispatch of 21 March, 1946, ff.C237929ff.

34. Copy in Queen's University Archives, J.J. Deutsch Papers, folder 1225. R. Cuff and J.L. Granatstein, *American Dollars/Canadian Prosperity* (Toronto, 1978), 197 ff.

35. See Queen's University Archives, Grant Dexter Papers, Memo, 22 Feb., 1947 and DEA, file 2-AE(s), Wilgress to SSEA, 25 April, 1947.

36. See Wilgress's letter to Pearson of 6 Nov., 1947 on *ibid.*, file 52-F(s).

37. *Ibid.*, file 2-AE(s), Wilgress to Pearson, 25 May, 1948. Smith's paper is on *ibid.*, file 52-F(s). On this paper, see the account in Don Page and D. Munton, 'Canadian Images of the Cold War 1946-7', *International Journal*, XXXII (Summer, 1977), 596-7.

38. Heeney Papers, vol. 2, Chapter XIV file, Diary entry, 21 May, 1955.

39. PAC, Escott Reid Papers, vol. 4, 'The First Rector of St Chad's Church', address by Reid, 22 Sept., 1968.

40. *Ibid.*, Writings #3, 'The Future of Canada', 21 April, 1921.

41. *Ibid.*, Writings #12.

42. University of British Columbia Archives, N.A. MacKenzie Papers, folder 6/4, Main Correspondence, Reid to Mackenzie, 18 Dec., 1929.

43. PAC, F.H. Underhill Papers, vol. 7, Reid file, Reid to Underhill, 9 Dec., 1929.

44. MacKenzie Papers, *op. cit.*, also Reid's 'Some influences on me in the interwar period, 1914-1939,' a copy of which Mr Reid gave to me.

45. See Reid Papers, 'Canadian Politics: Notes on Interviews 1930-2.

46. Escott Reid Papers (Ste Cécile de Masham), W.Y. Elliott to Reid, 14 June, 1932; J.L. Granatstein, *A Man of Influence*, 46-7.

47. Underhill Papers, vol. 7, Reid file, Reid to H.M. Margoluith, Secretary of Faculties, Oxford, 30 Jan., 29 Sept., 1933.

48. Published in *Papers and Proceedings of the Canadian Political Science Association*, IV (1932); *Contributions to Canadian Economics*, VI (1933); and *Canadian Journal of Economics and Political Science*, II (1936).

49. PAC, CIIA Papers, vols 6-7.

50. Bishop's University, T.W.L. MacDermot Papers, file/70, Claxton to MacDermot, 20 Feb., 1936.

51. Dexter Papers, Dafoe to Dexter, 23 Jan., 1937. See also Shelagh Grant, 'Search for a Northern Policy, 1940-1950: Impact of the CIIA,' B.A. honours thesis, Trent University 1981, 15-19, and B. Pearsall, 'Escott Reid, Canadian Foreign Policy and the CIIA, 1930-8', York University graduate paper, 1982, 23ff.

52. Cited in Michiel Horn, *The League for Social Reconstruction* (Toronto, 1980), 146.

53. Reid Papers, Writings #30, June, 1934.

54. 'Can Canada Remain Neutral?', *Dalhousie Review*, XV (1935), 148.

55. 'Canada and this Next War', *Canadian Forum*, XIV (March, 1934), 209.

56. Reid Papers, Writings #39, 'Canada and the Ethiopian Crisis', 26 Aug., 1935. For Reid on his 1930s views, see 'The Views of Escott Reid: The L.S.R. and Canadian Foreign Policy', 18 Oct., 1980, presented at a Toronto Conference on the LSR.

57. Scottish Record Office, Edinburgh, Lothian Papers, CD40/17/349/545-6, Reid to Lothian, 19 March, 1937.

58. 'Democracy and Political Leadership', *University of Toronto Quarterly*, IV (July, 1935), 547.

59. 'Canada and the Threat of War', *University of Toronto Quarterly*, VI (January, 1937), 242ff.; King Diary, 7 Feb., 1937; Reid Interview, 14 Oct., 1978.

60. House of Commons *Debates*, 19 Feb., 1937, 1054.

61. Reid Papers (Ste Cécile de Masham), Appointment to External Affairs Service file, Reid to wife, 16 Nov., 1936. Reid had known Skelton for some ten years. *Ibid.*, Skelton file, Diary notes, 8 Sept., 1927, etc.

62. Underhill Papers, vol. 7, Reid file, Reid to Underhill, 4 Nov., 1937.

63. Documents on Reid Papers (Ste Cécile de Masham), Appointment file.

64. *Ibid.*, Memo for USSEA, 3 Dec., 1942.

65. Dafoe Papers, Dafoe to J.M. Macdonnell, 16 Sept., 1940.

66. Reid Papers (Ste Cécile de Masham), Skelton file, Wood to Skelton, 10 Aug., 1940. and reply, 12 Aug., 1940.

67. Reid, 'One Man's Journey to the Cold War', 3, a chapter excised from *Time of Fear and Hope*. Mr Reid sent me this copy.

68. Reid Papers, vol. 5, file 10, 'The United States and Canada', 12 Jan., 1942. Similar views are expressed in 'Some Problems in the Relations between Canada and the United States', 16 April, 1943, *ibid.* and in 'United States Policy Towards Canada,' 29 Feb., 1944 in EAR, vol. 823, file 702.

69. Massey College, University of Toronto, Massey Papers, Diary, 17 May, 1943.

70. Reid Papers, vol. 5, file 10, 'The United States and Canada'.

71. *Ibid.*, Memo, 16 April, 1943.

72. *Ibid.*, vol. 5, file 7, Reid to Robertson, 23 Sept., 1944.

73. *Ibid.*, vol. 5, file 6, 'International Conference on Civil Aviation', Part II, Chapter IV, 14 Dec., 1944. For a British view of the Canadian role, see Dominions Office Records, documents on DO 35/1235.

74. See 'International Conference', *op. cit.*, 2.

75. Reid Papers, vol. 5, file 7, Reid to Wrong, 18 Dec., 1944.

76. Reid has prepared a draft manuscript on his role at San Francisco and after, 'The Making of the United Nations: San Francisco, London 1945-6', a copy of which he kindly gave me.

77. Reid Papers, vol. 5, file 8, 'Memo on Work of the [UN] Preparatory Commission', 4 Jan., 1946.

78. *Ibid.*, vol. 5, file 11, 'Prepared for P.M.'s Speech', 8 April, 1946.

79. *Ibid.*, vol. 5, file 8, 'Impressions of the First General Assembly of the United Nations', 27 Feb., 1946.

80. Dexter Papers, Memo, 17 March, 1946. Reid soon thought better of forcing the Russians out of the UN. See Reid Papers, vol. 5, file 11, Memo for Robertson, 29 Oct., 1947. Reid's recollection of this conversation with Dexter is some-

what different. Letter, Reid to author, 22 Sept., 1981.

81. 'An Approach to some of the Basic Problems of Foreign Policy', 9-11 Feb., 1946. Mr Reid gave me a copy of this paper.

82. Reid Papers, vol. 5, file 11, 18 Feb., 1947. See also DEA, file 52-F(s), Reid to Pearson, 10 Oct., 1947.

83. On UN reform, see also Reid's testimony before the House of Commons Standing Committee on External Affairs, 6 May, 1947, 60ff., and Reid Papers, vol. 5, file 8, 'The Summoning of a Revisionary Conference', 28 Oct., 1947.

84. Reid, 'Canada's Role in the United Nations', 13 Aug., 1947, *Statements and Speeches*, 47/12.

85. DEA, file TS 52-F(s). See also the responses to this paper on *ibid.*, and Page and Munton, 'Canadian Images', 577ff.

86. Escott Reid, *Time of Fear and Hope* (Toronto, 1977), 139. This is the best book on the organization of NATO.

87. This had also been suggested by Dana Wilgress in a dispatch, 25 April, 1947 on DEA, file 2-AE(s). Wilgress called Reid's memo 'very excellent', *Ibid.*, file 52-F(s). Wilgress to Pearson, 6 Nov., 1947.

88. For the achievement of the Treaty see docs on *ibid.*, file 283(s).

89. Bank of Canada, Louis Rasminsky Papers, file LR76-32, Wrong to Rasminsky, 12 Sept., 1945.

90. PAC, L.B. Pearson Papers, N1, Reid to Pearson, 3 May, 1957. Cf. *ibid.*, vol. 32, Heeney to Pearson, 19 Nov., 1948.

91. Department of State Records, 842.00/11-1945, Clark to Parsons, 15 Nov., 1945.

92. e.g., PAC, Hume Wrong Papers, vol. 5, file 30, Robertson to Reid, 9 Nov., 1948. Cf. A.P. Herbert, 'The Battle of Bunkum', (London) *Sunday Times*, 23 Dec., 1945.

93. PAC, N.A. Robertson Papers, vol. 2, Personal Correspondence, Heeney to Robertson, 16 Feb., 1949.

94. Pearson Papers, vol. 32, Pearson to Robertson, 5 April, 1947.

95. See Reid's article on 'The Revolution in Canadian Foreign Policy 1947-51', *India Quarterly*, XIV (April-June 1958), 188ff.

9. THE END OF THE MANDARIN ERA

1. PAC, Watson Sellar Diary, 11 Jan., 1956.

2. M.C. Urquhart and K. Buckley, *Historical Statistics of Canada* (Toronto, 1956), 621ff.

3. Based on interviews with Mitchell Sharp, 13 July, 1981, J.H. Warren, 15 May, 1979, and Louis Rasminsky, 30 Nov., 1978. See also Sharp's essay, 'Role of Economic advice in Political Decisions', in D.C. Smith, ed. *Economic Policy Advising in Canada: Essays in Honour of John Deutsch* (Montreal, 1981).

4. Keynes to Bryce, 10 July, 1935, printed, along with Bryce's paper, in D. Patinkin and J.C. Leith, eds., *Keynes, Cambridge and the General Theory* (Toronto, 1977), 127ff. Also Cambridge University, Faculty of Economics, R.B. Bryce file, Bryce to J.T. Saunders, 13 May, 1938. I am much indebted to Prof. Don

Moggridge for his great assistance in securing access for me to this very useful file.

5. R.B. Bryce interview, 28 Nov., 1978. The best account of Cambridge in the 1930s remains P. Stansky and W. Abrahams, *Two Roads to the Spanish Civil War* (New York, 1970), 201ff.

6. *The Sun,* cited in the *Globe and Mail,* 8 April, 1981; *The Toronto Sun,* 31 March, 1981; *The Financial Post,* 11 April, 1981.

7. Marshall Library, Cambridge University, Keynes Papers, black folder, Keynes to R.H. Simpson, 13 Feb., 1935. I am again indebted to Prof. Moggridge.

8. J.K. Galbraith, 'How Keynes Came to America', in Milo Keynes, ed., *Essays on John Maynard Keynes* (Cambridge, 1975), 137.

9. Cambridge Bryce file, Bryce to Saunders, 13 May, 1938.

10. *Ibid.,* Bryce to Sartain, 15 Feb., 1940.

11. *Financial Post,* 11 April, 1981; DEA, Washington Embassy files, file 27-3-12, tel. Washington to External, 10 April, 1957 and attached memo, Heeney to Farquharson, 30 April, 1957.

12. Bryce interview, 28 Nov., 1978.

13. *Ibid.*

14. See documents on PAC, Department of Finance Records, vol. 3444, Personal Correspondence 1938-9.

15. Cambridge Bryce file, Bryce to Saunders, 13 May, 1938 and Bryce to Sartain, 15 Feb., 1940; Board of Research Studies to Sraffa, 13 May, 1940.

16. Bryce interview, 28 Nov., 1978.

17. Department of Finance Records, vol. 3976, file E-3-0, 'Report on Memorandum regarding Proposed Adjustment of Exchange Value of Canadian Currency', [March, 1939]; 'The Effects on Canada of Industrial Fluctuations in the United States', *Canadian Journal of Economics and Political Science,* V (Aug., 1939); documents on Department of Finance Records, vol. 3381, file 03238-2.

18. *Ibid.,* vol. 3444, Personal Correspondence 1938-9, C.H. Herbert to Bryce, 27 April, 1939.

19. *Ibid.,* R.G. 19 E2(f), Statistics 1940 file, 'What Proportion of the National Income . . . ,' n.d. [fall 1939].

20. Bladen interview, 2 Nov., 1978.

21. See his paper, 'Some Aspects of Canadian Economic Relations with the United States', in S.E. Harris, ed., *Foreign Economic Policy for the U.S.* (1948), 134ff.; see also R. Cuff and J.L. Granatstein, *American Dollars/Canadian Prosperity* (Toronto, 1978), 59.

22. e.g., PAC, Privy Council Office Records, PARC box 287273, file D-100-E, Bryce to N.A. Robertson, 12 Dec., 1949 and attached memo for Robertson, 30 Nov., 1949.

23. W.L. White and J.C. Strick, *Policy, Politics and the Treasury Board in Canadian Government* (Don Mills, Ont., 1970), 33; also J.E. Hodgetts, *The Canadian Public Service* (Toronto, 1973), chap. XI. Bryce's account of Treasury Board role is in his 'Expenditure Control in Canadian Federal Financing', *The Tax Bulletin* (Sept.-Oct., 1952), 279ff.

24. White and Strick, 34-5.

25. See J.L. Granatstein, *A Man of Influence: Norman A. Robertson and Canadian Statecraft, 1929-68* (Ottawa, 1981), 241ff. See also Bishop's University, T.W.L. MacDermot Papers, /70, Notebook, entry, n.d. [late 1949].

26. Bryce interviews, 10 Jan., 13 Feb., 1979.

27. Sharp interview, 21 Feb., 1979.

28. Abbott interview, 11 Jan., 1979.

29. Bryce interview, 26 Oct., 1978.

30. Sellar Diary, 14 Sept., 1953.

31. House of Commons *Debates*, 30 June, 1942, 3795.

32. PAC, George Drew Papers, vol. 11, file 82, Drew to J. Bassett, 31 Oct., 1945; and Ontario Archives, Drew Papers, Ontario files, box 9, vol. 18, Drew to H.A. Bruce. I am indebted for these references to Mr Mark Gotlieb.

33. Sellar Diary, 16 Feb., 1945.

34. J.W. Pickersgill Papers (Ottawa), Lower file, Lower to Pickersgill, 21 May, 1954.

35. Sellar Diary, 26 March, 1952.

36. MacDermot Papers, /70, Ferguson to MacDermot, 1 March, 1952.

37. J.E. Hodgetts, 'The Liberal and the Bureaucrat', *Queen's Quarterly*, LXII (Summer, 1955), 182.

38. John Meisel, 'The Formulation of Liberal and Conservative Programmes in the 1957 Canadian General Election', *Canadian Journal of Economics and Political Science*, XXVI (November, 1960), 567. Also J.E. Hodgetts, 'The Civil Service and Policy Formation', *ibid.*, XXIII (November, 1957), 467ff.

39. (Toronto, 1977), 167.

40. 'Ottawa's Incredible Bureaucratic Explosion', *Saturday Night* (July-August, 1975), 27ff.

41. 'Bureaucrats and Politicians', *Canadian Public Administration*, XI (Fall, 1972), 426-7.

42. 'The Bureaucratic Elite and Policy Formation', in W.D.K. Kernaghan, ed., *Bureaucracy in Canadian Government* (Toronto, 1973), 73.

43. Eugene Forsey, *Freedom and Order* (Toronto, 1974), 91.

44. See Mitchell Sharp, 'The Role of the Mandarins', *Policy Options*, II (May-June, 1981), 44.

45. See, e.g., House of Commons *Debates*, 11 Dec., 1947, 189.

46. John Diefenbaker, *One Canada: The Memoirs of the Rt Hon. John G. Diefenbaker* (Toronto, 1976), II, 52-4.

47. Cited in House of Commons *Debates*, 6 Dec., 1957, 2012.

48. Peter Stursberg, *Diefenbaker: Leadership Gained 1956-62* (Toronto, 1975), 73.

49. James A. Roberts, *The Canadian Summer* (Toronto, 1981), 190.

50. 9 April, 1958.

51. 12 April, 1958.

52. Stursberg, 144, See also T. Van Dusen, *The Chief* (Toronto, 1968), 29, 32-3; Patrick Nicholson, *Vision and Indecision* (Toronto, 1968), chaps. IV-V on the 'Hidden report'; and Blair Fraser, 'Backstage at Ottawa', *Maclean's* (1 March, 1958), 2.

53. Charles Ritchie, *Diplomatic Passport: More Undiplomatic Diaries* (Toronto, 1981), 157-8.

54. On friendships between politicians and civil servants, see R.M. Burns, 'The Role of the Deputy Minister', *Canadian Public Administration,* IV (December, 1961), 360.

55. See A.D.P. Heeney, *The Things that are Caesar's* (Toronto, 1972), 150.

56. The *Globe and Mail,* 9 April, 1958; John Porter, *The Vertical Mosaic* (Toronto, 1965), 454-6.

57. Diefenbaker interview, 15 Feb., 1979.

58. Stursberg, 144.

59. Diefenbaker interview; Bryce interview, 26 Oct., 1978; Basil Robinson interview, 16 May, 1979.

60. Diefenbaker interview.

61. *Ibid.* For comparison to a later period, see Hon. Flora MacDonald's Address to the Canadian Political Science Assn., 3 June, 1980.

62. Robinson interview; Granatstein, *A Man of Influence,* 324-6.

63. PAC, R.B. Bryce Papers, Telephone notes, Feb., 1961, April, 1961 etc.

64. Robinson interview.

65. See Peter Newman, 'Backstage at Ottawa', *Maclean's,* 4 June, 1960, 2; Newman, 'The Ottawa Establishment', *Maclean's,* 22 Aug., 1964, 7.

66. The indecisiveness can be shown by the astonishing number of Cabinet meetings. e.g., Cabinet met 22, 23, 24, 27, 28, 29, 30, 31 January, twice on 1 February and once on 3 February 1958, and followed this pattern at several other points. Bryce Papers, Notebooks, Jan-Feb 58. Diefenbaker believed that Cabinet, not committees, should decide questions, with the result that discussions went on and on.

67. Letter, Bryce to author, 17 Sept., 1981.

68. On civil service anonymity, see Kenneth Kernaghan, 'Politicians, policy and public servants: political neutrality revisited', *Canadian Public Administration,* XIX (Fall, 1976), 451ff.; Burns, 361-2.

69. See, e.g., Christopher Armstrong, *The Politics of Federalism: Ontario's Relations with the Federal Government 1867-1942* (Toronto, 1981), chapter X.

70. See A.K. Eaton, *Essays in Taxation* (Toronto, 1966), 136; Reginald Whitaker, 'Images of the State in Canada', in L. Panitch, ed., *The Canadian State* (Toronto, 1977), 59.

71. See among others, James Eayrs, *The Art of the Possible* (Toronto, 1961), 36-7; Kernaghan, 'Politics, policy and public servants', 432ff.; Escott Reid's 'Responsibilities of a Public Servant', [December 1948] in PAC, Reid Papers, vol. 13; and R.D. Putnam, 'The Political Attitudes of Senior Civil Servants in Western Europe', *British Journal of Political Science,* III (1973), 257ff.

72. See George Grant, letter to editor, *Globe and Mail,* 28 Dec., 1981.

73. See, e.g. James Gillies, *Where Business Fails* (Montreal, 1981), 96ff.

74. See Robert Presthus, *Elite Accommodation in Canadian Politics* (Toronto, 1973), for one estimate of the 'decisive' role of the bureaucracy.

75. Mitchell Sharp, 'The Role of the Mandarins', *Policy Options,* II (May-June, 1981), 43-44; Gillies, 85, 92; R.D. French, *How Ottawa Decides* (Toronto, 1980), 2ff. Cf. Flora MacDonald, 'Ministers, Civil Servants and Parliamentary Democracy', *Dalhousie Review,* LX (Summer, 1980), 238ff. for the assessment of one minister who believed the bureaucracy still had too much of an influence.

76. R.B. Bryce, 'Public Servants as Economic Advisers', in D.C. Smith, ed.,

Economic Policy Advising in Canada, 68.

77. J.E. Hodgetts and O.P. Dwivedi, 'The Growth of Government Employment in Canada', *Canadian Public Administration,* XII (Summer, 1969), 229. In 1946, there were 116,657 federal civil servants; in 1956, 155,892; in 1966, 228,325.

78. Bryce, 53-56.

79. Colin Campbell and George Szablowski, *The Super-Bureaucrats* (Toronto, 1979) is the best account.

80. Report of *Royal Commission on Conditions of Foreign Service* (Ottawa, 1981).

81. Robert K. Merton, *Social Theory and Social Structure* (New York, 1968), 252.

82. In Canada, 'the senior civil servants' involvement in the policy process has been as close and continuous as anywhere in the world.' Eayrs, *Art of the Possible,* 32.

83. The Canadian consensus was paralleled in Britain. See Paul Addison, *The Road to 1945* (London, 1975).

84. See R. Miliband, *The State in Capitalist Society* (London, 1969), 59ff., for an account of class similarities among civil servants, politicians and businessmen in Western Europe.

85. Arthur Lower, 'Adam Shortt, Founder', *Historic Kingston,* No. 17 (January, 1969), 9.

BIBLIOGRAPHY OF MAJOR PRIMARY SOURCES

This listing comprises the major manuscript collections that have proved useful for this study, as well as a listing of interviews. Further primary sources and all printed materials are cited in the reference notes.

A. MANUSCRIPT SOURCES

CANADA

Private collections
Mrs C.H.A. Armstrong Papers (Toronto)*
Floyd Chalmers Papers (Toronto)*
Kenneth Skelton Clark Papers (Toronto)*
Prof. George Glazebrook Papers (Toronto)*
Mrs A.D.P. Heeney Papers (Ottawa)*
Prof. Brian Heeney Papers (Peterborough)*
W.D. Herridge Papers (Toronto)*
Margaret Clark Johnston Papers (Niagara Falls)*
J.W. Pickersgill Papers (Ottawa)*
Mrs A.F.W. Plumptre Papers (Ottawa)*
Escott Reid Papers (Ste Cécile de Masham, Qué.)*
Mrs June Wrong Rogers Papers (Ottawa)*

Massey College, University of Toronto
Vincent Massey Papers*

Queen's University Archives
Board of Trustees Minutes*
T.A. Crerar Papers

J.J. Deutsch Papers†
Grant Dexter Papers†
Norman Lambert Papers
Arthur R.M. Lower Papers†
W.A. Mackintosh Papers
Norman Rogers Papers
Adam Shortt Papers
D.A. Skelton Papers
J.A. Stevenson Papers
University Records†

University of British Columbia Archives
Norman MacKenzie Papers
Alan Plaunt Papers

Bishop's University Archives
T.W.L. MacDermot Papers*

Public Archives of Nova Scotia
E.N. Rhodes Papers

Bank of Canada Archives
Louis Rasminsky Papers*
Records*
Graham Towers Papers*

Department of External Affairs
Interviews*
Records†
Washington Embassy files†

* Closed records.
† Partly closed records.

Public Archives of Canada
Civil Service Commission, Historical
   Personnel files*
Department of External Affairs
   Records†
Department of Finance Records†
   Economic Advisory Committee
   Records
Department of Finance Records†
   Economic Advisory Committee
   Records
Department of Trade and Commerce
   Records†
Privy Council Office Records
   Cabinet War Committee Records

Laurent Beaudry Papers
R.B. Bennett Papers
Sir Robert Borden Papers
Canadian Institute of International
   Affairs Records
Loring Christie Papers
Brooke Claxton Papers†
J.W. Dafoe Papers
George Drew Papers*
W.L. Grant Papers
Bertal Heeney Papers*
Arnold Heeney Papers*
W.L.M. King Papers
Ian Mackenzie Papers
R.J. Manion Papers
L.W. Murray Papers
L.B. Pearson Papers†
Maurice Pope Diaries
John Read Papers
Escott Reid Papers†
N.A. Robertson Papers†
Newton Rowell Papers
Louis St Laurent Papers†
Watson Sellar Diaries*
O.D. Skelton Papers
F.H. Underhill Papers
Georges Vanier Papers*
Hume Wrong Papers†

UNITED KINGDOM

Public Record Office
Cabinet Records
Dominions Office Records
Foreign Office Records
Prime Minister's Office Records
Treasury Records

*Cambridge University, Faculty of
   Economics*
Records*

Churchill College, Cambridge
Burgon Bickersteth Papers

Marshall Library, Cambridge University
Lord Keynes Papers†

Bodleian Library, Oxford University
Mss. English History

Balliol College, Oxford University
College Records*

Rhodes House, Oxford
Records*

UNITED STATES

*United States Treasury Department,
   Washington, D.C.*
Records†

Library of Congress, Washington, D.C.
Felix Frankfurter Papers
Cordell Hull Papers

United States National Archives
Department of State Records
Hickerson files

Harvard University
J. Pierrepont Moffat Papers

* Closed records.
† Partly closed records.

B. INTERVIEWS

Hon. D.C. Abbott
Mrs C.H.A. Armstrong
J.R. Beattie
Vincent Bladen
R.B. Bryce
Ross Campbell
K.S. Clark
Rt Hon. John G. Diefenbaker
Mrs J.J. Deutsch
Graham Fraser
J. Douglas Gibson
George Glazebrook
Hon. Walter Gordon
Mrs Walter Gordon
Mrs A.D.P. Heeney
Brian Heeney
J.W. Holmes
Margaret Clark Johnston
H.L. Keenleyside

Douglas LePan
Rt Hon. Jules Léger
H.I. Macdonald
Mrs W.A. Mackintosh
David Mansur
Hon. Paul Martin
Hon. J.W. Pickersgill
Mrs A.F.W. Plumptre
Louis Rasminsky
Escott Reid
C.S.A. Ritchie
Mrs N.A. Robertson
R. Gordon Robertson
H. Basil Robinson
Mrs June Wrong Rogers
Hon. Mitchell Sharp
Walter Turnbull
George Watts
Dennis Wrong

INDEX